Rising East Asia

To Leling, Christine, and Alex

Rising East Asia

The Quest for Governance, Prosperity, and Security

Chien-pin Li

Kennesaw State University

FOR INFORMATION:

CQ Press, an Imprint of
SAGE Publications, Inc

2455 Teller Road

Thousand Oaks, California 91320

E-mail: order@sagepub.com

SAGE Publications Ltd.

1 Oliver's Yard

55 City Road

London EC1Y 1SP

United Kingdom

SAGE Publications India Pvt. Ltd.

B 1/I 1 Mohan Cooperative Industrial Area

Mathura Road, New Delhi 110 044

India

SAGE Publications Asia-Pacific Pte. Ltd.

18 Cross Street #10-10/11/12

China Square Central

Singapore 048423

Printed in the United States of America

Library of Congress Cataloging-in-Publication Data

Names: Li, Jianbin, author.

Title: Rising East Asia : the quest for governance,
prosperity, and security / Chien-pin Li, Kennesaw
State University.

Description: Los Angeles : Sage, [2021] | Includes
bibliographical references.

Identifiers: LCCN 2019044999 | ISBN 9781483344713
(paperback) | ISBN 9781483344706 (epub) |
ISBN 9781544399263 (epub) | ISBN 9781483344720
(ebook)

Subjects: LCSH: East Asia—Foreign relations—21st
century.

Classification: LCC DS518.14 .L5 2020 | DDC
327.5009/05—dc23

LC record available at https://lccn.loc.gov/2019044999

This book is printed on acid-free paper.

Acquisitions Editor: Anna Villarruel

Editorial Assistant: Lauren Younker

Production Editor: Vishwajeet Mehra

Copy Editor: Michelle Ponce

Typesetter: Hurix Digital

Proofreader: Sarah J. Duffy

Indexer: Jean Casalegno

Cover Designer: Candice Harman

Marketing Manager: Jennifer Jones

20 21 22 23 24 10 9 8 7 6 5 4 3 2 1

Contents

2 | Political Governance in China   33

3 | China's Pursuit of Economic Prosperity   71

4 | China's Pursuit of National Security 91

5 | Japan: The Foundations 113

11 | South Korea's Pursuit of Economic Prosperity   251

12 | South Korea's Pursuit of National Security   271

Preface

Countries in East Asia have experienced dynamic changes since the end of World War II. Stellar performances in economic growth, along with shifts in political dynamics, social order, and security landscapes, underscore the transformation of the region. The trajectory of these changes, however, has not always followed a linear, uniform pattern of development. Regression and contradictions sometimes coexist with growth and progress. The admirers and detractors of the region both can find support for their optimistic or pessimistic projections about the region. Whatever their position may be, the future of East Asia is likely to have major impacts on the rest of the world.

To help people understand the past and present of the region, and develop well-informed opinions about its future, this book tries to provide readers with an analytical tool that integrates the scholarly traditions of area studies and social sciences. The pioneering work of the Asian specialists, whose understanding and insight about the region's history and culture laid the foundation of the field, has been increasingly enriched by new generations of empirical scientific research. Thus, to benefit from the scholarship of both sources, the book maintains the knowledge base of the area studies while presenting the information from conceptual and theoretical angles when appropriate. The unique details of historical events and actors is deemphasized, but behavioral patterns across time and places are highlighted. In doing so, the book tries to promote analytical thinking instead of rote memorization.

While the goal of the book is clear, the best approach to achieving this goal is not. During the course of writing, it has been a constant challenge to determine where the right balance of the distinct scholarships might be and how best to blend them. Although the best effort was made at the time of writing, it surely has room for improvement.

Acknowledgments

I am grateful to CQ Press/SAGE for their willingness to support the idea of this book, which was first encouraged by Elise Frasier. Throughout the project, the editorial and production teams at CQ Press/SAGE have been incredibly patient, flexible, and helpful. I deeply appreciate the counsel and guidance from Charisse Kiino, Sarah Calabi, Nancy Matuszak, Scott Greenan, Anna Villarruel, Vishwajeet Mehra, and Gagan Mahindra, who have all been professional and efficient. It has been an absolute pleasure to work with them. I am also indebted to Raquel Christie and Lauren Younker for their hard work in reviewing the manuscript and paying attention to the details. A special thanks to Michelle Ponce, copy editor for this edition, and the numerous reviewers who provided constructive comments and suggestions for the drafts of the book at various stages. Together, they have helped make the book better.

I would like to express my gratitude to my academic home, the School of Government and International Affairs, College of Humanities and Social Sciences, Kennesaw State University. My colleagues' dedication and commitment to student success inspires me to find a clear and interesting way to deliver the course materials to my students, shaping my teaching philosophy and instructional approach. I am also grateful for the research support I received, particularly the assistance from Pamela Klomp and Mei Shih.

I wish to thank the reviewers of this first edition for their feedback during the development process:

Ming Wan, George Mason University

Guoli Liu, College of Charleston

Kenji Hayao, Boston College

Srobana Bhattacharya, Georgia Southern University

Zhiqun Zhu, Bucknell University

Diqing Lou, Rider University

Lastly, I would like to thank my family, Leling, Christine, and Alex, for their love, patience, and encouragement. I would not have been able to finish the work without their support and sacrifice. To them this book is dedicated.

About the Author

Chien-pin Li is associate dean and professor of political science in the College of Humanities and Social Sciences at Kennesaw State University in Kennesaw, Georgia. He received his PhD in political science from the University of Iowa. His teaching and research interests focus on the political economy in East Asia, including trade disputes, trade negotiations, and regional integration. He is author of articles in *Asian Survey, Pacific Review, International Studies Quarterly*, and other journals.

Introduction

China, Japan, and Korea in East Asia are societies of long history and tradition. In the premodern era, their civilizations thrived with indigenous creation coupled with cultural intermingling and grafting, facilitated by human migrations and interactions due to geographic proximity. They built effective governing institutions centuries before many modern states arose in Europe, Africa, or other parts of Asia. Of the three, China had been dominant in the region for at least a millennium given its size, resources, and cultural influence.

Beginning in the 18th century, as Europe and North America experienced economic expansion and technological innovation, scientific and economic developments in East Asia began to stagnate. The onset of the Industrial Revolution in Great Britain from 1780 to 1850 ushered in an era of commercialization of agriculture and mass production of industrial goods, creating large middle classes in urban centers requiring new methods of organization and management. The economic efficiency and productivity unleashed by these technological breakthroughs gave Great Britain and other industrialized societies in Europe unprecedented economic advantage and military prowess that, in turn, translated into their ability to shape the international environment and foreign affairs. In contrast, East Asian countries were slow to recognize the importance of industrialization and technological innovation for competition in the modern capitalist environment.

The arrival of the European and American powers in Asia in the mid-19th century significantly altered the development trajectories of the three states. The superior Western technology and military forces shattered the international order that was familiar to them. Late in catching up with the Western powers, the three countries struggled to adapt to a Western-organized new world order.

Simple statistics illustrate the enormous challenges they experienced. In 1820, two decades before the Europeans and Americans expanded their influence into East Asia, China and Japan by one estimate accounted for 36 percent of the world's total economic production (Maddison 2001). Chinese gross domestic product (GDP) at that time was nearly 30 percent higher than that of Western Europe and the United States combined. Nevertheless, by 1950, that is, more than a hundred years later, the gross production of these two countries regressed to merely 8 percent of the world total production. The statistical comparison revealed the struggle of a region that once enjoyed grandeur and splendor and was trying to regain its footing.

In the aftermath of World War II, with the devastating loss of human and physical capital sustained during the war, few people would have predicted the region's quick recovery and even rapid rise. To everyone's surprise, East Asia in the following decades experienced three waves of development with sustained, dynamic economic growth, making it the most vibrant region in the global economy.

Japan was first to emerge from the rubble of wartime destruction. Beginning in the early 1950s, its per capita GDP grew at an average rate of almost 7 percent each year for the next three consecutive decades. The newly industrializing economies (NIEs)—South Korea, Taiwan, Hong Kong, and Singapore—followed suit with their explosive growth since the mid-1960s. From 1965 to 1990, compared with middle-income countries that grew at 2.2 percent on average as estimated by the World Bank, Asian NIEs grew three to four times faster by world standards and at a level previously thought unattainable. A decade later, China joined the group for the latest round of spectacular growth, elevating millions of citizens out of poverty after it undertook the policy of opening and reform in 1978. Decades of dynamic economic success brought recognition by the World Bank, which labeled states in East Asia as "high performing Asian economies" to underscore their accomplishments.

The region's economic progression can also be seen in the hosting of the Summer Olympics—first the Tokyo Olympics (1964), followed by the Seoul Olympics (1988) and the Beijing Olympics (2008), with Tokyo ready for its second Olympics in 2020. It reflects the pride of the host countries in displaying their success, as well as the recognition by others of their accomplishments.

The growth spurts and the rapid ascent of the region spark debates on whether the 21st century will be the Asian Century. Supporters point to the economic vibrancy of the region and argue that, by 2030, Asia could have three of the largest four economies: China, India, and Japan. Skeptics, however, question the sustainability of its growth, given the aging populations and environmental and resource constraints in the region. Of course, making long-term predictions is a risky business, as projections are often based on assumptions that are bound to change. Arguments aside, the debates nevertheless underscore the deep interest in the future of the region, as well as the implications it has for the rest of the world.

What explains the reversed fortunes of these countries? The purpose of this book is to provide a comprehensive overview of the rise of China, Japan, and Korea in recent decades, including the challenges and struggles they encountered in gaining economic and political prominence. The analysis and discussion focus on three broad themes: political governance, economic prosperity, and national security, which are broad policy goals commonly pursued by leaders and publics in modern states. Whether in the early industrializing states such as European powers, or the late developers in Asia, it is desirable to achieve national wealth and security in a peaceful and stable political environment. Facing steep challenges from advanced industrial powers, East Asian states have been particularly keen on the importance of these policy goals for their survival. Did they take the same approach to these objectives? Comparing the policies and actions they took in each area offers insights on the parallel or divergent patterns of development of these states. The following is an overview of the theoretical basis and practical implications of these goals.

THEMES: POLICY GOALS

Political Governance

The etymological origin of the term *governance* comes from the Greek verb *kybernan*, meaning to pilot or steer a ship. Its Latin equivalent, *gubernare*, also conveys the notion to guide, direct, or rule. Thus, political governance pertains to questions such as these: Who has the power and authority to guide or rule? How should power and authority be distributed? Who should have them, and how do we decide who gets what? In a nutshell, political governance is the totality of structures and processes by which political power and public authority are distributed and exercised. It deals with the fundamental question of how the state, which is the collective of all the institutions and individuals that exercise power, is organized vis-à-vis society.

The conventional wisdom is that government, which acts as the ruling body in modern sovereign states, is empowered to do so. Historically, government serves two important purposes: to preserve law and order and to provide public goods. In the first function, government uses its monopoly of the coercive power such as the military and police to protect the life and property of its citizens. In the second function, it provides public goods and services, such as roads and dams, which benefit all members of a society. The coercive force deployed by government allows it to maintain an orderly society and to collect tax revenues to build infrastructures that otherwise would not be built if solely depending on voluntary actions of individuals. With rule-making and rule-enforcing authority that uses legitimate force, government could demand conformity for all forms of activities within its boundaries, with the support and assistance from the bureaucratic and security apparatus.

The State versus the Society

While government is a key player that exercises command and control over the state, there are other entities in political governance. In the case of failed states, government can be far less influential than other nongovernmental actors such as warlords or oligarchs. In regular, viable states, government may also need to contend with other social actors. For example, in European history, citizens in self-governing towns or cities had certain rights to participate in governance. While they enjoyed economic freedom to pursue their material interests in a capitalist economy, they needed political space to protect their property from arbitrary action by government, hence giving rise to the concept of civil (i.e., citizen) society. They organized civil society organizations (CSOs) as an intermediary between them and the government to express their needs and voice their demands. Situated outside the government and the market, modern-day CSOs, such as trade unions, civic organizations, professional associations, women's groups, environmental groups, and human rights organizations, are engaged in public discourse and collective action to protect and promote the interests and values of their members.

Civil society performs several important functions. First, it provides a platform to monitor or restrain the state power, holding public officials accountable. A vibrant civil society is a vital instrument in checking potential abuses of power and violations of law. Civic associations may investigate human rights violations, and the media can report cases of corruption or electoral irregularities. Without the checks and balances by civil society, government can be corrupt, serving only the interest of its political allies and clients. Second, it offers an arena for people to express and defend their interests in addition to political parties. Throughout the process of contestation and accomodation, citizens learn to develop political skills such as negotiation, compromise, and consensus-building. The practice helps educate citizens and develop future political leaders. Third, it creates a forum to bring people together, building a web of interests that cuts across class, religion, ethnicity, or other social cleavages to mitigate political conflicts and divisions.

Notwithstanding these advantages, government and political leaders may be apprehensive of the power sharing demanded by other political actors, including the civil society. Contention and cooperation between the state and the society reveal important information about how governance issues are handled.

Effective governance involves setting rules and creating institutions outside the narrow realm of government to include public and societal actors to manage the politial process and steer the society toward policy goals and preferred outcomes. Nevertheless, steering is a dynamic process, and the capability to steer is determined by two concpets: autonomy and legitimacy. While the state needs to be autonomous to act with authority above particularized interest for the greater good of the country, its authority has to be recognized and accepted as legitimate by other actors in the political process.

Autonomy and Legitimacy

Autonomy refers to a state's ability to exercise its power independently of other political actors, domestic or international. A state's autonomy originates from its central position as a sovereign authority to claim control over people and land within its boundary. It also derives from its capacity to formulate and implement policies deemed best for the country, irrespective of pressure politics. A strong, autonomous state will be able to mobilize required economic resources to carry out the governing tasks effectively. A state with a low degree of autonomy will act largely on behalf of dominant interests that control specific issues or policies. While in a good position to govern without being interfered with by the organized interests, an autonomous state may run the risk of suppressing dissenting voices and societal input. Effective governance needs to strike a balance between autonomy and dependency.

Another important element in effective governance is legitimacy, by which political leaders and institutions are recognized and accepted as proper and justified. Where there is legitimacy, public laws and obligations are obeyed with minimal use of coercion or punishment. Without legitimacy, political leaders have to rely on raw, brute force, or the threat of such force, to intimidate or overwhelm the public into submission and compliance. The governing capacity is severely curtailed when the public has little faith in the political process or institution.

German sociologist Max Weber (1864–1920) identified three sources of legitimacy: traditional, charismatic, and rational-legal. Traditional legitimacy appeals to custom, tradition, and historical symbolism to gain authority. How things were done in the past lends credence as to why it should be done today. On the other hand, charismatic legitimacy comes from political leaders who gain power and influence because of their heroic achievements or charming personalities. Finally, rational-legal legitimacy is grounded in rules by which people are governed. It stems from an appeal to a system of laws and procedures that is regarded as valid for all invovled. For example, citizens in a constitutional democracy would accept the outcome of the election, even though their preferred candidates may have lost.

Another way to view the source of legitimacy is to distinguish procedure-based (or input-oriented) legitimacy from performance-based (or output-oriented) legitimacy. Procedure-based legitimacy is similar to the rational-legal legitimacy discussed by Weber in that widely accepted democratic procedures for political decisions lay the foundation for people's faith in government. Performance-based legitimacy, however, depends on concrete outcomes delivered by government. Government's effectiveness in serving the common good and providing tangible benefits becomes an important element in earning trust and achieving legitimacy.

Economic Prosperity

The active pursuit of sustained economic growth is a relatively recent phenomenon, dating back only 300 or 400 years. For much of human history until the early 16th century, per capita production and income grew at a slow, steady pace. The Industrial Revolution that began in the mid-18th century in Britain ushered in a new era. Capitalist forms of production made it possible to produce more goods with fewer inputs at lower cost. The application of scientific knowledge and innovative technology to industrial production processes encouraged the pursuit of efficiency that increased profit while reducing cost.

Growth versus Development

The economic dynamism unleashed by the Industrial Revolution naturally led to intellectual interest in how and why economic growth and development took place. Although "economic development" and "economic growth" are often used interchangeably, there is a subtle distinction between the two. Economic growth is usually defined as an increase in national income or production, as measured by GDP or gross national product (GNP), whether at the per capita or aggregate level.

Nevertheless, these measures take into account only goods and services that are traded in the market or, if supplied by the government, have prices attached to them. They do not consider nonmarket activities engaged in by individuals or organizations that can affect, positively or negatively, a sense of well-being. To address this deficiency, the broader concept of economic development intends to go beyond the narrow focus of income or production and capture different aspects of economic and social change, such as improvement in education and human conditions, as well as elimination of poverty, unemployment, and inequality (Kuznets 1966; Schultz 1961; Seers 1969).

The broad definition of development means that economic decision making must consider not only issues of efficiency and growth but also the question of equality and distribution. In this book, the concept of economic prosperity encompasses the broad definition of economic development, including not only economic production and growth but also economic distribution.

Supply-Side Economics versus Demand-Side Economics

What causes sustained economic growth? Economists have analyzed growth elements from both the supply and demand sides. Supply-side economics emphasizes factors such as capital (K), labor (L), and technology (T). Economic production is considered the function of these growth factors:

$$Y_s = F\,(K, L, T)$$

Capital (K) represents durable physical inputs such as machines, factories, and buildings, while labor (L) denotes inputs associated with human effort, including the number of individuals in the workforce and the length of time they work. The third input, technology (T), is basically the knowledge (i.e., a blueprint or formula) that uses machines and workers to produce the finished product.

From the supply-side perspective, physical investment in machines, buildings, and infrastructure drives economic growth. If a country wishes to enhance its standard of living, the solution is simple and straightforward: increase the rates of saving and investment so that physical capital is accumulated at a higher rate. An economy that is unable to generate sufficient domestic capital may rely on external funds to supplement domestic saving and investment. Foreign saving in the form of aid, loans, and foreign direct investment could be added to domestic saving to stimulate economic growth. In the case of East Asia, rapid economic growth has been facilitated by relatively high savings rates, supplemented by foreign borrowing (South Korea) or foreign direct investment (China).

As increased physical capital stimulates economic growth, so does investment in education for productive human capital. In high-performing Asian economies, enrollment in primary education in 1960 was a good predictor for a significant part of economic growth from 1960 to 1985. The level of primary education was the most important economic contributor, accounting for 58 percent to 87 percent of the growth rate in different Asian economies (World Bank 1993).

On the other hand, demand-side economists such as Keynes and his followers believe that expanding societal demand for goods and services can promote economic growth. They consider the aggregate demand as the sum of consumer spending (called consumption, C), investment (I), government spending (G), and net exports (exports minus imports: X-M). A simple equation, equivalent to the calculation of the GNP, sums up these elements:

$$Y_d = C + I + G + (X-M)$$

Keynesian economists propose that government monetary and fiscal policies can be used to stimulate demand. For example, when an economy loses its momentum, a government can pursue an expansionary monetary policy by lowering the interest rate to reduce the cost of borrowing. Doing so encourages private sector investment in factory construction (I) to create new units of physical capital (K) or replace old capital, which stimulates demand. Alternatively, government may implement an expansionary fiscal policy either by cutting taxes to increase disposable income so consumers have more money to spend (C) or by increasing government spending (G) to stimulate growth. Monetary and fiscal policy tools target different growth components on the demand side. An economy can also engage in international trade and create demand-induced growth by expanding its exports (X-M).

Although demand is certainly important, particularly in the short run, economic growth in the long run must be sustained by the growth in its capacity to produce. Balanced growth can be achieved only if demands and supplies grow without disruption.

The Market versus the State

How best can an economy mobilize and distribute resources for economic prosperity? Which one is a more effective mechanism, the market or the state?

Classical and neoclassical economists argue that capital accumulation and technological innovation, which are instrumental to wealth generation and expansion, will naturally take place within the framework of a competitive market environment. They expect government to pursue market-conforming policies to stabilize macroeconomic environments, promote exports, invest in human capital, and create a legal framework for enforcement mechanisms to maintain a competitive market. Neoclassical economists emphasize the importance of economic fundamentals and minimal state interference (Balassa 1982, 1988; Hughes 1980; Little 1982) as they explain the economic growth of the Asian NIEs. In their view, much of the economic growth in the region can be attributed to macroeconomic fundamentals and market-friendly policies. So long as the government can maintain macroeconomic stability, including mild inflation, fiscal discipline, low taxes, and liberalized trade and investment environments, private enterprises will thrive.

At the opposite end are the statists who question the self-regulating virtues of the market, particularly for less advanced nations to catch up in a competitive international environment. Instead, they emphasize the importance of pro-moting economic development from national and strategic perspectives.

According to Gerschenkron (1962), late developers in Europe rely on state intervention to overcome their difficulties. While short on physical capital, late developers can learn from the lessons of earlier industrializers to know what to emulate and what to avoid. To catch up, they need to take short cuts by direct-ing limited resources to areas that have proven vital to early developers. As a centralized institution with coordination and enforcement power, the state must be the driving force for industrialization.

The statist perspective informs the model of "developmental state" in Johnson's (1982) pioneering study of the postwar Ministry of International Trade and Industry (MITI) in Japan. According to Johnson, MITI embodied the Japanese developmental state by planning for Japan's economic growth through direct and indirect forms of administrative guidance. Staffed by the best managerial talent from a small, elite bureaucracy, MITI and the Japanese developmental state were deeply involved in the economy through industrial policies such as strategic targeting and resource allocation, as they coordinated investment and production activities with the private sector. This thesis of the developmental state model has been used to explain the economic success of other Asian NIEs, too (Deyo 1987; Gold 1986; Haggard and Moon 1990; Johnson 1987; Koo 1984; Rodan 1989; Whang 1987).

National Security

While no one doubts the importance of national security, there may not be consensus on what constitutes national security and what needs to be made secure. National security in its traditional sense involves the military aspect of international politics, with special emphasis on state survival. As states com-pete for power, status, and wealth in the modern international system, it is imperative to safeguard their sovereignty and territorial integrity from foreign incursion. To do so, states rely primarily on their military capabilities to pro-tect themselves and gain influence.

In recent decades, the scope of national security has broadened. In the aftermath of the 1973 oil embargo imposed by oil exporting countries, people began to realize that economic instruments could be as effective as military means in undermining the welfare of a society. Similarly, environmental deg-radation that damages food and water supplies could be of equal importance as military security. Furthermore, the emergence of nonstate actors such as ter-rorists, separatists, or ethnonationalists heightens the importance of internal security, as opposed to external security.

Realism versus Liberalism

Whether national security is defined narrowly or broadly, two distinct schools of thought have influenced the security policies and decisions: realism and liberalism.

Realism is built on the assumption that power struggles in international politics are caused by human nature, which is driven by the lust for power and domination. Domestically, human instincts are constrained by the state, whose legitimate use of coercive force helps maintain public order. Internationally, however, there exists no supranational institution above sovereign states; states have to help themselves to survive in this kind of anarchic system. They cannot depend on other states to defend them even if they share common interests or ideology, nor can they rely on international law or international organizations for protection. To deter attack by potential enemies, states have to augment their power to ensure self-preservation.

For the realist, power is fungible, that is, one kind of power can be transformed into another. For example, while technological innovation, economic development, and population growth represent different aspects of national strength, they all help expand a state's military capabilities. To establish and maintain a favorable power balance in the international system, leaders of a state have to engage in power calculation constantly as they seek to improve the state's power standing vis-à-vis others.

The power equation is dynamic and subject to change. According to the power transition theory, significant changes in power structure could undermine international stability. When a rising power (a challenger) approaches parity with an established dominant power (a defender), conflict is likely, particularly if the challenger is dissatisfied with the status quo. Instability comes either from the revisionist challenger, who tries to redefine the international order, or from the defender, who attempts to maintain the existing order. The recent rise of China raises questions on power transition in East Asia, where the United States has held the hegemonic position since the end of WWII. Is China approaching power parity with the United States? Is the rising China dissatisfied with the international status quo? Will China challenge the U.S. military presence in the region?

Ironically, a rational decision by a state to increase its security could result in more insecurity, leading to a phenomenon called "security dilemma." As one state builds up its defense, its action may be perceived by another state as security threat, prompting the second state to react by enhancing its war preparedness. Soon, the action-reaction pattern from both parties can spiral into an arms race for military superiority. Taken together, what is seen by each side as legitimate self-defense effort could thus lead to a dangerous and expensive military competition. The existence of the security dilemma casts doubt on whether realist measures alone can fully address security concerns.

In contrast to realism, liberalism believes that human nature is capable of goodwill and cooperation. For liberal theorists, an anarchic international system may be a necessary condition for conflict and war but not a sufficient one. So long as appropriate processes and institutions are in place, the negative elements of international politics can be contained and possibly eliminated. Two distinct mechanisms are seen by liberals as particularly instrumental for international cooperation: economic interdependence and democratic norms.

The economic strand of liberalism argues that international trade and economic transactions bring societies together through the sharing of material benefits. Economic cooperation makes states interdependent, reducing tensions and promoting better political relations. When engaged extensively in trade and investment, the networks of contacts and exchanges between trade partners create interwoven functional linkages in multiple channels that can spill over to other areas for further cooperation. Additionally, complex interdependence raises the cost of conflict to both sides, hence dissuades the publics from military conquests and ventures.

The political variant of liberalism emphasizes the role of democratic norms and values in fostering peace. According to Immanuel Kant (1724–1804), liberal republics are more pacifist than other forms of government, as people in republics are more cautious about going to war, for they have to bear the human and economic costs of the war. Modern theory of democratic peace (Doyle 1986) argues that, while democracies have fought numerous wars with nondemocracies, democracies rarely if ever go to war with each other. Constrained by representation and respect of the rights of the others, liberal democracies exercise caution and settle their conflicts peacefully.

Realism and liberalism offer competing, but completely different, perspectives on security. Both traditions have continued to shape the thinking and dialogue on security. One perspective may dominate the other at any given time, but neither could totally eliminate the influence of the other.

EXPLANATORY VARIABLES

As discussed earlier, while these three goals are high on every state's agenda, each state may pursue those using different strategies and approaches. The decisions, however, are not made in a vacuum. What explains the choices and decisions made by these East Asian states? What drives policy makers' actions and behaviors? What shapes their governing, economic, and security policies? This book emphasizes the role of four distinct explanatory variables—interests, ideas, institutions, and international factors (or the four I's) in shaping public policies and explaining continuities and changes.

Interests

Broadly defined, interests include the tangible (such as resources and wealth) and the intangible (such as power and authority). Regardless of their types, they are important determinants of policy preferences. From the interest perspective, people are rational actors with clearly defined preferences, objectives, and goals. Weighing the cost and benefit of each option, they try to maximize gains and minimize losses. Although people may show different preferences for different interests, they in general view interests as something valuable and desirable.

Divergent interests between individuals or groups of individuals can cause competition and conflict. Lipset and Rokkan (1967) identified four social cleavages—regional, religious, urban-rural, and economic class (owner-workers)—as the primary bases for political and social divisions in a society. For example, city dwellers and rural residents tend to have opposing interest for food price. People in cities are more likely to work in commerce and industries, whereas rural residents in agricultural production. City people, as consumers of food, generally prefer lower food price, while people in the countryside, as food producers, would benefit from higher food price. Thus, government policy on food price would have opposite effects on economic benefits of these two groups. Similarly, workers and capitalists, and landlords and landless peasants, also have divergent interests. Workers generally prefer a distributive policy that transfers wealth from the rich to the poor, but capitalists favor less state intervention. In the same vein, landless peasants have economic stakes in land reforms that landowners are likely to oppose.

From the interest perspective, it is reasonable to assume that people will take actions to protect their real or perceived interests. But individuals usually do not act alone to guard their interests. In liberal democracies, people organize associations such as interest groups, trade unions, professional organizations, and political parties as vehicles to pursue and defend their welfare. Even in authoritarian states, political elites may form factions to advance their ambitions and protect their interests.

Nevertheless, it is not easy for people to act as a group in pursuit of their common interest, given what is known as the collective-action problem, or the "let-George-do-it" problem. People are less willing to spend their own time or resources on collective movements if they believe that the collective action will occur anyway without their contributions. This is particularly true when free riders can still share the benefits of the collective action, even though they did not contribute to the cause.

Literature suggests that, when benefits and costs are concentrated and directly related to a relatively small number of players, they are more likely to work together and take collective actions to pursue and defend their interests (Olson 1971). In contrast, when benefits are more diffused, collective action is less likely to materialize, for people are concerned about bearing extra burdens, while allowing other free riders to enjoy the benefits. The ability to overcome the collective action problem in part determines the power of interest groups.

While the interest perspective is plausible and straightforward, it leaves some important questions unanswered. For example, how do people define their self-interests? Can interest be understood apart from the idea of who the "self" is or what the individual's purpose may be? If not, factors outside the interest domain may need to be included to help us understand how people determine their interests and preferences, which leads to the discussion of the concept of ideas.

Ideas

Ideas encompass a variety of expressed thoughts, ranging from simple concepts such as freedom, justice, or equality, to highly structured, well-articulated ideologies such as conservatism, liberalism, or socialism. They are underlying beliefs, values, and worldviews ingrained in people's minds that consciously or unconsciously guide their attitudes and actions. Ideas inform people of who they are, what their purpose is, and how they should relate to the outside world. The ideational perspective assumes that people are meaning-seeking beings who not only try to understand the society in which they live but also seek to build it in accordance with ideals or values. Even the most powerful interest groups recognize that simply pushing for their self-interests would not take them very far. Instead, they need to present their arguments in light of norms and values to gain legitimacy.

Ideas matter; they inspire and guide political actions. When invoked, they appeal to people's emotion and imagination and influence their thoughts and behaviors. Ideas frame people's perspectives and can constrain or expand their understanding of events and outcomes. Innovative ideas promote new thinking and alternative vision, serving as a catalyst for social, political, and economic changes.

When new ideas are transmitted and broadly shared, they may begin to shape political agendas that in turn can have a transformative impact on policy outcomes. The process involves two stages: first, the collapse of the reigning paradigm, and second, the consolidation of a new paradigm. In the first stage, the prevalent idea gradually loses its credibility and legitimacy. The widespread dissatisfaction with the conventional wisdom then paves the way to the emergence of replacement ideas that consolidate to become a new paradigm.

The rise of the macroeconomic Keynesian policies illustrates this point. During the Great Depression of the 1930s, the traditional economic approach was to cut government expenditures when revenues declined during economic downturn, which unfortunately worsened unemployment and prolonged economic slump. To reverse the vicious economic cycle, Keynes proposed the opposite policy of stimulating demand through budget deficits in economic recessions. The idea was initially considered by many as problematic. With its gradual acceptance by the community of economists, several governments began to implement Keynesianism during the Great Depression. Eventually, the success made Keynesianism a standard practice after World War II.

Clashes between competing ideas and interests often lead to political conflicts. The battle between socialism and capitalism was the dominant theme in international politics for much of the 20th century, particularly in the Cold War era as the world was divided along two ideological camps. Similarly, conservatism and liberalism are opposing ideas that continue to influence domestic politics in many states. Additionally, ideas could be in conflict with vested interests, setting up political battles between the two, as seen in the clash between the norm of environmental protection and the interest of powerful polluters and between the principle of democracy and the political interests of dictators.

Competition between ideas and interests takes place in social and political institutions, within which politicians and political groups act to pursue what is deemed desirable. These institutions provide rules and structures so that political conflicts and disagreements can be contained and managed and cooperation achieved—a subject to which we now turn.

Institutions

Institutions are organizations, structures, and patterns of activity that define and shape what is possible and appropriate in political life. Basic governmental structures such as the executive, legislature, courts, the civil service, and the military are examples of formal political institutions created under law and constitution. Additionally, insitutions such as electoral systems and party systems provide linkages between political organizations and government and establish structures and channels for political participation.

Why do institutions matter? Institutions set the stage and provide the forum in which divergent ideas and interests compete with one another before government officials and bureaucrats transform them into public policies. Institutional arrangements, however, are not necessarily neutral. Rules embodied in institutions, in effect, construct incentives and disincentives for political actors, steering them toward what is appropriate. For example, if democratic procedures take root and the public accepts democracy as "the only game in town," then politicians need to respect the democratic principles; otherwise, they risk losing their political careers. Thus, institutions shape, enable, or constrain political behaviors.

Once established and accepted as legitimate, institutions tend to be resilient and stable. They become self-perpetuating, enduring beyond the turnover of political leaders and their idiosyncratic personalities. With legitimacy, institutions command authority and demand compliance. Furthermore, those who benefit from their existence are likely to guard and preserve the existing institutions, viewing any adjustment or change as a potential threat to their interests. Together, they become a formidable force to prevent change. Any attempt to reform institutions, even for those unproductive or inefficient ones, usually encounters resistance. Institutional stability is the rule; major change is the exception.

Along with the "stickiness" of the institution is the phenomenon of "path dependence" of policies and political outcomes. The fact that certain political behaviors are encouraged and sustained by existing institutions implies that some political "paths" are more likely, which further demonstrates the importance of institutions. Choices made in the past in a particular context will persist to shape the choices in the future. Thus, it is critical to understand not only how institutions may shape policies and events but also how institutions emerge and change: What are the rules of the game in politics? Why are they established? How are they designed and enforced?

A constitution can provide some answers to these questions. It is a formal document that declares how power is divided and distributed in a state, whether it is federal or unitary, presidential or parliamentarian. When the locus of power does not conform to the formal arrangement stipulated in the constitution or law, it suggests that some informal institutions such as political conventions and behaviroal patterns need to be closely examined. Although informal institutions are unwritten and unofficial, they could be just as powerful as the formal ones in regulating political processes.

Furthermore, a constitution guards the fundamental rights of the people against power abuse by government, as seen in the principle of constitutionalism that repects the practices such as rule of law, limited government, and legally enforceable rights. Drafting and passing a document called a constitution does not necessarily mean that a state in fact rules in accordance with constitutionalism. When a constitution merely provides a cover for a dictatorship whose power rests on an extraconstitutional basis, it does not meet the basic element of constitutionalism.

International Factors

International forces have always been an important factor shaping domestic politics. As stated earlier, the arrival of the European and American powers in the mid-19th century significantly changed the development trajectory of East Asia. Of course, the phenomenon was not unique to Asia. Colonialism and modern imperialism have influenced domestic politics and international relations in other parts of the world, including Africa, Latin America, and the Middle East. In the 20th century, the fierce competition between major powers led to the two World Wars, underscoring the influence of international geo-economic-strategic interests.

In the post-WWII era, connections between countries have expanded in scope, depth, and speed. As the Allies met in Bretton Woods, New Hampshire, in 1944, to rebuild the postwar economic order, they envisioned a system functioning under greater collaboration between governments. The three key international institutions under the Bretton Woods System—the International Monetary Fund (IMF), the World Bank, and the General Agreement on Tariffs and Trade (GATT)—intended to harmonize member states' policies in foreign exchange, currency convertibility, and trade. The norms established by these international organizations, in essence, imposed restrictions on the member states, hence reducing their control over their own economies. Subsequently, the creation of the United Nations, the European Union, and numerous regional and international organizations reflects another aspect of the international order—the necessity to promote international coordination and cooperation.

Innovation and improvement in communication and transportation technologies in the postwar environment further encourage movement of goods, capital, and people across borders. Operating in expanded international trade and investment networks, multinational corporations (MNCs) and international banks can produce and distribute their goods and services more efficiently on a global basis. The ability of the MNCs to create jobs and expand tax bases in home and host countries gives them an advantage in influencing public policies and regulations.

In light of the trend of globalization, the distinction between international affairs and domestic politics is increasingly blurred. The rapid dissemination of news and information on a global basis makes it difficult to contain any ideas, interests, and institutions within national boundaries. Many aspects of domestic politics are under the influence of international forces. Networks of international organizations, whether governmental or nongovernmental, set standards, shape expectations, and enforce rules on a range of issues, hence challenging state autonomy and capacity.

Together, the analysis of the independent and interactive effects of the four I's—interests, ideas, institutions, and international factors—helps us reflect on policies and actions in China, Japan, and Korea, as they pursue the goals of governance, prosperity, and security. While the prominence of each factor may vary in different countries at different times, the systematic examination of these factors collectively paints a comprehensive picture for the accomplishments and future challenges of these states.

ORGANIZATION AND APPROACH

This book is divided into three sections. Chapters 1 through 4 in Section One deal with China. Chapter 1 provides a brief survey of the historical background to lay the foundation for the understanding of post-WWII China in political governance (Chapter 2), economic prosperity (Chapter 3), and national security (Chapter 4). Parallel structures apply to Section Two (Chapters 5 through 8) for Japan and Section Three (Chapters 9 through 12) for South Korea. Parallelism in structure reflects a deliberate choice. For readers interested in studying one country at a time, they can follow the sequence of the book. For audiences that would like to focus on themes, they can select the relevant chapters from each section and read them as a group. Comparing and contrasting developments from a comparative lens helps to understand the factors contributing to similarities and differences between these countries.

The discussions in the book try to bridge the gap between area studies and social sciences. Literature in Asian studies provides rich information and insights on the histories and cultures of these three countries that highlight the uniqueness of the states. On the other hand, modern social science theories identify commonality in human experiences for comparison, with the goal of finding generalizable trends and patterns of these societies. Both approaches are valid, as they provide insights from different angles. This book tries to integrate the two and include the unique and the shared in its discussions.

Given the depth and complexity of the civilizations of these societies, it would be impossible to focus on the details of all events and personalities. Rather, the book tries to identify some distinct patterns or major trends in these societies for in-depth discussions. In so doing, it does not imply that these are the only narratives about the region across all the periods or the only lines of evolution or progression for their development trajectories. Any attempt to make such a claim is likely to oversimplify the reality. Nevertheless, many of these trends and patterns are an important part of the national memories or cultural imprints of these civilizations and are instrumental for our understanding of the contemporary societies.

Personal names in this book follow the East Asian tradition with surnames (or family names) first. The Chinese phonetic system of spelling (*pinyin*) is used for Chinese names and terms, except for the established and widely accepted spellings of Tibet, Confucius, Kuomintang, Chiang Kai-shek, and Sun Yat-sen. Japanese words and names are Romanized according to the modified Hepburn system. Korean names generally follow the McCune-Reischauer system, with the exception of well-known names such as Seoul, Pyongyang, Syngman Rhee, Park Chung-hee, Kim Il-sung, Kim Jong-il, and Kim Jong-un. Korean given names consisting of two syllables are hyphenated in this book.

DISCUSSION QUESTIONS

1. What does political governance mean? What are the roles and functions of the state in political governance? How do the concepts of autonomy and legitimacy describe the dynamic relationships between the state and civil society in governance?

2. Is the market, or the state, more effective in promoting economic development? Compare the different views of the neoclassicals and the statists, and discuss whether their differences can be reconciled.

3. What are realist and liberal strategies in achieving national security? What explains their differences? How would you evaluate the effectiveness of each approach?

4. Provide a definition for "ideas," and give some examples. Based on those examples, explain how they may affect people's beliefs and contemporary politics.

5. Give some examples of political institutions. Based on the examples you provide, discuss the possible functions they may perform in politics, economics, or national security.

1

China

THE FOUNDATIONS

PEOPLE AND GEOGRAPHY

China is the most populous country in the world (1.39 billion people) and the second largest in land area (3.6 million square miles, after Russia). Its territory covers vastly different typographies and climates. Over 90 percent of its population lives on the eastern half of the country, which consists of fertile lowlands and is the origin of Chinese civilization. Major river systems such as the Yellow River (*Huang He*) in the north, the Long River (*Chang Jiang*) in the middle, and the Pearl River (*Zhu Jiang*) in the south provide key lifelines for irrigation and transportation but may also cause floods leading to significant loss in life and property.

The mountain ranges in the southwest (the Himalayas and the Altai) and the desert in the northwest (Xinjiang region) are difficult to cross and form natural geographic barriers. The Qinling mountain range, extending east from north of Tibet, divides China into north and south. Farmers of the northern plains produce millet and wheat in a dry climate, while farmers in the south grow rice and tea in fertile plains and hills.

The north, where Chinese civilization first originated, is connected to the south through the Grand Canal. Dug in the 7th century and extended in the 13th century, it brought rice from the southern plains to supply the armies and the government in the north.

The confluence of size, geography, and resources historically contributes to a Sino-centered worldview for its people. The name China, meaning the "Middle Kingdom" in Chinese, reflected the Chinese perception that they were at the center of civilization. Even when the country had been weakened by internal conflicts, natural barriers provided security protection to the Chinese in the premodern era.

The majority of the people in China are the Han ethnic group. Approximately 8.5 percent of the total population (or 115 million people) belong to 55 government-designated minority nationalities, who are concentrated in the border regions that are rich in natural resources such as oil, coal, gold, and other minerals. The largest groups are Zhuang in the southwest, Hui (Muslim) in the west and northwest, and Manzu in the northwest.

Because arable land accounts for only 15 percent of China's territory, the pressure to produce enough food to feed the population has been a chronic challenge for China throughout its history. The nature of China's population challenge, however, has changed significantly in the past several decades. In 1953, according to the first population census, the total population was 582 million. By the late 1970s, the number had nearly doubled, leading to fear that the runaway population growth would produce economic stagnation and social instability. To counter the growth trend, the government instituted in 1979 the one-child policy that limited urban couples to a single child. The policy effectively reduced China's fertility rate from 2.8 children per woman in 1979 to 1.6 in 2016. Nevertheless, the steep decline in the fertility rate, which is below the replacement level of 2.1 children per woman needed to maintain population size, contributes to the aging of the population and increases burdens in health care and social welfare (China Power Team 2017). Although the government in 2015 replaced the one-child policy with a two-child policy, the action might be too late to reverse the demographic trend. The projection is that the Chinese population will peak in the late 2020s or early 2030s, followed by a steady decline thereafter.

THE HISTORICAL ROOTS

The ancient Chinese civilization dates back to the Shang dynasty (ca. 1600–1046 BCE), as evinced in archaeological excavations of the weapons, oracle bones, and bronze vessels from that period. Shang was an agrarian, feudal society controlled by an aristocracy that maintained a standing army of cavalry and chariots. Inscriptions on oracle bones and tortoise shells represented the priestly attempts to seek divination from the spirit world and were the earliest known form of the written Chinese characters. Shang was succeeded by the Zhou dynasty (Western Zhou, 1046–771 BCE; Eastern Zhou, 770–256 BCE). It was during the formative years of Zhou that a number of enduring governing ideas and institutions emerged.

Mandate of Heaven

Emperors of Zhou, bearing the title of the "Son of Heaven" (or *Tianzi* in Chinese), purported to rule based on the "Mandate of Heaven." They justified their military actions against Shang on grounds of change in mandate, pointing to social disorder and natural disasters in the late Shang dynasty as evidence that the original mandate had been shattered by morally corrupt Shang emperors, hence the disharmony between Heaven and Earth.

Although the myth of mandate intended to lend legitimacy to the ruler, it implicitly created a performance standard by which rulers were judged. While

Chinese emperors faced no formal legal constraints on their ruling power, the concept of mandate formed the moral basis for justified rebellion to depose a ruthless tyrant.

During the latter reign of Eastern Zhou, the state affairs degenerated into the period of disorder as feudal lords fought with one another to expand their domains and spheres of influence. Ironically, it was at this time that Chinese civilization and intellectual tradition first developed and grew. The strong Chinese influence on the region was in large part due to its ability to develop institutional innovation early on, such as sophisticated governance structures and practices, including specialized state functions and coherent political philosophy.

Confucianism

Competing schools of thoughts flourished during the latter era of Zhou when the imperial control weakened, as people aspired to establish an ideal social and political order. The instructions of Confucius (551–479 BCE) laid the philosophic foundation of Chinese political order. Confucius, a teacher and a philosopher living in a time with widespread political instability and disorder, believed that the best way to achieve an orderly and harmonious society was to cultivate ethical and virtuous behaviors such as humanity, righteousness, propriety, wisdom, and integrity.

For Confucius, proper behaviors, manifested in relationships between emperor and subject, father and son, as well as husband and wife, led to enduring social and political order. Subjects should be loyal to their emperor, the emperor righteous and just toward subjects. Sons and daughters should show filial piety toward their parents, and parents should show kindness to their children. Husbands should provide for wives, and wives should be faithful and obedient to husbands. The teaching provided practical codes of ethics and conduct for different roles in the society. Emperors and political leaders had moral obligations to be just and responsible, acting as guardians of the public interest and welfare. Even though such expectations were never codified in law or enforceable at court in premodern China, they became an institutional constraint to manage public affairs fairly and wisely.

More than any other individual in Chinese history, Confucius offered a code of conduct and ethics with broad applications in all aspects of the society. With its implicit emphasis on social harmony, deference to authority, and hierarchical nature of society, Confucianism is seen as a conservative belief system in support of existing political order and power.

Political Centralization

Division and disorder in Zhou ended when the ruthless Qin First Emperor (*Qin Shi Huang Di*, 221–210 BCE) conquered his rivals with an efficient military machine in 221 BCE. After unifying the country, he constructed a governance structure comparable to a modern state in its ability to extract resources and control people's behaviors, laying down the foundation of the Chinese imperial system.

Under Qin, people had to pledge their allegiance to the central government, not to their traditional masters such as the landowners or feudal lords. The measure gave the government a huge reservoir of work force for military service and public projects such as roads, canals, royal tombs, and sections of the Great Wall. To centralize political power, Qin First Emperor created regional administrative units, appointed nonhereditary officials, implemented uniform laws and taxes, as well as promoted standardized weights, measures, and written characters.

Since then, for more than two thousand years and with more than 20 dynastic turnovers, the form and substance of the core governing institutions within a single, centralized Chinese empire were remarkably stable and remained essentially unchanged.

In an attempt to clean up the past and create new loyalties, Qin went to the extremes to order the burning of all books, except those in agriculture, medicine, and divination. Scholars who disobeyed the command were executed or buried alive. Qin's cruel and totalitarian control of public affairs led to widespread uprisings that quickly ended the regime in 206 BCE.

Meritocratic Bureaucracy

The Han dynasty (206 BCE-220 CE) that succeeded Qin was comparable to its contemporary, the Roman Empire, in area and population. To enhance the governing capacity of the emperor, imperial leaders developed a selection system to recruit and promote officials based on merit and experience. This practice marked an early attempt of developing a meritocratic, professional bureaucracy, rather than appointing officials based on their aristocratic pedigree—an idea that did not emerge in other parts of the world until centuries later.

The utility of the Confucian doctrine in promoting virtuous behaviors to maintain social harmony and political stability was not lost to the Han imperial court. Han rulers began to elevate Confucianism above all other contending schools of thoughts as officially sanctioned political ideology and established an imperial academy to train Confucian officials.

The bureaucratic selection system gradually evolved into the civil service exams in the Tang Dynasty (618–907 CE). Civil servants who served the emperor were recruited through competitive civil service examinations based on their knowledge of the Confucian classics. For centuries, rote memorization of the ancient Confucian texts was the only effective strategy to pass the exams, which had a long-term pass rate of less than 10 percent (Eisenstadt 1967). Notwithstanding the remarkable advances in science and technology of the world, the exam and its criteria stayed virtually unchanged well into the early 20th century.

Because the examination was open to commoners, the system promoted social mobility and served to break the dominance of hereditary aristocracy. From Tang onward, China gradually evolved into a society with greater social mobility. While the meritocratic bureaucracy lent support and legitimacy to imperial rule, the examination system helped promote education and popular literacy in China.

Political Governance

At the top of the political structure of the Chinese imperial system stood the emperor, the holder of the Mandate-of-Heaven claim. The emperor served as a symbol of unity, although the real power might vary in each case.

Ministers and official-scholars (the mandarins) recruited through the civil service exams played an important role in political governance under the imperial system. They administered public affairs in various ministries in the central government. Some of them, serving as advisors and counsels to the emperor, could, in fact, constrain the power of the emperor.

The vast majority of the population in the traditional Chinese society were farmers, while others were engaged in crafts or commerce. Together, they shouldered most of the tax burden and uncompensated labor service such as building levees and bridges.

Most of the people were governed at the local level by government officials in respective administrative jurisdictions. The local administrative apparatus, however, was not entirely autonomous, for there were other power contenders in the governing system. The gentry class of the landlords, for example, was usually influential in local affairs. They tended to collaborate with local officials in governance, collecting taxes, and maintaining social stability. Corrupt officials might take the opportunity to enrich themselves.

Advanced farming techniques such as irrigation systems, waterwheels, and multiple cropping boosted productivity to support China's large population. The strength of the Chinese agricultural economy gave the imperial system great staying power. During the time of agrarian crisis and famine, however, farmers sometimes rose up against the heavy tax burdens imposed by the officials and gentry class. Some prominent examples in the premodern era included the Yellow Turban Rebellion (named for the scarves that the rebels wrapped around their heads) in the Han dynasty (184 CE) and the Red Turban Rebellion (1351–1368) against the Mongol-led Yuan dynasty.

One achievement of imperial China was its remarkable ability to hold the country together. Despite periods of division, and the rise and fall of more than 20 dynasties throughout history, Chinese governing institutions effectively maintained law and order and extracted resources for governance purposes like a modern state. As a polity commanding the world's largest landmass and population, the Chinese state was able to bring together diverse subcultures and ethnic groups, maintaining its integrity since the Qin dynasty without breaking up into separate states like those in Europe. By the 14th century, an estimated forty thousand bureaucrats were involved in collecting taxes and administering laws. From the 13th century to the end of the 19th century, each year the bureaucracy organized the largest grain shipment, moving hundreds of thousands of tons of taxed grain through the Grand Canal to feed the population in the capital and other large cities in northern China. A common cultural identity, the communication and transportation infrastructure, and the massive bureaucratic apparatus all seemed to contribute to the unification of the country in the premodern era.

Foreign Relations: The Tributary System

During the Han dynasty, China entered a period of military conquest to expand its territories and extend its frontiers. International trade and foreign exploration were encouraged in the Han dynasty. The Silk Road, trade routes between China and Europe through Central Asia, helped promote commerce and cultural exchanges. At the height of its power, the territories of the Han dynasty almost reached the modern-day Chinese frontiers, from its base in the north China plain to modern Vietnam and from the Pacific coast to Central Asia.

Unlike modern diplomatic practices based on the principle of equality and reciprocity between states, Han China managed its relations with neighboring states through the "tributary system." Foreign rulers offered tribute (i.e., native products or other precious commodities) to the emperor; in return, they received the nominal status of a vassal and the permission to have commercial and cultural contact with China. While the presentation of tribute signaled subservience to the Chinese emperor, these tributary missions were in fact opportunities to conduct trades for both sides. Additionally, they facilitated cultural exchange for foreign scholars to collect Chinese books and learn the latest cultural trends.

With its immense size and sophisticated governing system, China's military power and cultural influence prevailed in the region. At the beginning of the 14th century and on the eve of the European Renaissance, China held superior technological advances in areas such as metallurgy, gun power, shipbuilding, papermaking, block printing, and silk and porcelain production. Its maritime technology was more advanced than that of Europe at the time, as evidenced by its seafaring expeditions to Southeast Asia and the Indian Ocean in the early Ming dynasty (1368–1644).

Zheng He (1371–1433), a Ming eunuch and admiral, launched the first voyage in 1405, 87 years before Columbus's trip. Under Zheng's command, more than 20,000 people boarded 300 plus ships on his first voyage, compared to Columbus's four boats and 150 sailors. From 1405 to 1433, Zheng conducted seven expeditions, blending commerce with politics to display China's power and wealth.

Ming China, however, turned inward in the 15th century, terminating foreign trade missions and private trade. The policy shift was justified on the grounds that potential invasion from Mongolia or Manchuria demanded real-location of resources from overseas missions to inland defense. The isolation policy, reinforced by the sense of self-sufficiency and self-confidence of the Sino-centric worldview, continued well into the last dynasty in China, the Qing dynasty (1644–1912).

The Qing dynasty, established by foreign ethnic Manchus in 1644, ruled over a country of approximately 300 million people. Though a foreign regime, Qing emperors adopted the Chinese governance model. A series of success-ful territorial expansions by Qing emperors expanded the Chinese empire to modern-day Xinjiang and Tibet.

Under the isolation policy, Chinese merchants in southern China traded with Southeast Asia and restricted trade with Russia took place in the north. Trade with Europeans, however, was limited to the southern port of Guangzhou.

CHINA IN THE AGE OF IMPERIALISM

External and Internal Upheavals

At the time when Europe advanced rapidly through the Renaissance and Industrial Revolution, China's technological development and innovation began to languish. The Chinese were largely unaware that scientific, techno-logical, political, and social revolutions had transformed Western Europe and North America into major players on the world stage. Improved technology and enhanced productivity brought by the Industrial Revolution led to over-supplies of manufactured goods in Europe, creating the urgent need to look for new markets and trading opportunities. Asian markets, particularly the Chinese market, appeared to be an ideal outlet for those goods.

As European powers sought to trade with China, Qing emperors dismissed these overtures as inferior vassal states seeking trading privileges with China. Frustrated by the fact that their requests to greater market access were repeat-edly rejected by Qing emperors, the European powers relied on their supe-rior military power to open the Asian markets. From the 1840s to 1860s, by force and by coercion, European states, particularly Great Britain, succeeded in prying open Chinese markets.

Britain easily defeated China in the Opium War (1839–1842) and secured a number of economic and political concessions. In the Treaty of Nanjing (1842), China was forced to pay the British a large indemnity restitution, cede Hong Kong to Britain, and open five treaty ports to foreign trade under "fair and reasonable" tariffs, as determined by the British. An 1843 agreement supplemented the treaty, granting "extraterritoriality" and the "most-favored-nation" status to the British. Under the principle of extraterritoriality, British citizens were exempt from all Chinese taxes and from any accountability to Chinese laws, while the most-favored-nation clause automatically gave Britain all privileges that China might grant to other countries. The Chinese, however, did not have the same rights in Britain, thus making the treaty unequal. Other Western states soon followed the example, securing rights and privileges through unequal treaties with China. By the end of the 19th century, 50 treaty ports in China had been opened to foreign trade.

Within treaty ports, foreign powers could acquire concessions, which were areas designated for occupancy of their residents. Foreign communities were responsible for governing themselves in concessions by the laws of their own country rather than by the laws of China, as extraterritoriality suggested. As many Westerners lived their separate lives with as little contact with the native Chinese population as possible, racial tension and conflict sometimes erupted. Treaty ports, however, also became a transmission belt of Western thoughts and ideas. Western concepts such as freedom, equality, nationalism, and constitutionalism came through treaty ports unhindered and gradually became part of the vocabulary in Chinese political discourse.

Foreign incursion aggravated social disorder, which had been built up by rampant official corruption and prolonged economic stagnation for decades beneath the surface of political stability. Between the first Opium War and the Second Opium (Arrow) War (1856–1860), major uprisings erupted, including the most devastating Taiping Rebellion (1850–1864) that swept through some of China's wealthiest and most productive areas for 14 years and caused an estimated 20 million deaths. Together, these rebellions led to widespread economic dislocation and seriously undermined the foundation of the Qing dynasty.

Early Modernization: The Self-Strengthening Movement

In the aftermath of the Second Opium War and the Taiping Rebellion, the highest priority for the governing elites in Qing China was defense. The inadequacy of the navy and army in dealing with the Western invasions and domestic rebellions called for fundamental reforms. Anti-Taiping generals such as Zeng Guofan and his protégé Li Hongzhang began to advocate for self-strengthening. Facing the dynastic decline, they emphasized maintaining social and political order with Chinese core values, while selectively adopting elements of Western technology, particularly military technology, for modernization purposes. The selective adoption of Western technology and institutions was to be carefully balanced with the preservation of the traditional social, political, and cultural order.

For the first decade, the focus was on manufacturing machines and weaponry. In 1865, with permission from the imperial court, Zeng and Li established the Jiangnan Arsenal in Shanghai, which became the first builder of modern guns and cannons in China. Its translation bureau translated foreign works into Chinese, assisting in the adoption of Western knowledge and technology. A machine-building factory was established in Tianjin and a naval yard in Fujian. Young Chinese students were sent to the United States to study the latest thoughts on military and international affairs.

Subsequently, from the 1870s to the 1890s, the focus expanded to other defense-related fields, including steamships, railroads, mining, and manufacturing to generate wealth. Li created a few state-sponsored firms in shipping, mining, telegraphs, and textiles. These firms received government loans and were overseen by government officials, but private merchants were responsible for their day-to-day operations. The model resembled some elements of a state-led economic modernization. Additionally, Li founded the Tianjin Navy Academy (1880) and built Beiyang Fleet in 1888. Overall, with its primary focus being on defense and military technologies, the approach was still narrow.

While Western technology helped lay the foundation for Chinese industrialization, the scope, however, was limited. As discussed earlier, the proponents of the self-strengthening movement advocated using all valid means, including Western weapons, to maintain the country in its existing form. Their thinking could be summed up in a slogan: "Chinese learning for substance, Western learning for practical use." Thus, Chinese political leaders never entertained the radical notion of Westernization. Industrial projects were often initiated by provincial governors such as Zeng and Li based on their own vision and interest. There was no centralized or coordinated effort to transform the economy based on the Western model.

The absence of a unified vision for broader social reform underscored deeper governance problems in Qing court: the division between factions in competition of political power. Beginning in 1861, Empress Dowager Cixi was the de facto ruler of China for almost half a century. She twice manipulated emperor succession (in 1861 and 1875) to maintain her regency for two young emperors. She was willing to entrust Han Chinese officials such as Zeng and Li as provincial governors and to support the self-strengthening movement. Under her leadership, the Qing government instituted a modern customs service and created the first Chinese foreign service office. Nevertheless, she was never fully committed to a consistent progression toward reform, for she manipulated factional rivalry in the imperial house to maintain her position, satisfying different groups at different times.

A significant number of Manchu aristocrats in the Qing court were conservatives who harbored deep distrust of Westerners. They advocated hostile and militant responses to confront foreign powers. Hence, Cixi's policies and attitudes toward modernization were not always consistent, pending the prevalent direction of political undercurrents at a particular time.

More External and Internal Upheavals

While the Qing court offered no unified, enthusiastic leadership on modernization, neighboring Japan took a different course of action (Chapter 5). During Meiji Restoration, with central planning and strong government intervention, Meiji leaders quickly and successfully transformed Japan into a rising power with expanded regional ambition.

In spring 1894, Korea, China's traditional tributary state, sought military assistance from China to put down a rebellion. As China sent its troops, the Japanese perceived the Chinese intervention as a threat and moved troops into Seoul first. After the rebellion was defeated, neither party withdrew their troops. In July, the Japanese initiated military action against China, sinking a Chinese ship. Clashes between China and Japan over Korea escalated into the first Sino-Japanese war (1894–1895), in which the better trained and better equipped Japanese army and navy scored quick victories on land and sea and advanced into Manchuria.

In 1895, the Qing officials had no choice but to accept the humiliating terms of the Treaty of Shimonoseki as dictated by the Japanese government: recognizing the independence of Korea; ceding Taiwan, the Pescadores, and the Liaodong Peninsula (in southern Manchuria) to Japan; and granting Japan commercial concessions. Additionally, China was required to pay 200 million taels (a traditional Chinese unit of weight) of silver to Japan. The huge indemnity was more than twice China's annual revenue at the time.

From the perspective of national defense, the loss of the Liaodong Peninsula would have placed Japanese troops close to Beijing, making China particularly vulnerable. Wary of Japan's expansion, and its potential threat to its own national interest, Russia intervened. Russia, along with France and Germany, forced Japan to return the Liaodong Peninsula to China for additional indemnity. Japan acquiesced reluctantly.

The war was a huge setback for the Qing court self-strengthening movement. Seeing China's weakness, Western powers were emboldened to exact territorial concessions. For the next several years, they competed with one another to divide China into different spheres of influence. Germany moved into Shandong, Russia entered Manchuria, France expanded in southwest China, and Britain took central China as its sphere of influence, besides taking over the Kowloon Peninsula opposite Hong Kong Island. China was on the brink of partition, with a status worse than a colony, having to answer to multiple foreign powers.

The aggressiveness of foreign powers created a new sense of urgency in China. While supporters of the self-strengthening movement had emphasized defense and military affairs, some intellectuals and officials began to realize the significance of institutional and economic reforms in the wake of the Sino-Japanese War.

After Cixi's retirement in 1898, young Emperor Guangxu was anxious to find a solution to the worsening condition of the country. Beginning in June 1898, urged by more radical reformers, he initiated a series of radical and hastily prepared reforms, including the overhaul of the education and examination system, the restructuring of the government, and the promotion of agriculture, mining, and trade. Although the reform measures produced no concrete results, they provoked the conservatives, who brought Cixi out of retirement. In September 1898, Cixi took over the administration. The emperor was detained and six of the reformers executed. The reform movement, known as the Hundred Days Reform, was over before it could begin.

Decades of foreign domination had caused economic stagnation in China, as foreign commercial penetration displaced local workers and industries. Financial burden to pay for wars and indemnities increased tax load for the public. Widespread social discontent was a breeding ground for political instability.

In Shandong, a band of people called the Yihequan (or "Righteous and Harmonious Fists," mistranslated as "boxers" in the West) believed that a certain kind of boxing art would render them mysteriously invulnerable to firearms. Disturbed by German advances there, they began to stage antiforeign, anti-Christian uprisings that were covertly encouraged by the provincial governor.

By 1900, the Boxer Rebellion grew in strength, openly attacking Chinese Christians and Western missionaries and destroying all things foreign, including churches and railways. They laid siege to the foreign legations in Beijing and Tianjin. Thousands of Chinese Christians and roughly 250 foreign nationals (mostly Christian missionaries) were killed. The Western allied army that came to rescue quickly defeated the unorganized and poorly armed Boxers in August 1900 and occupied Beijing. The Qing government was forced to pay an enormous indemnity to Western powers, adding to China's already crushing burden of foreign payments.

Republican Revolution

China's humiliating defeat by Japan also spurred radical movements that called for complete political and social revolutions. One prominent revolutionary was Dr. Sun Yat-sen (Sun Zhongshan). Educated in Hawaii and Hong Kong, he founded an anti-Manzhou revolutionary group, the Revive China Society (*Xingzhonghui*), in October 1894 in Honolulu to plot uprising activities. Sun participated in a failed attempt to capture Guangzhou in 1895. Afterward, he lived in exile in Europe, Japan, and the United States for 16 years, raising money from the overseas Chinese communities while coordinating revolts with revolutionaries in China. His revolt attempts, however, all ended in failure. In October 1911, an armed rebellion not directly under Sun's control broke out in Wuhan, Hubei province. With the Qing provincial governor fleeing the scene, the rebels managed to control the provincial government. Soon afterward, other provinces announced their break with the Qing. By December 1911, more than half of China declared its independence from the Qing government. Sun returned to China and was elected provisional president of the new government.

CHINA IN THE REPUBLICAN ERA

Political Governance in the Early Republican Period

The establishment of the first republican country in Asia, however, did nothing to change the existing political culture and structure. The country remained in the hands of the powerful military leaders of the Qing regime.

Among them, Yuan Shikai was the dominant figure. He was trusted by the Qing court and regarded as the indispensable person to restore unity. In a three-way settlement, Sun resigned his position in February 1912 in favor of Yuan; Yuan promised to establish a republican government; and the Qing court proclaimed the decree of abdication, ending its rule of China and paving the way to power transition. Yuan was elected the first president of China but was tangled in power contention with the former revolutionaries.

The majority of the members elected to the first National Assembly (parliament) in February 1913 were former revolutionaries from the Nationalist Party, or Kuomintang (KMT). They drafted a constitution that placed the executive power in the cabinet accountable to the National Assembly rather than to the president. Afterward, Yuan revoked the credentials of the KMT members and dissolved the parliament. The presidency reverted to a dictatorship.

Following the outbreak of World War I in 1914, Japan joined the Allies and seized Germany's land possessions in Shandong. In January 1915, Japan secretly delivered twenty-one demands to Yuan, making claims to rights and concessions that would turn China into a Japanese dependency. These demands sought Chinese recognition of Japanese privileges in newly acquired territory in Shandong and special privileges and concessions in Manchuria. They also called for granting Japan greater access to Chinese ports and railroads, as well as political and police affairs. In May 1915, under the pressure of 48-hour ultimatum, Yuan accepted all but the most extreme conditions (i.e., to grant Japanese advisors the power to control Chinese financial, political, and police affairs). The public was outraged, calling for a boycott of Japanese goods.

In the wake of the humiliating concessions, Yuan launched a movement to revive the monarchy, only to encounter strong oppositions from other political leaders and his own subordinates. In March 1916, Yuan was forced to abolish the new monarchy and died three months later. With Yuan's death, regional military leaders, the warlords, carved up China.

Frustrated by the warlords' attempt to sabotage the republican revolution, Sun in 1917 established a rival government in Guangzhou, joined by some 100 members of parliament. Military men soon dominated the southern government, forcing Sun to leave Guangzhou. Nevertheless, the split between north (Beijing government) and south (Guangzhou government) continued. The Beijing government was the one recognized internationally as the legitimate Chinese government.

The collapse of Yuan's regime produced a power vacuum, leading to a decade of war and chaos as China disintegrated into several regions dominated by military warlords. Warlords competed for territorial bases, which were the source of revenue and manpower. Competition for territory brought on unceasing wars and conflicts. To finance their armies and sustain their war efforts, military rulers and their subordinates taxed the people heavily, taking money away from education and other government services. Merchants and bankers were forced to provide "loans" to the military. Ironically, while warlords contended for power and territory, they were less interested in prescribing any particular ideology. As a result, college students and intellectuals had more freedom to speak their minds and debate about ideas.

In late April 1919, the powers at the Paris Peace Conference decided that Germany's rights and possessions in Shandong should be retained by Japan, rejecting China's appeal to regain full control. On May 4, thousands of patriotic students demonstrated in Tiananmen Square. Waves of protests soon spread to other cities. Joining the students, merchants and workers joined the mass demonstrations, urging the Beijing government not to sign the Treaty of Versailles.

This May Fourth Movement marked a new stage in China's attempt for modernization. It came to represent not only a political or nationalistic campaign but also a cultural and intellectual movement. Participants advocated the ideas of democracy (for individual liberty and equality) and science (for a scientific, practical approach to solving the country's problems, free of the restraints of culture and tradition). Seeking deeper reforms of China's institutions than the self-strengthening movement or the republican revolution, the movement created new momentum for national revolution, as led by the KMT and the Chinese Communist Party (CCP).

Political Struggle between the Nationalist and the Communist

With the patriotic upsurge in 1919, Sun revived the name of the KMT. He returned to Guangzhou the following year and established the party headquarters there. In 1921, a few intellectuals who had been inspired by the Bolshevik revolution in Russia in 1917 established the CCP in Shanghai.

In 1923, Soviet advisors arrived in Guangzhou and assisted Sun with the reorganization of the KMT based on the Leninist centralized party structure. With the help of Soviet funding, Sun established a military academy near Guangzhou to build a KMT army. Chiang Kai-shek (Jiang Jieshi), a close associate of Sun, was appointed the first commandant of the academy. In 1924, the CCP members were advised by the Soviets to join the KMT while maintaining their separate party identities in the CCP.

Within the KMT, members of the two parties began to compete for control over policies, organizations, and members. After Sun's death in 1925, the KMT-CCP alliance fell apart. Chiang, now commander of the National Revolutionary Army, took actions to purge the Communists. The CCP revolted but was quickly defeated. Under Chiang, the Nationalist government in Guangzhou launched the military campaign called Northern Expedition in 1926 against the warlords and armies in the north. By 1928, the major warlords were defeated. In October 1928, the Nationalists formally established the National Government in Nanjing and quickly received diplomatic recognition by foreign powers.

Although military separatism continued in some areas, the Nationalist government was able to expand its governing capacity. It created a coherent monetary and banking system, expanded the public education system, improved transportation and the communication system, and encouraged industry and commerce. The KMT closely allied with business in urban centers and landlords in the countryside but did little to improve the rural economy.

The government also had limited success in restoring sovereignty. It reclaimed tariff autonomy and regained control over some concession areas. Nevertheless, most of the unequal treaties remained unchanged. The KMT achievement in economic modernization was seriously undermined by corruption, mismanagement, the continuous threat of civil war with the CCP, and Japanese invasion.

In September 1931, Japan's Guangdong Army engineered a bombing incident near Mukden (Shenyang), leading to the Japanese occupation of Manchuria and creation of a puppet state of "*Manzhouguo*" with the last Qing emperor as the head of state. Incidents of Japanese territorial encroachment and seizure continued for the next several years in Manchuria and neighboring Mongolia and northern China.

While external threats escalated, the internal threat from the Communists also intensified. The Communists created rural bases in central China. One of the largest, the Jiangxi Soviet (1931–1934), was established in November 1931 by Mao Zedong (1893–1976) and Zhu De (1886–1976). They had their own military, tax, and financial systems and implemented land reforms by distributing farm land from landlords to landless farmers to attract support from the poorer classes.

Facing both the external and internal threats, the Nationalist government decided to implement the policy of "Unity before Resistance," hoping to suppress the Communist uprisings first before fighting with the Japanese.

Chiang intensified the military campaign against the Communists in late 1934, forcing the Communists to abandon their bases and retreat. Many of the later Communist leaders, including Mao Zedong, Zhu De, Zhou Enlai, and Liu Shaoqi, joined in the Long March (1934–1935), a circuitous retreat that covered 6,000 miles through some of China's roughest terrain. Around 400,000 people started out, but only 40,000 made it to Yan'an, a remote rural base in northwestern China. During the Long March, Mao took the CCP leadership position in 1935.

Before then, Mao's revolutionary strategy was at odds with other CCP leaders, who mostly advocated the conventional Marxist strategy to encourage a Communist revolution relying on industrial workers in the urban centers. In contrast, Mao believed that the Communist revolution in China needed to depend on peasants, drawing on his observation of peasant uprisings in Chinese history. Mao's experience in building Jiangxi Soviet in a rural base with the farmer army lent him the credibility in reorienting the revolutionary movement toward the farmers.

The China embroiled in civil war was considered by Japan as the perfect opportunity to expand the Japanese empire to the rest of Asia. In 1937, Japan launched a full-scale invasion of China. The Japanese army moved swiftly and captured several major Chinese cities. By December, they occupied Nanjing. To trade space for time, the Nationalist government relocated its capital to the city of Chongqing in mountainous Sichuan province for the duration of the war. Frustrated that the fall of Nanjing did not result in China's surrender, the Japanese army brutally killed more than 300,000 unarmed civilians in the city in December 1937. Repeated denial of the occurrence of the Nanjing Massacre by some Japanese officials continues to cause diplomatic tensions in the post-WWII era.

The Japanese invasion of 1937 profoundly reshaped the course of the civil war between the KMT and the CCP. Although both parties ostensibly formed a united front against the Japanese, they continued to battle each other. The CCP took the opportunity to regroup and recover, consolidating its territorial hold. It recruited from the rural population and young students from the cities, organizing them for food supply and guerrilla warfare, and steadily grew during the war.

In contrast, the Nationalist government had difficulty managing the wartime economy. With limited sources of revenue, it resorted to printing money to support a large bureaucracy and an army of more than three million soldiers, causing runaway inflation. Factional politics and corruption further weakened the Nationalist government. As the war prolonged, the morale of the bureaucracy and military steadily declined. Under the name of national security, the government used violence to suppress dissidents and critics.

By the time the Sino-Japanese war ended in 1945, the CCP had expanded its membership and commanded support in much of the countryside. It successfully mobilized the farmers to form an army, resorting to guerrilla warfare tactics. In contrast, the KMT was weakened, as its traditional urban support was shattered by war.

The civil war between the KMT and CCP resumed shortly after the Japanese surrender. The Soviet Union, who received the Japanese surrender in Manchuria, turned over Japanese weaponry and factories to the Communists, further strengthening their power. In 1949, the Communist forces entered Beijing unopposed and established the People's Republic of China. Chiang and the KMT supporters fled to the island of Taiwan.

DISCUSSION QUESTIONS

1.   What are some of the basic teachings of Confucianism? Discuss how they shape the attitudes and behaviors of the people in contemporary China.

2.   China turned toward isolationism beginning in the 15th century. How did the policy affect its political and economic development since?

3. Why do you think China stayed as one state for thousands of years without breaking up into separate states? What brought the country together and kept it together?

4. Describe China's early modernization attempts such as the self-strengthening movement. What kind of criteria would you develop to evaluate its efficacy?

5. How did the focus of Chinese modernization efforts change after the self-strengthening movement? Why did people participating in the May Fourth Movement believe that China was in need of broader reforms?

2

Political Governance in China

On October 1, 1949, Mao Zedong, chairman of the Chinese Communist Party (CCP), stood atop Tiananmen Square in Beijing to announce the formation of the People's Republic of China (PRC). At the dawn of a new era, he proudly proclaimed that "the Chinese people have stood up." Flanked by his top CCP associates such as Zhu De, Zhou Enlai, and Liu Shaoqi, Mao was confident that the new China would bring back long lost pride and honor after more than a century of humiliation.

Turning that rhetoric into reality, however, was a daunting task. Decades of political instability from revolutions, civil wars, and the Japanese invasion had devastated the economy. Agricultural and industrial production had fallen significantly amid hyperinflation and rising unemployment. The economy was almost exclusively agricultural, with limited industrialization in pockets of northeastern and eastern China. There were also great disparities between regions and social groups. The preexisting governing apparatus was plagued by inefficiency and rampant corruption. Thus, mobilizing grassroots support, consolidating political power, building governing institutions, revitalizing economic growth, and maintaining law and order had to be accomplished all in tandem. Additionally, the new regime would need to overcome the diplomatic isolation in the context of the emerging Cold War and secure foreign trade and investment in an increasingly hostile environment.

The Chinese leaders initially were successful in establishing governing structures and stabilizing the economy. As time went on, policy debates over the path to development escalated into bloody power struggles between top leaders and threw the country into near-paralysis by the mid-1970s. Beginning in the late 1970s, a series of reforms that combined elements of market economy with political authoritarianism gradually steered the country toward greater stability and economic success. Sustained economic growth has attracted foreign investments to China, significantly improved the standard of living, and made the country an integral part of the global economy. In 2010, China overtook Japan and became the second largest economy in the world. Has it found the right formula for governing? Will its governance structure be sustainable? Is it possible to have economic freedom with limited political freedom? This chapter will review the PRC's history of political governance, the evolution of its governing principles and institutions, its policy swings and adaptations, and its achievements and challenges.

FROM THE SOVIET MODEL TO MAO'S RADICALIZED POLITICS: 1949–1977

Building the Governance Foundation

Governance Structure: A Party-State. Following the Communist takeover, the vision of the CCP leadership was clear: to bring together the fractured society and to speed up economic recovery. To that end, it is essential to develop an effective administrative apparatus that could maintain order and promote economic growth. The CCP, as a revolutionary organization that specialized in guerrilla warfare in remote rural areas, now needed to be transformed into a governing body to manage national commerce and economy in urban centers and industrial complexes. What should be the blueprints for political integration and social reconstruction? What should be the model of political governance and economic development? And what role should the CCP play in the governance structure?

From the beginning, the PRC adopted the Soviet governance structure of a party-state—including a tight relationship between the party and the government, with the CCP playing the dominant leadership role. The CCP is regarded as the sole source of all political power in China and has the exclusive right to control all other political organizations.

The highly centralized party-state structure was deemed most appropriate for China for both governance and development purposes. Through economic planning and resource allocation on a national scale, the model could effectively mobilize resources for rapid industrialization and modernization, while overcoming the resistance of regionalism from powerful local party bosses in order to balance regional disparities.

The CCP's supremacy over other state institutions such as the State Council (the executive branch on the government side) and the National People's Congress (the legislative branch) is achieved through structural design and personnel appointment. At each administrative level (i.e., the national, provincial, prefectural, county, and township), the party and the government are structured in a parallel yet joined manner. The party is pervasively embedded in the fabric of governance to ensure compliance with party directives; it is present in all government units (including ministries), the military, factories, schools, enterprises, and so on.

Additionally, the party controls personnel decisions through a *nomenklatura* system—a list of positions to be filled by party appointment. Key officials in the party and government are appointed and dismissed by the party, and the party secretary implanted in the government unit often enjoys greater power and authority than the formal head of the unit.

Within the CCP, the National Party Congress (PC) ostensibly holds the highest power. The PC elects the Central Committee, which acts on its behalf to manage party affairs until its next session. In reality, at the top of the structure is the Politburo of the CCP. Power can be further consolidated in the hands of a single preeminent leader (such as Mao Zedong) or a group of leaders in the Politburo Standing Committee (PSC).

International Environment. The international environment also played a role in facilitating the Sino-Soviet alliance. At the end of World War II, the U.S.-Soviet rivalry intensified. The Soviet Union's support of international Communist movements heightened the United States' fear of Communist takeover in Europe and elsewhere. In March 1947, in a speech to a joint session of Congress, President Harry S. Truman declared that the United States would provide political, military, and economic assistance to all democratic nations to forestall Communist domination. The announcement was a de facto declaration of the Cold War. The Berlin blockade of 1948–1949 and the creation of NATO in April 1949 by the United States highlighted the rising tension of the Cold War.

The loss of the Chinese mainland to the Communists in October 1949, despite the considerable military aid from the United States in support of Chiang Kai-shek and the Nationalists during the Chinese Civil War, was a huge diplomatic blow to the United States, putting pressure on the Truman administration to draw the line of containment in Asia. The PRC was viewed as an aggressor in a Moscow-orchestrated attempt to spread communism and was excluded from participation in any international or diplomatic forums outside of the Communist bloc. After the outbreak of the Korean War in June 1950, the United States imposed a total trade embargo on China. In the face of hostility from the West, the PRC adopted the policy of "leaning to one side" to learn from the Soviets in the initial period of consolidation and reconstruction.

The signing of the Sino-Soviet Treaty of Friendship, Alliance, and Mutual Assistance in February 1950 formalized the alliance between China and the Soviet Union. With the assistance of loans and technical support from the Soviet Union, Soviet policies and institutions became an integral part of the new Chinese regime.

Governance Process: Collective Leadership. During the revolution era, the CCP followed a decentralized decision-making structure and granted substantial autonomy to party units at local levels due to the need of guerrilla warfare. In 1948, in anticipation of the military victory over the Nationalists, and with the aim to reduce the power grip of local party chiefs, Mao and the CCP leadership called to strengthen the CCP party committee system on the basis of "collective leadership." The principle instructed that important problems be discussed collectively in party committees at all levels before decisions were made and that resolution of important issues would not be left to individuals. The practice of collective leadership was built on the organizing principles of the "mass line" proposed by Mao, and the "democratic centralism" proposed by Lenin.

Democratic centralism was embraced by all Communist parties as a means to achieve unity in action while having free discussions. In reality, centralism trumps democratic discussions, allowing the Communist party leadership to dominate all other party-state organizations. The principle nevertheless emphasizes the important process of consultation and investigation for party leaders.

Mao's "mass line" (i.e., "from the masses, to the masses") depicts an ideal form of political communication between the CCP and its constituencies. Party officials and leaders are expected to seek ideas based on the needs and demands of the ordinary people (from the masses) and then translate them into practical policies and plans that can be embraced by the people (to the masses). The broad discussions and consultations with all the constituents also illustrate the democratic element of Lenin's democratic centralism.

Based on this principle, the 1956 Eighth Party Congress reinstituted the PSC, which had not been in session since the 1945 Seventh Party Congress. The six-member PSC, presided over by Mao as chairman of the party, brought together the heads of the party, government, and military hierarchies for collective decision making. Subsequently, in 1958, the CCP Central Committee and the State Council supplanted the structure by establishing "leading small groups" in the following areas: financial and economic, political and legal, foreign affairs, science, and cultural and education. Each of these small groups would bring together principal government ministries in their respective policy sector and report directly to the Secretariat.

Elite Politics. Under the collective leadership, how did political actors express ideas, interests, or grievances within the one-party structure behind the façade of unity? In the absence of legitimate means to do so, political actors naturally colluded to form factions to promote favorable policies and defend their own interests. Personal ties within the faction helped provide mutual support to advance political career and power, as well as protect against political uncertainty and abrupt changes that were often associated with a political system deficient in transparency and accountability.

Formed by the mixture of institutional, geographic, and generational factors, CCP factions usually cut across formal organizational structures and belonged to the realm of informal politics. Operated behind closed doors and hidden in code-word exchanges, faction politics was usually shielded from public eyes until members of a faction were removed from office or publicly denounced. Newspaper commentaries and policy speeches were often the venues for such political attack, delivering an early sign of faction conflict.

Scholars have used different models to analyze CCP politics under Mao. The first is the Policy Choice Model (Barnett 1974) that explains elite conflicts based on differing policy preferences resulting from different ideological stances, which shape the perspectives on how problems are defined and solved. The second model is the Power Struggle Model (MacFarquhar 1974). This approach argues that CCP elite conflicts are feuds over power and status, resulting in the resolution of policy debates or personality clashes through political power struggle. A third model is the Bureaucratic Model (Lieberthal and Oksenberg 1988), explaining conflict and policy outcomes based on the bureaucratic interest and institutional structure of policy making. Because authority is fragmented internally among various divisions and geographically through the center and provinces, political actors articulate interests through bureaucratic institutions and engage in protracted bargaining processes to seek consensus. While these models provide valuable analytical tools for our understanding of faction politics, it is possible that these explanations are not mutually exclusive, and something of each motivates faction leaders and their followers.

On one hand, factions operating under the principle of collective leadership serve as competing interest groups to perform checks and balances for policy discussions, avoiding calamitous mistakes. On the other hand, challenges from dissenting factions might be viewed as destabilizing or even treasonous when infighting intensifies. Legitimate policy and ideological differences might be viewed as pretexts for a power struggle, hence undermining the credibility of policy debates in the public realm.

Establishing the New Order through Socialist Transformation

Land Reforms. As a revolutionary regime, the CCP promised to end social injustice and economic exploitation, but it took different approaches in the countryside and the cities in the early stages of the postrevolutionary transition. Relatively familiar with the rural environment, the CCP took a bolder approach right away in the countryside to eliminate "class enemies" and solidify its power. In traditional Chinese society at the time of the Communist takeover, most of the lands were controlled by a small number of landlords; nearly 90 percent of the people lived in rural villages, with two-thirds of them owning less than 20 percent of the land. Landless tenants paid exorbitant rents to landlords, sometimes up to 60 percent of their production. Prior to its final victory in October 1949, the CCP had implemented land reform in areas under its control and redistributed landlords' property to the peasants. It then expanded the program through the newly created Peasants' Associations. Using "struggle meetings" and "people's tribunals" to prosecute (and, oftentimes, to execute) landlords, local CCP cadres confiscated and transferred lands from landlords to farmers. The success in land reforms created a new interest pattern and solidified the CCP's political control in rural China. While execution of as many as 800,000 landlords and "counterrevolutionaries" demonstrated to the rural masses that the Party was now the source of political authority, breaking up land ownership into small lots for individual holdings provided new incentives for farmers to increase agricultural production and stimulate economic gains.

Urban Transformation. In the cities, the CCP proceeded more carefully to encourage cooperation of the urban middle classes to ensure economic recovery and political stability. The government took over private businesses and industrial enterprises but compensated the owners based on a percentage of the total value. It left smaller businesses of urban handicrafts and small enterprises in private hands for a few more years before merging them into cooperatives. By the mid-1950s, urban private enterprises were either state-owned or state-private jointly owned.

At the same time, the CCP gradually tightened social control through mass campaigns, mobilizing people to engage in thought reform. The 1951 "Three Anti-Movement" (anticorruption, antiwaste, and antibureaucracy) targeted primarily the bureaucrats and officials considered "politically unreliable" due to prior association with the Nationalist regime or alleged betrayal of revolutionary ideals. In 1952, another round of mass campaigns, the "Five Anti-Movement" (against bribery, tax evasion, fraud, theft of government property, and theft of state secrets), was launched. A large number of industrialists and business owners were put through humiliating public trials with massive fines and taxes that they could not pay. In the end, the government took over their businesses, paving the way for the First Five-Year Plan (1953–1957, though announced in 1955).

While the CCP seemingly fulfilled its promises to the peasants who brought it to power, a close analysis of the PRC's economic policy in Chapter 3 reveals that urban centers and industrial sectors were the true beneficiaries of the government's growth strategy. Private land ownership in the countryside was only transitory; it soon gave way to the socialist push by the Communist party-state.

From the Soviet Model to the Maoist Model

Sources of Conflicts: Ideas or Interests? As observed by Harding (1981), there were at least three distinct sources of theories on how China should be governed in the aftermath of the revolution: the Chinese bureaucratic history and tradition, the practices of the Soviet model, and the experience of the CCP during the revolutionary years in administering their rural bases. These sources, however, could not yield a clear, coherent set of governance principles, and policy debates over appropriate governance structure have persisted from the 1950s to the present day. Questions continue to emerge about the governing role of the CCP and its relations with nonparty elements such as state administrative units and the civil society. Should the CCP exercise complete control and domination over nonparty elements in the political sphere, or should nonparty entities enjoy greater autonomy? Furthermore, questions arise in economic decision making about the role of directive planning versus market incentives and the responsibility of the central government versus local government. Competing ideas and institutions at different stages of the PRC political history have provided different answers to these questions.

Since the mid-1950s, the three sources gradually evolved into a clash between the revolutionary camp and the bureaucratic apparatus, depicted as a conflict between "Red" versus "Expert." Red represented the die-hard ideologues and revolutionaries who firmly believed in the Communist doctrines and were skillful in mobilizing the masses. They showed little interest in technical knowledge or administrative expertise; instead, they strongly emphasized the commitment to ideological purity and revolutionary fervor through purges, class struggles, and political education campaigns, until the total defeat of the "class enemies."

In contrast, Expert represented those who were better educated and well trained in their technical areas, such as scientists, technicians, teachers, managers, intellectuals, and bureaucrats. They were less interested in revolutionary slogans and emphasized the importance of efficiency and economic rationality in planning and management.

Moving in the direction of Redness meant mobilizing people and arousing their revolutionary enthusiasm through continuous political campaigns and struggles. Expertness represented reliance on technical expertise and scientific knowledge and, if necessary, bending some ideological restrictions for market mechanism and economic regularity in order to achieve economic growth and development.

The ideological difference between Red and Expert began to reflect tensions between rural Communist cadres and urban intellectuals and the gap between Mao's development concept based on China's huge, indigenous human resources and the Soviet development model based on capital input.

What was described by Mao as "two-line struggle" between Red and Expert could have been more than policy debates over governance models or development strategies. It could also have been a pretext for political maneuvering and power struggle between opposing factions at the top leadership in an opaque system with little transparency. Political rhetoric, nevertheless, provides a valuable window to observe and analyze the political dynamics in PRC.

Transition to the Maoist Model. With financial and technical assistance from Moscow, the PRC's First Five-Year Plan (1953–1957) brought some positive results. Nevertheless, the CCP leadership was concerned. Economically, the growth was skewed between sectors; namely, heavy industries had expanded far more rapidly than agriculture. This raised the question about the sustainability of the Soviet development model, for if the trend continued, stagnant growth in agriculture and a dwindling supply of raw materials would limit expansion of the manufacturing sector. Furthermore, Soviet financial assistance, though modest, had been instrumental for the initial spurt of China's economic recovery and growth. Short on investment capital, China could hardly continue this mode of capital-intensive production on its own.

Politically, Mao also questioned the industry-centered, planning-based Soviet development model. In his mind, centralized, bureaucratic-driven programs propelled by modern technology and technical expertise would elevate the status of the technocrats and the intellectuals and promote elitist and "bourgeois" attitudes at the expense of the original purpose of the proletarian revolution. For Mao, running the country according to the Soviet model would direct the attention to routinized and bureaucratized economic affairs and away from the ideological and political emphasis that had defined the party in its old revolutionary days. Convinced that a true revolutionary ought to guard against the creeping influence of the capitalist class and be vigilant of the loss of revolutionary zeal, Mao began to hatch plans to abandon the Soviet model and press on with class struggle to protect the integrity of the revolution.

After the uprisings of 1956 in Eastern European Communist states in Poland and Hungary, the CCP encouraged the people to express their opinions about the party and its policies in the Hundred Flowers Campaign (1956), with the slogan "Let a hundred flowers bloom and a hundred schools of thought contend." Yet the CCP leadership was ultimately unprepared for the harsh, extensive criticisms it elicited. Many intellectuals came forward with opinions that were highly critical of the party and its policies. The experience confirmed Mao's suspicion of "expert" and convinced him that class struggle was absolutely necessary to eliminate the exploitative bourgeois attitudes of the capitalist class. The Hundred Flowers Campaign turned into the Anti-Rightist Campaign (1957–1959), in which an estimated four hundred thousand "Rightists," many of them intellectuals who had played an important role in education, science, and engineering, were imprisoned or sent to labor camp for reform and rehabilitation. The Anti-Rightist Campaign effectively silenced all the critics and marked the beginning of radicalized politics. For the next 20 years, a series of political campaigns and rectification movements were launched to identify and cleanse the "bad" elements of the society.

In retrospect, Mao's move in the direction of "Redness" starting in the late 1950s was more than a reversal in merely economic policy; this had profound implications for PRC's political institutions and mode of governance. Through the process, Mao consolidated his power and transformed the PRC's political and economic system in accordance with his revolution scheme. The increasing extremism and violence in those political campaigns ripped apart political leadership and governance structures, taking the entire country onto a path of turmoil and disorder.

The Great Leap Forward. To lessen China's reliance on Soviet expertise and assistance and to wrestle policy-making power from economic technocrats, Mao advocated a growth model based on his concept of "mass movement," using China's most abundant resource—its people. The Great Leap Forward (GLF), launched in 1958, represented Mao's attempt to leap dramatically forward to achieve not only economic development but a Communist utopia. However, with no concrete plans or clearly defined objectives, the GLF was, at best, a set of uncoordinated policies based on principles of self-reliance and mass mobilization, driven by the belief that political enthusiasm and a spirit of teamwork were more important than skills, knowledge, and planning.

For Mao, the key to a successful revolution was to stimulate human spirit. He believed that people's passion and energy, once released, would overcome any limitation and hardship. The same philosophy was applied to economic growth: rather than relying on capital input, inspiration of political activism and enthusiasm, along with changes in labor force utilization, would be sufficient to enhance economic productivity.

Agricultural collectivization was an integral part of Mao's development strategy, as seen in the establishment of people's communes to promote political governance and economic production. The new economic institutions, however, created serious dislocations in both agriculture and industry (Chapter 3). At the same time, the Sino-Soviet alliance fell apart (Chapter 4), leading to the abrupt withdrawal of Soviet economic and military assistance in 1959. The combination of the GLF and the Soviet withdrawal set the stage for additional economic hardship.

At an enlarged Politburo session at Lushan in July 1959, veteran CCP leaders such as Defense Minister Marshal Peng Dehuai voiced concerns about the GLF. But Mao threatened to lead the farmers in a new revolution against the government if GLF and communes were overturned. The Politburo yielded to Mao's wish. Months later, Peng and other prominent critics of Mao were purged as "anti-Party cliques," and Lin Biao was appointed to succeed Peng as the Defense Minister. Eagerly embracing Mao's policies, Lin intensified political education and ideological indoctrination in the military, deprioritizing professional training and technical expertise. Furthermore, Lin's staff compiled Mao's quotations in a "Little Red Book," which subsequently became the Red Guard's Bible during the Cultural Revolution.

Peng's purge ran counter to the CCP tradition of collective leadership that encouraged candid discussions in party committees and collectively made decisions. This signaled a shift in party politics and future decision making.

The economic situation worsened after the renewed mandate of the GLF. For reasons discussed in Chapter 3, grain production plummeted from 200 million tons (1958) to 143.5 million tons (1960), causing a famine with estimated deaths of 25 to 50 million people (Grasso, Corrin, and Kort 1991). Shortages of food and raw materials further affected industrial production and the life of urban workers.

The catastrophe of the GLF eventually strengthened the position of Liu Shaoqi (president of the PRC) and Deng Xiaoping (vice premier and general secretary of the CCP); they forged a collective leadership to curb Mao's influence. While Mao remained the CCP chairman, Deng was responsible for the daily operation of the CCP Central Committee Secretariat. As pragmatists, Liu and Deng restored greater central control over industrial planning and management. They introduced a series of moderate policies to reverse the damage caused by the GLF. Plans for rural industrialization were scaled back, and agricultural production decisions were transferred from communes to lower units and, even in some cases, families. Material incentives were reinstated to encourage productivity. Farmers were allowed to keep the harvest from their private lots to themselves, while workers could receive bonuses for superior performance.

For Mao, these measures represented corrupt, capitalist efforts to achieve economic growth at the expense of socioeconomic equality and Communist ideals, the basis of the Chinese revolution. He sought, unsuccessfully, to reverse these policies at the Tenth Plenum of the Central Committee in September 1962.

Policy differences between Mao and Liu/Deng began to spill over into other areas such as education, cultural policy, and the party apparatus. For Mao, the education system as it existed in the mid-1960s was still a "class-based" institution. College students were mainly the children of party cadres and the urban middle class; farmers and workers were significantly underrepresented. Arts and literature continued to promote capitalist values without recognizing the struggle of workers, farmers, and soldiers. In Mao's mind, these problems indicated that government leadership had been held by those "taking the capitalist road."

For Mao, state bureaucracy, reflecting the entrenched vestige of the corrupt and elitist forces of the past, had to be removed to eliminate the values and practices of the old societies. As Mao tried to centralize power to maintain control without bureaucratization, what he did was essentially substitute state bureaucrats with party bureaucrats. Thus, the role of the CCP changed from setting broad, general directions for the state's programs in accordance with party values and goals to making detailed plans and policies for the state and overseeing their implementation. Party officials simultaneously held administrative or managerial posts and intervened on the basis of political expediency with no respect for expert opinions. The fusion of these roles and functions made the CCP a supervisor, an enforcer, and a decision maker, cementing its absolute leadership power over the state.

The Radicalization of Politics. To halt the capitalist revival and to regain control over the progress of revolution, Mao launched the Cultural Revolution in 1966. To preempt Mao's move, Liu and Deng had tried to convene a special Central Committee Plenum in June 1966, but the attempt was blocked by Lin and the military. With Lin's support, Maoists excluded more than half of the regular Central Committee members to convene their own Plenum (the Eleventh Plenum of the Central Committee) in August 1966 to demote Liu and name Lin the vice chairman. The focus of the Cultural Revolution was expanded from educational and cultural sectors to virtually all the political and economic organizations in China. By the mid-1960s, PRC developed a new organizational trinity where party, state, and the military were intertwined in the leadership structure and evolved into a form of totalitarian control (Schurmann 1968).

During the Cultural Revolution, the Central Cultural Revolution Small Group bypassed the party Secretariat and, to a large extent, the Politburo, and made final decisions on behalf of the party-state. Political ideology permeated all aspects of the Chinese people's everyday life; newspapers and periodicals were full of quotations from Mao, Marx, and Lenin, indoctrinating the importance of continuous class struggle and "proletarian dictatorship" against alleged enemies, both internal and external. Through endless political campaigns, mass movements, self-criticisms, and purges, continuous revolution centered on class struggle aimed to ensure the integrity of the revolutionary spirit.

Mao heightened the level of popular participation and mass mobilization in the Cultural Revolution. Millions of youths, the Red Guards, responded to Mao's call to cleanse the party and government of "counterrevolutionary" elements. They mobilized to supervise, criticize and, if necessary, dismiss leaders and officials at schools, universities, factories, enterprises, party organizations, and government offices without regard for laws or regulations. Persecuting and torturing hundreds of thousands of people, the Red Guards searched houses, confiscated properties, and ransacked government buildings. Their attacks on the governance structures and institutions, whether formal or informal, were relentless, leading to the destruction of the bureaucratic apparatus and the paralysis of the government system. Rival groups of the Red Guards, some backed by the officials under attack, battled with one another in violent clashes in major cities all over China, destroying books, properties, and cultural artifacts. Streets turned into battlegrounds between contending factions, throwing the country into extreme violence and chaos and severely damaging the national economy.

In January 1967, Mao ordered the military to intervene to restore order. The military seized the opportunity to fill the leadership vacuum and became another power contender. It established revolutionary committees to replace the party committees at all levels of governing structures. In early 1967, Mao engineered the removal of Liu and Deng from the Politburo in a close vote, and in the summer of 1968, he disbanded the Red Guards. Liu was stripped of all his offices and arrested in the fall of 1968, dying in prison in late 1969.

Now firmly in control, Mao convened the Ninth Party Congress in April 1969 to select Lin as "Comrade Mao's close comrade-in-arms and successor." A large number of members of the Politburo, the Central Committee, and provincial leadership were replaced. The new Politburo appointments consisted of three contending factions: the Maoists (the radical leftists), the military under Lin, and the surviving elements of the state bureaucracy under premier Zhou Enlai.

Jiang Qing, Mao's fourth wife, led the Maoists. She, along with her protégés Wang Hongwen, Zhang Chunqiao, and Yao Wenyuan, were members of the Cultural Revolution Committee. Collectively, they were known as the "Gang of Four."

To check the rapid rise of the military, Mao joined forces with Zhou in restoring the CCP as the primary political institution. Mao and Zhou presented a draft of the new Constitution in 1970 that would eliminate the office of the chairman of the PRC, a title formerly held by Liu and now coveted by Lin. In 1971, Lin and supporters attempted to flee to Russia after a failed coup, but the plane crashed in Mongolia. Lin's death and Mao's deteriorating health served to strengthen Zhou's position. He was able to gradually restore rational economic policies and, with Mao's consent, rehabilitate party officials purged during the Cultural Revolution. Deng resumed his post as vice premier in 1973.

With failing health and now caught between Jiang's group and the restored state bureaucratic leaders, Mao designated Hua Guofeng as his successor. Hua was a compromise, as he lacked a following in either group. In January 1976, Zhou passed away. Zhou's death emboldened Jiang's group to attack Deng. In April 1976, on a traditional Chinese holiday in memory of the ancestors (i.e., *Qingming*), crowds gathered in Tiananmen Square to lay memorial wreaths to Zhou. Knowing that the move was a subtle protest over the Maoist policies, Jiang's group ordered the dispersion of the mourners, causing violent reactions from the crowds. Blaming Deng as the mastermind behind the incident, the Gang of Four removed Deng from all leadership positions and organized a national campaign against him. In September 1976, Mao died and was succeeded by Hua. Within a month, Hua arrested the Gang of Four. However, their trial was not held until November 1980.

The Cultural Revolution set the PRC back for decades through its ensuing violence and destruction. Political instability caused stagnation in economic growth and industrial production. Agricultural production could barely keep up with population growth. The political and economic conditions placed the CCP in a serious legitimacy crisis.

INITIAL PHASE OF THE POST-MAO REFORMS: 1978–1992

In July 1977, the Central Committee restored the 73-year-old Deng to his former posts. The reformers gradually consolidated their power to undertake a major shift in policy, endorsed by the watershed Third Plenum of the Eleventh Central Committee in December 1978. In an attempt to regain public trust in the CCP's ability to lead, Deng and the reformers laid the ideological foundation of the reform era, dropping Mao's priority of waging class struggle and revolutionary warfare and redirecting the nation toward "socialist modernization." The goal was to build a "modern agriculture, industry, science and technology, and national defense" (or four "modernizations") by the year 2000.

Economic and Political Reforms

Economic modernization began with a more decentralized economic system to allow for greater local autonomy and marketization. In the countryside, selective decollectivization of agriculture was implemented, leading to significant increases in grain output. Subsequently, sustained economic development in rural areas spurred the growth of the township and village enterprises, creating employment opportunities for nearly 100 million people in the countryside.

In the urban areas, reforms centered on price reform and granting greater autonomy to economic enterprises. Pricing control was loosened to allow adjustments based on market forces of supply and demand. Economic decision making regarding industrial production and management was gradually decentralized, turning over the power to enterprises or subnational units. Additionally, the leadership adopted the "open door" policy to encourage foreign trade and investment. As a result of these reforms, China began to experience sustained high growth rates starting in 1978, which has translated to an increase in personal income and improvements in standard of living.

In light of the fact that many reform measures ran counter to socialist theories and principles, how was it possible for the reform faction to overcome resistance from the leftists or supporters of the Soviet model? The broad consensus shared by the senior leadership was to affirm the CCP's monopolistic power and authority, notwithstanding changes in economic policies. As declared by Deng in 1982, the CCP would practice "socialism with Chinese characteristics" as it pursued modernization. Economic growth and development were framed as a means to build political support to strengthen the legitimacy of the party and advance socialism. As discussed in Chapter 3, economic reforms were marked by gradual and cautious steps, reflecting compromises between central planning and market forces.

Concurrent political reforms were driven by the concern for efficiency in order to build up state capacity and to facilitate economic development. Reform efforts could be summarized by twin goals of "institutionalization" and "legalization" (Horsley 2010). To prevent the recurrence of the Cultural Revolution that destroyed the legal foundation of political authority, the Third Plenum of the Eleventh Central Committee sought to protect the integrity of the political and legal institutions deemed critical for economic and social modernization. Economic growth required a competent administrative state with well-trained bureaucrats and experts shielded from undue political interference.

The first step toward institutionalization was to restore and restructure political organizations and institutions of the party and the state. The totalitarian party-state system built by Mao had to be rebalanced to maintain the proper role of the party and the state. While recognizing the importance of maintaining party leadership, Deng called for a clearer distinction of the responsibilities between the party and the state to grant greater operational autonomy to the government. Thus, the 1982 Constitution affirmed the leadership of the CCP but restored a system of government to uphold the socialist legal system. A civil service system was gradually established to recruit professional appointees to the government through meritocratic exam, while the party retained control over political appointees.

Under Mao, the regularly scheduled Party and People's Congresses were convened rather sporadically. For example, the Eighth Party Congress was convened in 1956, but the Ninth was in 1969, and the Tenth 1973. There were no People's Congresses from 1965 to 1974 during the Cultural Revolution. Since the early 1980s, the regular convening of the National Party Congresses and National People's Congresses according to the party charter and state Constitution (every five years) has contributed to the continuity and stability of Chinese politics.

Legalization reflected the reformers' desire to "rule *by* law." The concept was meant to address the problem of "rule of man" that characterized Mao's era. As the law is viewed by the state as an instrument to regulate the public, the public would be expected to obey and comply with the law, and no organization or individual would be above the law. The 1982 Constitution reflected this concept, stipulating that no one, including the state, the military, and all political parties, was above the law and the Constitution. Nevertheless, that goal remains elusive in practice.

To encourage the promotion of younger and more educated cadres to replace old revolutionaries in leadership transition, Deng instituted term limits and a retirement system for the party and state posts. Up until then, the PRC had no formalized rules to deal with political succession. Political leaders, including the general secretary of the CCP, the president of the state, the premier, and other important officials, were allowed to serve, at most, two five-year terms in office (i.e., 10 years). Term limits not only helped prevent the reemergence of a dictator but also facilitated healthy leadership turnovers to accommodate generational changes. Deng also enforced retirement of a whole generation of veteran leaders who were over a certain age limit. To ease their concerns of losing power and prestige, Deng established the Party Central Advisory Commission in 1982 to provide a formal channel for senior party leaders to influence policy making. To set an example for other old revolutionaries, Deng ceded all formal power in 1989 and relinquished all informal influence in 1994.

Elite Politics

Despite the goal to institutionalize rules and norms, the Chinese leadership system throughout the 1980s and the early 1990s remained highly personalistic. The locus of power did not necessarily correspond to the formal organizational structure; rather, informal factors such as the pre-1949 revolutionary background, the post-1949 political activism, and personal connections—not necessarily official positions—became the real source of power. Deng never occupied the formal top positions in either the party or the government; he preferred to leave those posts to his loyal lieutenants. The fact that he was the "paramount leader" and the most powerful individual in China for two decades in the post-Mao era without a top position speaks volumes about the importance of informal politics in PRC.

There were differences in how factions and elite politics operated between Mao and Deng. Under Mao, factions were defined by ideological terms and personal ties. Faction members were exceptionally loyal in a fierce political competition of "win all or lose all." Under Deng, conflict was handled with greater civility, and factions were organized primarily around policy lines and bureaucratic interests rather than ideology (Dittmer 2003).

Deng did not have the enormous power and authority enjoyed by Mao. Although he was first among equals, he maintained careful balance by consulting, and often making compromise with, other key leaders such as Chen Yun, Bo Yibo, and Li Xiannian.

Early tensions centered on the official evaluation of Mao's legacy. Members of the reform wing wanted to repudiate Mao, whereas conservatives wanted to uphold Mao's legacy. As a compromise, the resolution adopted by the Sixth Plenum of the Eleventh Central Committee on June 27, 1981, acknowledged the "gross mistakes" Mao made during the Cultural Revolution but concluded that "his contributions to the Chinese revolution far outweigh his mistakes. His merits are primary and his errors secondary."

Subsequently, policy differences emerged between the progrowth group, led by Deng, and the prostability group, led by Chen Yun and Peng Zheng. Chen joined forces with Deng in the historic Third Plenum of the Eleventh Central Committee in November-December 1978 to wrestle control from the Maoists, but his views of economic policies were different from Deng's.

Deng's pragmatism could be seen from his expressions of "seeking truth from facts" and "It doesn't matter whether the cat is black or white, as long as it catches mice." In his mind, result and performance, not preconceived ideological notions, should guide action. Chen, however, supported orthodox planned economies. He was concerned about the loosening controls over the economy and the excessive reliance on market mechanism. Peng, a Politburo member and the chair of the National People's Congress (NPC), also preferred a command economy and was critical of the use of capitalist measures. Chen and Peng had the support of the economic bureaucrats, who naturally resisted the trend toward marketization, for it took away their power to plan and control.

A Setback to Reforms

By the mid-1980s, problems began to emerge in economic and political realms. While reforms brought new economic opportunities, not everyone benefited equally from the policies. Decentralized control and marketization led to a rise in unemployment and inflation, while corruption and growing crime along with economic dislocation created social instability. In 1986, student demonstrations broke out in a number of cities, in protest of inflation, official corruption, and government control. The conservatives blamed Hu Yaobang, the general secretary of the CCP and Deng's protégé, for being too sympathetic to students and intellectuals, allowing them to spread "bourgeois liberalism," a code word for Western values. In January 1987, Hu was abruptly dismissed and was replaced by Premier Zhao Ziyang, another Deng supporter. Li Peng succeeded Zhao as premier.

Hu had become a symbol of reforms, and his death in April 1989 drew thousands of mourning students to the streets in Beijing. From April to June, students, workers, and ordinary citizens joined together in demonstrations in cities throughout China, protesting against a multitude of issues, including inflation, job insecurity, official corruption, and lack of political freedom and participation. By mid-May, an estimated 1.2 million people gathered at Tiananmen Square.

The Chinese leadership was divided over how best to handle it. Zhao advocated compromising with students in order to resolve the situation peacefully, whereas other conservative hardliners, including Premier Li, supported suppression by force. Ultimately, the latter course prevailed. Martial law was declared, and soldiers and tanks moved into the city and cleared the Square on June 4, 1989, leading to considerable loss of life. Zhao was dismissed and put on house arrest until his death in 2005. Jiang Zemin, then party secretary in Shanghai, replaced Zhao as the general secretary of the CCP. Jiang was promoted for firm but decisive action that prevented bloodshed in similar protests in Shanghai.

Afterward, the PRC went through a few years of political oppression and economic retrenchment. The crackdown of the Tiananmen demonstrations significantly damaged Deng's reputation, but he survived the crisis and was able to hold the balance between the conservatives and the moderates. A few months after the Tiananmen crackdown, he stepped down from the chairmanship of the Central Military Commission (CMC) and promoted Jiang Zemin into the post. The strategic purpose of the move was to pave the way for the takeover of the third-generation leadership, with Jiang at its core. In addition to his positions as general secretary of the CCP and chair of the CMC, Jiang became president of the PRC in 1993, the first time that the three positions were held by the same person.

The Push for Further Reforms

The CCP leadership faced grave challenges in the aftermath of the Tiananmen Square incident. Western governments and media denounced China's actions; the United States and the European Union imposed an arms embargo on the PRC. Later in 1989, the Soviet satellite states in Eastern Europe collapsed, followed by the implosion of the Communist Party of the Soviet Union in 1990. Under isolation and with a strong sense of urgency, the CCP leadership undertook considerable analysis and introspection to search for a formula to survive the post-Soviet world (Shambaugh 2008). Not giving up its supreme position as a single ruling party anytime soon, the CCP, however, was willing to adapt and change. While there was no set course of action, the general aim was to enhance the legitimacy of the regime through economic growth and nationalism. It also worked to enhance the capacity of the party and the state to be more responsive to the grievances and demands of the people while balancing various societal contradictions.

To further solidify the proreform forces, Deng in 1992 went on a "southern tour" to visit cities such as Shenzhen and Shanghai where economic openings had produced economic growth. He launched broad criticisms against conservative leaders, paving the way for a change in the political atmosphere for the 14th Party Congress later that year with a call for the creation of a "socialist market economy" in the Congress's political report. Deng further engineered the ouster of a group of conservative leaders to ensure a smooth power transition to Jiang. In 1992, when Deng fully retired from politics at the 14th National Party Congress, he dissolved the Party Central Advisory Commission, which was one of the platforms leading to the downfall of the two general secretaries, Hu Yaobang and Zhao Ziyang. By outliving his opponents (with Chen Yun passing in April 1995 and Deng two years later in February 1997), Deng sealed the deal for future reforms. Ironically, while his reforms stressed the importance of institutionalization, Deng operated outside the bounds of formal institutions to maintain the course of reforms.

POLITICAL GOVERNANCE IN THE REFORM ERA: 1992–PRESENT

In the post-Deng era, the basis of power came from political leaders' education, experience, performance, and, most importantly, positions. They worked their way up the bureaucratic ladder step by step as technocrats or party generalists. Their strengths were in planning, managing, and problem solving. As China's economic reforms widened and deepened, would they have the political skills and governing ability to lead the PRC to meet internal and external challenges?

Politics under Jiang Zemin

Coming into power at the time of grave uncertainty in the post-Tiananmen crackdown, Jiang Zemin (general secretary 1989–2002, PRC president 1993–2003, chair of CMC 1989–2004) attempted to both extend and redefine Dengism in political and economic realms. Under Mao, the legitimacy of the regime came from revolution and ideology. In the reform era, economic performance became the basis of legitimacy. Jiang continued the path of economic reforms, introducing greater marketization in commodity and labor markets, downsizing smaller state-owned enterprises (SOEs), and encouraging private entrepreneurship. In 1997, during the 15th Party Congress, Jiang declared the party's general task to be "economic development." Under Jiang, the Chinese economy became more open to the outside world in trade and investment, culminating with its entry into the World Trade Organization (WTO) in 2001. In 2002 (the 16th Party Congress), Jiang refined the goal as to "build a moderately prosperous society" by 2021, the party's 100th founding anniversary.

Economic development was accomplished under the close watch of the central government, which exerted its authority over personnel selection and management to promote sustained growth. Economic performance became an important criterion in the promotion of provincial officials (Chen, Li, and Zhou 2005; Maskin, Qian, and Xu 2000). Under the policy of "grasping the big; letting go of the small," the central government privatized the smaller, less efficient SOEs but retained control over the large SOEs in strategic areas such as defense, electricity, petroleum, and telecommunications, thus maintaining monopolies over the "commanding heights" of the economy. Premier Zhu Rongji undertook administrative and tax reforms to enhance the fiscal capability of the central government. Under Jiang's watch, the PRC grew to be a major economic power.

Politically, Jiang continued Deng's institutionalization effort by applying the two-term limit to the premiership and other senior government posts. In 1997, he introduced the rule of retirement-at-70 for members of the Politburo Standing Committee (PSC), except the general secretary. While the rule was used to sideline his rival Qiao Shi, it helped eliminate lifelong tenure for senior leaders. Unlike in Deng's era, informal gatherings of retired officials were no longer the final authority in decision making. Decisions were made through formal party, government, or military bodies.

The policy to separate the party and the state was modified. Jiang strengthened the role of the leading small groups (LSGs), personally chairing the ones concerning Taiwan affairs, foreign affairs, and national security, to expand his reign. Some of these LSGs were ad hoc, others permanent, and they brought together relevant units from the party and the government for consultation and coordination before final decisions were made by the PSC. Decision making thus became more consultative and consensual. It recognized the bureaucratic pluralism in the party-state structure, while minimizing individualistic tendencies.

Jiang also made some progress in inner-party democracy within the CCP. A series of rules and regulations were implemented to make elections and selections of party cadres more competitive. Members of standing committees at various levels were required to report their work to the plenary sessions of party organizations for accountability purposes.

As the Chinese economy became more vibrant and diverse after more than two decades of reform and opening, Jiang realized that the CCP needed to expand beyond the traditional base of workers and farmers and embrace the entrepreneurial forces that are critical to China's economic growth. Thus, he proposed the idea of "three represents," to make the CCP a representative of "the advanced productive forces in society," "the advanced modern culture," and "the interests of the vast majority of the people." Formally incorporated into the party charter in 2002, the principle of "three represents" intended to draw professionals and entrepreneurs into the party to expand its ruling capacity.

While Jiang found it necessary to be ideologically flexible and pragmatic, he continued to view liberalism and constitutional democracy as subversive Western plots. Viewing political stability as the top priority, Jiang's regime began to shield the Chinese Internet behind a "great firewall" to censor and filter the information flow. Fearful of the rise of any organized political rivals, it created more legal barriers for social and civil organizations to register and banned the Falun Gong, a religious group that it deemed as "spreading superstition." Jiang was also unwilling to extend village elections to the level of townships or counties.

Although formal rules and structures gained traction under Jiang, there was still room for political patronage. To expand his circle of support, he systematically promoted former aides and associates from Shanghai, collectively known as the "Shanghai faction/clique," that was instrumental in ensuring that the agenda of reforms and opening could remain intact. During Jiang's era, the membership of the PSC expanded from five to seven, and then to nine, for the purpose of having more of his loyalists on the committee to retain his influence. When transitioning out of the office, Jiang undercut the idea of institutionalization by holding onto the position of chairman of the Central Military Commission for two more years.

Politics under Hu Jintao

When Deng assisted Jiang for leadership transition in 1992, he also appointed Hu Jintao (general secretary 2002–2012, president 2003–2013, chair of CMC 2004–2012) to the PSC as Jiang's successor. Following in the footsteps of former General Secretary Hu Yaobang, Hu Jintao was promoted through the system of the Communist Youth League. While Jiang came from Shanghai, the affluent commercial center of the coastal region that had benefitted from reform and opening, Hu's career was mostly based in the poor, interior regions. Experiencing firsthand the realities of poverty and hardship in an unbalanced economic development, Hu and his associates put greater emphasis on social justice, the root issue of most political and social contentions.

Unbalanced Growth. Since the economic reform in 1978, sustained economic growth has brought enormous improvement to the standard of living for most Chinese, lifting 500 million people out of poverty. Yet the cost of China's growth model has also become apparent. Relentless pursuit of economic development came with the price of corruption, resource depletion, environmental and ecological destruction, and increasing income disparities. Social grievances and dissatisfaction became widespread, as the public began to voice concerns for food safety, clean air, and affordable housing. While economic growth has been an importance source of political legitimacy for the CCP in the reform era, the unbalanced and unsustainable growth has begun to undermine its legitimacy.

The 2008 Beijing Olympics illustrated both the achievements and problems of the Chinese growth model. On the one hand, the Olympics was a long-awaited opportunity for China to showcase its economic success. The "Bird's Nest" stadium, the "Water Cube" aquatic center, and Beijing Airport's Terminal 3 were iconic displays of China's economic and technological prowess. Designed by some of the most renowned architects in the world, these buildings symbolized a new China with wealth and a global vision.

However, fast-paced economic growth with unbridled greed stripped the state of its ability to enforce regulations and legal rules, which was evident in two events. The extraordinary efforts undertaken by the Chinese state before

the games to combat Beijing's smog and improve its air quality, such as closing factories for weeks and adopting an odd-even road rule for automobiles
based on the license plate, revealed a significant cost of economic development
—environmental degradation. Additionally, days before the opening of the
Olympics, Fonterra, a New Zealand–based dairy firm and the joint venture
partner of China's dairy giant Sanlu Group, learned that Sanlu's powdered-
milk product had been contaminated with melamine, a toxic chemical commonly used in producing plastics. According to Fonterra, it was unsuccessful
in pressing Sanlu for an immediate recall, and the top executives of Sanlu,
appointed by the Hebei party committee, tried to cover up the scandal particularly during the Olympics. It was not until a month later, after the news
broke, that Sanlu finally issued a massive recall of its infant formula. By that
time, the melamine-laced milk product had sickened more than 56,000 infants
and young children, and four babies had died from kidney failure by the end
of September.

The incident shook public confidence in food safety. More important, it
illustrated a bigger problem—fast economic growth with unbridled greed had
overtaken the state's ability to enforce rules and regulations.

Fully aware of the rise of social tensions and discontents, Hu intended to
shift governance focus from economic development to economic distribution.
He proposed a "scientific development" approach to building up a "harmonious society." The term *scientific* referred to a better way of economic development that intended to redirect economic activities from a sheer pursuit of
higher GDP to a more sustainable path with broader support.

To address regional imbalance, Hu and premier Wen Jiabao in early 2004
had begun to redirect the macroeconomic resources to less developed western
and northeastern regions. With the call to "build a new Socialist countryside,"
the government nearly doubled its spending between 2004 and 2007 in rural
areas to improve infrastructure, education, and health care. Agricultural taxes
were formally abolished in 2006 to ease farmers' burden. Yet, despite the leadership's intention to change the development paradigm and promote social
justice, the situation deteriorated under Hu's watch. While China overtook
Japan in 2010 as the second largest economy, the governing institutions effective in promoting prosperity and stability were unable to rebalance the growth.
The income gap between the "haves" and "have-nots" widened in the 2000s.
The richest 10 percent of families had 65 times the income of the poorest 10
percent (Wu 2011).

Corruption and Social Discontent. Amid the widening income gap, the public's perception that wealth is accumulated not by talent or hard work but by
corruption and abuse of power fueled greater distrust and discontent. Huge
amounts of government revenues and state assets remained in the hands of
the powerful party-state apparatus and those with good connections. The
asset value of national SOEs tripled from 2002 to 2009, highlighting a trend
in which wealth had been diverted from citizens and the private sector to the

government (Wu 2011). The 2008 global financial crisis further exacerbated the trend, as massive 4-trillion-RMB ($586 billion) stimulus funds were channeled to SOEs for growth stimulation to counter the economic downturn. The growing weight of the state sector runs against the marketization effort of the post-1978 reforms and provides enormous opportunities to government-affiliated elites to become wealthy and corrupt.

Illegal or arbitrary actions of local officials were another source of social discontent. Uncompensated transfer of land, mismanagement of construction projects, a dubious procurement process, and poor interpretation and implementation of government regulations were examples of power abuse by officials, contributing to people's grievances toward governance.

The sharp increase in social protests was an indicator of the rising social tension. The statistics of mass incidents (*qunti shijian*, i.e., strikes, riots, or demonstrations) showed increased frequency and higher levels of violence throughout the 2000s. Over 180,000 mass incidents were recorded in 2010, more than double the number reported in 2006 (Zheng 2012). These incidents were instigated by a broad range of issues, from corruption to environmental pollution to ethnic conflicts. Unlike in the past when the incidents were mostly limited to small towns and rural areas, the protests have taken place in major cities, where collective actions can be organized through social media and microblogs (*weibo*, the Chinese version of Twitter).

Governance Approach. The Hu regime reacted to social discontent with a two-prong approach. On the one hand, the government increased its budget to build a coercive apparatus that would respond to "emergency incidents" through a nationwide "social management" system that connects police, People's Armed Police (PAP), and the People's Liberation Army (PLA) with offices at county and city district levels. In 2002, the central government's spending on domestic security was 135 billion RMB. In 2013, the public security budget rose to 769 billion RMB, exceeding China's announced defense budget of 720 billion RMB (Fewsmith 2013). The numbers revealed that the political leadership was quite concerned about its internal threats.

On the other hand, the Chinese authorities began to establish channels for policy consultation and deliberation. As the 2008 global financial crisis rendered the prospect for sustained economic growth less certain, Hu and Wen attempted to regain legitimacy by opening up informal channels for citizens to participate in policy deliberation. Whereas Western democracies formulate policies through electoral procedures and representative politics to meet the interests and demands of the people, the Chinese party-state sought to respond to popular demands through consultative and deliberative mechanisms.

Technology was applied to governance in a similar manner. Using the e-government approach, the party-state expanded consultations beyond the traditional face-to-face meetings to include online bulletin boards and chat rooms for informal bargaining. Online comment sections maintained by the administrative and legislative branches were created for the general public to provide feedback on the drafts of laws and regulations. Tools such as citizen input boxes, online petitions, online opinion polls, and Q&A with officials became regular features on government websites.

Nevertheless, there was another side to the party-state's cyber presence. Recognizing the popular use of microblogs to discuss politics and news, public security agencies and offices were actively engaged in those spheres (Noesselt 2014). A large number of Internet police and monitors were deployed at all levels of the party-state to take part in an extensive censorship program (King, Pan, and Roberts 2013). The purpose of censorship was not necessarily tracking and eliminating the postings that were critical of the party-state. On occasion, comments on social problems and bureaucratic mismanagement were allowed to be posted and circulated; when these postings attracted widespread attention or angry reaction by netizens, the government took swift action to address the issues. Microblogs have therefore served as transmission belt to connect the party-state and society by offering a new platform for the general public to address their grievances. Government censorship instead focuses mostly on the mobilization potential of the postings. Comments that have the potential to generate collective action such as protests or public gatherings are more likely to be censored, regardless of their contents.

However, to engage the public via digital channels has proved only partially effective. In 2012, Japan's move to nationalize the disputed Diaoyu/Senkaku Islands in the East China Sea triggered massive, and sometimes violent, protests and demonstrations against Japan across the PRC. Yet the demonstrations were more than nationalist outbursts. Many protesters used the opportunities to voice their true concerns, carrying banners and signs calling for democracy, anticorruption, food safety, and economic equality. The events revealed a society full of anger and frustration.

Elite Politics. The Hu regime took no action on political reforms. Amid the rising social unrest, the economic dominance of the SOEs, and the widespread influence of social media, Premier Wen repeatedly called for political reforms, including separation of the party from the state and expanding democracy through elections. However, another member, Wu Bangguo, chairman of the Standing Committee of the NPC, proposed five "no's" to resist any genuine political reforms. Others on the PSC, including Hu, did not side with either member. It was clear that the leadership was fragile and divided. The collective leadership in the PSC functioned with very little coordination between its nine members (Zheng 2012). While each member was responsible for a specific policy domain, they could veto each other. The checks and balances among them created policy paralysis, leading to ultimate failure to exercise leadership over major economic, social, and political issues.

Growing income inequality ignited the debate between Maoism and Dengism. Maoists blamed China's social problems on the market reforms undertaken by Deng. Refuting privatization and globalization, they called for a return to the socialist economy dominated by the state sector with strengthened party leadership. Bo Xilai (son of Bo Yibo, a major figure in the Chinese revolution) was a proponent of Maoism. As a charismatic Politburo member and party chief in the city of Chongqing, he used Mao's tactics of mass mobilization and political campaigning to promote the so-called Chongqing model that imposed law and order to crack down on corruption while emphasizing government leadership in social and economic development.

Hu never visited Chongqing to show support of the Chongqing model. Instead, he visited Guangdong province to show his support of the role of the market in leading development, a Dengist model.

In 2012, Bo's wife Gu Kailai was arrested in a murder case involving a British businessman. Bo himself was accused of being responsible for power abuse during the anticorruption campaign in Chongqing and was sentenced to life imprisonment in September 2013.

When stepping down from the office in 2012, Hu did not hold on to any other position. The size of the PSC was changed again (from nine to seven), to streamline the policymaking process.

Politics under Xi Jinping

Xi Jinping was chosen as Hu's successor in the 17th Party Congress (2007) by members of the Central Committee and retired party leaders. Xi is one of the "princelings" (children of high-ranking officials); his father, Xi Zhongxun, was a Communist revolutionary and one of the founding fathers of the PRC. When Xi took over the party and the military in 2012, the common perception was that he would be severely limited by Jiang's and Hu's factions. However, Xi has proven otherwise by successfully consolidating his power and is en route to becoming the most powerful leader of China since Mao.

Two examples illustrate his power status. First, his name was written into the CCP charter in 2017, and the PRC Constitution in 2018: "Xi Jinping Thought for the new era of Socialism with Chinese characteristics." The direct mention of his name elevates him to a status similar to Mao's and Deng's; while Jiang and Hu had their doctrines of "three represents" and "scientific outlook of development" mentioned in the Constitution and party charter, their names were not preserved. Xi's vision to build a "modern Socialist country" by the PRC's 100th anniversary in 2049 in the "new era of Socialism with Chinese characteristics" will provide an ideological framework to guide the party agenda for the next three decades.

Second, the constitutional revision of 2018 eliminated the two five-year term limits on the posts of PRC president and vice president. Analysts debated over the implication of the change. Some noted the ceremonial role of the position and argued that the revision merely brings the top state position in line with that of the party (i.e., general secretary) and the military (i.e., chair of the CMC)—none of which have term limits. Others believed that the step was primarily to extend Xi's tenure beyond 2022. Whatever the reason may be, the move clearly stood against the once-popular idea to institutionalize leadership transition in the reform era. Presidential term limits, in a way, formed the constitutional basis for Jiang and Hu to serve only two terms as the party leader. The abolition of the term limit removes the only constitutional constraint for the top leadership. Reversing a trend engrained in the reform era demonstrates Xi's powerful leadership.

Why was Xi able to consolidate power so swiftly? As a proud member of the CCP revolutionary tradition, he had reached back to Mao's legacy to reinvoke the idea of a "mass line," reminding party officials to better understand, represent, and prioritize the wishes of the people. To ensure that the entire party follows its economic and political line, he launched a major "rectification campaign" in June 2013 to combat "four devils": corruption, bureaucratic behavior, hedonism, and extravagance. The campaign, called "Mass Line Education and Practice Activities," reflected Mao's style, asking the cadres to be moral role models and be closer to the masses through self-purification, self-reformation, self-criticism, and self-education.

Anticorruption Campaign. Associated with the campaign is an unprecedented anticorruption drive that reaches far and wide to bring the cadres and armed forces under stricter control. The central leadership dispatched inspection groups to all provinces and organizations to investigate corrupt behaviors within the elite. Since its inception, over 200 senior officers and executives of state-owned enterprises have been investigated. Many have been arrested and indicted, including four senior national leaders: Zhou Yongkang (PSC member in charge of the security apparatus), Guo Boxiong and Xu Caihou (both Politburo members and vice chairs of the CMC), and Ling Jihua (Central Secretariat member and Hu's confidant).

Although some may question whether this is a true anticorruption campaign or an old-style power struggle to consolidate Xi's power, it seems that the breadth of the campaign has carried beyond factional enemies. It, in fact, reflects Xi's deep concern for the party's governance capacity, as the party's reputation in recent years has been damaged by corruption and lax practices.

Political Agenda. Restoring public confidence in the CCP is only the first step toward ensuring continued party rule and maintaining its preeminent position over the state and the society. Xi revealed an ambitious reform agenda in 2013, outlining a 60-point decision with 300 reforms in seven policy sectors—economy, ecology, law, culture and media, social management, military, and party—all to be completed by 2021, the centennial anniversary of the CCP. A Leading Small Group for Comprehensively Deepening Reform was established in 2014 to coordinate implementation of the reforms.

He reaffirmed the importance of Marxim as a guide for action and rejected the influence of "Western ideas and theories," such as constitutional democracy and universal values. Instead, he promoted traditional Chinese culture through selective interpretation of Confucianism to bolster the claim of "Socialism with Chinese characteristics."

He believes that the CCP can offer the best leadership to the state and society, with little need for external oversight or checks from nonparty organizations. For Xi, complete loyalty to the CCP is expected of not only party members but all other members of society. Control over new social media and nongovernmental organizations (NGOs) was tightened. New rules were issued to impose greater restrictions upon lawyers and law firms deemed disruptive or threatening to national security, primarily targeting "rights protection" lawyers who advocated rights for citizens. Under the Xi regime, many lawyers and human rights activists have been arrested and indicted for subversion of state power.

Xi also inserted himself in virtually all policy spheres. He has taken over as head of a number of leading small groups, including foreign affairs, Taiwan affairs, cyber security and information, economics and finance, and "comprehensive deepening of reform."

Even with tight control, social unrest continues. A particularly notable development involved retired PLA soldiers. Several thousand of them surrounded the PLA headquarters building in Beijing in 2016, protesting economic hardship and insufficient retirement payment.

Economic Agenda. While the anticorruption drive broke down vested interest groups, economic restructuring is a long-term and multifaceted project. It was clearly understood by Xi and Premier Li Keqiang that the easy phase of economic development is coming to an end. The old growth model that relied on labor-intensive exports and state-led investment could not continue to generate growth. The PRC is in need of new growth drivers, including shifting from exports to domestic consumption, and upgrading to higher end products and industries to minimize the environmental impacts of the pollution-heavy industries in coal, steel, and other traditional sectors.

Who should lead the charge in economic transition, the market or the state? It seems that Xi and Li emphasized both. On the one hand, they stressed the important role of the market in allocating resources, creating social wealth, and sustaining economic development. Thus, they argued for setting utilities prices such as water, gas, electricity, and telecommunications through the market mechanism.

On the other hand, Xi and Li would like to maintain state engagement in economic development to retain control over key sectors of domestic economy through SOEs, similar to the economic model of Japan and South Korea. Under Xi, the state plays a more active role in Chinese overseas investment. To be more integrated into regional economic cooperation, the PRC has taken the lead in the establishment of the Asian Infrastructure Investment Bank (AIIB) to finance infrastructure construction such as overland railroads, highways, ports, and pipelines. The Belt and Road Initiative (BRI) proposed by Xi since 2013 intends to connect China to the Eurasian continent and Southeast Asia through trade expansion and infrastructure construction. Calling on countries along the original Silk Road (i.e., countries in Central Asia, West Asia, the Middle East, and Europe) and the "21st Century Maritime Silk Road" (i.e.,

Southeast Asia, Oceania, and North Africa) to participate in the BRI, Xi tries to achieve economic policy coordination for smooth movement of goods, people, and capital along the longest economic corridor. There are also definite domestic economic calculations behind the BRI, as Chinese authorities seek to spur economic growth in its less developed western region, reduce regional imbalance, and strengthen political stability against separatist movements.

As the strongest political leader since Mao, Xi is well positioned to implement his political and economic agendas. It remains to be seen whether he can translate his power into effective governance to solve the political and economic dilemmas faced by the PRC in accordance with his vision.

GOVERNING INSTITUTIONS

The PRC Constitution

In 1948, eight minor political parties sanctioned by the CCP, collectively known as "democratic parties," pledged support to the CCP's leadership. Together, they adopted the Common Program as a provisional constitution on September 29, 1949, two days before the formation of the PRC. The Common Program provided the guiding principles and fundamental laws as the new revolutionary leadership consolidated its power and authority.

The PRC's first formal constitution was promulgated in 1954. It drew heavily on the constitutional tradition of the former Soviet Union with strong emphasis on the socialist principles. Unlike the federal system adopted in the Soviet model, it established a unitary system in which the central government had the exclusive power to change or revoke any decisions by provincial or local governments deemed inappropriate.

On paper, the 1954 Constitution survived for 20 years. In reality, political and legal orders based on the 1954 Constitution ended at the beginning of the Cultural Revolution in 1966. The radicalism manifested in the Cultural Revolution found its way into the next two state Constitutions, the 1975 and 1978 Constitutions, emphasizing class struggle under the proletarian dictatorship.

The current Constitution, enacted in 1982, adopts many of the principles of the 1954 Constitution as it reestablishes political order through reforms in the aftermath of the Cultural Revolution. Subsequent amendments took place in 1988, 1993, 1999, 2004, and 2018. The continuation of the 1982 Constitution reflects the effort to stabilize and institutionalize the political and constitutional order in the reform era. Over the years, as reforms deepen and widen, it gradually incorporates the support and endorsement of a market economy, rule of law, nonpublic ownership, and protection of human rights. The 2018 amendments, besides the abolition of the two five-year term limits on the posts of PRC president and vice president, reaffirmed that "the leadership of the CCP is the most essential characteristic of socialism with Chinese characteristics."

The Chinese Communist Party

The Structure and Organization of the CCP. The CCP dominates state and society in China and maintains a permanent monopoly of power. As of the end of 2018, it had approximately 90.6 million members, making it the largest political party in the world. The published data indicate that about 27 percent of them are women, and more than 48 percent of the members hold a college degree or higher. Occupation distribution shows that the CCP is broadly based, drawing members from all walks of life. The party consists of the most outstanding and accomplished members of society. In the eyes of its critics, however, people increasingly join the party to further personal careers, rather than "to serve the people."

The CCP is organized hierarchically. According to the CCP charter (a separate document from the Constitution of the PRC), the highest leading bodies of the party are the National Party Congress (PC) and the Central Committee it elects. But the organizational chart of the CCP does not always reflect the true locus of power. Since the CCP was formed in 1921, 19 PCs have been convened (the last one being in 2017). With the gathering of more than 2,000 party delegates from all over the country, PC meetings are major events attracting national media and societal attention. Very little debate and deliberation occur during PC sessions. They perform mostly public relations functions for party leaders to review their past achievements and chart the course for the future. Party leaders use the occasion to set a general tone and direction for policies and provide official formulation on ongoing debates. A comparison of the language used in a series of political reports issued by the PC frequently provides an indication as to how the official view evolves.

Another function performed by the PC is to elect the Central Committee, which acts on behalf of the PC to manage party affairs until its next session. PC delegates usually receive a recommended list for the Central Committee membership from the party authority and have only marginal influence on the outcome of the election. Since 1987, the CCP has adopted a more competitive procedure for the elections to have more candidates than seats. As a result, some candidates favored by top leaders could in fact lose the election.

The Central Committee consists of approximately 350 members (full and alternate) who represent the top elites in the CCP, generally of four backgrounds: central party apparatus, the state systems, provincial leaders, and the military. Women and minorities are usually underrepresented; only 10 percent of the members of the 19th Central Committee are women, and 11 percent are minorities.

Meeting once or twice a year, the Central Committee is charged with electing the Politburo, its Standing Committee, and the general secretary—a group of leaders with real political clout in China. Lieberthal (1995) aptly observed the reverse relationship between the size of the political body in China and its political power: "In theory, the larger the body, the more powerful it is. In reality, the opposite is true—the smallest committee is the most important structure."

The seven members of the PSC are the most powerful leaders in China; each member has executive responsibility for a particular area of policy.

The actual functions or powers of the Politburo have never been clearly defined in the party charter, which merely states that the Politburo carries out the work of the Central Committee when it is not in session. The Politburo contains two dozen or so members, with careful balance in backgrounds between the party and the state, as well as between the central administration and provincial leadership to prevent any institutional bloc from dominating others. Members of the Politburo deliberate over major policies and personnel decisions in closed-door sessions. Occasionally, there are leaked reports on division between the Politburo members, but the decision making is normally based on consensus.

Analysis of the backgrounds of the Politburo members reflects an interesting trend that matches the path of modernization and development in China. Prior to the 1978 reforms, the CCP leadership came primarily from the backgrounds of farmers and soldiers. During the 1990s and early 2000s, the leadership composition changed, with 60 percent to 70 percent of the Politburo members having some technical expertise, especially in the fields of science and engineering. The rise of the technocrats reflects their role in and contribution to China's economic growth and development. In recent years, degree patterns have become more diverse, with more in humanities and social sciences than technical fields (Li 2013; Miller 2018). It remains to be seen whether this diversity in education and occupational background will interject different dynamics in decision making and whether it will shift policy priority from economic development to legal and judicial development.

The supremacy of the CCP leadership is not just mentioned in the state Constitution; it is also manifested in political practice as well. For example, the leadership transition in the post-Mao era follows a two-stage pattern that implies the pivotal role of the CCP. The transition of the political leadership first takes place when the PC meets in the fall to appoint top-level posts in the CCP. The composition and ranking of the members of the Politburo and its Standing Committee in the CCP then give indications as to what the top posts in the PRC state would look like when the NPC meets the following spring to confirm the leadership of the state. The sequence has strong symbolism in affirming the party leadership over the government.

The Central Military Commission. The Central Military Commission (CMC) is the key organization in charge of overseeing the Chinese armed forces. It exists as a dual organization in both the party and the government, overlapping entirely in membership and function. The CMC is the highest command authority for military operations, and the highest military policy-making body for military affairs, directly supervising the PRC Ministry of National Defense. The chairman of the CMC is the commander in chief of the People's Liberation Army and always a top party leader. Deng held the position from 1977 to 1989. Since then, Jiang, Hu, and Xi have held the position to oversee the military.

In the past, the CMC exercised leadership through four departments: staff, political affairs, logistics, and armaments. Under Xi's military reform, the CMC has undertaken major restructuring to streamline the command structure to directly oversee the military services and theaters of operations. Along the lines of Xi's anticorruption campaigns, three agencies (i.e., the Disciplinary Inspection Commission, the Politics and Law Commission, and the Office of the Auditing Administration) report directly to the CMC and enhance its ability to ensure accountability in the military.

The National Government

National People's Congress. Government authority, ostensibly belonging to the people, is exercised by the people through the NPC at the top and people's congresses at the provincial, county, and township levels. These congresses are the legislative branch of the government and are empowered to supervise the work of the "people's governments," the executive branch.

The NPC, the "highest organ of state power," is a unicameral legislature with three thousand members serving a five-year term. It performs functions usually reserved for a parliament, such as law making, budget approval, and oversight of law enforcement. The NPC meets once a year for about two weeks. Given its immense size, only a handful of full plenary meetings are convened to approve reports. Most of the time, delegates are divided into working groups, according to regions, to discuss matters of national concerns. Although in recent years there have been more delegates casting dissenting votes that contradict the party line, it is clearly not a democratic or deliberative body.

Compared with legislatures of other countries, the NPC has some unique power such as amending the PRC Constitution and electing the PRC president and vice president. The presidency of the PRC is mainly a ceremonial position; its duties include meeting with other heads of state, awarding state honors, and receiving the credentials of foreign ambassadors. In the early stage of reforms, the office was held by leaders of high party rank, such as Li Xiannian, president from 1983 to 1988, and Yang Shangkun, 1988–1993. As China's international profile grows, the diplomatic functions performed by the office become increasingly important.

When the NPC is not in session, the Standing Committee of the NPC serves as its executive body. It, too, performs some unique functions such as interpreting the Constitution and enforcing martial law in the event of domestic disturbances.

In the reform era as China strives to develop its economy, lawmaking becomes increasingly important. To attract foreign investors, it is necessary to develop a sound legal system to protect property rights, enforce contracts, and resolve conflicts. Thus, the NPC is gaining more autonomy and greater stature as demands for quality laws and regulations increase. Its growing reliance on public hearings, subject matter experts, and written public input indicates the trend to make the legislative process more transparent and participatory (Horsley 2010).

Delegates of people's congresses are elected through direct or indirect elections. At the township- and district-level, delegates are directly elected by their constituencies. For congresses above the district level (i.e., county/municipal, provincial, and national), they are elected indirectly by the congresses one level below. In the reform era, these elections have become competitive (i.e., the number of candidates may be 20 percent to 50 percent more than the number of positions available) and are decided by secret ballots.

By law, independent candidates (i.e., those not nominated by the party-state) are eligible to run in direct elections. In reality, the party-state has tightened the rule to discourage such practice (Yung Sun 2013). For indirect elections, the party-state plays an active role in managing the electoral process and vetting candidates. Prior to elections, it would carefully determine the demographic makeup of the congress, distribute quotas to each of the social groups, and recommend candidates accordingly (Y. Sun 2014). In recent years, the party-state makes efforts to recruit entrepreneurs, managers, technical professionals, and leaders of civic associations as candidates.

State Council. The State Council is the highest executive body and the chief administrative authority of the Chinese government. It consists of the premier, vice premier, state councilors, and ministers in charge of ministries and commissions. The premier is appointed and removed by the PRC president, with the approval of the NPC.

The structure and configuration of the State Council's ministries and commissions have gone through several rounds of changes. The purpose of these administrative reforms was threefold (Burns 1993, 2003; Yeo 2009). First, they aimed to streamline or downsize government agencies, partly for budget reasons to reduce government financial burden and partly for functional rationalization to eliminate duplication. In the late 1980s, the State Council had more than 40 ministries and commissions; it has since decreased into the range of the 20s. While units appear to have reduced or positions eliminated, the excess administrative staffers usually were not dismissed but transferred to service units (*shiye danwei*) affiliated with government agencies, such as research institutes, economic enterprises, schools, or hospitals. Despite the downsizing efforts, the total number of employment in core organs and service units has grown consistently (Ang 2012). Public employment remains an important source of political patronage, used as a tool to maintain political support and social stability.

Second, the reforms sought to adjust the function and scope of government to meet the needs of an increasingly marketized economy. Agencies responsible for allocating human resources or approving production quotas were no longer necessary in the new economic system, whereas those in charge of taxation, audits, industry, commerce, and statistics needed to be strengthened and expanded.

Third, the reforms tried to enhance the quality and education attainment of government personnel. Policies were implemented to instill a competitive process in personnel selection, impose a mandatory retirement age to replace the older generalists with younger technocrats, and improve salary scales to boost morale and enhance performance (Burns 2004). The Civil Service Law of 2006 aimed to formalize the categorization of civil servants in the public sector.

THE STATE–CIVIL SOCIETY RELATIONS

Civil society, in the standard definition, refers to self-governing nongovernmental and nonprofit organizations that are formed voluntarily by their members. Different theoretical lenses have been used to describe the relationship between the state and the civil society organizations (CSOs) in China. Some emphasized the dominance of the state in controlling and regulating social organizations (Pearson 1997; Ru and Ortolano 2008). Others (Frolic 1997; He 1997) focus on the efforts of the social actors in confronting the state to expand their autonomy. Still others (Shieh 2009) argue that it is a relationship too complex and dynamic to fit into any single pattern, because the interactions between the state and civil organizations may vary, depending on the functions and roles of the CSOs and the state's perception of the benefits and threats they may pose.

Civil Society Organizations in the Pre-Reform Era

The 1949 Communist takeover resulted in strict control of civil society. Under the party-state structure, private and civilian interests were supposedly subsumed under the public and state interests. CSOs were regarded as antagonistic to the party-state, despite the fact that citizens were supposed to have freedom of association according to the Constitution.

Mao's "mass-line" idea, however, opened some doors for mass organizations. Although the mass-line model assumed direct communication between the party and the grass roots, mass organizations and professional associations were subsequently developed as intermediaries or transmission belts to mediate these contacts. For example, the All-China Women's Federation, All-China Federation of Trade Unions, and Communist Youth League were assigned the function of representing the interest of women, workers, and youth, respectively (Wu and Chan 2012). Before 1978, there were only about 100 national social organizations in China (Zheng 2010). Almost all social organizations were funded by the party-state and were subordinate to its governance structure.

Civil Society Organizations in the Reform Era

Proliferation of the CSOs. Economic reforms since 1978 brought fundamental changes to the structure of the society and encouraged the development of CSOs. As private entrepreneurs actively participated in the national economy, professional associations, chambers of commerce, and trade organizations began to emerge. By 1989, the total number of national CSOs reached 1,600. They served as new intermediaries to bridge the party-state and the increasingly diversified economic and social interests. At this stage, no single government ministry was responsible for regulating civil society organizations. Nearly every public agency could approve and take charge of certain types of organizations under this decentralized regulatory environment.

In the aftermath of the 1989 Tiananmen crackdown, CSOs, particularly independent student unions and trade unions, were perceived as a threat. The fear was that CSOs would be cover for groups engaged in political activities and cause social unrest. To tighten its control over CSOs, the party-state instituted a "dual supervision" model in 1989.

Supervision of the CSOs. According to the 1989 Regulation on the Registration and Management of Social Organizations, a CSO first needed to be sponsored by an "administrative supervising unit" (*yewu zhuguan danwei*), such as a government agency, a state-owned enterprise, or a public institution (e.g., a university), before it could file for registration with the Ministry of Civil Affairs or a local civil affairs department. Under this rule, the party-state placed CSOs under the supervision of both the civil affairs departments and the administrative supervising units (i.e., the "dual supervision") to ensure political and social stability. Furthermore, the 1989 Regulation established the "noncompetition" principle, allowing only one organization in the same category for the same administrative region. For example, if an environmental protection association already existed in Beijing, then no other environmental group would be approved. In many cases, government-sponsored organizations could easily take up the entire quota, leaving little space for voluntary-based organizations to register.

The 1989 Regulation on the Registration and Management of Social Organizations was amended in 1998 to incorporate the CSOs more closely into the party-state structure (Saich 2000). The 1998 Regulation specified in greater detail the role of the supervising units. The supervising unit would be held responsible for the organization's actions and needed to guarantee that the social organization would not engage in illegal or antigovernment activities. Under normal circumstances, a government agency would have very little incentive to sponsor a CSO. Furthermore, a CSO with nationwide membership was prohibited from establishing regional branches so that no horizontal, cross-regional alliances could be formed.

In 2016, a new Foreign Nongovernmental Organization Management Law tightened the registration process for foreign nongovernmental organizations (Wong 2016). Foreign groups would be required not only to find an administrative supervising unit but also to register with the local public security bureau (i.e., the police), which became authorized to scrutinize all aspects of their operations, including finances. The transfer of registration from civil affairs to the public security departments reflects the broader effort under Xi to limit Western influences on Chinese society.

While the party-state is unwilling to lose control over the CSOs, it also recognizes the value of their services and contributions. For example, in the wake of the devastating magnitude-7.9 earthquake in Sichuan province in 2008, it was the CSOs that actively and effectively mobilized volunteers and donors and coordinated relief work. Their ability to identify social needs and to mobilize resources to meet needs demonstrated the growing capacity of grassroots-based activism and volunteerism in China (Shieh and Deng 2011; Teets 2009). The social services and relief provided by some of the CSOs for the poor and the elderly contribute greatly to social stability, particularly as the Chinese society is rapidly aging with widening income gaps.

Thus, the Chinese party-state has devised a pragmatic approach of "graduated control" (*fenlei guanzhi*) to deal with the CSOs (Kang and Han 2008; Wu and Chan 2012). Based on their purpose, source of funding, and operational scale, the party-state would exercise differentiated levels of control over the CSOs. For example, it maintains minimal supervision over the organizations that deliver social services to the poor, the elderly, and children, particularly if they operate at the local community level. In fact, they could even be eligible for government funding, acting as a service arm of the administration. Nevertheless, the level of surveillance is heightened over the CSOs that advocate for rights of marginalized groups such as migrant workers, AIDS patients, and dislocated urban residents, as they may work with lawyers, social workers, and medical professionals for technical support, thus increasing the risk of social mobilization and collective action. The government would monitor their activities more closely if they received funding from overseas entities. Finally, the CSOs engaged in democracy movements, ethnic separatism, and human rights promotion draw the closest scrutiny from the security apparatus and face harsh, vigorous crackdowns because of their capability to organize collective action to challenge the party-state.

Responses from the CSOs. How effective is this supervision system? It appears that the system is effective in discouraging the registration of the CSOs but not as effective in deterring the growth of CSOs or the development of civil society (Howell 2007; Shieh 2009).

Given the restrictive rules regarding registration, a growing number of the CSOs decided not to register with the government. They found it more convenient to register as business organizations or to simply operate illegally outside the system. Currently, there are more than 400,000 associations registered with the Ministry of Civil Affairs. Estimates of unregistered CSOs range from a few hundred thousand to over two million.

Many of them found alternative, creative ways to circumvent registration barriers. They may establish partnerships with existing organizations or embed themselves as research groups or project centers. The widespread use of the Internet and social media provides flexible platforms for social organizations to form loose networks without relying on conventional structures.

Chinese CSOs are not passive actors when dealing with state supervision or intervention. While they may not enjoy as much autonomy as their counterparts in the West, they continue to have social space to pursue their goals. In fact, the pursuit of organizational autonomy has rarely been the goal of the Chinese CSOs, for it could minimize their influence and effectiveness. For them, activism embedded in the state structure is a preferred approach. They would deliberately blur the line between themselves and the state so that they can influence policies from within (Salmenkari 2014).

Evidence has shown that the relationship between state and civil society is dynamic and reciprocal (Salmenkari 2013; Wu and Chan 2012). The Chinese CSOs tend to seek direct access to the state and use personal contacts and networks to gain official support. Rather than acting as an independent watchdog to investigate cases on their own, they would report the problems and violations to the government and resolve the issues through official intervention. An important strategy for the Chinese CSOs to gain influence is to provide information and research to the state. In so doing, they could interject new perspectives in policy making. While the state is undoubtedly the stronger party, resistance or contestation from CSOs could reshape the process of the state-society interactions.

VILLAGE ELECTIONS

The Origin of the Village Elections

After communes were dissolved in the reform era, some villagers began to experiment with various forms of self-government such as village committees to manage public works, maintain public security, and restrain corrupt and abusive officials who acted as "local emperors."

Village committees were recognized in the 1982 Constitution as self-governing bodies. Members of the village committee, however, were generally appointed by the township government. In the late 1980s, as local officials began to arbitrarily impose higher taxes or levies on farmers to make up for the lost revenue from decollectivization, many farmers retaliated with violence, such as arson, vandalism, and even killing of local cadres. Village elections were seen as a solution to ease farmers' grievances and reduce the "tax riots." The partial devolution of policy-making power was meant to preserve social stability and political order by curbing power abuse by local officials and reducing local rebellions.

The passage of the 1987 Organic Law of the Village Committees (Experimental) introduced the direct election of the chairman, deputy chairman, and members of the village committees on a trial basis. The idea of direct elections encountered strong opposition from the more conservative elements of the CCP. Its chief proponent, Peng Zhen, then chairman of the Standing Committee of the NPC, made a forceful argument that direct elections of the village committees would allow farmers to be the masters of their own affairs. Learning and practicing socialist democracy is consistent with the mass-line policy of the CCP, according to Peng.

Although the electoral process was initially met with strong skepticism from farmers, it gradually became an institutionalized practice in rural China. Elections were introduced in a top-down manner by provincial governments. Once the provincial government decided to hold village elections, all villages in the province would implement the decision within a few years. Villages had very little say in the timing of introduction of elections.

The 1998 Organic Law of Village Committees further consolidated the development of grassroots democracy. The law stipulated that competitive elections be held every three years and that candidate nominations be open to all villagers.

Rural Democracy

How do we assess the grassroots democracy? Are the elections meaningful, or are they pro forma? Do they make a difference for the governance structure and policy implementation? Will democratic elections spread upward from the village to the township, county, provincial, or even national level?

Given that some 60 percent of the Chinese population lives in the rural areas and that regular, direct elections occur only at the village level in China, implications of this kind of grassroots democracy have attracted a lot of interest. Many studies noted the positive effects of the elections. Although village elections were introduced primarily for the purpose of social stability, not for a commitment to democracy, the practices are becoming more than "window-dressing" activities. From the angle of democratic procedures, Chinese village elections represent limited but genuine contestation for offices (O'Brien and Han 2009; X. Sun 2014). The elections are generally competitive, for the number of candidates must exceed the number of open seats. For most places, balloting is conducted by members of an independent election committee selected by village assemblies, or assembly representatives, to ensure that the election is fair and open.

For the substantive benefits, direct elections have helped limit corruption, while enhancing accountability and transparency in village governance (Jakobson 2004; Kennedy, Rozelle, and Shi 2004; Manion 2006; Martinez-Bravo et al. 2011). Elected village officials are viewed as more accountable to villagers than appointed cadres, as regular elections have made them more aware of their public image. The possibility of being ousted from office serves to reduce corruption and arbitrary use of authority at the grassroots level. The introduction of direct elections has also enhanced public goods and services, as funding for irrigation systems and schools tends to increase as a result of election.

These positive developments notwithstanding, conflicts between villagers and village committees in Taishu Village (in the Panyu District of the Guangzhou City, 2005) and Wukan Village (in Lufeng County, Guandong province, 2011) revealed that elections have not necessarily eliminated corruption. In both cases, officials sold community farmland to outside developers without properly compensating the villagers.

Questions remain as to whether elected village officials have real power. The distribution of power between the village committee and the village party committee is not always clear, creating tension between the elected village committee and the party branch in the same village. Some party members, inspired by the electoral practice, have demanded direct election of the village party secretary by party members, but these have remained isolated cases. Article 3 of the Organic Law of Village Committees (1998) affirms the party committee's "core role in leadership" in the village. Thus, the appointed party secretary, members of the village party committee, and party leaders at the township could exercise de facto control over village affairs and subvert the electoral process.

Finally, the prospect of democratic spillover beyond the village level remains doubtful. Between 1998 and 2004, a handful of isolated experiments were initiated by some local officials to elect magistrates at the township level that, by law, should be elected by the township people's congresses. The CCP leadership reacted negatively to these innovative attempts, declaring them "unconstitutional." But it took no further action to annul the election results or punish the officials.

From the viewpoint of the party-state, township-level elections would have elevated political activities to a much higher level than in villages. Campaigns could attract large-scale gatherings, and campaign organizations connecting multiple villages may lead to the formation of political groups or even political parties that are forbidden by law (Jakobson 2004).

After a series of regime changes in the former Soviet Union and the Balkans during the early 2000s (i.e., the so-called color revolution), the party-state began to tighten its control over these "experiments." The CCP leadership continues to harbor distrust of the concepts of election and democracy, viewing them as part of Western conspiracies to change China's political system, rather than as an indigenous effort to deepen reforms (Liu 2010).

Research has shown that, besides changing policy outcomes at the local level, grassroots democracy has affected villagers' political attitudes. Villagers' experience with fair and free elections have increased their trust in local government and their support for democracy (X. Sun 2014). Competitive elections project an image of trustworthiness for the government, which could increase regime popularity and diffuse social discontent. Thus, the party-state is in a dilemma. Its fear of elections in fact could be counterproductive as it seeks to achieve broader legitimacy.

DISCUSSION QUESTIONS

1. The CCP plays a dominant role in the PRC's governance structure. Describe the characteristics of the party-state structure, and explain how the CCP interacts with other government organs and societal groups.

2. The PRC replaced the Soviet development model with the Maoist model in the mid-1950s. How did the Maoist model differ from the Soviet model? What were the reasons for the change? What impact did it have on the Chinese economy in the late 1950s?

3. Unbalanced growth and official corruption have led to social discontent in China. How did the Chinese government under Hu Jintao handle these issues? After Xi Jinping took over, what has he done to address these issues?

4. The CSOs have grown in China in the reform era. How are they managed and supervised by the government? How do the CSOs respond to government policies?

5. Why did the PRC promote village elections? Evaluate their effects on political governance and discuss whether elections at the village level spill over to other administrative levels.

CHAPTER

3

China's Pursuit of Economic Prosperity

ECONOMIC DEVELOPMENT IN THE PRE-REFORM ERA: 1949–1977

At the time of Chinese Communist takeover in 1949, the national economy had suffered from enormous losses of human and physical capital after years of civil wars and Japanese invasion. Industrial and agricultural productions had fallen below the levels of the 1920s. With massive unemployment and hyperinflation in the country, economic conditions looked quite bleak.

Most employment and economic production came from the agricultural sector. Nearly 90 percent of the population lived in rural areas and used traditional labor-intensive farming techniques. Industrialization was limited. Manchuria, Shanghai, and Chongqing (the wartime capital of the Nationalists) were the only areas of significant industrial capability. The manufacturing facilities in Manchuria were established by the Japanese after their occupation of the land in 1931 as a military supply base for Japanese war efforts. At the end of World War II, most of the industrial assets in Manchuria were taken away by the Soviet army assigned there to receive surrender. The loss, estimated at $3 billion at 1945 prices (Deng 2014), was a huge setback for China's industrial programs.

Growth Strategies

Industrialization. Though China was a low-income, agrarian economy at that time, the People's Republic of China (PRC) leaders set an ambitious goal to overtake the United Kingdom and the United States in 10 to 15 years in iron and steel production. To that aim, they adopted the Soviet model of command economy to pursue the big push for rapid industrialization. All aspects of economic activities (i.e., production, distribution, and consumption) were placed under state control. Economic bureaucrats, not markets, decided price and production targets; they also determined the supply of energy and raw materials and the distribution of finished goods.

To promote industrialization, the party-state used low-interest loans and underpriced materials to subsidize industries, particularly heavy manufacturing and defense industries. Mobilizing intellectual and economic resources for defense industries led to breakthroughs in the development of nuclear bombs in the 1960s and satellite technology in the 1970s. Industrial investment, however, disregarded light, consumer industries.

Although the countryside was the seedbed for the Chinese revolution, the Chinese Communist Party (CCP) leadership placed economic emphasis on industries and urban centers. By 1953, key agricultural products such as grain and cotton were subject to price controls to provide cheap raw materials for industrialization. Under the device of "scissors pricing" (Deng 2014), prices for industrial goods were artificially raised to inflate China's industrial gross domestic product (GDP), whereas state procurement prices for agricultural products were suppressed to deflate the agricultural GDP. The practice not only made the economy more "industrialized" on paper but also constituted indirect taxes on the agricultural sector. Under this scheme, cotton farmers sold their cotton to the state at cheap prices but had to purchase cotton goods from the state at high prices. The pricing difference was equivalent to a stealth tax on farmers to support industries.

Rural Industrialization. Mao believed that industrialization should expand beyond urban centers; for him, rural industrialization held the key to China's balanced development. The decision to produce iron and steel in the Great Leap Forward (GLF) reflected his goal of rural industrialization. In the 1960s, as China became isolated due to the growing military presence of the United States in Vietnam and diplomatic competition with the Soviet Union, Mao pursued an extreme form of self-reliance, or autarky, to counter potential war threats from either of the two superpowers. At that time, China's industrial bases were located predominantly in Manchuria and Shanghai and were vulnerable to potential attacks by the Soviet Union and the United States. Rural industrialization became a defense and economic strategy; it served to spread national defense capabilities beyond those areas and to redress regional imbalance. Mao's goal was to create new, secure production centers for coal and steel in western China and the mountainous hinterland, particularly in the provinces of Sichuan, Gansu, Guizhou, and Yunnan.

Surging state investment in these provinces led to rapid industrialization and output growth, but the projects were inefficient. The idea to construct these enterprises far away from population centers failed to consider transportation lines for sources of energy and other raw materials. Although the sheer amount of capital investment under Mao was high (accounting for a quarter of China's GDP), so was the waste. Duplication and poorly planned industrial investments explained why, at the end of Mao's era, the Chinese economy remained industrially underdeveloped, with the primary sectors (i.e., agriculture and extractive) still the main sources of employment.

Economic Institutions

Communes. To raise agricultural production to support the industrial needs, the party-state envisioned the creation of large collective farms that combined government administration (at the township level) and economic production into a centralized authority called people's communes. Equivalent to traditional townships, communes were generally comprised of 2,000 to 5,000 households with 10,000 to 22,000 farmers. Within communes, production brigades (equivalent to villages) and teams (neighborhoods) were created to organize farming and distribute tasks.

The rural labor force was organized as military-like in its production elements to increase agricultural output. Farmers were expected to pool their talents and resources to fulfill the commune's production target; they were not allowed to keep their private plots or engage in sideline businesses. They turned over ownership of land, animals, farm equipment, and houses to the commune in exchange for "five guarantees"—provisions of food, clothing, housing, medical care, and burial service. Individuals received "work points" over the course of the year for their work. The true value of these accumulated points was determined when the net income of the communes had been calculated after the harvest, grain being the dominant form of payment for work points. As such, the commune became a multifunctional, multipurpose unit, coordinating administration, economy, welfare, public health, and public works.

To make communes self-sufficient and highly productive during the GLF, they were encouraged to engage in innovative projects and initiatives. People were instructed to be bold and ambitious in setting production targets and using novel production methods even though they might well defy basic economic rule and rationality. Local and provincial officials competed with one another in reporting inflated production figures and in establishing more and bigger "communes." Exaggerated claims by local cadres about grain yields in 1958 gave government leaders a false impression that collectivization had achieved a great leap in productivity.

From 1957 to 1958, under the false impression of significantly boosted agricultural productivity, the government mobilized over 100 million farmers to undertake large irrigation and water conservancy projects and to produce industrial goods such as iron and steel, using simple "backyard furnaces." The ill-conceived attempt to engage in these industrial projects not only wasted resources but also diverted labor from agricultural production, leading to a drastic fall in food production. While grain-sown areas were reduced, grain output was overreported by local cadres. Based on false figures, the government increased state procurement of grains, leading to severe shortages of food available in the countryside, further depressing labor productivity. Diversion of labor from agricultural production and excessive procurement demands from the government accounted for a significant portion of the decline in grain production (Li and Yang 2005). Economic mismanagement and policy failure were exacerbated by floods and droughts in 1959 and 1960, leading to widespread famine and starvation.

The dire state of food supplies in the countryside and the enormous human loss eventually brought the GLF to an end. President Liu Shaoqi and Vice Premier Deng Xiaoping took over economic affairs, working to restore economic order by reintroducing material incentives in agricultural and industrial production. Farmers could farm on private lots to supplement their basic incomes, and bonus systems were restored for laborers. Rural production of iron and steel was abandoned; farmers returned to farming. Economic conditions improved in 1962 and gradually were back on track for positive growth. Yet Mao retained much of his power and was able to launch the Cultural Revolution later. Economic institutions introduced in the GLF campaign, such as communes and collective farming, were kept in the Chinese countryside for the following 20 years.

State-Owned Enterprises. After 1949, private businesses and industries were gradually nationalized. Most urban laborers came to be employed in state-owned enterprises (SOEs) controlled by line ministries or collective enterprises owned by local governments. Under the direct control of ministries, SOEs fulfilled production targets assigned by state officials and sold their products at predetermined prices. They were told where to buy materials and where to sell their products. Their survival did not depend on the ability to find the lowest prices for supplies, the most profitable markets, or the best technologies. SOEs operated in well-protected markets with ample profits. Their operating funds came directly from state budgets, with profits transferred to the state and reinvested in SOEs.

When implementing the First Five-Year Plan (1953–1957), central planning agencies encountered serious problems in coordinating the economy. Central ministries were overwhelmed by information sent from the provinces, while the provinces complained that central directives and targets were unrealistic. The number of enterprises and the types of goods necessary to economic planning had increased substantially because of expanded nationalization, which further complicated the task of economic coordination.

To resolve bottlenecks, the government decided to delegate part of the planning power to provincial governments. Central ministries lost part of their economic planning power, handing over SOEs to provincial or municipal governments, who were given more autonomy in the highly centralized planned economy.

Most SOEs were midsized and located in urban areas. They provided not only jobs but also benefits, subsidies, and a range of social services such as housing, education, medical care, and retirement protection. Taken together, these benefits and services formed a comprehensive system of "from-cradle-to-grave" welfare coverage. In 1978, on the eve of reform, SOEs accounted for 77 percent of the industrial output; collective enterprises accounted for 14 percent.

Rural-Urban Divide. While rural populaces were managed by communes, urban workers were assigned to SOEs or collective enterprises. Rural communities and urban centers were segregated by the household registration system (i.e., *hukou*), which limited geographical mobility, since rural populations were not allowed to move to cities. After the Great Leap Forward, rural communities were relatively isolated and inward looking. They were cut off from cities and were expected to be economically self-sufficient, depending mostly on their own resources for investment and welfare.

A huge disparity existed between rural and urban areas in terms of benefits provided by government. Urban residents received state subsidies for health care, education, housing, and welfare, but these benefits did not extend to people in the countryside. The government assisted urban residents with job assignments but was not obligated to provide jobs for people in rural areas. Prices for daily necessities and consumer goods were kept at low levels for the benefit of urban residents.

The Regulations on Labor Insurance (1951), patterned after the Soviet model, were the foundation of China's social policy prior to the 1978 reforms. Various benefits, based on the principle of lifetime employment ("iron rice bowl"), were extended to all urban workers, including SOE workers, government employees, and labor forces in schools, universities, and health fields (Salditt, Whiteford, and Adema 2007). The scheme was financed through employer contributions and administered by local trade union committees. After the Cultural Revolution, when trade unions were closed down, individual enterprises assumed the responsibility for pensions and other "cradle-to-grave" benefits.

Farmers, constituting the majority of the workforce in China, were not covered under the scheme. The rural welfare system, which guaranteed provisions of food, clothing, housing, medical care, and burial service, was offered through communes after the GLF. Since the welfare scheme was financed by income from production teams, the standard and quality of the provisions varied according to the financial condition of the communes.

THE REFORM ERA: 1978–PRESENT

As discussed in Chapter 2, the reformers in 1978 were able to consolidate their power and forge a broad consensus in the senior leadership by reaffirming the monopolistic political power of the CCP. Economic development was framed as a means to build up productive forces to advance socialism and strengthen the legitimacy of the party, despite the fact that many reform measures contradicted socialist tenets and doctrines.

In the reform era, the economy expanded at an average annual rate above 9 percent during the 30-year span from 1982 to 2011, even faster than the long growth spells of Japan (6.5 percent; 1951–1980) and South Korea (7.7 percent; 1966–1995). This rapid and sustained growth was made possible by reforms in economic structures and institutions that stimulated expansion of manufacturing and service. As a result of the reforms and growth, over 500 million people have been lifted out of poverty (World Bank 2013). In 2010, China surpassed Japan as the second largest economy in the world.

The Initial Stage of Reforms: 1978–1992

Reform Strategies. China's economic transformation began when there was virtually no private property or private ownership in the country. The market was weak or nonexistent when rapid economic growth took place.

The initial steps of reform were gradual and piecemeal, reflecting a compromise between continued central planning and the newly formed market. The operational framework was predominantly planned and socialist, as the reform was characterized as "planned commodity economy" (1979–1983) and "socialist commodity economy" (1984–1991). To address the economic malaise, PRC leaders experimented with policy measures along the lines of decentralization and marketization. Decentralization delegated greater administrative authority to local governments, including fiscal and taxation authority, investment, and financing authority, and the power to manage enterprises. Marketization meant less control on prices, greater reliance on material incentives, fewer restrictions on foreign trade and investment, and more tolerance for private or semiprivate forms of ownership.

Rural Reforms. As discussed earlier, agriculture under Mao had been heavily taxed and repressed. In fact, per capita agricultural productivity in 1977 was slightly over the 1952 level, barely keeping up with population growth. To improve productivity, reformers tried to decentralize and incentivize agricultural production through the household responsibility system—a system initiated by desperate farmers in Anhui province to escape poverty and starvation. The core concept in the responsibility system was to link income to output through family farming. Communes would distribute the land and production quotas to individual households, who then assumed the responsibility of meeting the allotted quotas but could retain surpluses for themselves. The arrangement enhanced households' incentives to produce, as they could sell the surpluses on the open market for profits, after paying taxes and meeting quotas.

The system proved to be effective and successful in yielding bumper crops, despite objections from some central and provincial leaders. Between 1978 and 1984, agricultural output increased by over 61 percent, with most of the increase due to the change from the production-team system to the household responsibility system (Lin 1992; McMillan, Whalley, and Zhu 1989). By the end of 1982, over 90 percent of agricultural households practiced some form of family farming.

Higher rural incomes followed. The boom in agriculture helped propel economic growth and lifted millions of people out of poverty. Eventually, communes were dismantled, and townships were reestablished.

Growth in the rural economy was also spurred by the rise of township and village enterprises (TVEs). TVEs existed in Mao's era as part of the strategy for rural industrialization, but they accounted for a much smaller percentage of industrial output (9 percent) compared to that of SOEs (77 percent) and collective enterprises (14 percent). It was extremely difficult to differentiate public versus private ownership of TVEs, as they either were collectively owned by townships and villages (Naughton 2007; Rodrik 2006) or were private enterprises located in townships and villages (Huang 2011). The diverse forms of party ties, government connections, and entrepreneurial backgrounds accounted for the mixed nature of these enterprises in different areas. TVEs clearly operated entirely outside of the state plan, as they received almost no subsidies from the state budget, and the salaries their workers received were signficantly lower than those of state enterprise workers.

In the era of economic reforms, TVEs took advantage of openings in previously monopolized industrial sectors and began to compete with state enterprises over producing much-needed consumer goods using their wage advantage. The bias against light industries in planned economies offered TVEs vast markets and huge profit potentials. As an important part of the nonstate sector, the share of TVEs in GDP grew quickly from 13 percent in 1985 to 31 percent in 1994. Between the late 1970s and mid-1990s, TVEs created over 90 million jobs and were the most dynamic force in the Chinese economy. After the mid-1990s, however, the deepening of reforms created an increasingly competitive market that was difficult for many traditional TVEs to sustain, due to their outdated technologies. The overall growth rate slowed significantly, and many TVEs were restructured as private businesses.

At a time when institutional protection of property rights was weak or nonexistent and when private ownership still faced ideological and political restrictions, TVEs became the second-best institutional arrangement to private ownership. As a legacy from the Maoist era, TVEs were politically protected by local governments and had access to markets and resources because of their government connections. TVEs helped reduce local unemployment by hiring surplus labor released from collective farming, while local authorities gained tax revenues by supporting TVEs for enterprise expansion. TVEs offered local authorities rights to revenue streams and gave local officials an avenue to promote economic growth (Li 1996; Oi 1999). Local governments and TVEs became mutually dependent; this synergy promoted the growth of local economies.

Economic restructuring was facilitated by dual-track price reforms. Free market prices coexisted with prices set by the planning agencies, with the state gradually scaling back its control from agricultural products to consumer goods, then to intermediate goods. Artifically suppressed planned prices were gradually raised along the way to match the market prices. By the end of 1994, prices for 80 percent to 90 percent of the goods were determined by markets.

Foreign Trade and Investment. In 1977, on the eve of economic reform, China's total trade accounted for merely 0.6 percent of the world trade. To attract foreign direct investment (FDI) and to develop export-oriented industries, Guangdong province in 1979 pilot tested the idea of "special economic zones" (SEZs). Despite strong skepticism and fierce debate at the top level, the central government approved the establishment of four SEZs in Guangdong and Fujian provinces in 1980 (Zhao 2010). Strategically targeting overseas Chinese communities in Taiwan, Hong Kong, Macao, and Southeast Asia, SEZs offered cheap land, labor, preferential tax rates, and duty-free imports (if used for re-export) to encourage foreign investment for export processing. The influx of foreign investments brought in capital, technology, and management practices essential for economic growth. SEZs also became testing grounds for various social and economic experiments before national reforms were implemented.

After initial experiments, conservatives led by Chen Yun voiced concerns over foreign influence. Deng toured the SEZs in early 1984 and gave his personal approval to retain SEZs. After returning to Beijing, Deng convened a high-level meeting to further expand the idea to create a number of "open cities" on China's coast. Chen did not attend the meeting.

The resulting Coastal Development Strategy allowed all types of firms, including TVEs, in coastal provinces to engage in export processing and assembly contracts. The Pearl River Delta and the Long River (or Yangtze River) Delta began to develop and attract a significant amount of foreign investment.

SOE and Fiscal Reforms. New market entrants, such as TVEs, began to compete in markets previously monopolized by SOEs, who could no longer depend on government protection to generate surpluses. Reformers in the early phase of industrial restructuring did not attempt to privatize SOEs; instead, they focused on the management issue of SOEs. While maintaining the organizational structures of SOEs and their ties to respective ministries and bureaucracies, reformers experimented with various incentive devices such as profit sharing and profit contracting, trying to duplicate the successful experience from agricultural reforms. Managers in SOEs, who previously had little flexibility and few rewards, were granted more autonomy in purchasing materials, hiring workers, and selling products.

Increased managerial authority and decreased government oversight, however, created opportunities for corruption. Officials and SOE managers had ample opportunities to illegally transfer public assets for personal benefit and private gains, or to buy and sell goods using price differentials between planned and market prices and pocket the difference. These problems revealed that SOEs needed fundamental reforms to define property rights and delineate corporate governance structures.

Furthermore, separating the issue of management from ownership lost sight of the overall financial problems confronting SOEs. Burdened with the welfare and financial obligations to current employees and retired workers, SOEs became less flexible within their cost structures. Many SOEs became fiscal drains on state budgets, relying on state support to survive.

By 1984, the principle of decentralization had spread to fiscal arrangements as well. The central government began to negotiate a "fiscal contracting system" with provincial governments. Wealthy provinces had to remit a certain portion of revenue to the central government, while poor provinces received prearranged subsidies. The tax system, however, treated fast-growing provinces more favorably by reducing the contribution rate once a target level of revenue had been remitted. As a result, total remittance to the central government declined between 1985 and 1990. As the wealthy provincial governments retained an increasing percentage of tax revenues, the central government had limited funds to transfer to poor, interior provinces, leading to the widening gap between regions.

Reform Setbacks. Taken together, these reform measures spurred economic growth and raised living standards. Higher incomes created greater demands for a variety of consumer goods and services, better entertainment, and improved housing and transportation. Nevertheless, negative consequences of reforms began to emerge, too. Gaps between the haves and the have-nots, between the city and the countryside, and between coastal areas and inland regions were growing. Heightened interest in moneymaking and materialism gave rise to higher crimes and social instability. Official corruption drew the most criticism, as the party-state officials took advantage of rapid growth and weak rules and regulations to enrich themselves and their families.

The expansion of economic reforms inevitably raised sharp ideological clashes in the late 1980s. Mao's programs, though disruptive and radical, were largely consistent with the ideals of communist revolution. Reform measures such as replacing collective communes with private economic activities, however, posed direct challenges to Communist party ideology. Conservatives believed that the negative effects justified a slowdown, or even a rollback, of reforms, whereas some reformers argued that such problems called for bolder and deeper reforms, including political openness and liberalization. Against this backdrop, the violent crackdown of the 1989 prodemocracy movements in Tiananmen Square invited international condemnation and economic sanctions, including the United States revoking China's most-favored-nation (MFN), or nondiscriminatory, status. Reforms went on hold.

Three years later, in mid-1992, Deng relaunched the reforms during his "southern tour." During the trip to Wuchang, Shenzhen, Zhuhai, and Shanghai—areas where economic boom was associated with economic opening to the outside world—he delivered an important speech to guide reform while avoiding ideological conflict. Late that year, in the 14th Party Congress, the CCP announced its intention to build a "socialist market economy" and continue economic reform. These announcements dispelled doubts about China's policy direction and unleashed a new round of reforms.

Deepening of Reforms: 1992–Present

China's economic growth has been fueled by two essential drivers: export and investment. The rising labor cost in Japan and other newly industrialized economies (NIEs; i.e., South Korea, Taiwan, Singapore, and Hong Kong) pushed manufacturing industries to look for cheaper production bases elsewhere. After China reaffirmed its commitment to promarket openings and reforms, investments from Hong Kong and Taiwan poured in and were followed by accelerated inflow of FDIs from Japan, the United States, and the European Union. While the inflow of FDIs boosted China's role in export processing, migrant workers from rural China provided abundant labor supply to keep China competitive in labor-intensive manufacturing.

Another notable phenomenon in China's fast economic growth is its high investment. Investment share in GDP since 1996 has been very high by international standards. From 2003 to 2017, gross fixed capital formation has accounted for over 40 percent of China's GDP. In comparison, the average for middle-income countries was only 27 percent. Massive and rapid investment growth in manufacturing and real estate built up production capacity and contributed to its GDP growth.

Regional and Global Integration for Export-led Growth. In 1994, the United States restored China's (nonpermanent) MFN status. Advanced Asian economies accelerated the relocation of lower value-added manufacturing processes to China, retaining control of key production components and high-tech inputs. Materials, parts, and goods shipped between headquarter economies (i.e., Japan and the NIEs) and factory economies (i.e., China) created Asian production networks and global value chains. Imports and exports between China and other economies were not simply trade between states. A considerable portion of the trade flow was carried out by multinational enterprises that transported parts, materials, and finished products based on their global manufacturing strategies.

FDI has been an important element for China's economic expansion. In comparison with Japan and South Korea, whose incoming FDI accounted for less than 1 percent of the GDP during the period of rapid growth, the Chinese economy was more open to foreign capital, with the FDI/GDP ratio in the range of 3 percent to 5 percent. Much of the early FDI went to China because of tax incentives, which compensated for the lack of preexisting businesses and infrastructure known for accommodating foreign investment. A significant portion of the early FDI was in labor-intensive export industries, helping China expand international trade to become a "world factory."

In 1996, China implemented a trade liberalization program to reduce an average of 35 percent of tariffs for 4,900 items (i.e., over 76 percent of all existing tariff items). On one hand, the tariff reduction of 1996 reduced the cost of imported raw materials and advanced machinery and equipment, which enhanced China's export competitiveness and facilitated technological upgrades. On the other hand, it increased competition pressure on agriculture and inefficient industries.

Tariff reform also paved the way for China's accession negotiations in joining the World Trade Organization (WTO)—a goal initially set by China in 1986 to be a member of its predecessor, the General Agreement on Tariffs and Trade (GATT). In 1999, China and the United States entered into a bilateral agreement for China's entry into the WTO, expediting the negotiation process. In December 2001, China became an official WTO member, marking a milestone in its opening to the world and creating conditions for stable, healthy, long-term economic growth.

SOE Reforms. The deepening of the reforms propelled the government to address the issue of public ownership. Industrial privatization began in 1995 under the policy of "grasping the big; letting go of the small." The central government decided to maintain control over the largest and more important SOEs, but privatized or even closed some 90,000 small SOEs through sales, mergers, or employee buyouts. The policy was based on the recognition that large and medium-sized SOEs performed better than small SOEs and TVEs, many of which were simply too small to exploit economies of scale and become profitable. In 1998, reforms extended to business investments made by the People's Liberation Army, which was instructed to withdraw from its enterprises so that these could be managed more efficiently by civilians.

During the restructuring, tens of thousands of SOEs and collective firms were closed and millions of workers (about 40 percent of the SOE workforce) were laid off. The impact of economic restructuring and dislocation would have been more disruptive if it were not for China's rapid economic growth.

In 2003, ownership of many SOEs was transferred from line ministries to the state-owned Assets Supervision and Administration Commission (SASAC) under the State Council. The purpose of the move was to limit the role of the government to regulator, rather than owner and supervisor of the enterprises at the same time. SOEs were transformed into corporate entities. The corporate structure of SOEs modeled that of their international competitors, with senior management staffed by a new generation of highly trained professionals.

The share of SOEs in gross industrial output declined from 77 percent in 1978, to 49.6 percent in 1998, to 26.2 percent in 2011. It is projected to further drop to 10 percent by 2030 (World Bank & Development Research Center of the State Council, PRC, 2013). In contrast, the private sector has become a vibrant economic force, especially in the highly competitive IT sector. Companies such as Alibaba, Huawei, Sina, and Baidu are prominent examples. The technological capability of the private sector, accounting for 60 percent of research and development (R&D) spending, is expected to grow.

Despite their recent decline in the domestic economy, Chinese SOEs continue to be viewed as formidable opponents by foreign businesses. Since the 2008 global financial crisis, the party-state has strengthened investment in SOEs and state monopolies. To counter the economic downturn triggered by the crisis, the Chinese government deployed a 4 trillion RMB fiscal stimulus package and 10 trillion RMB bank loans to stimulate the economy, with most allocated to SOEs. Although government subsidies have been substantially reduced in recent years, the share of bank loans extended to SOEs continues to be disproportionately larger than that extended to private companies. This may reflect the lingering bias in favor of SOEs in the predominantly state-owned banking sector (OECD 2010).

Supply-side Structural Reforms. In dealing with the 2008 global financial crisis, the PRC government not only employed economic stimulus programs but also implemented plans to boost employment and growth in key industries. While these measures helped stabilize the economy, they led to a massive increase in domestic production capacity, particularly in areas such as steel, cement, and aluminum. Overcapacity meant declined profits and higher debts. To address these problems, the PRC government began to implement the Supply-side Structural Reforms (SSSR) in 2015, aimed at cutting industrial overcapacity, clearing the large inventory of unsold properties, curbing corporate debt, reducing business costs, and improving weak industries.

As part of SSSR, the 13th Five-Year Plan (2016–2020) issued targets to individual provinces to reduce industrial capacity. To take care of workers that were laid off because of reduction in production, the government provided funds for labor resettlement and training. Local governments converted stocks of unsold or unoccupied housing units into affordable rental properties for rural migrants. While SSSR attempted to address structural problems in the Chinese economy, it went against the direction of market economy and encouraged an interventionist role for the government.

Growth versus Distribution. During the 1990s, the central government used its personnel power to promote economic growth. Economic development, measured by provincial GDP growth rate, provincial GDP per capita growth rate, or relative performance between provincial and national growth, weighed disproportionately in promotion decisions for provincial officials (Chen, Li, and Zhou 2005; Li and Zhou 2005; Maskin, Qian, and Xu 2000; Tsui and Wang 2004). As a result, provincial governors and officials competed with one another in soliciting and attracting investment projects to meet the growth target.

The pursuit of fast economic growth in the 1990s, however, came with the price of increased inequalities between coastal and inland regions, between urban centers and rural areas, and between rich and poor households in both rural and urban China. Of the 100 wealthiest counties in China, 93 were located in the coastal provinces (Li 2014). Incomes earned by urban dwellers were three and a half times higher than those made by rural residents, the highest urban-rural income gap in the world (Yao 2010). The increase in inequality, measured by the change in Gini coefficients, was considered by the World Bank (1997) as "by far the largest of all countries for which comparable data are available" in terms of magnitude and pace.

The export-led growth model that relied on the nine coastal provinces for 90 percent of its total exports was an unbalanced development strategy. Entrepreneurs from urban centers in coastal regions benefited most from this breakneck growth, while farmers and workers, especially those living in inland provinces, suffered most in the rapid economic transformation due to job loss and downward pressure on wages. For millions of farmers and workers, who were the social bedrock of the Chinese Communist revolution, the loss of the traditional socialist safety net during economic transition created significant needs in health care and social security. By 2010, the urban-rural and coast-inland divides had become sources of contention for resource allocation and policy decisions.

Furthermore, economic opportunities were skewed in favor of those with political connections. The number of private entrepreneurs who belonged to the CCP, also known as "red capitalists," grew rapidly. Even with improved social upward mobility, economic development had only a limited effect in mitigating public anger about inequality in China (Lu 2014). The uneven distribution of economic gains and losses in reforms, and the rapid rise of the "new riches" gave the general public a sense of depravation, giving rise to distributional conflicts. Labor disputes skyrocketed almost sevenfold between 1994 and 1999, rising from fewer than 8,000 cases to over 55,000 (Wang 2000). Protests, demonstrations, riots, and petitions rose to over 40,000 cases a year in the early 2000s.

As growing inequality threatened to undermine the legitimacy of the Communist regime, based on egalitarian principles, the Chinese government stepped up its efforts to establish social policies. Under the slogan of building a "harmonious society," Hu Jintao shifted the emphasis from urbanites and elites to the less privileged. The government scaled back China's growth ambitions and made a commitment to broader social development. Hu and Premier Wen Jiabao adopted a populist style by visiting miners, farmers, and victims of natural disasters in poor, remote areas. The symbolic gesture was to convey a loving and caring attitude toward the general public.

In the 10th Five-Year Plan (2001–2005), the development of inland provinces became a top priority. To narrow the regional gap, transfer payments to western provincial governments increased, as did centrally funded infrastructural projects such as the high-elevation Qingzang railway linking Qinghai and Tibet (completed in July 2006), the first to connect Tibet to other provinces. The State Development Bank of China was also instructed to provide subsidized loans and credits for infrastructural projects to western provinces. Critics of these infrastructural projects were skeptical of their effect on egalitarian development, arguing that the real purpose was for resource extraction and political control.

The government expanded its support of rural areas through subsidies, income transfers, and tax relief. In the 11th Five-Year Plan (2006–2010), the government called for "Building a New Socialist Countryside." Recognizing the growing rural-urban divide, the government implemented policies to address issues concerning agricultural production, living standards of farmers, and quality of life in rural communities. Government expenditures on rural areas nearly doubled between 2004 and 2007 for infrastructure building and social development (OECD 2009). All formal and informal fees and taxes on farmers were abolished beginning in 2006 to further ease their financial burden, and rural school children between the ages of six and 15 were exempt from tuition and fees.

These efforts have yielded some positive results. Income inequality measured by Gini coefficient has declined; the index dropped to 0.465 in 2016, after its peak at 0.49 in 2008. The ratio of urban-to-rural disposable income has also narrowed. In 2005, 30 percent of the rural population lived below the poverty line; the number fell to 5.7 percent in 2015 (OECD 2017b).

The Evolution of Social Policies. As discussed earlier, communes and SOEs in the Mao era served as not only production units but also social security providers. In the reform era, the breakdown of these institutions created the need for new social safety nets.

Parallel to the change in economic institutions was the need for new social policies. As boundaries between public and private ownership began to shift, so did the responsibilities between individuals and the state. Pensions and other benefits such as housing, education, and medical care, having previously been viewed as social services provided by the state free of charge, were increasingly treated as commodities with monetary value. Individuals were expected to assume greater responsibility in paying for these services.

During the early 2000s, the government began to develop a more equitable social policy, as social development became a government priority. One notable example was the extension of the coverage of social insurance schemes. Migrant workers, rural residents, and employees in private enterprises have gradually been included in different forms of social protection, particularly in contributory social schemes. A subsistence allowance program covers needy people in rural areas, such as the elderly and the disabled. However, the average level of benefits for rural populations remains modest. Additionally, the unemployed and the disabled in urban areas now receive minimum living standard guarantees and unemployment benefits, although the level of entitlements is locally determined. Finally, public medical insurance is nearly universal, extending coverage to rural populations, although the benefits are minimal. As of 2014, approximately 1.3 billion people were under health insurance coverage, a dramatic improvement from the reported 200 million in 2004 (OECD 2017b). Nevertheless, the public still feels that good quality healthcare is unaffordable and inaccessible.

China's public social spending stood at 8 percent of the GDP in 2013–14, exceeding levels of other emerging economies such as India but lower than the OECD average of 21 percent (OECD 2017a). An increased effort in this area expects to have the combined social insurance and social assistance programs cover all residents in urban and rural areas by 2020.

AN ANALYSIS OF CHINA'S GROWTH

The Chinese economy has come a long way since the 1978 economic reforms. Accelerated economic growth over the last three decades has made China the second-largest economy in the world and the largest exporter and manufacturer. China is expected to be an engine of growth that will play an important role in the global economy for the foreseeable future.

In retrospect, China's growth experience illustrates the economic catch-up process previously experienced by Japan (Chapter 7) and South Korea (Chapter 11). Taking advantage of "economic backwardness" (Gerschenkron 1962), China followed the well-established path of economic growth by adopting the technologies, production structures, and economic organizations of the more advanced economies. The strategy was low risk and with low cost, calling for increased labor input, capital accumulation, and gains in productivity.

A large influx of migrant workers from rural areas to urban centers, called the "floating population," provided an abundant supply of cheap labor to fuel China's economic growth. The floating population, estimated around 30 million in the early 1980s, rose to 70 million by the late 1980s. By the end of the 1990s, the number might have been close to 100 million (Chan 2001). Furthermore, rising savings rates allowed rapid capital accumulation to translate to high investment rates to sustain growth. Finally, distortions and misallocations of resources under the planned economy, once removed, led to quick gains in productivity.

None of this would have happened without the series of pragmatic, market-friendly reforms discussed earlier. The household responsibility system, emergence of TVEs, establishment of SEZs, extensive price liberalization, fiscal decentralization, restructuring and privatization of SOEs, tariff reductions, and WTO accession all contributed to building a favorable macreconomic environment for sustained growth. This raises two questions regarding the role of the Chinese government in economic growth. First, did the government use industrial policy to promote industrial transformation, and if so, was it successful? Second, in a broader sense, how did the government guide the process of instituional transformation to facilitate the transition from a command economy to a largely market-based, but still evolving, system?

Industrial Policies

In the 1980s and 1990s, the automotive industry was designated as a "pillar industry," but it did not develop as planned. Support to nurture iron and steel producers also had limited success (World Bank & Development Research Center of the State Council, PRC 2013). In recent years, the goal of the government has been to keep absolute control of strategic industries and maintain a strong influence in pillar industries. Industries such as defense, electricity generation and distribution, petroleum and petrochemicals, telecommunications, civil aviation, and waterway transport are considered strategic, while machinery, automobiles, information technology, construction, steel, base metals, and chemicals are pillar industries. Foreign companies are excluded from strategic sectors and are heavily regulated in pillar industries. Although minority equity shares of these SOEs may be traded on domestic and international stock markets, the state's majority ownership makes it difficult for foreign businesses to expand within China through merger and acquisition.

A group of 120 enterprise groups was selected to be "national champions" across industrial sectors in the defense industry, energy, telecommunications, and transportation. The central government intended to channel financial support to the larger enterprises to create dynamic and globally competitive companies, much like the Japanese *keiretsu* and South Korean *chaebol*. Through interventions in interest rates and credit allocation, the government moved resources to the targeted industries via the four largest state-owned banks (i.e., the Bank of China, the Industrial and Commercial Bank of China, the China Construction Bank, and the Agricultural Bank of China). Even though their production is about one-third of the national output, SOEs and large firms took a lion's share of all bank loans, accounting for 70 percent of them (Nolan 2014). Consequently, small and medium enterprises have had significantly less access to formal financial support.

These policies appear to be somewhat successful. SOEs have grown rapidly and earned large profits. In 2002, 11 Chinese SOEs were listed on the Fortune Global 500. By 2017, the number had grown to 109 (Chiang 2018). In 2015, SOEs comprised 5 percent of total Chinese industrial enterprises but accounted for 38.8 percent of total assets. The scale-focused industrial strategy has definitely had traction.

Chinese SOEs, however, are hardly competitive globally. The majority of their sales revenue comes from a well-protected domestic market that shields them from direct competition with the world's leading competitors. Although China's export structure has changed from toys, textiles, and other labor-intensive consumer products to machinery, appliances, and other information and communication technology products, most high-value goods are produced by subsidiaries of global firms within China, who retain control over key design and production components and high-tech inputs elsewhere. These firms are not indigenous entities.

In recent years, the Chinese government has intended to use foreign capital to achieve national development priorities in scientific innovation, industrial upgrades, and regional balance. Attracting capital-intensive, high tech, and high-value-added projects in other economic sectors became a priority. Foreign investment in high-end manufacturing, and in high and new technology industries, is encouraged. Enterprises that can establish R&D centers in China or engage in R&D cooperation with domestic partners are particularly welcome.

Institutional Transformation

Chinese reformers did not design reform policies or institutions according to a fixed ideology. Instead, they took gradual, incremental steps in small areas, experimenting with new policies in an evolutionary approach, before implementing them in other places. Measures such as the household responsibility system and SEZs illustrated this process. Two systems, market (experimenting) versus planned (nonexperimenting), often coexisted, as seen in practically every aspect of the reform measures, including price liberalization, enterprise restructuring, foreign exchange management, and central-provincial fiscal arrangements. This dual-track arrangement allowed new and old institutions to operate together, promoting innovation without directly challenging vested interests. Through this gradual, dual-track approach, China implemented a "reform without losers" and moved slowly, but progressively, to a well-functioning economic system.[1] The approach was different from that of other transition economies such as the former USSR and Eastern European states, which began reforms a decade later but opted to go through a "big bang" shock to transplant the whole set of capitalist systems and institutions within a short time period (Sachs and Woo 2000).

Different conclusions have been drawn about the implication of this experimentalist strategy. One school of thought contends that, because of this evolutionary approach, China has created a unique development model built on an all-powerful political leadership to manage social and economic affairs. They believe that the "Beijing Consensus" offers an alternative growth model for developing countries, as opposed to the Washington Consensus (Ramo 2004). In the aftermath of the 2008 financial crisis, marked by excessive borrowing and risky investment of U.S. financial institutions and the ongoing Eurozone sovereign debt crisis, the spectacular performance delivered by the Chinese model appears particularly attractive.

The second school of thought, however, argues that gradualism is simply a temporary political compromise. It does not represent a feasible, sustainable economic model. The arrangement, though enabling China to achieve stability and growth in the transition process, creates a number of economic bottlenecks such as income disparities and consumption-investment imbalances (Lin 2013) or even becomes politically unsustainable (Callick 2007; Hutton 2006).

As China becomes a well-known investment destination, foreign investors are now more concerned with the overall regulatory regime and policy stability than with incentives. This is consistent with the broad empirical research

---

[1] Huang (2008) disagreed with the characterization of gradualism and argued that the Chinese economic growth in the 1980s occurred precisely because it had satisfied the institutionalist tenets such as private ownership, financial liberalization, and secure property rights. According to Huang, it was only in the 1990s when reforms experienced a decade of reversal and China resorted to state capitalism with heavy economic control and intervention in the urban sectors that we witnessed rising social tensions, inequality, and corruption.

in current literature, which found that institutions, reflected in rule of law and quality of bureaucracy, are an important determinant of FDI flows for transition economies (Campos and Kinoshita 2003).

Labor Policy

It is widely recognized that China's "population dividend" is about to disappear; the labor supply is likely to decline very soon, given the projected demographic trend. While the 1979 one-child policy helped lower China's fertility rate from 2.8 children per woman in 1979 to 1.6 in 2016 (below the replacement level of 2.1 children per woman needed to maintain population size), it also incurred political and social cost. Political coercion and economic penalties created not only social discontent but also serious gender imbalance among China's younger population as many couples used sex-selective abortions to ensure their only child was male. The steep decline in the fertility rate, coupled with increased life expectancy, contributed to the aging of the population. By 2025, more than 14 percent of the Chinese population will be over 65 years old, making it an "aged" society (Sheehan 2017). By 2050, 39 percent of the Chinese population will be above the retirement age, adding significant burdens to social welfare and elderly care (China Power Team 2017).

Thus, demographic trends signal future labor shortages, wage increases, and profit declines, culminating in economic slowdown. In 2015, the government officially repealed the 1979 one-child policy and replaced it with a two-child policy to address the aging issue of the population. Nevertheless, the new policy is unlikely to reverse the demographic shift anytime soon. The Chinese population is projected to peak in the late 2020s or early 2030s with a steady decline thereafter.

Thus, the development of a flexible labor market will be instrumental for sustained economic growth. The continued practice of the *hukou* system, however, may have led to an inefficient labor market. The *hukou* system no longer restricts moving from rural to urban areas; migrant workers can obtain temporary residence permits and identity cards by paying a fee to local government. Yet, without formal urban residency status, migrant workers are still denied access to social entitlements that urban residents enjoy, such as health care, education, and housing. Further liberalization of the *hukou* policy is opposed by local governments, which claim that they cannot extend public services to migrants and their families due to the lack of financial resources. The dual status of citizens not only increases inequality but also discourages labor mobility. The solution, however, will require closer examination of the role of government in social welfare.

In April 2019, to promote integrated urban-rural development, the Central Committee and the State Council released guidelines to eliminate restrictions on rural-to-urban settlement by 2022, in hopes that the *hukou* reform could significantly increase labor supply and enhance the economy's potential growth.

Land Policy

While farmers now have more autonomy, land remains in the hands of the state. Farmers receive the use-rights of land, with a typical lease for 15 to 20 years, which is not ideal for long-term improvement. Furthermore, local governments have sole rights to requisition agricultural land for urban purposes at its agricultural, not market, value. As trends of urbanization continue, demands for land expand. Local cadres have colluded with commercial interests to acquire farmland at acquisition prices, then sell it at market prices, leading to social injustice and rural unrest. In 2017, agriculture accounted for approximately 8 percent of the Chinese economy and employed 27 percent of the total workforce, down from half of total employment in 2000. These numbers revealed not only a decline in the relative importance of agriculture within the national economy but also the low productivity in agricultural labor. Strengthening land use rights for farmers could create incentives for land improvement and productivity growth.

Trade Conflicts with the United States

Besides these internal issues, China's trade relations with the United States are becoming an unknown factor in its future course of economic development. In March 2018, the United States invoked Section 301 of the Trade Act to impose tariffs on Chinese products in aerospace, information communication, and machinery on the grounds that China had engaged in unfair trade practices, including theft of U.S. intellectual property. In retaliation, China in April 2018 imposed tariffs on U.S. products, including aluminum, cars, soybeans, and pork. Since then, tensions have escalated with both adding more tariffs on an ever-expanding list of goods, despite multiple rounds of high-level negotiations between the two sides.

For the United States, while the dispute began with its huge trade deficits with China, the heart of the conflict involves broader, structural concerns. Besides the allegations of intellectual property theft, the United States accuses China of unfair industrial policies to protect its SOEs, as well as its investment practices to force foreign enterprises for technology transfer. U.S. officials who take a hawkish view on trade disputes believe that these practices constitute a long-term threat to U.S. prosperity, and even national security.

Heightened tensions, coupled with the lack of trust between the two sides, have politicized trade and economic issues, making it difficult to find feasible solutions. Hardliners in China tend to view the entire package of U.S. demands, particularly those about technology, as a revival of U.S. containment strategy aimed to derail China's 2049 centennial goals for economic development. As trade conflict persists, there is a high risk that the hostility and the strategic rivalry will carry forward, leading to deteriorated Sino-U.S. relations in the long term. Trade conflicts between China and the United States have created huge uncertainty over the economies of the two countries and the global economy. It remains to be seen whether the leadership on both sides can find satisfactory solutions to address these core concerns.

DISCUSSION QUESTIONS

1. What were the growth strategies under Mao? Discuss how the urban and rural economies were affected differently by the strategies.

2. In the late 1970s, how did the reformers address the problems in the agricultural economy? What kind of policies were implemented, and what were the results?

3. The state-owned enterprises (SOEs) were a key component of the command economy under Mao. What were some problems they encountered in the reform era? Describe the various SOE reforms undertaken by the Chinese government, and discuss the challenges the SOEs may face in the future.

4. Many economists consider economic growth and economic distribution as conflicting goals. Which did the Chinese government emphasize in the reform era? What kind of problems has it created? What has the government done to address the imbalance?

5. "The population dividend," an advantage for China's economic development in the past, is about to disappear. Besides the demographic challenges, what are the other potential challenges China would need to overcome to ensure sustained growth in the future?

4

China's Pursuit of National Security

While the People's Republic of China (PRC) leaders have experimented with different governance ideas and economic policies since 1949, their security goals and priorities remain largely unchanged. For both Chinese leaders and the public, the historical memory of the century of humiliation, beginning with Qing China's defeat in the Opium War (1839–1842), calls for the defense of the Chinese state's sovereignty, self-determination, and territorial integrity (Z. Wang 2015). PRC leaders have rarely wavered from these security goals, irrespective of shifts in economic policies and ideological orientations, although their strategies may vary.

In recent years, with its economic prowess and military strength, China has achieved the status of a major power. On one hand, the growing need to sustain economic dynamism has made it necessary for China to expand its security definition beyond traditional military security. On the other hand, the rise of China has profound implications for the stability of the international system. As the power transition theory suggests (Introduction), a rising power may seek to challenge the existing rules and order. At the same time, the established power, feeling threatened by the power transition, may be reluctant to accommodate the rising power's revisionist demands. Conflict is likely the outcome of this scenario. Will the rising PRC expand its security conception to contest global order? How will other key players in the international system, such as the United States, respond to the power transition? This chapter will discuss the evolution of the PRC's security strategies and policy-making institutions and review various security relations and contexts to shed light on these questions.

SECURITY GOALS AND STRATEGIES

Security Goals

In July 2015, the National People's Congress (NPC) passed the National Security Law (NSL). According to Article 2 of the NSL, China's national security refers to "a status where the national regime, sovereignty, unity, and territorial integrity, welfare of the people, sustainable economic and social development, and other fundamental national interests are immune from danger and external and internal threats, and the capability to maintain this status of security." It is evident that, with this list, China takes a broad view of national security, ranging from political, military, and economic to human security that touches nearly every aspect of China's society. Although the document is quite recent, it clearly identifies the PRC leaders' principal security goals since 1949: sovereignty, regime security, and development (Atanassova-Cornelis 2012; Medeiros 2009; Nathan and Scobell 2012; Roy 2013; F.-l.Wang 2005).

Sovereignty represents the broad concern for national independence, territorial integrity, noninterference, and unification. The concern for sovereignty ranges from securing China's land and maritime borders, addressing territorial disputes, and preventing foreign incursions to reunification with lost territories such as Hong Kong, Macao, and Taiwan. In April 1955, at the Afro-Asian conference at Bandung, Indonesia, Zhou Enlai proposed the five principles of peaceful coexistence: mutual respect for sovereignty and territorial integrity, mutual nonaggression, noninterference in internal affairs, equality and mutual benefit, and peaceful coexistence. These principles continue to serve as guidelines for Beijing's foreign and security policies.

Regime security relates to internal security and, more specifically, the continued monopoly of political power by the Chinese Communist Party (CCP). For PRC leaders, a unique feature of China's history is the interconnectedness of foreign threats and domestic disorder (J. Wang 2011). Throughout the century of humiliation, foreign invasions coincided with internal uprisings. In the Qing dynasty, the Taiping Rebellion occurred after the British victory in the Opium War. During the Republican era, fighting between warlords and conflicts between the Kuomintang (KMT) and CCP correlated with the Japanese incursions. Since the establishment of the PRC, the perceived open or covert foreign threat to its political survival reinforces the distrust and fear of foreign power. The PRC leaders believe that the CCP safeguards the national interest of the PRC; hence, the Communist regime's survival is critical to the national security of the PRC. The apprehension of internal security, and the international source of domestic disturbances, is manifested in the party-state's close monitoring of domestic stability, including the separatist movements in Xinjiang and Tibet.

Besides the preservation of national sovereignty and domestic stability, the CCP builds its legitimacy on its ability to promote economic development—key to the improvement of the living standards of Chinese people—and the revival of China as a major power. As proposed by Jiang Zemin at the 16th Party Congress in 2002, the goal to "build a moderately prosperous society" by 2021, the party's 100th founding anniversary, remains the aspiration for China to become a stable, prosperous power with a sizable middle class.

Thus, recent trade conflicts between the United States and China over tariffs, trade imbalances, and intellectual property rights are not simply trade or economic issues for the PRC leaders. They clearly view it from the lenses of strategy and security. What is unclear, however, is the type of actions they will take and the extent of geographic or territorial perimeter deemed within its core economic interests. To include economic development and sustainability in the formulation implies that the PRC would be determined to engage in competition for strategic resources. It remains to be seen how far Beijing will go to promote and sustain its economic interest.

The Evolution of Security Strategies

While these goals are interrelated, policy emphasis may vary in response to the changing international and domestic environments. The PRC leaders have pursued different policies and used different tools to pursue these goals. For the first several decades after 1949, the strategic security environment faced by the Chinese leaders was shaped by diplomatic competition and military confrontation between the two superpowers, the United States and the Soviet Union. The Sino-Soviet-American triangular relations have often been analyzed from the realist balance-of-power model (D. Wang 2017). The PRC first allied with the Soviet Union against the United States (1949–1963) in hopes of achieving international communist revolution. Following the Sino-Soviet split, Beijing then pursued an independent, nonaligned policy against both superpowers (1963–1972). Mao's self-reliant development strategy during the Great Leap Forward and the Cultural Revolution was to ensure that neither superpower could extort economic concessions from China. In the aftermath of the border clashes with the Soviets in the late 1960s, China reoriented its foreign policy. The Sino-U.S. rapprochement in the early 1970s, in essence, created a "tacit alliance" against the Soviets (1972–1982).

Since the era of "reform and opening," China abandoned its revolutionary stance in favor of the new "peace and development" approach to pursue its modernization program in a peaceful environment. It began to improve relations with its Asian neighbors and join international organizations. In 1980, it rejoined the International Monetary Fund and the World Bank, accepting aid from both. While claiming to follow an independent, nonaligned foreign policy, it sought closer economic relations with the United States, Japan, and other Western developed countries in order to obtain market access and technical expertise.

In the aftermath of the 1989 Tiananmen crackdown, to overcome diplomatic isolation, Deng Xiaoping prescribed the foreign policy strategy of "keeping a low profile while striving for achievement" (*taoguang yanghui, yousuo zuowei*). Deng suggested that China should be moderate and cautious in its international conduct. He emphasized the importance of pursuing economic growth while maintaining friendly relations with all countries, and he advised against "raising a banner" or taking a leadership role in international affairs (Yan 2014). Following closely the first part of Deng's formulation (keeping a low profile), Chinese leaders sought to avoid international controversies, unless the issues involved the immediate national interests. By not challenging the dominant role of established powers (such as the United States), China hoped to ease fears other countries held over its rapid growth.

Peace in the post-Cold War era sustained China's economic growth and modernization efforts, preserved its domestic political stability, and strengthened the legitimacy of the CCP. Increased economic resources and capacity enhanced not only China's material power but also its soft power—its political and ideological influence (Nathan and Scobell 2016).

In part because of increasing confidence in its major power status and also because of the U.S. policy of rebalancing to Asia that was widely seen as constraining China's rise, the PRC leadership began to show more assertiveness and activism in its foreign policy. Since 2012, Chinese policies have displayed a notable shift to the second part of Deng's advice: "striving for achievement." In disputes involving the East and South China Seas, the PRC has shown tougher stances, escalating tensions with Japan, Vietnam, the United States, and the Philippines.

Additionally, China now actively resorts to economic statecraft (Beeson 2018). The creation of the Asian Investment and Infrastructural Bank (AIIB) could be viewed as a challenge to the U.S.-led World Bank and the Japanese-led Asian Development Bank. The Belt and Road Initiative (BRI) has opened new opportunities to strengthen China's economic ties and infrastructural connections with countries in Eurasia and Southeast Asia.

In November 2014, Xi Jinping called on China to "develop a distinctive diplomatic approach befitting its role of a major power." Central to this new approach is establishing "strategic partnerships" with individual states and groups of states. These partnerships are not necessarily security or military alliances; rather, they intend to build long-term commitments to improve all aspects of bilateral relations, including economic, cultural, political, and security (Struver 2017).

Frequent visits by PRC top party and state leaders to these partnership states reinforce mutual relations. Prior to the reform era, Chinese leaders were less engaged in foreign visits. Since then, leadership and military diplomacy efforts have increased significantly to enhance the PRC's international visibility and promote its diplomatic and security priorities.

SECURITY INSTITUTIONS AND POLICY MAKING

Security policy making in China has tracked closely with the prevailing governance model in terms of institution and process. Under Mao and Deng, the paramount leader enjoyed unparalleled authority in making national security decisions, as both possessed revolutionary and military credentials and had extensive contacts in the military and security apparatus. Mao made the decision to enter the Korean War in an enlarged, specially convened Politburo meeting in October 1950 (Hao and Zhai 1990). Although the majority of the participants were deeply concerned about China's inability to win a war against the United States, Mao's strategic analysis, based on the long-term U.S.

threat to China, carried the day. Similarly, he made all key decisions during the Taiwan Strait crises in the late 1950s and during the war with India in 1962.

Under the Deng era, even with the reaffirmation of the principles of professionalism and collective leadership, Deng was in a privileged position to make final decisions (Yun Sun 2013). In 1978, he made the decision to normalize relations with the United States, despite the fact that both sides still had unresolved disagreements over the continued American arms sales to Taiwan. A year later, in 1979, he gave the approval to launch an attack on Vietnam.

In the post-Deng era, the governance model of collective leadership means that security policy making usually involves senior leadership (Cabestan 2009). The process of consultation and approval may not follow a single pattern, as it varies by the nature and importance of the issue. Routine national security affairs are usually within the purview of the top leader, who has taken the three highest positions in the party, the military, and the state since 1993: the CCP general secretary, the Central Military Commission (CMC) chairman, and the PRC president. For emergency and crisis management, members of the Politburo Standing Committee (PSC) are often involved. If the crisis involves military components, the CMC may be brought in. When new policies and changes in existing guidelines and principles are needed, members of the Politburo, or even the Central Committee, may be consulted for review and approval.

One notable development is the diminishing role of the People's Liberation Army (PLA) in security policy making (Scobell and Saunders 2015). In recent years, particularly under Xi's leadership, the party has tightened its control over the PLA to strengthen the military's loyalty, discipline, and professionalism (Chang 2018). The organizational reforms implemented since 2015 (Chapter 2) that separate the operational command and the administrative functions of the PLA reinforce the military's subordination to central authorities.

The PRC leadership has found it a challenge to involve all the bureaucratic units and agencies from different systems for coordination and information sharing. The process becomes particularly inefficient during crisis, which requires timely response. Beginning in the late 1990s, the Chinese leadership has been searching for a strong and unified platform to enhance policy-making and crisis management. The establishment of informal leading small groups (LGSs) on foreign affairs, security affairs, and Taiwan affairs reflects an attempt to streamline government and party representation for coordination, consultation, communication, and decision making. LGSs, however, are ad hoc committees with no fixed participants for each meeting. Members are invited as needed. When they do join the LSG meetings, they tend to advocate for their own command channels and bureaucratic interests, making it difficult to reach across functional areas to achieve coordination and integration.

In April 2014, the creation of the National Security Commission based on the U.S. National Security Council model represent the latest attempt in streamlining security decision making (Hu 2016; Lampton 2015). So far, the operations of the NSC remain nontransparent, with no published record of meetings, decisions, or even membership.

INTERNAL SECURITY

The Chinese party-state closely monitors all aspects of social life for purposes of internal stability but pays particular attention to the Tibet Autonomous Region and Xinjiang Uyghur Autonomous Region. Governance in both regions has been complicated by history, economics, religion, and culture. Disputes over historical boundaries, competitions over lands and natural resources, and clashes over the use of ethnic minority languages in school and their religious practices have heightened tension between the Chinese government and local minorities, with policies alternating between soft and hard approaches for greater autonomy or more centralization.

Both regions sought some form of independence between 1911 (the Republican revolution) and 1949 (the founding of the PRC). During that time, Tibet declared independence from China and exercised self-rule until October 7, 1950, when nearly 80,000 Chinese troops invaded and occupied Tibet to integrate it with the "motherland." Outnumbered by the Chinese forces, Tibet surrendered to China on October 15, 1950. In Xinjiang, various warlords governed the area after 1911. The establishment of the Turkish Islamic Republic of East Turkestan (1933–1934) and the East Turkestan Republic (1944–1949) marked attempts for independence. In 1949, Chinese troops entered Xinjiang and established control.

Tibet shares borders with India, Nepal, Bhutan, and Myanmar, while Xinjiang is next to Pakistan, Afghanistan, Tajikistan, Kyrgyzstan, Kazakhstan, Russia, and Mongolia. The complexity of cross-border interactions between the minority groups and the neighboring states has long reinforced the Chinese suspicion that external forces have influenced the separatist movements in both regions.

Tibet

Since the PRC annexation of Tibet in 1951, there has been constant resistance from Tibetans against the Chinese rule. Political trust between the Chinese central government and the Tibetan authority soon shattered after the signing the Seventeen-Point Agreement in May 1951. The agreement guaranteed Tibetan autonomy, respected its Buddhist religion, and accepted its leader Dalai Lama's power and authority in a self-rule political system. Despite the promise made by the CCP leadership not to pursue "democratic reforms" for another six years, the Tibet Work Committee began to initiate reforms by the end of 1956. Additionally, the Chinese government claimed that the Seventeen-Point Agreement applied only to the areas under the Dalai Lama's direct jurisdiction, not to those outside of it.

In 1958, the CCP leadership carried out the Great Leap Forward campaign in areas of Sichuan, Yunnan, and Qinghai—regions heavily populated by ethnic Tibetans but outside of the Dalai Lama's jurisdictional control. Collectivization and land redistribution directly contravened the age-old economic practice that put Tibetan monasteries as the largest landowners based on the value and ideology of Tibetan Buddhism. Conflict erupted. Many Tibetans formed guerrilla groups to rebel against the Chinese rule.

Rebellions in ethnic Tibetan regions were met with brutal reprisals from the PLA. Additionally, a large number of Han Chinese began to settle in ethnic Tibetan areas such as Sichuan and Qinghai, further raising fear among ethnic Tibetans of a takeover plot. By February 1959, the Tibetan rebellion escalated to a full-scale movement. In March 1959, mass demonstrations in Lhasa resulted in open rebellion, but they were violently suppressed by Chinese troops. The Dalai Lama escaped to India. Before the Chinese troops could seal Tibet's border, an estimated 80,000 Tibetans had followed the Dalai Lama into exile in India. The PRC dissolved the Tibetan government, replacing it with a military regime to initiate many economic reforms. In 1965, the Tibet Autonomous Region was created.

Relations between China and India, already fraught with border disputes, further deteriorated after India granted asylum to the Dalai Lama. China launched two attacks on Indian positions in late 1962. From 1960 until the mid-1970s, Tibetan exiles based in Nepal formed guerrilla forces and carried out armed attacks along the border.

During the Cultural Revolution, Red Guards were encouraged to destroy religious and cultural artifacts. Tibetan Buddhism suffered violent suppression, which deepened Tibetan resentment toward the PRC government.

Since the 1978 reform, Chinese policy toward Tibet has vacillated between tolerance and suppression. It began with a moderate policy in the early 1980s, liberalizing control over the cultural and religious activities. Monasteries were rebuilt, and monks quickly grew in number. The growing number of monks and monasteries, however, caused grave concerns for the Chinese authority, who then gradually reversed the liberal policy in the 1990s, controlling Buddhist curriculum, limiting the number of monks and nuns, and implementing compulsory registration of Tibetan Buddhist sites.

Migrants of Han Chinese and Muslim backgrounds have moved to areas previously dominanted by Tibetans. The massive inflow of Chinese immigrants has changed the economic and cultural landscapes in Tibet. Beijing has developed crops of wheat and rice in Tibet to make the region more attractive to Chinese immigrants. From Beijing's perspective, the policy of sinicization, as seen in the promotion of tourism and market economy, along with strong cultural assimilation, has effectively improved the local economy and raised the living standards in Tibet. From the Tibetan perspective, the assimilation policy, sustained by political violence and human rights abuse by the Chinese party-state, intends to undermine not only their cultural and religious heritage but also their political autonomy. Hence, Tibetan refugees continue to flee to India and neighboring states.

In March 2008, pro-independence Tibetans attacked Han neighborhoods in Lhasa; ransacked police stations, government offices, and businesses; and caused 19 deaths and over 300 injuries. The riots soon spread to other ethnic

Tibetan areas in Gansu, Qinghai, and Sichuan and became one of the most massive protests in recent decades. Since then, there have been frequent clashes between Tibetans and the Chinese authorities, leading to arrests, injuries, and deaths. In recent years, self-immolation has become a new and extreme form of protest in Tibet.

Over the years, the PRC government has strengthened its miltiary position in Tibet to improve its strategic options. The Chinese government has built a sophisticated military infrastructure in Tibet, including five air bases, several helipads, and extensive networks of roads and railroads. This infrastructure will facilitate the rapid deployment of military forces not only in Tibet but also along the border against India (Malik 2012).

Xinjiang

Xinjiang is rich in natural resources, including petroleum, coal, gold, and uranium. Located along the trading route of the ancient Silk Road, it is now a major logistics hub of China's ambitious Belt and Road Initiative. Of the 13 different ethnicities in Xinjiang, Uighurs, who are Muslim and have linguistic and cultural ties to Turkic peoples in Kazakhstan, Kyrgyzstan, and Tajikistan, are the largest group. Historically, the Uighurs are opposed to Chinese rule. In 1955, Beijing established the Xinjiang Uighur Autonomous Region and began to encourage migration from Han Chinese, who now are the second largest group (40 percent of the population).

The Xinjiang Production and Construction Corps (XPCC), a quasi-military organization that reports directly to the State Council, is responsible for implementing the state economic development strategy in the region. Staffed mostly by Han immigrants, it operates industrial and commercial enterprises, as well as numerous farm complexes. With superior skills and training, economic migrants are more competitive in job markets and enjoy higher incomes than local residents.

Many Uighurs view the XPCC as an economic instrument for Beijing's colonizing effort and consider the Han Chinese as chief beneficiaries of exploited natural resources and economic opportunities. While the majority of the Muslim Uighurs reside in southern Xinjiang, most of the economic investment made by the PRC government goes to infrastructure and heavy industries in the northern part of the region. Thus, economic development has not closed the income gap between the Han Chinese and ethnic minorities.

The PRC government has alternated between "soft" and "hard" policies toward the Uighurs and their Islamic faith. To win the support of the ethnic minority population, the government may tolerate the religious practices and construction of mosques. However, when Islam is perceived as a threat to security, the state implements the hard policy to impose restrictions.

The PRC leaders have always viewed international intervention as a contributing factor for political instability in Xinjiang. For them, the 1962 Yili-Tacheng Incident, in which 60,000 Kazakhs and Uighurs fled from

Xinjiang to the Soviet Union—apparently with Soviet encouragement and support—attests to that internal-external connection. After the dissolution of the Soviet Union in 1991, the newly independent Central Asian Muslim states attracted transnational Islamic movements. For China, the rise of Islamic fundamentalism has the potential of encouraging separatist and secessionist movements, particularly as a sizable number of Uighurs currently reside in Kazakhstan and Kyrgyzstan (Davis 2008). After the 9/11 terrorist attack in the United States in 2001, the PRC intensified its suppression of Muslim dissidents, labeling them "terrorists." The government has banned the wearing of headscarves, hijabs, and veils. Students and government employees are prohibited from attending Ramadan fasting gatherings. These strict and heavy-handed restrictions on Islamic practices have radicalized many Uighurs.

In 2009, protests in Xinjiang escalated into widespread riots directed at government and police property as well as Han Chinese property. Chinese vigilante groups responded by attacking the Uighurs. As a result of the violence, 200 people died, and 1,700 were injured. Since then, Xinjiang has experienced chronic violence in the form of protests, demonstrations, riots, bombings, and guerrilla attacks. The party-state has reacted with more repression, increasing the number of security personnel and deploying government employees to local districts to monitor situations. Festivals and cultural events are often canceled to prevent large public gatherings. A large number of Uighurs are held in detention centers and indoctrination camps.

The government blames terrorist organizations such as the "Turkestan Islamic Party" and the "East Turkestan Islamic Movement" for instigating instability and points to their connections to jihadist groups such as al-Qaeda and ISIS. Critics, however, argue that the protracted instability is the result of failed economic, cultural, and religious policies.

EXTERNAL NATIONAL SECURITY

International and domestic factors, including contending ideas and interests at both levels, have shaped security relations between China and other states. Although China's security relations are increasingly expanding, this section focuses on the evolving relations between China and major powers such as the United States, the Soviet Union/Russia, and India. It also discusses China's involvement in the South China Sea (SCS). Sino-Japanese security relations are discussed in Chapter 8.

Sino-U.S. Security Relations

Hostility and Confrontation: 1949–1972. In the first decade after the founding of the PRC in 1949, China adopted the policy of "leaning to one side" and formed an alliance with the Soviet Union in February 1950. Eight months later, the Chinese troops, under the name of the Chinese People's Volunteer

Army, crossed the Yalu River and took part in the Korean War. Mao advocated for military intervention in the Korean peninsula on the grounds that, if the United States seized Korea, it would gain a platform to launch attacks against China, and possibly all across Asia. The Chinese involvement ultimately forced a stalemate on the Korean peninsula.

Alarmed by the Chinese intervention, the United States responded by isolating China economically, diplomatically, and militarily. It imposed a total economic embargo on China and dissuaded countries from recognizing the PRC or admitting it to the United Nations. To contain China's military expansion, the United States concluded a series of bilateral and multilateral mutual security treaties with South Korea (August 1953), with Taiwan (December 1954), and with Britain, France, Australia, New Zealand, the Philippines, Thailand, and Pakistan under the Southeast Asia Treaty Organization (September 1954).

Furthermore, the U.S. Seventh Fleet entered the Taiwan Strait to neutralize the area, protecting the KMT regime from the PLA. For PRC leaders, the U.S. support of Chiang Kai-shek's KMT regime in Taiwan undermined the sovereignty and territorial integrity of the PRC, reflecting the century-old imperialist aggression against China.

To counterbalance the U.S. encirclement, Mao in the 1950s twice took military actions against Taiwan (Chen 2001). In September 1954, the PLA began an intense artillery bombardment of the KMT-occupied island Jinmen (or Quemoy), located two miles from the mainland Chinese city of Xiamen. Heavy bombing soon expanded to another KMT-held island, Mazu (or Matzu), 10 miles from the city of Fuzhou. Tensions deescalated after the U.S. Congress authorized President Eisenhower to defend Taiwan in January 1955, and U.S. officials made public comments about using tactical atomic weapons to defend these offshore islands.

In August 1958, in the midst of revolutionary zeal from the Great Leap Forward, Mao resumed the bombardment of Jinmen and Mazu and launched a blockade against Taiwan's supplies and shipments to the offshores. The United States reacted swiftly. American ships escorted Taiwan supply vessels to Jinmen but stayed at least three miles offshore to avoid exchanging fire with the PLA. The United States also provided Taiwan with advanced air-to-air missiles to maintain air superiority over the battlefield.

The 1958 Taiwan Straits Crisis was a turning point in Sino-Soviet relations. While Mao was displeased with the lack of support from the Soviets, the Soviet leaders viewed Mao's action to precipitate military crisis as reckless. In 1960, Moscow withdrew technical experts from China and terminated most economic assistance programs, which practically ended the Sino-Soviet alliance.

In October 1964, China's successful detonation of its first atomic bomb significantly boosted its prestige and influence, signaling its great power status. The rise of the PRC as a nuclear power led to a significant reconfiguration of the global security structure—the emergence of the Sino-U.S.-Soviet triangular politics.

In 1965, as the United States began to deploy combat troops in Vietnam amid escalating conflicts there, Chinese leaders were deeply concerned with a possible U.S. invasion in southern China. Meantime, the Soviet Union steadily increased the number of Soviet troops along the Sino-Soviet border, putting pressure on the PRC's northern border. In 1966, Mongolia signed a defense treaty with the Soviet Union to allow Soviet troops to be stationed in Mongolia. By 1967, nearly 100,000 Soviet troops moved to Mongolia. Considering the Soviet Union a greater threat than the United States, Chinese leaders began to reassess their defense strategy in the triangular frame.

In March 1969, Beijing and Moscow were involved in border clashes at Zhenbao Island along the Wusuli (Ussuri) River. While the incident helped Mao mobilize the nation through patriotism during the tumultuous Cultural Revolution, it also led to increasing military pressure, including nuclear threat, from the Soviet Union.

Rapprochement: 1972–1989. Beijing and Washington came together in the early 1970s to balance against the common threat from the Soviet Union. U.S. National Security Advisor Henry Kissinger made a secret visit to Beijing in 1971, laying the groundwork for President Nixon's visit to China. In October 1971, the PRC was admitted to the United Nations as the sole legal representative of China. In February 1972, Nixon visited China and signed the Shanghai Communique with Zhou Enlai, creating a "tacit alliance" between the two. On this basis, unofficial relations between the two began to develop. In 1973, liaison offices were established. China broke its diplomatic isolation and became an active player on the world stage.

In the late 1970s, international and domestic factors drove China closer to the United States. The alliance treaties that the Soviet Union signed with Vietnam and Afghanistan heightened anxiety among the Chinese leaders over Soviet encirclement. Although Beijing continued to express antihegemonic rhetoric against the two superpowers, its real target was the Soviet Union.

Domestically, the dire need for economic development after the destruction of the Cultural Revolution was a compelling reason for China to seek assistance from capitalist economies such as the United States, Japan, and other Western countries for capital and technology. In January 1979, the PRC and the United States established formal diplomatic relations and signed a trade agreement in July to provide mutual most-favored-nation (MFN) treatment. At that time, bilateral economic interactions were minimal. China ranked as the 23rd largest market for U.S. exports and 45th as the source of U.S. imports. Bilateral trade was merely $2 billion in 1979, accounting for 0.5 percent of the total U.S. trade that year (Morrison 2018).

During the annual congressional hearing about China's MFN status, critics of China often pointed to human rights records and labor conditions in China, questioning the moral basis of the bilateral relations. Nevertheless, geopolitical calculations to counterbalance the Soviet Union with China trumped other considerations. In the aftermath of the 1989 Tiananmen Square crackdown, the U.S. administration imposed economic sanctions on Beijing, suspending arms sales and export licenses to China.

Competition and Cooperation: 1989–2012. As the Cold War came to an end, the strategic framework of the Sino-U.S. cooperation developed by Nixon and Mao became obsolete and irrelevant. The bilateral relations needed a new basis for cooperative relations. Geo-economics replaced geopolitics as the central theme for the Sino-U.S. relations during this period.

For the PRC, economic development remains the central task and key national goal. To sustain growth momentum, it is imperative for Beijing to maintain friendly relations with all major powers, particularly the United States, in a peaceful international environment. For the United States, liberalism, which emphasizes the positive effect of economic engagement in fostering peace and instilling democratic norms (Introduction), became the new rationale for U.S.-China relations. "Constructive engagement"—engaging China economically in hopes of peacefully transforming its authoritarian regime to a democracy—became the dominant narrative of the "strategic partnership" developed under the Clinton administration.

One important development was China's entry into the World Trade Organization (WTO) in December 2001, 15 years after its bid in 1986 to join the General Agreement on Tariff and Trade (GATT), the predecessor of the WTO. Concluding an agreement with the United States represented the most difficult hurdle for China's admission during the protracted accession negotiations.

In the face of strong resistance from state planning organizations, state-owned enterprises, and local governments, Jiang Zemin and Zhu Rongji skillfully used U.S. pressures to overcome domestic opposition for much-needed market reforms. China introduced four rounds of tariff reductions and signaled its willingness for more cuts to bring tariffs down to levels comparable to those of other developing countries. In the end, both sides were able to overcome obstacles and reach an agreement in November 1999, paving the way for China's admission to the WTO.

Despite economic cooperation, there were political tensions as well. In June 1995, Taiwan's president, Lee Teng-hui, visited the United States and gave a speech at his alma mater, Cornell University. Concluding that Lee's intention was to promote separatism and Taiwan independence, Beijing retaliated with off-and-on military exercises in the Taiwan Strait from 1995 to 1996. In 1996, Beijing launched missile tests and simulated a naval blockade of Taiwan just prior to Taiwan's presidential elections, causing concerns that China might use force to reclaim Taiwan. In the end, the United States intervened by sending two carrier battle groups into the area to defuse the crisis.

Tensions flared again in the late 1990s and early 2000s. The U.S.-led NATO forces during the Kosovo War accidentally bombed the Chinese embassy in Belgrade in 1999, causing three Chinese deaths. In 2001, the U.S. EP-3 reconnaissance plane was involved in a mid-air collision with a Chinese fighter jet near Hainan Island. The Chinese pilot died in the incident, whereas the U.S.

plane crew landed in Hainan and were detained by Beijing for 11 days. These cases led to public pressure on the CCP leadership to be tough on the United States.

Given the importance of the U.S. market, investment, and technology for the PRC's economic growth, the PRC leaders in the 2000s took a pragmatic approach to Sino-U.S. relations. While in official discourses the PRC leadership maintained uncompromising positions or voiced tough rhetoric toward Washington, it also tried to stabilize its relationship with Washington by carefully controlling the expression of nationalistic sentiments at home to avoid escalating tensions beyond control.

More Confrontation Ahead? 2012–Present. China's rising economic and military power, along with its growing belligerence in maritime disputes in the South China Sea (to be discussed later), has led to speculation about further intensified power contests between the United States and China.

In November 2011, President Obama announced America's "pivot" policy to return to the Asian Pacific after the decade-long U.S. war on terrorism in Iraq and Afghanistan.

The "pivot to Asia" or "rebalancing" policy had three essential pillars: military, diplomatic, and economic. The military aspect involved U.S. efforts to strengthen ties with traditional allies such as South Korea, Japan, and Australia and to forge new partnerships with India and Indonesia. The diplomatic strategy promised deeper engagement with the Association of Southeast Asian Nations (ASEAN) and related Asian regional institutions. Finally, the economic component of the policy was marked by the negotiation of the Trans-Pacific Partnership (TPP) agreement—a comprehensive trade agreement that reflected U.S. priorities and values.

Although President Trump withdrew from the TPP in January 2017, he kept the economic pressure on China. A series of tariff increases were imposed on Chinese imports on the grounds that China had not fully implemented its WTO obligations. The U.S. administration charged the Chinese government with engaging in widespread cyber-theft of U.S. trade secrets and with unfair trade practices to protect its domestic sectors and firms deemed critical to China's future economic growth.

Underlying U.S. economic concerns is the chronic trade deficit with China, which reached an all-time high in 2018 at approximately $419 billon. The deficit is seen by many as an indication of an unfair, unbalanced relationship that could damage the vitality of the U.S. economy. Tensions over Chinese currency manipulation and job losses in U.S. manufacturing reflect these long-term concerns.

Beijing has responded to the U.S. challenges with its own counter strategies. The shift in policy emphasis from "keeping a low profile" to "striving for achievement" is manifested in its economic and diplomatic initiatives of the AIIB and the BRI. Although the United States has decided to stay out of the AIIB and has actively lobbied its allies to do the same, there is strong support from countries in and out of the region, including the United Kingdom, Russia, France, Germany, Australia, New Zealand, South Korea, and Singapore.

The PRC is also supportive of the Regional Comprehensive Economic Partnership (RCEP), a free trade agreement initiated by the ASEAN states. The fact that the United States is not included in the RCEP might be taken as an indication that the PRC intends to use it to counterbalance the TPP.

Furthermore, PRC leaders have stood firm on trade conflicts, meeting the U.S. tariff threat by increasing tariffs on American imports, particularly agricultural products. Even if the latest round of the Sino-U.S. trade war can be peacefully resolved through further negotiations, other conflicts or crises are likely to occur soon if leaders from both countries are driven by a zero-sum mentality in managing their relationship. It is conceivable that the two countries will be involved in long-term competition over ideas, markets, resources, and technologies. While it remains to be seen whether the PRC and the United States can achieve mutual accommodation and trust, it is clear that Sino-U.S. relations will be an important determinant of global peace and conflict in the 21st century.

Sino-Soviet/Russian Security Relations

As discussed previously, China and the Soviet Union transitioned from allies to enemies during the Cold War. Different attitudes toward the world communist movement, conflicting views on the fundamental relations between the communist and capitalist camps, and varying interest in power politics drove the two countries apart (Hsu & Soong, 2014).

In the early 1980s, given the emphasis on economic development, China began to seek peaceful and cooperative relations with both superpowers. In the meantime, Secretary General Mikhail S. Gorbachev initiated domestic reforms, known as *perestroika* and *glasnost*, and reoriented Soviet foreign policies. In 1986, Gorbachev proposed to China a number of foreign policy initiatives aimed at reducing tensions, such as withdrawing troops from Afghanistan and Mongolia, and called for greater bilateral cooperation. Sino-Soviet relations improved significantly in the late 1980s. In 1989, in the final years of the Soviet Union, China and the Soviet Union restored their relations and jointly declared that their bilateral relations would be based on the five principles of peaceful coexistence.

In the post–Cold War era, Sino-Russian relations have been marked by pragmatism and gradual rapprochement, as both countries act on shared interests and common objectives. After the dissolution of the Soviet Union, Russia's power and influence declined. This decline coincided with Chinese double-digit economic growth in the first half of the 1990s. The reversed fortunes ironically opened up new opportunities for win-win cooperation. For China, Russian arms, energy, and raw materials are essential for its pursuit of modernization and development. For Russia, the influx of hard currency from the sale of oil, natural gas, and military equipment benefits its economy.

Economic Relations. Bilateral trade and investment have steadily increased. China exports consumer goods such as textiles, apparel, and footwear to Russia and imports energy and industrial materials such as metals, chemicals, wood, and paper from Russia. In 2010, China overtook Germany to become Russia's largest trading partner.

One key area of mutual economic cooperation lies in the energy sector. China purchases Russian oil for two reasons: to diversify its supply beyond the current sources of the Middle East and Africa and to build up strategic reserves to meet future demand. Two Russia-China pipelines from the East Siberia–Pacific Ocean system are currently in operation to transport 30 million tons of Russian crude oil to China annually. On natural gas, Beijing and Moscow signed a landmark $400 billion 30-year framework agreement in 2014 to construct a 1,250-mile pipeline to deliver 38 billion cubic meters of Russian natural gas to China annually.

Diplomatic Relations. Mutual relations were characterized as a "constructive partnership" in the 1994 summit between Jiang Zemin and Boris Yeltsin, who then upgraded the relations in the 1996 summit to a "strategic partnership" to strengthen mutual political and economic ties. The 2001 Sino-Russian Treaty of Good Neighborliness and Friendly Cooperation signed by Jiang Zemin and Vladimir Putin aimed to expand economic, diplomatic, and military cooperation. It stated that the two countries would consult each other if either party felt its security interests were threatened.

China and Russia share common security interests in Central Asia (Weitz 2012). For both countries, regional security in Central Asia is imperative as they try to contain Islamic groups for internal security: China in Xinjiang and Russia in the North Caucasus. In April 1996, China, Kazakhstan, Kyrgyzstan, Russia, and Tajikistan signed the Treaty on Deepening Military Trust in Border Regions in Shanghai. The same countries then signed the Treaty on Reduction of Military Forces in Border Regions in April 1997. In 2001, with Uzbekistan joining the group, the Shanghai Cooperation Organization (SCO) was formally established. Beginning as a counterterror organization, SCO's mission expanded to regional economic and security collaboration in 2004. It provides a multilateral framework for Russia and China to manage their interests in Central Asia.

For decades, territorial disputes have troubled Sino-Soviet/Russian relations. The efforts to resolve border disputes and to demilitarize common borders began in the 1990s and finally resolved in 2008, when Yinlong Island (known as Tarabarov Island in Russia) and half of Heixiazi Island (Bolshoi Ussuriysky Island) were returned to China. Peaceful resolution of border disputes eliminates an important source of tension between the two countries.

Military Relations. In the 1990s and early 2000s, China and Russia became perfect partners in the arms trade (Wezeman 2017). For Russia, its defense industry desperately needed new markets, after losing major clients in the former

Eastern European communist states following the collapse of the Soviet Union. For China, after the 1989 Tiananmen Square crackdown, Russia was one of the few countries willing to sell weapons to China in the wake of arms embargos imposed by the West. Russian weapons were compatible with the PLA's equipment from the Soviet era and were reasonably priced compared to those from the West.

From 1992 to 2006, China was the biggest buyer of Russian military equipment and technology, including combat aircraft, warships, submarines, and armored vehicles. The transfers accounted for 30 percent to 60 percent of Russia's annual arms sales.

However, there were concerns in Russia. Critics argued that military transfers to China could potentially build up a competitor who could compete with Russia in the global arms market, or, in the worst case, develop a threat to Russia's national security and survival.

China has indeed become a competitor with Russia in the global arms market since the late 2000s, as its arms industries have reverse engineered Russian weapon systems and begun selling indigenous copies of them. China's demand for complete Russian weapon systems has fallen steadily since 2007, although it still depends on Russia for key parts and components.

Beyond arms sales, Sino-Russian defense cooperation has become more institutionalized and integrated, evident in three areas: joint military exercises, military-technical cooperation, and contacts between high-level military leaders.

China and Russia held their first combined military exercise in 2003. From then until 2017, the two conducted approximately 25 joint exercises that were increasingly complicated, in terms of the level of integration and coordination. The scope of cooperation expanded to include missile defense in 2016, reflecting their common position in opposing the U.S.-led missile defense network in Asia.

In recent years, China and Russia have pursued joint military-technical research across a wide range of sectors, including the development of next-generation heavy-lift helicopters, advanced conventional submarines, and space-grade materials.

Finally, China and Russia have maintained ongoing dialogues between ranking military officials. Exchanges between high-level military officers provide opportunities for defense officials to discuss regional and global security concerns and facilitate greater cooperation in military exercises and research collaboration.

While the strategic partnership between China and Russia is broad, it has its limits. Both countries have emphasized that their strategic partnership is not an alliance aimed at a third country. While they share a common interest in countering U.S. hegemony, they have not succeeded in overcoming some U.S. policies, such as ballistic missile defense.

In fact, the development of a formal Sino-Russian alliance is unlikely, due to continued difference and ambivalence in areas of distrust and disagreement. China and Russia display rather ambivalent stances toward each other's policies and behaviors. For example, while China never openly criticized Russia's policies and actions in the Russia-Georgia war of 2008, or Russia's annexation of Crimea in the Ukraine crisis of 2014, China does not openly support Russia either. Similarly, Russia has never publicly questioned the legitimacy of China's claim in the South China Sea, but it does not openly express support.

Sino-India Security Relations

While India was the first non-communist state to establish a diplomatic relationship with the PRC in 1949, a long history of disputes and rivalry has since marked the relations between the two. Border disputes led to open hostility in the 1962 Sino-Indian War. In the aftermath of the war, India immediately severed diplomatic relations with the PRC and did not restore the relations until 1976. Bilateral interactions and exchanges have since grown steadily. In recent years, common economic ties between the two have strengthened. China has been India's largest trading partner since 2008. Nevertheless, even with the growing common interest, bilateral relations remain fraught with geopolitical competition.

Tibet and Territorial Disputes. Central to the bilateral relations are Tibet and border issues (Holslag 2009; Panda 2013). The border issue relates to the disputed status of the McMahon Line, which was the borderline drawn by British India and Tibet in the 1914 Simla Convention. While India recognizes this line as an established border line with China after the British departed, China opposes the validity of the line on the grounds that Tibet was not a sovereign state and did not have the legal power to execute treaties. Protracted disputes involve the western region Aksai Chin, occupied by China, and the eastern area of Arunachal Pradesh, controlled by India.

In April 1954, China and India signed an agreement regarding Tibet based on the five principles of peaceful coexistence. India recognized Tibet as a "region of China," and nullified all previous agreements it had signed with Tibet. The treaty legitimized China's annexation of Tibet and was an enormous concession to China by the Nehru government.

In spite of this agreement, China believed that India remained involved in covert operations to support the Tibetan resistance, with the intention of transforming Tibet into a buffer zone between India and the PRC. After the 1959 Lhasa rebellion, India initiated a Forward Policy to place outposts along the border. The Indian government not only granted the Dalai Lama political asylum but also allowed him to organize and maintain quasi-government structures in the Tibetan exile community in India. India also provided training, arms, and support to several Tibetan military organizations. From the Chinese viewpoint, active Indian support of Tibetan resistance activities poses a major challenge to China's rule in Tibet.

In August 1959, a bloody border incident occurred between Chinese and Indian garrisons at Longuju, an eastern section of the border. Two months later, another border clash occurred at the Kongka Pass on the western section of the border, resulting in the further deterioration of relations. In October 1962, the PLA launched attacks against the Indian army along the border. Over 1,300 Indian troops were killed, and nearly 4,000 were captured.

Several rounds of border talks since 1981 have failed to resolve the disputed claims.

In 1986, nearly 200,000 Indian troops were mobilized along the border, after having discovered increased Chinese military presence. The mobilization pushed both sides to the brink of war. To ease the tension, both sides in 1988 agreed to create a Joint Working Group (JWG) to make concrete recommendations to resolve border disputes and maintain peace. In the 1990s, several agreements were reached to reduce border tensions with confidence-building measures, such as reduction of border troops, withdrawal of offensive weapons, and regular meetings between local military commanders.

After 2003, border negotiations were institutionalized through appointed special representatives to explore the overall relationship, but no breakthrough has been achieved. In the meantime, border incursions by Chinese troops establishing camps inside India's Line of Actual Control reinforced mutual distrust.

In 2017, tension flared up in Doklam (or Donglang in Chinese), a disputed territory between China and India's ally Bhutan. In June 2017, Indian troops entered Doklam to keep Chinese troops from building a road there. In August, after a 73-day standoff, both sides pulled back.

Geopolitical Competition. The Sino-Indian territorial disputes are merely symptoms of a sustained, multifaceted geopolitical rivalry, as seen in competing alliances, nuclear development, and overlapping spheres of influence. Their bilateral relations appear to follow the action-reaction dynamics of the concept of security dilemma (Garver 2002).

Maintaining a solid, strategic alliance with Pakistan is a key component of China's attempt to constrain India. China's support for Pakistan's military capabilities, particularly in its missile and nuclear programs, creates a serious security risk to India. With Pakistan on its western border and China on its northern border, India faces a two-front threat.

China's successful nuclear test in October 1964 made India feel vulnerable. To combat China, India signed the Treaty of Friendship and Cooperation with the Soviet Union in 1971. It was a significant departure from India's previous nonalignment policy in the Cold War. In May 1974, India tested a nuclear explosive. Shortly after India's nuclear test in 1974, China began to assist Pakistan with acquiring nuclear weapons technology. The assistance expanded to ballistic missile technology in the late 1980s. In May 1998, India conducted five nuclear tests. Pakistan responded in June 1998 with its own nuclear testing.

Besides Pakistan, Beijing has established and expanded political and security relations with countries in South Asia, an area traditionally viewed by India as its security zone. China's collaborations with Bangladesh, Nepal, and Myanmar (Burma) in the region aim to counter India's influence. Beijing has invested heavily in building ports and overland transportation links in Pakistan, Sri Lanka, Bangladesh, and Myanmar, with the goal of developing navy support stations and supply lines along the North Indian Ocean.

To counter Beijing's moves, India has expanded its cooperation with the United States since the mid-1990s. In 2005, India and the United States signed the New Framework for India-U.S. Defense to increase military cooperation. Subsequently, the United States and India have conducted multiple joint military exercises. India's participation in the Quadrilateral Security Dialogue with the United States, Japan, and Australia is widely seen as a strategy to restrain China's expanding strength and influence in the Asia-Pacific and Indian Ocean regions.

The parallel rise of India and China in the 21st century has complicated the security landscape in the region. India's fast economic growth and diplomatic activism have attracted increasing attention from the PRC. India's pursuit of great power status can be seen in its effort to join Brazil, Japan, and Germany as a member of an expanded United Nations Security Council—an idea that has not received much support from China. While China has invited India to take part in its economic initiatives such as AIIB and BRI, it has also sought to limit India's participation in the East Asia Summit, the Asian-Pacific Economic Cooperation (APEC) forum, and the Asian Development Bank. The ambivalence reflects a volatile relationship that oscillates between competition and cooperation.

Security Relations in the South China Sea

The SCS is an area of immense strategic and economic value. Resources and raw materials that fuel the economic growth in East Asia are transported through the SCS each day, and the area itself is reportedly abundant in hydrocarbons that could sustain the future growth of the region.

Brunei, China, Malaysia, the Philippines, Taiwan, and Vietnam are the six parties to SCS disputes with conflicting claims to various features, reefs, and islets in the region. Sino-Vietnamese and Sino-Philippine relations have been the most contentious of all, involving armed conflicts in the 1980s and 1990s. China and Vietnam both claim historical control over the Paracel Islands (known as Hoang Sa in Vietnam and Xisha in China) and the Spratly Islands (Nansha in China and Truong Sa in Vietnam). Conflicts between China and the Philippines center on the Mischief Reef and Scarborough Reef.

In 2009, conflict intensified as states tried to meet the deadline for submitting applications to extend continental shelves beyond the 200 nautical miles set by the Conference of the States Parties to the United Nations Convention on the Law of the Sea (UNCLOS). A Vietnamese submission and a joint Vietnam-Malaysia submission prompted respective counterprotests from China and the Philippines. The so-called nine-dash line map used by China appeared to claim the SCS in its entirety, yet China would not clarify the nature and scope of its claim.

In January 2013, the Philippines initiated arbitration against China at the Permanent Court of Arbitration in The Hague, asking an arbitral tribunal to rule on whether China's nine-dash line is a valid maritime claim. In July 2016, the arbitral tribunal supported the Philippines, finding no evidence that China had historically exercised exclusive control over the waters or resources. Thus, according to tribunal, there is no legal basis for China to claim historic rights over the nine-dash line. The ruling, however, did little to resolve the conflict, as both China and Taiwan, which currently administers the largest naturally formed feature in the Spratlys—Itu Aba (or Taiping Island, as called by Taiwan)—refused to accept the ruling.

Beginning in 2014, China has undertaken massive land reclamation projects at seven features in the Spratlys: Fiery Cross, Cuarteron, Hughes, Johnson South, Mischief, Gaven, and Subi. This reclamation project has permanently changed the ecology and landscape of these features. More importantly, China has built helicopter pads, wharfs, lighthouses, buildings, observation posts, and communication centers on these features. The construction of an airstrip as well as the installation of radar facilities on some features are particularly significant, for they provide China the capability to project its power in the SCS. Whatever its intentions, these actions have transformed the nature of SCS disputes from competition over resources (i.e., fish, oil, and gas) to a battle of security.

In response, the U.S. Navy has increased its presence in the SCS. Taking a neutral position on the territorial disputes, the United States instead insists on the protection of the overflight and navigational freedoms in the SCS waters. For China, the U.S. naval actions constitute a threat to its sovereignty and interest in the region. The United States, however, justifies the actions based on the perceived militarization of the SCS. Although it is unlikely that all parties involved in the SCS disputes will be involved in a direct, large-scale military confrontation, the possibility of unplanned and unexpected clashes has increased, as security becomes a dominant concern.

DISCUSSION QUESTIONS

1. The Chinese government takes a broad view of national security. What are some of the security priorities? How would they affect China's relations with other major powers in the region?

2. Discuss whether the Chinese security strategies have changed from Deng Xiaoping to Xi Jinping, and explain what may be the reasons for the change, or lack of change.

3. In the Chinese view, internal security and external security are interrelated. What explains this perception? Is there any evidence to support this view?

4. Competition and cooperation have both been part of Sino-U.S. security relations since the end of the Cold War. Discuss whether the power transition theory is helpful in explaining Sino-U.S. relations. Why or why not?

5. Describe Sino-Russian security relations in the post–Cold War era. What are some of the key domestic and international factors influencing the relations?

5

Japan
THE FOUNDATIONS

PEOPLE AND GEOGRAPHY

Japan is a country of islands and mountains. The Japanese archipelago consists of four main islands—Hokkaido, Honshu, Shikoku, and Kyushu, a few sizable nearby islands, and nearly 7,000 islets. The long, thin chain of islands extends from the northeast to the southeast, along the western edge of the Pacific Ring of Fire, an area of frequent earthquakes and volcanoes that often cause tsunami tidal waves along the coastlines. In average, there are 1,500 recorded earthquakes in Japan each year. The country is also vulnerable to seasonal torrential typhoons and monsoon rains.

With gross land area of approximately 146,000 square miles, Japan is slightly larger than Germany and a little smaller than California. In comparative terms, Japan's population (127 million in 2018) is almost half that of the United States, but its landmass is less than 4 percent of that of the United States, making it one of the most densely populated countries in the world.

Mountainous terrain, devoted mostly to forest and pasture, accounts for approximately 75 percent of the land surface. Only about 16 percent of its territory is arable. Most of its population is concentrated in areas from northern Kyushu, through the Inland Sea, to the three urban centers in Honshu—*Kansai* (Osaka-Kobe-Kyoto), *Tokai* (greater Nagoya), and *Kanto* (greater Tokyo). The large, fertile plains along this east-west axis have been the foundation for Japan's political, economic, and cultural life. With roughly 80 percent of the people living in urban settings, Japan has a high rate of urbanization.

Besides its shortage in habitable and arable land, the country is poorly endowed with natural resources. It has practically no petroleum and insufficient quantities of lead, copper, and magnesium. Iron and coal deposits are sparse. It depends on imported raw materials to sustain its industrial economy. Limited agricultural base and natural resources have contributed to the sense of economic insecurity and vulnerability.

Most rivers are short and too shallow to navigate. Before the construction of modern roads and railways, Japanese people had to rely on sea transportation to move goods between many natural harbors along the coast. Difficulty in land communication hindered the development of centralized political rule in the premodern era, as feudal lords controlled their own fiefdoms. Regionalism and localism were the dominant features. Although Japan enjoys a high degree of racial, ethnic, and linguistic homogeneity, regional tensions between southwest and northeast Japan have persisted for centuries in the form of political and cultural rivalries. The emergence of the notion of "Japanese-ness" as a coherent nation with a common identity is a modern creation since the mid-19th century.

Japan's closest continental neighbor is Korea, which is about 130 miles west across the Sea of Japan. China is farther west, about 475 miles across the East China Sea (or the Yellow Sea). While these distances were close enough to allow sea journeys in the premodern era, they were far enough to give Japan a clearly defined national frontier to separate from the outsiders. Historically, the Korean peninsula served as a conduit for Japan to import culture and technology such as fine arts, religions, and architecture from the Asian mainland and places beyond. In the 13th century, the Mongols and Koreans mounted two separate attacks on Japan and were twice repelled by typhoons. Throughout most of their history, the Japanese were able to concentrate on domestic issues with little concern of external security.

THE HISTORICAL ROOTS

In Japan, there is evidence that early Japanese society existed around 200 to 300 BCE. Nevertheless, it was not until the middle of the 3rd century that a primitive state emerged, founded by a ruler (*Jimmu Tenno*) of the Yamato clan who claimed to descend from the Sun Goddess (*Amaterasu Omikami*). The worship of the Sun Goddess and other divine and sacred beings (*kami*) in nature formed the basis of the indigenous Shinto (or "the way of the gods") religion. Many *kami* were closely connected to the agricultural cycle and local community, and some were worshipped as protectors of powerful political families, including the imperial family. Thus, Shinto rites and rituals were closely intertwined with government affairs.

The Rise and Fall of the Imperial Court

Buddhism and Confucianism first came to Japan from Korea in the 6th century. In the early 7th century, the state of Yamato sent a 600-member mission to Tang China. The visit led to the Taika Reforms of 645 CE that adopted key elements of the Chinese governing ideas and institutions, particularly the system of a centralized state with an absolute sovereign, along with architectural styles, modes of dress, and the Chinese written language.

Nara, located in the Kansai region of the main island of Honshu, was the first capital of Japan. It was modeled after the Tang capital for its rectangular grid pattern. During the Nara period (710–794), the court aggressively imported Chinese civilization, sending diplomatic envoys to Tang China every

20 years. Nevertheless, it made significant modifications to Chinese ideas and institutions.

One important modification was about the "Mandate of Heaven." Although the Japanese, like the Chinese, linked the origin of imperial authority to Heaven, they did not develop a "Mandate of Heaven" type of legitimacy claim as the Chinese. The Yamato rulers preferred to be legitimized by divine descent rather than by the ongoing scrutiny and judgment of their virtue and performance. A genealogical line was constructed to trace the imperial origin through 28 legendary rulers to 660 BCE.

Another modification related to the Chinese concept of the meritocratic civil bureaucracy. Although the examination-based administrative system was introduced, it quickly evolved into a bureaucracy determined by inherited family status, rather than by individual merits, as the established elite sought to protect their own interests.

In 794, the capital was moved to Heian, present-day Kyoto. During the Heian period (794–1185), wealth and political power gradually shifted from the urban-centered imperial government to landed nobles or feudal lords (known as *daimyo*). A number of nobles ruled as sovereigns while the emperors had little more than ceremonial significance as priests in the Shinto tradition. Aristocrats linked to the imperial court first ruled the country, followed by military families of diverse backgrounds. Different clans and factions vied for control of land and labor, leading to a period of continued warfare.

Against this background, the warriors (known as *bushi* or *samurai*) serving in the imperial court or aristocratic families grew increasingly powerful. The first military government, called a *bakufu* (or tent government), was founded in Kamakura near present-day Tokyo in 1185, when its chief, Minamoto Yoritomo, seized power by force and ushered in the feudal age.

Feudalism

Although he emerged as the most powerful person, Minamoto felt a need for formal recognition by the court. The emperor conferred the title of *seii tai-shogun* (or Barbarian-subduing Great General) to confirm his legitimacy in 1192. While Kyoto remained the official capital, and the imperial court stayed there, political power was completely transferred to *shogun*, who acted as the commander in chief of the imperial army and de facto rulers of Japan. Since then, three shogunates (the Kamakura, 1185–1333; the Ashikaga, 1336–1573; and the Tokugawa, 1603–1867) ruled over Japan for seven hundred years. All drew legitimacy from the imperial court by accepting the title of *shogun*.

This fact illustrates an important cultural practice in Japan, where harmony is promoted through an outward display of agreement and conformity. A formal authority retains the hierarchical order of authority and remains the source to confer legitimacy on those below them, even when it does not have the real power. Thus, although the emperors had very little influence over public affairs, the imperial institution was important in symbolizing state unity and in legitimizing the authoritative relations of the political system.

Matters of governance were the responsibility of the *shogun*, who in turn delegated power to military governors loyal to him. As supreme hegemon, the *shogun* maintained his political power through military strength that relied on a system of personal loyalty and allegiance. The high political status of military leaders in this type of feudal structure was a clear contrast to the Chinese experience.

Relations with China and Korea

Although Japanese elites drew inspirations from the cultural achievements of China, they were unwilling to accept the subordinate position in the Chinese tributary system. In fact, Japan was concerned about its vulnerability at the hands of China. The Mongols under Kublai Khan attempted to invade Japan in 1274 and 1281. Both times, the Mongols landed on the shore of Kyushu and the *samurai* from the Kamakura shogunate fought them to an initial standstill. Twice, the arrival of typhoons wrecked the Mongol fleet, forcing the invaders to withdraw.

Three hundred years later, Japan launched its own attack of the Asian mainland under Toyotomi Hideyoshi (1536–1598). He invaded Korea in 1592, with the ultimate goal of conquering China to build a Japanese empire. The Japanese forces captured Seoul in three weeks, causing great casualties and economic loss for the Koreans. Korea appealed to China for assistance. Joint efforts by the Chinese attacks on land and Korean naval campaigns at sea finally halted the Japanese advance, leading to a stalemate. His second campaign against Korea was launched in 1597. The Koreans and their Chinese allies stopped the Japanese army before Seoul and slowly pushed them back toward Pusan. Following his death in 1598, the Japanese troops retreated.

The Japanese invasion, however, left deep and long-lasting hostility and suspicion in Korea toward Japan. Culturally, Japan benefited by acquiring from Korea the technologies of porcelain making and movable-type printing.

Tokugawa Shogunate: 1603–1867

In 1600, Tokugawa Ieyasu defeated his military rivals and successfully unified Japan. The imperial court conferred upon him the title of *shogun* in 1603, beginning the reign of the Tokugawa shogunate for the next two-and-a-half centuries. Ruling from Edo (Tokyo) while the emperor resided in Kyoto, Tokugawa tried to reestablish order and stability after a century of warfare. Confucianism was officially recognized as the guiding ideology, and its norms were used as a conceptual framework to build a strict social hierarchy.

At the top of the Tokugawa regime were the *shogun*, nobles, and local *daimyo*, followed by four broad social classes: warrior-bureaucrats (*samurai*), farmers, artisans, and merchants. The social structure reflected the belief in an agrarian economy in which farmers were the primary producer, whereas commercial activities (and the status of the merchants) were deemed insignificant. The class distinction between the nobility and the commoners (the farmers and below) was strictly maintained, hence limiting the likelihood of social mobility.

Notwithstanding the strong influence of Confucianism, the Japanese desired to build their political and cultural identities with their own traditions. The feudalism developed since the 12th and 13th centuries was distinctively Japanese; Confucian values were used to reinforce the feudal order. There was also scholarly reaction against foreign influence, primarily directed toward China. During the Tokugawa period, the idea of *kokutai* (national polity, national character, or national essence) began to emerge, reflecting the attempt to build a Japanese identity by emphasizing its unique features, including the Shinto religion and Japanese classic literature.

The control mechanism created by Tokugawa Ieyasu and his successors reflected their strategic thinking on political governance. First, feudal domains were distributed based on political loyalty. The lands surrounding Edo were given to Tokugawa's family and his close allies. Others were forced to relocate to outer domains in the far reaches of southwestern Japan. Only limited land was under Tokugawa's direct control; the remaining territory was divided into 260 feudal fiefdoms, each headed by a *daimyo*. Second, feudal lords were required to alternate their residences between Edo and their domains. They were required to stay in Edo every other year, working on behalf of the *shogun*. When they traveled back to their feudal lands the next year, their families had to stay in Edo, under the pretense of populating the capital with provincial families when in fact they were held hostage by the shogunate. Dual residence and biennial processions were extremely expensive, hence preventing the lords from accumulating resources to challenge the shogunate. Tokugawa further demanded the lords to contribute to expensive public works such as bridges, dams, and dikes in various parts of Japan. These governance institutions helped produce a long period of peace in which the concerns of the *samurai* began to turn from military skill to civil administration.

Diplomatic isolation was another tactic used by Tokugawa shogunate to maintain political power. From the 17th century onward, Tokugawa Japan pursued a policy of national isolation (*sakoku*, or "closed country") that severely restricted trade and forbade its own people from leaving the country. Western merchants and missionaries had to stay within prescribed areas and operate under strict rules imposed by the government. Licensed trade with the Dutch and Chinese was limited to the port of Nagasaki in southern Kyushu, while some trade with Korea was permitted. The isolationist stance intended to minimize foreign intervention and to prevent the feudal lords from accumulating wealth through the gold and silver brought over by foreign merchants. Altogether, these practices helped solidify the *shogun's* political authority.

During the long peace under the Tokugawa shogunate, the socially despised merchants ironically were able to accumulate significant wealth through the sophisticated trading networks they built. The wealth they accumulated, however, gradually led to inflation. As inflation went unchecked, the economic situations for *samurai* and farmers worsened. Most of the *samurai* lived on a fixed rice stipend that lost its value because of rising inflation; many were hard pressed even to support their families. Farmers also suffered, as they were asked to deliver more to feudal lords to compensate for the lost value of their production. Toward the end of the Tokugawa era, economic hardship led to increasing social discontent and revolts.

BUILDING A MODERN STATE

The Meiji Era: 1868–1912

Ten years after the British pried open the market in China, the West turned its attention to Japan. U.S. Commodore Matthew C. Perry (1794–1858) steamed into Edo Bay in July 1853 with four ships, demanding the opening of Japanese ports for trade. In February 1854, he returned with a larger fleet of nine ships. The display of superior naval forces by Perry set off a chain reaction that eventually brought down the shogunate.

After centuries of peace under diplomatic isolation, the Tokugawa government did not have the military capacity to fight the Americans. Negotiations with the United States persuaded the Tokugawa leaders to agree to open two ports to American ships in need of supplies and to provide for American consular representation in Japan. The second U.S.-Japan treaty in 1858 further augmented U.S. rights in Japan, opening five more treaty ports to Americans, setting favorable duties for U.S. trade, and granting American citizens "extraterritoriality" rights in Japan. Several European powers quickly seized the opportunity and forced Japan to grant similar concessions to them in "unequal treaties."

Many feudal lords viewed the shogunate's concessions to foreigners as a betrayal of the Japanese nation. Mounting opposition led to political chaos. In 1868, a small group of junior *samurai* and aristocrats mostly in their early thirties undertook a coup to overthrow the shogunate. Many of them came from the most remote domains: Satsuma and Hizen in Kyushu, Choshu in the extreme southwestern section of Honshu, and Tosa in southern Shikoku. While their motives were varied, historical animosity toward Tokugawa and dissatisfaction with the suppressed *samurai* status played a role.

They justified their action by restoring to the emperor to his rightful ruling position. The 16-year-old Emperor Mutsuhito (1852–1912), who took the reign name Meiji ("enlightened rule") as Japan's 122nd emperor upon his father's death in January 1867, went along with the new regime. The emperor moved to Edo, which was renamed Tokyo and designated as the national capital. The restoration leaders—usually called the Meiji oligarchs—never meant for the emperor to be restored to the powers claimed by the Nara court. Instead, they themselves formed core leadership in civil and military affairs, taking the country on a path toward industrialization and modernization.

Political Governance. The Meiji oligarchs quickly forged a clear vision to "enrich the country, strengthen the military" (*fukoku kyohei*), linking economic development to military power. Guided by this vision, they consolidated political power to establish the institutional foundation for the modernization program. The feudal structure was dismantled, and feudal domains were converted to centrally controlled administrative units. They abolished the restrictive class system, allowing people to pursue their preferred occupation. The *daimyo* and *samurai* were persuaded to give up their privileges and rights for financial arrangements and government bonds. A peerage system was devised to award "outstanding services to the country"; titles were bestowed based on political support to the new regime. A new conscription army was established in 1873.

Early on, the Meiji leaders were aware that knowledge and expertise are integral to the process of modernization. More than 3,000 foreign advisers, engineers, and technicians were employed in Japan during the Meiji era. Nevertheless, these were considered short-term solutions; the government sought to replace them with Japanese personnel as soon as they could be trained. Over 11,000 Japanese people were sent abroad to study Western institutions and to identify models that Japan could adopt. For this purpose, education played a key role in producing bureaucrats, workers, and managers for political development and economic growth. Mass public education was introduced. Many of Japan's most famous universities such as Tokyo, Kyoto, Keio, and Waseda were established during this period.

Meiji leaders built a modern, centralized bureaucracy based on merit. They recruited former *samurai* who were literate, respected, and had administrative experience to implement modernization programs. Recognizing that Western strength was more than just weapons and technology, they borrowed and adopted a wide range of institutions and ideas, determined to learn and emulate the best models available in order to catch up with the West. Compared with Chinese elites who were unwilling to abandon their "Middle Kingdom" mentality, Japanese leaders' turnaround was swift and complete.

Yet it did not mean that there were no divisions among the oligarchs. One of the key differences among the oligarchs was the extent of political liberalization for the new political system. The conservative wing of the oligarchs, represented by Ito Hirobumi, preferred an authoritarian regime that governed with efficiency and effectiveness, while the populist wing of oligarchs such as Okuma Shigenobu and Itagaki Taisuke sought implementation of broader liberties.

After resigning from the Meiji government in protest over the factionalism within, Itagaki established the political societies that were the precursors of today's political parties to build grassroots support beyond the inner circle of the oligarchs. He founded the Society of Patriots (*Aikokusha*) in 1875, which drew inspiration from the Western concept of the fundamental, inalienable rights enjoyed by people. In 1881, Itagaki organized the Liberal Party (*Jiyuto*), Japan's first political party. Along with the Constitutional Progressive Party (*Rikken Kaishinto*) formed by Okuma in 1882, they led the nationwide popular movement for tax reform and civil rights in the early 1880s. The division between the authoritarian and liberal traditions evolved into the mainstreams in Japan's political development.

Political institutions were formally established in the Meiji Constitution of 1889, which was presented as a token of imperial benevolence. According to the constitution, all executive power was vested in the emperor, who appointed the cabinet ministers, commanded the armed forces, and retained the prerogative to sanction and promulgate laws. In reality, despite the affirmation of imperial sovereignty, the emperor continued to be a figurehead.

The oligarchs created a Privy Council based on the British model and filled it with their political allies. The Council advised, and in fact constrained, the emperor on matters of legislation and imperial ordinances.

The Meiji Constitution established the first Japanese parliament, the Imperial Diet, based on the Prussian model. The British and American models were deemed by many of the oligarchs as too liberal in granting too many rights to the legislature. The bicameral Imperial Diet consisted of a popularly elected House of Representatives and a House of Peers comprised of aristocrats (the former *daimyo* and court nobility). Members of the House of Representatives were chosen by a limited franchise; only 1 percent of the population in Japan was eligible to vote based on the tax requirement in the first parliamentary election in 1890.

In 1898, Itagaki and Okuma joined forces to form the Constitutional Party (*Kenseito*) that had an overwhelming majority in the House of Representatives in the Diet. Ito, the architect of the Meiji Constitution, realizing that the constitutional design was insufficient to contain the populist movement, began to form his own political party, the Political Friends Party (*Seiyukai*), in 1900.

Although Okuma's *Kenseito* and Ito's *Seiyukai* had divergent roots in authoritarian and liberal traditions, they did not compete along these values or ideals. Instead, trying to survive fierce political competition, these two major political parties appealed to big business for financial support. They were not mass based or tightly organized; rather, they were built on the basis of a leader-follower relationship. Cliques and factions were prevalent in the political parties, a pattern that has persisted into the contemporary period.

Guided Economic Development. At the beginning of Meiji Restoration, Japan was a prototypical agrarian economy. Handicraft industries such as the production of raw cotton, textiles, dyeing, silk, sake, and paper had emerged in rural Japan by the mid-19th century, with the bulk of their outputs produced in small rural workshops or factories. The free trade regime imposed by foreign powers through the "unequal treaties" seriously threatened their survival, as Western goods entering the Japanese market through the open ports easily outsold the domestic products.

Determined to be able to compete with the West, the Meiji oligarchs were strategic in promoting industrialization. Compared with free market economies, the Meiji state played an active role in the economy, building formal and informal relationships with private sectors and mobilizing resources intentionally for developmental goals. The state used different approaches in different industries to adapt to the changing environments.

The government provided limited support in textile and light manufacturing industries, for they were sufficiently competitive. Entrepreneurs in silk and cotton industries were able to react and adapt to the market conditions without government intervention. The success of the textile industries laid the foundation for macroeconomic modernization and led to Japan's industrial growth in the late decades of the 19th century.

In heavy manufacturing, however, it was more difficult to persuade the private sector to invest because of the amount of capital required for initial investment in those areas. Thus, in cases of iron and steel, automobiles, and shipbuilding, the government provided the most subsidies to achieve the fastest technological change. The protectionist measures offered by the Japanese state were commonly used elsewhere by other governments for those industries.

The government also founded and operated a large number of state factories and enterprises in key heavy industries such as chemicals, cement, paper, and sugar but had to privatize many of them during the 1880s due to their inferior performance compared to private enterprises.

Many of these corporations were taken over by former *daimyo* and *samurai* who had acquired capital funds in the form of bonds in return for renouncing annual stipends previously arranged. Most of the privatized enterprises subsequently evolved into giant industrial conglomerates known as *zaibatsu* (or financial cliques) and maintained close links to the government. The ties between big business and government have endured since then.

National Security. The Meiji Restoration became the first successful modernization program undertaken by a non-Western country. As envisioned by the Meiji leaders, economic enrichment strengthened the country, giving Japan the ability to turn economic power into military supremacy. Its neighbors, Korea and China, became the first targets as it sought to expand to ensure its national security.

Japan used Western "gunboat diplomacy" against Korea. In 1875, Japan displayed naval power along the coast of Korea. After being fired upon by the Korean defenders, the Japanese troops came back in 1876 and forced Korea to sign the Treaty of Kanghwa, which opened two ports for Japan to trade, allowed the Japanese to reside in treaty ports, and gave Japan the right of extraterritoriality.

The treaty paved the way for Japan to intervene in Korean politics, including an attempted coup in 1884. In 1894, both China and Japan sent troops to Korea to quell a rebellion, but neither was willing to withdraw afterward. The incident escalated to the Sino-Japanese War of 1894–1895, which ended with Japan's decisive victories on land and sea (Chapter 1). In the wake of the war, the huge indemnity paid by China to Japan was equivalent to three times that of Japan's annual revenue at the time. Japan also acquired its first colony, Taiwan, but had to renounce the Liaodong Peninsula under the tripartite intervention by Russia, France, and Germany. Russia's intervention, however, led to public outcry in Japan, particularly after the Russians obtained a 25-year lease of the Liaodong Peninsula from China in 1898.

Japan's victory in the Sino-Japanese War brought international recognition of its major power status. It succeeded in renegotiating the unequal treaties with the West to eliminate their extraterritoriality rights and to restore Japan's tariff autonomy. Additionally, Japan formed an alliance with Great Britain in 1902 to safeguard their respective interests in China and Korea. The Anglo-Japanese alliance (1902–1923) was the first military pact concluded on equal terms between a Western and non-Western nation.

Japan declared war against Russia in February 1904, after terminating their diplomatic relations. Both countries suffered heavily in the Russo-Japanese War (1904–1905), but Japan's final victory over Russia earned great respect from the international community. The Treaty of Portsmouth mediated by President Theodore Roosevelt formally ended the war. The treaty recognized Japan's paramount interests in Korea, and Russia agreed to turn over its lease of the Liaodong Peninsula as well as the southern half of Sakhalin Island to Japan (now commonly known as the Northern Territories or Kurile Islands). Manchuria was nominally restored to China.

Domestically, the public was furious at the peace settlement, which did not produce any indemnity or territorial gain as expected. The nationalist rallies turned violent, leading to massive riots in Tokyo. After the war, popular unrest grew more common. Besides the nationalists, socialists became increasingly militant and radical. In 1910, the authorities arrested and executed socialist sympathizers in the High Treason Incident for their plot to assassinate the emperor. In 1911, a Special Higher Police was established. Known as the "Thought Police," they were responsible for investigating and controlling political groups and ideologies deemed a threat to internal security.

After the Russo-Japanese war, Japan tightened its control over Korea. In November 1905, it forced Korea to become a protectorate. In 1910, Japan formally annexed the whole Korean peninsula as its second colony with no international opposition.

Ascendancy and Defeat: 1912–1945

Because of its alliance with Great Britain, Japan joined World War I (1914–1918) on the side of the allies. It declared war on Germany and seized German-leased territories in Shandong Peninsula in China. World War I provided a welcome boost to the Japanese economy, enabling it to fill the market gap left vacant by the warring European powers. The short supply of German drugs, fertilizers, and dyes offered the Japanese chemicals industry an opportunity to expand to meet the market demand. Its iron- and steel-making capacity was also enhanced. By 1920, the industrial share of the Japanese gross domestic product (GDP) had surpassed the agricultural sector.

At the Paris Peace Conference that ended World War I, Japan was recognized as one of the "Big Five," along with Great Britain, the United States, France, and Italy, and obtained a permanent seat in the Council of the League of Nations.

Taisho Democracy, 1924–1932. The Meiji Constitution emphasized imperial sovereignty, not popular sovereignty. Hence, political parties and elected politicians had only a minor role in the governmental process. They ruled as partners with other political elites, such as the Meiji oligarchs and their successors, the military leaders, the ranking bureaucrats, and the big businesses. Neither the military nor the bureaucracy was accountable to the Diet. Military leaders could act independently of the prime minister, for they reported directly to the emperor, who was the supreme commander of the military. Similarly, bureaucrats were appointees of the emperor and were insulated from the Diet. In fact, the oligarchs, through their appointment to the Privy Council, helped ensure that the party leaders would not contradict the wishes of nonparty elites.

Despite these limitations, elected politicians in the House of Representatives held the budget power to approve the expenditures and revenues of the government. This power gave political parties in the House crucial leverage to bargain for policies they favored. During the reign of the Taisho emperor (1912–1926), there were signs pointing to change in the direction of democracy. From 1924 to 1932, commonly known as the period of Taisho democracy, the institutions of parliamentary democracy gained ground.

After decades of economic development, Japan was becoming a country of diverse economic and political interests. Export expansion drove up the prices of goods in Japan, and inflation caused riots and disturbances. The country in the 1920s was marked by considerable political debate and social unrest. People demonstrated in the streets. Labor unions were formed; left-leaning movements and activism grew and gained strength. The growing middle class demanded more voices and rights, laborers asked for better working conditions, and farmers petitioned for less onerous taxes. Political parties became the channel for political inclusion and participation. Efforts to institute democracy produced some positive results, such as electing the first commoner as prime minister in 1918 and extending suffrage to all males over age 25 in 1925.

The liberalization trends, however, encountered resistance, too. There was widespread distrust about the political parties and politicians, because of their cozy relations with *zaibatsu*. Corruption in the form of bribes to party officials was common. Conservative groups were also alarmed by the rising appeal of the socialist movement, concerned about the possible breakdown of the social and political order.

In 1925, conservatives enacted the Peace Preservation Law to suppress political dissidents. It banned organizations and movements aimed to "change our national essence (*kokutai*)," a term so broad and vague that it gave the Special Higher Police (the "Thought Police") the power to outlaw virtually any form of dissent.

Military Adventurism, 1932–1945. In the early 1930s, the Great Depression and global protectionism weakened the Japanese economy, causing further labor unrest and social instability. Against this backdrop, ultranationalists and militarists, who were increasingly frustrated with civilian politicians' domestic and foreign policies, began to take actions.

In 1931, officers from the Japanese Guandong Army in the Liaodong Peninsula engineered a bombing incident near Mukden (Shenyang) to create an excuse to invade all of Manchuria. The civilian government was powerless to stop it. Prime Minister Inukai Tsuyoshi tried to control the military, but he was assassinated in May 1932 by a small group of young military officers. By 1932, all Manchuria was under Japanese military control. The Japanese established a puppet state of "*Manzhouguo*" with the last emperor of China, Puyi, as the head of state. In February 1933, after its own investigation, the League of Nations condemned Japan's actions. Japan promptly withdrew from the League.

The Inukai assassination marked the end of the brief period of democracy. From this point on, the military was virtually unchecked. A number of prime ministers emerged from the ranks of army and navy. The military budget was increased greatly, and heavy industries were promoted for war preparation. The military ascendancy eroded the democratic institutions in Japan and took Japan down the path of expansionism.

In July 1937, Japanese and Chinese troops exchanged fire near the Marco Polo Bridge outside Beijing. The armed clash soon escalated into the second Sino-Japanese War (1937–1945). Japan captured Shanghai in August and attacked Nanjing in December.

The occupation of the eastern part of China put a strain on Japan's economy. The need to mobilize resources became urgent as the war progressed. In July 1938, under pressure from the military, the Diet passed the National Mobilization Law, authorizing the bureaucracy to issue orders to control material and human resources at the time of national emergency without the approval of the Diet. This law extended state control over the economy and reoriented the purpose of economic activities from making profit to winning the war. Some businesses were closed down to free up the workers for defense industries, and many people were drafted to work in factories. In October 1940, at the initiation of Prime Minister Konoe Fumimaro, all Japanese political parties merged into a single party, the Imperial Rule Assistance Association, to promote the New Order in Asia. Journalists and politicians made concerted efforts to satisfy the military.

Japan signed a Tripartite Pact in September 1940 with Nazi Germany and fascist Italy to form an alliance. The three countries agreed to assist one another if any of them were attacked by a country not already involved in the war.

Seeking to curb Japanese imperialism, the United States imposed economic sanctions on Japan, including an embargo on oil and steel. In response, Japan attacked Pearl Harbor in December 1941 and extended its sphere of influence into Southeast Asia in an attempt to establish a Greater East Asia Co-Prosperity Sphere under Japanese control. The ambition to build an empire finally ended in a crushing defeat in 1945.

DISCUSSION QUESTIONS

1. Japan often builds its own identity by mixing foreign ideas and institutions with traditional ones. Give some examples of how some of the ideas and institutions, namely from China, were adapted in premodern Japan.

2. Describe the governance institutions built by Tokugawa shogunate, and explain how they helped maintain its political power.

3. Compare the modernization programs initiated by Japan and China in the 19th century in terms of their scope and depth. How were they different? What explained their differences?

4. After the Meiji Restoration, Japan's rise was followed by wars with China, Russia, and the United States. To what extent can the phenomenon be explained by structural reasons, such as the power transition theory?

5. How did the Meiji oligarchs shape political institutions in the Meiji Constitution? To what extent did the institutional design of the Meiji Constitution contribute to the unchecked rise of militarism?

6

Political Governance in Japan

The U.S.-led Allied forces occupied Japan following its defeat in August 1945 with the U.S. atomic bombings at Hiroshima and Nagasaki. In theory, the occupation was a joint operation by the United States and its allies; in reality, it was almost exclusively an American operation. During the occupation, the Japanese continued to operate the government, but they were subject to American direction and supervision. Policies and programs implemented during that time have had a profound impact on Japan. A series of political and economic reforms created new interest patterns in the society and effectively transformed Japan from an authoritarian regime into a parliamentary democracy. To legitimize and preserve the outcomes of the reforms, a new constitution, drafted by the Americans and remarkably liberal and uniquely pacifist, was promulgated in November 1946 and came into force in May 1947. In the meantime, Japan changed from a defeated enemy to the most important and valued U.S. ally in East Asia. The new constitution and political order seemed to resonate widely with the Japanese people and achieved broad acceptance and support. Yet, throughout the postwar years and even until today, policy debates have centered on the pacifism of the constitution and U.S.-Japan relations, creating division between politicians and political parties.

In the 1950s, labor unrests and ideological conflicts over the constitution and the U.S.-Japan Mutual Security Treaty frequently led to massive demonstrations and violent clashes on the streets, until the ruling Liberal Democratic Party (LDP) built broad social consensus in the early 1960s to steer the country toward economic development. Japan successfully closed productivity and technology gaps with advanced economies during the high-growth era of the 1960s and the 1970s, changing from a low-income state to a mature manufacturing economy with high standards of living. The LDP and the Japanese "developmental state" (Johnson 1982) were credited for their ability to engineer this economic miracle.

In the 1980s, overextended credit expansion and reckless investment led to grossly overvalued property assets and inflated stock prices, forming the "bubble economy," which finally burst in the early 1990s. The imploded asset prices led to an estimated loss of $16 trillion (Kingston 2013), more than four times Japan's 1991 gross domestic product (GDP). This triggered the most serious fiscal and financial crisis and the longest recession in Japan's postwar history. Economic stagnation persisted for the next two decades with weak recovery, deflated commodity and asset prices, falling capital investment, and persistent unemployment.

Even with the prolonged economic malaise, the LDP continues to maintain its political dominance in electoral politics. In fact, the LDP has ruled over Japan since 1955 except for two brief periods (1993–1994 and 2009–2012). Thus, the quality of Japan's governance has been closely associated with the strengths and weaknesses of the LDP government. What accounts for the LDP's success? What explains its opposition's failure? This chapter will review postwar Japan's party systems and the evolution of its governing institutions to shed some light on these questions.

OCCUPATION AND RECONSTRUCTION: 1945–1952

Rebuilding the Governance Foundation

Ideas of Democracy and Pacifism. President Harry S. Truman appointed General Douglas MacArthur as the Supreme Commander of the Allied Powers (SCAP, a term often used to refer more generally to the occupation authorities) and head of the Allied occupation of Japan. When the occupation troops arrived in Japan, they found the country in ruins and people in despair. Wartime destruction had heavily damaged the country's economic infrastructure, and political leadership were demoralized and discredited. The SCAP moved quickly to rebuild postwar Japan along the lines of democratization and demilitarization.

The goal of democratization began with the drafting of a new constitution. The Meiji Constitution of 1889, largely modeled after the Prussian system, was built on the principle of imperial sovereignty. The emperor held the ultimate source of sovereignty, and his authority was considered "sacred and inviolable." He had the sole power to appoint cabinet ministers, enter into treaties, and make emergency decrees. In fact, the constitution was presented as a gift from the emperor to the people; only the emperor could amend the constitution. The SCAP helped draft a new constitution to remove authoritarian aspects of the Meiji Constitution and to institute democratic principles to represent the will of the people.

Drafting a new constitution was only the first step toward developing a democracy. To promote democratic values and ideals in the Japanese culture, the SCAP also undertook sweeping reforms in the political, economic, and educational systems. Broad social engineering included unionizing labor, liberalizing education, enfranchising women, establishing an effective judicial system to protect human rights, redistributing lands, and dismantling the *zaibatsu* (powerful financial and industrial conglomerates that had worked closely with the military during the war). Altogether, the reforms aimed to benefit a broad array of groups and social strata that would have a vested interest in supporting and sustaining the liberal and democratic order.

Political parties that had been banned in the prewar era were revived, including the Socialist Party and the Communist Party. The reconstitution and reshuffling of the parties was, in part, encouraged by the occupation authorities, whose New Deal liberal tendencies favored groups advocating social change.

Nevertheless, the SCAP did very little to change the Japanese civil service that assisted the prewar regime in carrying out programs of economic modernization and total war mobilization. Most of the bureaucrats in the government were kept to help implement the occupation policies and exercised discretion in reorienting programs or reinterpreting policies as they turned directives into concrete plans. As such, they were able to exercise strong influence over the direction of policies and programs during and after the occupation.

As for demilitarization, the SCAP disbanded the imperial military, converted and dismantled the arms industry, and prosecuted those who were guilty of war crimes at the Tokyo War Crimes Tribunal. Article 9 of the Constitution, also known as the Peace Clause, states that Japanese people "forever" renounce war as a "sovereign right" and also renounce "the threat or use of force as a means of settling international disputes." The purpose was to consolidate the goal of democratization and ensure that Japan would not be a military threat to others in the future.

Governing Institutions: A Parliamentary Democracy. The new constitution places sovereignty in the hands of the Japanese people, who elect the members of the Diet (parliament), which is the "highest organ of the state power" and the "sole lawmaking organ of the state." The Diet consists of the lower house, the House of Representatives, and the upper house, the House of Councillors.

The prime minister and the majority of ministers of the cabinet must be selected from among Diet members and are answerable to the Diet. If there is disagreement between the legislative and the executive branches, the prime minister resigns or calls for a general election.

The first postwar election of the House of Representatives took place in 1946. Members were elected from large, prefecture-wide electoral districts; depending on the district size, each district elected two to 14 people, and voters cast two to three votes. The conservative Liberal Party won the election, and Yoshida Shigeru (prime minister 1946–1947 and 1948–1954) formed the cabinet after the election. Yoshida, a former diplomat, kept some distance from the military during the war and was briefly jailed in April 1945 for his call for an early surrender. His antipathy toward war and his knowledge of Western societies made him the perfect candidate for the position in the eyes of the occupation authorities.

The conservative parties, fearful of the rising influence of the leftist parties, reinstituted the 1925 electoral rule with the blessing of the SCAP. The 1925 election system used medium-sized, multimember districts. Each district, depending on its size, would elect three to five members. The electoral system presumably favored the more established parties at the expense of smaller parties like the Communists. Yet, in the general elections of April 1947, the Socialists won a slim plurality and formed a coalition government. Intraparty bickering and political scandal, however, plagued the coalition of the leftist parties, which eventually lost power in 1949 to Yoshida and his Liberal Party.

Yoshida was prime minister and his own foreign minister for most of the occupation years. Although in disagreement with MacArthur on many policies, he managed to cooperate with MacArthur in governing of the country through the early postwar years.

Global Security and the "Reverse Course"

Interaction of International and Domestic Politics. After 1947, the Cold War intensified, and the U.S. geopolitical interest led to a "reverse course" in the policies of the occupation authorities. Containing Communism became a higher priority than reforming Japan. In March 1948, George F. Kennan, the director of the policy planning staff at the Department of State, advocated the early restoration of Japanese power through economic recovery and recommended early termination of war crime trials. U.S. policy toward Japan was hence switched from reforms to recovery. Reform measures were relaxed or abandoned.

Subsequently, a series of domestic and international events made the occupation authorities more determined to accelerate the policy reversal. In the general election of January 1949, although Yoshida's Liberal Party won the majority of the seats, the Communist Party of Japan increased its number of Diet seats from four to 35, showing growing influence and popularity. This heightened concerns in Washington that Japan could be the next target for Communist expansion. In October 1949, the Chinese Communist Party took over the Chinese mainland and established the People's Republic of China. Then, in June 1950, Communist North Korea launched the Korean War by attacking South Korea.

Amid escalating security concerns, the occupation authorities launched a massive "Red Purge" to remove thousands of Communists from the government and business. At the same time, a large number of conservative politicians who were formerly purged for war crimes were allowed to be rehabilitated and to rejoin national and local politics. Hatoyama Ichiro (prime minister 1954–1956), Tanzan Ishibashi (prime minister 1956–1957), and Kishi Nobusuke (prime minister 1957–1960) were a few examples.

The "reverse course" had an enormous impact on Japanese politics. With the return of the rehabilitated conservative politicians as leaders, postwar Japanese political parties carried on with their prewar logic and approach. Furthermore, political rivalry between Yoshida and Hotoyama also split the conservative camp. In 1954, Kishi and his faction broke from the Liberal Party to join Hatoyama, forming the Democratic Party. In opposition to Yoshida, they proposed to amend the pacifist constitution to rearm Japan and restore its honor and status. In terms of foreign policy, they advocated a more independent foreign policy vis-à-vis the United States.

The Korean War. The outbreak of the Korean War in June 1950 profoundly altered Japan's postwar status, changing it from an American enemy to ally.

First, Yoshida used the Korean War as a lever to forge a new partnership with the United States. His vision, later called the Yoshida Doctrine (Sugita 2016), was to form an alliance with the United States for economic development and security protection. He believed that Japan should focus exclusively on economic development, for a speedy economic recovery could help Japan regain major power status. In political and security affairs, Japan should follow U.S. leadership as much as possible, without being involved in world politics. In essence, Yoshida outlined an economy-first policy for Japan.

As the staging ground for United Nations and U.S. troops in Korea, Japan was embraced as a "bastion of democracy in East Asia." In September 1951, with the signing of the San Francisco peace treaty that formally ended the war, Japan was welcomed back into the international community. Immediately after the peace treaty ceremony, the United States and Japan signed a Mutual Security Treaty to permit an American military presence in Japan.

Second, the Korean War boosted Japan's economy. Special procurement orders from the U.S. Army for war materials, as well as other goods and services to support the soldiers in the Korean Peninsula over the three-year period of the war, helped Japan revive its key industries. The inflow of U.S. dollars, equivalent to one-third of Japan's foreign income at that time, stabilized Japan's economic condition. By the end of the Korean War, Japan had returned its industrial production to prewar levels. Yoshida privately called such an economic stimulus "a gift from the gods."

Third, the Korean War led to a limited rearmament of Japan. SCAP pressured Japan to take on significant rearmament to protect itself so that the bulk of the occupation troops could be deployed to Korea. Yoshida, however, objected to large-scale remilitarization. Politically, he understood that repealing the pacifist constitution would set off a huge political storm and energize the left-wing forces. Economically, it would be less expensive for Japan to rely on U.S. protection rather than have a full military buildup. Thus, his support for pacifism was based on realist calculations.

In July 1950, Yoshida agreed to form a 75,000-person National Police Reserve, expanding it to the National Security Forces of 110,000 people in 1952 and the Self-Defense Forces (SDF) in 1954. Within the constraints of Article 9, the SDF could not participate in any collective security arrangements or be sent abroad.

GOVERNANCE UNDER THE 1955 SYSTEM: 1952–1993

Formation of the 1955 System

Ideological Conflicts in the Early 1950s. The party system was highly fractured in the 1946 election, with as many as 33 parties winning at least one Diet seat. Mergers and consolidations since then have gradually reduced the number of political parties. The Japan Socialist Party (JSP), whose roots could be traced back to the Socialist Study Society of 1898, represented the liberal, progressive camp on the left. The majority of its organizational and financial support came from labor unions, with particularly close ties to the more militant Sohyo federation (General Council of Japanese Trade Union) connected to public-sector employees. While its goal was to promote economic equality and worker's rights, the party did not have a coherent ideology.

From 1951 to 1955, the JSP split into a "left faction" and a "right faction." The left faction sought a revolutionary transformation of the capitalist system based on orthodox Marxism and opposed a security alliance with the United States. The right faction accepted reforms within the current economic system and a partial security arrangement with the United States but objected to U.S. military bases in Japan.

Further to the left of the Socialists was the Japan Communist Party (JCP). Founded in 1922 with support from the Soviet Union, it was popular among white-collar professionals and intellectuals such as attorneys and teachers who were drawn to the peace movement. Like the Socialists, there was a division in the JCP between those in favor of violent revolution and those in support of reforms through parliamentary politics. Its small but loyal group of supporters were disciplined and organized, producing consistent turnouts in elections.

On the conservative side stood Yoshida's Liberal Party that dated back to Itagaki's Society of Patriots and the Liberal Party (*Jiyuto*) in the early Meiji Restoration. The term *liberal* was used in its original sense to support liberal democracy, capitalism, and private ownership, rather than the modern meaning of promoting social equality.

Hatayama's Democratic Party was another conservative party. Leaders of the Democratic Party argued vigorously for Japanese rearmament to regain political status for Japan and to establish full independence from the United States as soon as possible. Their state-centered conservatism called for rollbacks of various reform measures, especially in the fields of education, police, and labor, so that the political institutions would be more compatible with the traditional preference for stronger and more centralized state power. Both conservative parties, however, pursued similar tactics in building political coalitions with bureaucracy and big business. Hatoyama led the Democratic Party to become the largest party in Japan after the February 1955 general election.

The 1955 Mergers. In October 1955, the Right Socialist (the moderate wing) and Left Socialist (the revolutionary wing) reunified and recreated the JSP. To check the rise of the Socialists, the conservative Liberal Party and the Democratic Party decided to join forces to form the LDP. The 1955 system was hence established, marked by the ideological split between the LDP and JSP.

The split was reinforced by demographics such as age and education in the 1950s (Watanuki 1967). Young and better-educated voters such as intellectuals, college students, and white-collar professionals were more inclined to vote for left-wing parties, while the older and less educated group, including farmers and self-employed merchants, supported the conservative camp. Besides ideological contention, competition between the LDP and the JSP was also about conservatism versus progressivism and tradition versus modernism.

The liberal and progressive camp was optimistic about its future, projecting that trends of social and economic modernization in Japan would be in its favor. Some also envisioned that the relationship between the LDP and the JSP would evolve into a vibrant two-party system taking turns in organizing the government. These scenarios never materialized. The LDP managed to establish continuous dominance from 1955 to 1993 until the party suffered a major split and was dislodged from power.

Instead of a two-party system, the 1955 system was described as a "One and One Half Party System" (Scalapino and Masumi 1962), with the JSP being the "one half party." In elections, the JSP, at most, could win only one-third of the seats in the House of Representatives, insufficient to mount any serious challenges to the LDP, which regularly controlled about twice as many seats as the JSP. The bitter ideological clashes between the two parties in the 1950s not only led to a decade of political turmoil but also went a long way in shaping their political fortunes thereafter.

Conflicts of Ideas. The reform measures implemented by the occupation authorities, followed by the "reverse course," had intensified the ideological divide between the conservative and the liberal camps. The liberal camp, feeling betrayed by the American reversal, tried to defend the original ideas of peace and democracy, whereas the conservative camp was eager to roll back the "excesses" of occupation reforms. The end of the occupation in 1952 raised the political stakes for both sides, as they strove to turn the political tides in their favor. This set the stage for intense, and sometimes violent, ideological showdowns in Japanese politics.

Political conflicts in the 1950s revolved around two issues—constitution revision and the U.S.-Japan Security Treaty. While there were sharp differences between the left and right, serious divisions also existed within them. Kishi and Hatoyama were both against the pacifist constitution, regarding it as something imposed by MacArthur. Nevertheless, a significant number of LDP members, worried about the excessive political cost of revision, supported the constitution. At Hatoyama's request, an advisory commission on the constitution was formed to study the matter, but the Socialists, who supported the constitution and the postwar reforms, boycotted it. Hatoyama also advocated emergency executive powers in times of crisis to limit civil liberties in hopes of controlling the radical left.

As for the U.S.-Japan Security Treaty and the presence of U.S. troops in Japan, liberals believed that if war broke out between the Soviet Union and the United States, military entanglement with the United States could lead Japan to another war. Furthermore, according to the treaty, crimes perpetrated by U.S. soldiers fell under the jurisdiction of American military justice. This brought back the unpleasant memory of extraterritoriality and the unequal treaties that Japan signed with foreign countries in the 19th century.

In 1957, Kishi succeeded Hatoyama as prime minister and began to aggressively promote revision of the Constitution and the U.S.-Japan Mutual Security Treaty. He organized a Research Council on the Constitution in 1958 to explore options for revision. His idea of expanding police power previously curtailed by the occupation authorities angered the left, leading to protests and demonstrations by workers and students. In 1959, Kishi negotiated in secrecy with the United States to change the terms of the security treaty before it was up for renewal in 1960. In his mind, the renegotiated treaty was an improvement, as it ended extraterritoriality and limited the duration of the treaty to 10 years. To his surprise, it drew strong opposition from the liberal camp, which objected to the fact that American troops would still be allowed to be stationed in Japan.

The liberal camp, mindful of their minority status in the Diet, resorted to extraordinary measures to boycott parliamentary sessions. They organized protests outside the Diet to rally against ratification of the revised treaty, framing the issue as de facto occupation of Japan by the United States and a loss of Japan's national sovereignty. Labor unions, student groups, Communists, Socialists, and even the ultra-right-wing nationalists all actively participated in the massive demonstrations.

In June 1960, Kishi called in the police to drag the JSP members out of the Diet. The LDP members then voted to renew the treaty with no presence of the opposition. The move infuriated the public; hundreds of thousands gathered on the Tokyo streets and surrounded the Diet building, creating one of the most serious political crises in postwar Japan. In the end, Kishi resigned. President Dwight D. Eisenhower, who had planned to visit Japan to celebrate the treaty's renewal, canceled his trip.

Electoral Politics

The opposition parties showed their organizational strength at these mass rallies and demonstrations during the time of ideological clash, but they also reached their peak. Subsequently, the LDP outmaneuvered them in defining national political issues, in delivering tangible policy benefits, and in building electoral support. The LDP demonstrated remarkable flexibility in adapting to change, resetting political agendas, and adopting policies of its opponents. The political climate became calmer, and ideological confrontation was gradually replaced by political accommodation and compromise.

Economic Development. Soon after the 1960 conflict, the LDP leadership, along with the bureaucrats and business leaders, decided to reset the political agenda and reinvent itself as a party with broad appeal. Steering clear of divisive issues such as constitution revision, they re-emphasized economic modernization and development. From that point on, raising standards of living became the mainstay of the LDP platforms and policies. It was an implicit bargain: silencing political opposition with rapid economic growth and development.

Prime Minister Ikeda Hayato (1960–1964), a Yoshida protégé, announced in 1960 the National Income Doubling Plan, aiming to double Japan's personal incomes and gross national product (GNP) in 10 years. The plan proved a great success. Incomes actually doubled in seven years.

Ikeda essentially proclaimed a growth contract between the conservative establishment and the general population. The theme of economic and industrial growth became a new unifying ideology that inspired people to take part in the pursuit of shared growth. With talent and hard work, everyone could enjoy and share in the growing wealth. Economic growth was no longer simply for the sake of reestablishing national status and grandeur. The ensuing success in economic development solidified the LDP's political legitimacy and credibility and helped the party to attract educated urban white-collar workers.

In the 1970s, the LDP once again was effective in managing political issues in response to the changing political environment. As industrialization expanded, environmental destruction caused by irresponsible industries led to pollution-related diseases and health problems for workers and residents. Urbanization also caused affordable housing shortages in major cities, where citizens were also concerned about food safety and quality. The probusiness LDP government was initially passive or unresponsive to these quality-of-life issues. It gave an opening to progressive candidates as they took the lead to propose welfare and environmental initiatives at the local level.

In the late 1960s and early 1970s, progressive politicians began to make significant gains in the urban centers. At one point, major cities in the *Kanto* (Tokyo-Yokohama-Kawasaki), *Chubu* (Nagoya), and *Kansai* (Osaka-Kobe-Kyoto) regions were all headed by progressive mayors or governors. Alarmed by the electoral gains of the progressives, the LDP began to co-opt their policies and initiatives. Prime Minister Tanaka Kakuei (1972–1974) declared 1973 as the "First Year of the Welfare Era" to institute major expansions in elderly care, medical programs, and pension systems. He also strengthened environmental laws, making it easier for victims to seek compensation and medical care. Although the government subsequently had to cut back on the welfare programs because of a significant revenue shortfall caused by the oil crisis of 1973, it was successful in regaining support in urban areas. In the end, the LDP successfully transformed itself from a conservative party to a catchall party that emphasized pragmatism over ideology to maximize support from as many voters as possible.

The U.S.-Japan Mutual Security Treaty was renewed peacefully in 1970 without causing much discontent. No major political controversies ever emerged again to divide the Japanese society as they once did, an indication of the LDP's effectiveness in setting the political agenda and managing issues.

In contrast, parties on the left were struggling to find a theme that could be politically relevant and significant as ideological debates diminished in importance. During the growth spurts of the 1960s and the 1970s, the fruits of economic development were widely shared. An overwhelming majority of Japanese began to think of themselves as part of a large middle class and became less interested in class warfare. Nevertheless, the JSP adhered steadfastly to its Socialist position. Holding onto the belief that peaceful Socialist revolution was inevitable despite the popular perception to the contrary, the JSP adopted "A Road to Socialism in Japan" as the official party line in 1964. The JSP's persistent pursuit of an ideological agenda made it less relevant and attractive to Japanese voters. It did not abandon the Socialist party line until 1986.

From the second half of the 1960s onward, the JSP suffered significant declines in electoral support. The weakening of the JSP also related to the membership decline in organized labor. The proportion of union members among Japanese workers declined from about 35 percent in 1970 to 25 percent in 1990, particularly among the left-wing unions affiliated with *Sohyo*.

LDP's Coalition-Building. Besides the traditional support base of bureaucracy and big business, the LDP ruling coalition included farmers and owners of small and medium-sized enterprises (SMEs). Favorable policies and tangible benefits were provided to these specifically targeted groups to solidify their support.

Over 90 percent of Japanese firms are SMEs with fewer than 300 employees. Many of them were associated with big conglomerates, acting as suppliers or subcontractors in manufacturing, retail, and wholesale. Most of the owners and employees of the SMEs turned out for the LDP, and the LDP government purposely eased their tax burdens and chose not to enforce rules strictly. Tax evasion by SMEs was widespread.

Policy benefits were also extended to farmers, who were staunch supporters of the LDP. Throughout the 1950s, the LDP government collaborated with large agricultural cooperatives in the countryside to purchase rice at inflated prices to win over the farmers. In return, the agricultural cooperatives mobilized votes for the LDP candidates at elections. In 1961, the LDP government instituted subsidies, import controls, and additional price support through the Basic Law on Agriculture to expand its protection of farmers. Despite intense pressure from the United States and other trading partners for Japan to open its agricultural market to foreign imports, the LDP government would not renounce these protectionist measures.

Construction projects and infrastructure programs were another way for the LDP government to secure rural support. Public works expenditures as a share of GNP were two to three percentage points higher in Japan than in Western advanced economies from the 1970s to the 1990s (Higuchi 2008). Financed mostly by urban tax money, these pork-barrel policies, in essence, transferred wealth from city to countryside to solidify the LDP's rural support.

Malapportionment (i.e., making districts unequal to prevent equitable representation) further enhanced the LDP's rural advantage (Christensen and Johnson 1995). As rural populations moved to cities at the time of rapid industrialization and urbanization, the LDP government was slow to reallocate Diet seats from the rural areas to the growing urban centers, despite rulings from the Japanese Supreme Court that the imbalance was unconstitutional. Rural districts were consistently apportioned more legislators per capita than urban areas, yet only one-third of the votes were needed to elect a candidate in rural areas compared to those in urban districts (Krauss and Pekkanen 2008). Combined with the LDP's rural strength, malapportionment created a large number of safe seats for the LDP beyond the reach of the opposition parties. Thus, the overrepresentation of the rural districts in the House of Representatives further strengthened the LDP's hold on power.

Fragmentation of the Opposition. Division within the opposition also contributed to the LDP dominance. The moderate faction of the JSP, mainly members of the former Right Socialist, left the JSP in 1960 to form the Democratic Socialist Party (DSP). It advocated democratic socialism and supported the U.S.-Japan alliance. In 1962, the moderate federations of the labor unions (Sodomei and Zenro) formed the Domei (All Japan Labor Federation) to support the DSP.

Komeito (or the Clean Government Party) was formed in 1964. It drew support from a popular new Buddhist sect called *Soka Gakkai* (i.e., the Value Creation Society). Although the party maintains an ostensible separation from the religious organization due to the principle of separation of religion and state in the constitution, the two are closely connected. Komeito positioned itself between the LDP and JSP and offered a moderate, centrist alternative to voters. It supported the pacifist constitution and the capitalist system. With many of its supporters being the lower middle class in urban areas, it advocated stronger welfare programs and eradication of corruption. It soon became the third largest political party in Japan.

JSP, DSP, Komeito, and the JCP were the core of the opposition to the LDP in the 1955 system. They competed for all the anti-LDP votes, yet none of them could be seen as a credible alternative to the LDP. For nearly four decades, the opposition parties were frustrated by their inability to shake the LDP dominance. They were practically reduced to checking government excesses, as the possibility of forming an alternative government was quite slim.

The Electoral System and Money Politics

Under the 1955 system, the electoral system for the House of Representatives consisted of multimember districts. Each district, depending on its size, typically elected two to five Diet members. Despite the fact that constituencies elected more than one Diet member, voters had only one vote in this kind of single, nontransferrable vote system.

From the party's perspective, to win a majority of seats in the Diet, it would have to win a majority of seats in districts. Thus, the LDP usually had multiple candidates running against one another in the same district to compete for votes, and the LDP supporters could choose only one of the candidates. Thus, multimember districts created interesting problems for voters and candidates.

Money Politics. The multimember electoral system was often criticized for promoting factionalism and corruption in Japanese politics. Anticipating intense intraparty competition in elections, potential candidates found it beneficial to join a faction within the party and seek sponsorship from a senior, established faction leader who could provide contacts and connections for them. Once elected, they would continue receiving help from their faction leader through committee assignments and party posts.

Additionally, when campaigning against fellow party members, candidates had to build their own personal support groups (*koenkai*) and maintain a core of loyal supporters. Cultivating and nurturing personal relations with *koenkai* members required large sums of money. Faction leaders usually raised money from business donors and then distributed funds to their faction members.

The need for a large amount of campaign funds could easily lead to under-table deals and corruption scandals. To fund the *koenkai* and election campaigns, faction leaders and individual Diet members were under constant pressure to raise money from business groups, local or national. In return, business interest groups enjoyed a cozy working relationship with politicians. Factional politics and money politics thus created "structural corruption" (Johnson 1995).

Under the 1955 system, money politics was a prevalent feature of Japanese politics. Hardly a decade went by without some major corruption scandal: the "black-mist" scandals in the 1960s, the shipbuilding scandal and the Lockheed scandal in the 1970s, and the Recruit scandal in the 1980s.

The Case of Tanaka. Prime Minister Tanaka Kakuei's career path illustrates how LDP politicians interacted with their constituents and how money politics worked in Japanese politics. Unlike many of his predecessors, Tanaka came from a humble background without even finishing high school. He made his fortune in construction, and his business connections helped him raise money and expand personal networks for his political career.

Given his construction background, he was one of the architects of the "construction state" (*doken kokka*) with a vision to "remodel the Japanese archipelago" through massive infrastructure projects such as an atomic power plant, the new Tokyo International Airport in Narita, an undersea tunnel linking Hokkaido Island to the main island of Honshu, and many others.

As he rose in the LDP party ranks, he was chosen for several key cabinet posts, including the most powerful positions such as the minister of finance, minister of posts and telecommunications, and minister of international trade and industry. At the time when Japan's economy was taking off, these political offices helped him bring more benefits to his home prefecture, the construction industry, and himself.

Tanaka built a huge local support group in his rural home prefecture Niigata and was responsive to the residents' requests for patronage and government-funded pork-barrel projects. Massive public works projects were brought to his home prefecture, including a highway, a tunnel, and *shinkansen* (high-speed rail line) between Tokyo and Niigata at a cost of millions of dollars per kilometer. These construction projects not only helped raise living standards for his home region but also offered business opportunities for his former business partners, who in turn contributed to Tanaka's coffers.

He then spread money around in support of young candidates. Over the years, Tanaka gathered large sums of money for aspiring Diet members to build up his own faction. He took care of them and made sure that they were appointed to important posts.

In 1974, the Japanese media reported on Tanaka's questionable land deals. His LDP rivals seized the opportunity and opened a public inquiry in the Diet that eventually led to his resignation as prime minister. Yet he remained a Diet member and the leader of his faction. In 1976, U.S. congressional investigations of corrupt U.S. overseas business practices revealed that several Japanese government officials, including Tanaka as prime minister, had received large bribes from the American airplane manufacturer Lockheed in return for their support of a large sale to Japan's SDF.

The Japanese prosecutors indicted Tanaka, along with 15 other people. As the Lockheed trial dragged on, he continued to receive overwhelming support in his constituency. His faction grew from 70 plus members prior to his 1976 arrest to 150 by 1981, becoming the largest faction, with more than one-third of the LDP Diet members.

Tanaka was found guilty in 1983, seven years after the indictment, and was sentenced to four years in prison. He refused to resign from his Diet seat and decided to appeal his conviction. His action drew strong reactions from the opposition parties, which demanded a vote to remove him from office. Prime Minister Nakasone Yasuhiro, elected because of the support from Tanaka's faction, declined to do so. The subsequent monthlong boycott by the opposition parties forced Nakasone to dissolve the Diet and call for a new election in December 1983.

Tanaka won the election—for the 15th time—by an unprecedented margin in December 1983, receiving the most votes in his entire career. Two years later, he suffered a paralyzing stroke but continued to exercise power behind the scenes. His poor health eventually forced him to relinquish his control of his faction to others, who themselves became embroiled in corruption scandals of their own. Tanaka died in December 1993.

More Scandals and Little Action. The 1989 Recruit Scandal was another corruption case that further shook public confidence in the LDP government. The Recruit company gave Diet members generous political contributions, cheap loans, and, in particular, company shares prior to its public offering. The company's share prices soared after it went public; all recipients made a quick and handsome profit. After this "stock-for-favors" scandal broke out, some 20 Diet members, including Prime Minister Takeshita Noboru and his predecessor, Nakasone, resigned over their involvement in Recruit. The scandal, among other things, contributed to the LDP's stunning loss in the 1989 House of Councillors election. The LDP, for the first time, lost the majority in the upper house.

Afterward, some LDP reformers sought to initiate reforms to curb corruption, but the LDP leadership was slow in delivering reform. Strong resistance came from the LDP factions and their *koenkai* supporters, as the adjustment of districts would inevitably affect the existing *koenkai*. The need for consensus among faction leaders prevented any significant policy initiatives from happening.

In the meantime, new scandals continued to emerge. Prime Minister Uno Sosuke, the successor of Takeshita, was brought down by a sex scandal after only two months in office. Then, in 1992, it was revealed that Sagawa Kyubin, a parcel-delivery company, donated illegally to approximately 200 Diet members and leading local politicians, with the largest sum going to vice president of the LDP Kanemaru Shin, a career politician and longtime Tanaka follower. Sagawa had also helped Kanemaru establish contacts with one of Japan's leading organized crime syndicates. He was forced to resign for violating the 1975 Political Funds Control Law by not reporting the contributions. Yet charges against most other Diet members were dropped as there was no documented evidence for the causal relationship between contributions and favorable policy decisions.

Again, the LDP was slow to enact any reform proposal, despite promises from two consecutive LDP prime ministers—Kaifu Toshiki (1989–1991) and Miyazawa Kiichi (1991–1993)—to make electoral reform their top priority. Miyazawa insisted that the scandal was caused by corrupt individuals, not by a corrupt system.

Mismanagement of the Bubble Economy

The LDP government was also indecisive and ineffective in handling the economic trouble of the 1980s. Despite the oil crises of 1973 and 1979, Japan's economy continued to perform well into the early 1980s. Its large trade surplus with the United States and other trading partners, however, led to many anti-Japanese comments and actions in the West.

To address this trade imbalance, the financial leaders of the G-5 nations (i.e., France, Germany, Japan, the United Kingdom, and the United States) convened a meeting in 1985 at New York's Plaza Hotel and agreed to devaluate the dollar relative to the yen. The yen rose and doubled its value in three years, but the appreciation of the yen against the dollar did little to redress the U.S. trade deficit. Contrary to American expectations, American goods did not make significant inroads into Japan.

Trying to ease the pressure of the appreciating yen on business, and to stimulate domestic demands, the Japanese government decided to keep interest rates at a low level at home. Low-interest loans were made available to corporations, who in turn used the nearly free money to speculate on real estate and stock markets. The price of land, which was used as collateral against loans, soared to absurd levels. At one point, the paper value of the land in the immediate vicinity of the Imperial Palace in Tokyo reportedly was the same as all of California. These inflated asset values created the "bubble economy" of the 1980s.

Beginning in 1989, the LDP government took a series of actions to curb inflation. The central bank rate was raised five times from 2.5 percent (May 1989) to 6 percent (August 1990). The abrupt and drastic measures popped the economic bubble: the stock market plummeted, and asset prices collapsed. The sudden loss of trillions of dollars of value led to a steep decline in consumption and consumer confidence, and the economy entered into a deep recession. The government then reversed its actions in 1991 to revive the economy. However, none of the stimulus measures worked. The country's growth engine failed to restart, throwing the economy into prolonged stagnation. Corruption scandals and economic mismanagement raised serious questions about LDP leadership. Deeply disappointed by the inability of the LDP leadership to deal with the issues promptly and effectively, the public was ready for a change.

THE 1993 SYSTEM: 1993–PRESENT

Formation of the 1993 System

A period of turbulent change in Japan's party system began in 1993 with a split in the LDP. The collapse of the 1955 system ended nearly four decades of predictable routines and brought new dynamics to Japanese politics. Since then, a number of "reform parties" have emerged to respond to popular calls for clean politics and effective leadership in the post–Cold War international environment. While parties positioned on the left (i.e., Communist), the right (the LDP), and the center (Komeito, renamed New Komeito in 1998) remained essentially the same, a series of party splits, mergers, and transformations have occurred, and may continue to occur, indicating that the new system is still fluid and evolving.

The Downfall of the LDP in 1993. In May 1992, Hosokawa Morihoro, a former LDP Diet member and prefectural governor, launched the Japan New Party in protest of the corruption scandals. In June 1993, when the opposition parties introduced a vote of no confidence to oust LDP Prime Minister Miyazawa, a group of LDP Diet members, led by Ozawa Ichiro (also a Tanaka protégé), joined the opposition and supported the no confidence vote. The Miyazawa cabinet lost the vote and was forced to call an election.

More than 50 LDP Diet members then left the party to join the Japan New Party, or to form the Japan Renewal Party (*Shinseito*) and the New Party Harbinger (*Shinto Sakigake*). The Japan Renewal Party had more Diet members, and some were prominent leaders of the LDP's younger generation. All three parties promoted reform, supporting measures to end corruption.

In the July 1993 general election, the three new parties together won over 100 seats. Ozawa worked behind the scenes to build a seven-party coalition to form a government under Hosokawa, ending the continuous dominance of the LDP and the 1955 system.

In less than a year, Hosokawa was forced to resign in April 1994, partly because of a corruption scandal, partly because of the difficulty in maintaining a unified position on key reform measures. Though short-lived, the Hosokawa coalition government was able to pass a reform package, including new electoral rules, regulations of political donations, and public funding for political parties. The strong public support behind these reform measures made it difficult for any politicians to publicly oppose them, in fear of being labeled as obstructionist.

The New Electoral System. In 1994, Japan adopted a mixed-member majoritarian (MMM) electoral system that combines single member districts (SMDs) and proportional representation (PR). On election day, voters may cast two ballots, one for a candidate in the SMD and one for a party in the PR region. The 300 SMD seats (reduced to 295 in 2014 and 289 in 2017) are elected by a plurality first-past-the-post system, whereas 200 PR seats (reduced to 180 in 2014 and to 176 in 2017) are elected from 11 multimember regional districts. Prior to the election, the political parties rank order their candidates in each region, and the seats are allocated according to the party's proportional vote and the candidates' ranking on the list.

Candidates in this new system can run in an SMD and be on the PR list at the same time. SMD winners can then have their names taken off the party's PR list. Those who lose in an SMD may still be elected to the Diet if they win in the PR region. In the SMD, conservative candidates from the LDP would no longer compete against each other. The non-LDP opposition parties could also cooperate in coordinating their nominations at the district level to avoid vote fragmentation.

The hybrid system provides mixed incentives for political parties. The plurality requirement makes it difficult for smaller parties to survive and win in the SMDs, hence it encourages them to consolidate in the direction of a two-party system. Yet the PR formula pulls political parties in an opposite direction by encouraging smaller parties to resist mergers and retain their own identities. Thus, due to these contradicting forces, smaller parties continue to find sufficient reasons to form in the postreform era.

Regulating Political Finance. Campaign fund-raising and political finance in Japan are regulated by three important pieces of law (Woodall 2015): the Public Offices Election Law, the Political Parties Subsidy Law, and the Political Funds Control Law. Japan has had strict rules on political campaigns. The 1994 revision of the Public Offices Election Law retained most of the restrictions, including limits on the official campaign period (12 days before the election), media access, campaign literature, offices, and expenditures. The new provision added a guilt-by-association clause to void election results if a candidate's aides or family members engaged in vote-buying activities. The enormous restrictions on voter outreach, however, encouraged the candidates to continue to rely on traditional practices such as *koenkai* as an important aspect of their campaigns (Christensen 1998).

Under the Political Party Subsidy Law, enacted in 1994, all political parties with at least five members in the Diet, or 2 percent of the popular vote in the most recent lower or upper house elections, are entitled to government funding. The pool of public funds is assessed on the basis of ¥ 250 per citizen and distributed to qualifying parties according to their representation in the Diet. This system of subsidies to political parties aims to ease pressures on political fund-raising and to prevent corrupt exchanges between politicians and businesses.

At the same time, the rules on political donations have changed. The 1994 revision of the Political Funds Control Law tightened restrictions on fund-raising. Political fund-raising responsibility was shifted from individual politicians to parties. Individual politicians and their funding organizations could no longer accept donations from private groups such as corporations and labor unions; the donations are now required to go to political parties. Previously, politicians could create several political organizations to evade the maximum limit of donations from a single source. The new law allows politicians to form only one political funding organization.

Realignment of Political Parties

The Demise of the JSP. In June 1994, JSP president Murayama Tomiichi (1994–1996) formed a coalition government with his longtime rival party, the LDP, and became the prime minister. In retrospect, the Socialist-LDP marriage of political convenience damaged the Socialists more than the LDP.

The JSP traditionally drew electoral support from its position as a defender of the pacifist constitution. In July 1994, Murayama reversed the Socialist position, declaring in the Diet that the SDF were constitutional. The Socialist party approved Murayama's position two months later, abandoning the longstanding position of unarmed neutrality. The party lost the 1995 House of Councillors election and changed its name to the Social Democratic Party (SDP) in 1996. Most of its Diet members left the JSP and joined the newly created Democratic Party of Japan. The SDP soon suffered a disappointing defeat in the 1996 general elections. By the late 1990s, it lost its status as a major opposition force.

The Rise and Fall of the Democratic Party of Japan. Another important development in the 1993 system was the launch of the Democratic Party of Japan (DPJ). Founded in 1996, it soon attracted defectors from the LDP and the JSP and received full organizational support from Rengo (Japan Trade Union Confederation, established in 1989 by a merger of the two national groups of labor unions, Sohyo and Domei). In 1998, the party merged with four smaller parties and was later joined by a fifth grouping. In the 2000 elections, it grew to become the largest opposition party, primarily at the expense of the JSP/SDP.

Although most of the party leadership is comprised of former centrist or center-right LDP lawmakers, the regular members, including a number of former JSP members, have a left-of-center political orientation. Not surprisingly, the amalgamated nature of the DPJ has led to considerable internal contradiction, primarily between the party's hawkish/conservative and pacifist/liberal wings. Nevertheless, the DPJ was able to present a unified front to win a resounding majority in the 2009 House of Representatives election (308 out of 480 seats). It was the first time that the LDP failed to win a plurality of seats in the lower-house election and the second time it did not act as the ruling party.

During the DPJ's three-and-a-half years in office, however, it failed at governing the country. The party was embroiled in controversy and instability, leading to a rapid turnover of three different prime ministers and finally a landslide defeat by the LDP in 2012.

The DPJ lost again in the 2014 House of Representatives election and continued to struggle over its future direction. In March 2016, DPJ and several fragmented opposition parties reorganized the party as the Democratic Party (DP). In the run-up to the October 2017 House of Representatives election, DP leadership dissolved the DP caucus, in an attempt to coordinate campaigns with rising politician Koike Yuriko, Tokyo's first female governor and former LDP member. Some DP members joined the Koike's Party of Hope, founded in September 2017. Others joined the left-leaning Constitutional Democratic Party (founded in October 2017 by Edano Yukio, a DP member); still others ran as independents. It remains to be seen whether the fragments of the DP can be reunited.

The LDP–New Komeito Coalition. Komeito rebranded as the New Komeito in 1998. In 1999, the New Komeito joined the LDP to form a governing coalition, which lasted for a decade until the LDP lost to the DPJ in 2009. The partnership resumed after the LDP returned to power after 2012. Since then, the LDP scored victories in the House of Representatives elections (2014 and 2017) and House of Councillors elections (2013 and 2016). The wins have resulted in a stable two-thirds majority in coalition with Komeito.

Despite their differences in political ideologies and party platforms, the two parties supported each other in election campaigns. The rural strengths of the LDP complemented the Komeito's urban advantages, as Komeito supporters would mobilize votes for LDP candidates in rural SMDs, while the LDP would choose not to run candidates against the Komeito in some urban districts. Additionally, the Komeito provided the critical support for the LDP to secure the majority in the Diet for some controversial bills. While the Komeito lost its independence on foreign and national security policies, its status was elevated from a perpetual opposition party to part of an enduring ruling coalition. In the 2015 legislation on SDF engagement in collective defense, Komeito used its position to ensure that SDF dispatches must be consistent with international law, must have Diet approval, and will not be in areas of active combat.

Governance under Koizumi

While the 1993 downfall of the LDP created different factions of "reformers" (mostly former LDP politicians), none of them was able to replicate the

LDP's broad base of support or displace its dominance. The LDP regained control of the government in 1996 when Prime Minister Hashimoto Ryutaro replaced Murayama to form the first exclusively LDP cabinet since 1993.

In April 2001, the charismatic LDP politician Koizumi Junichiro (prime minister, 2001–2006) was elected as party president and prime minister. Domestically, he undertook revolutionary measures to attack entrenched economic interests. Internationally, he closely followed U.S. foreign policy after the 9/11 terrorist attacks and sought to make Japan a "normal state" in its participation in world affairs and collective security. During his five-year tenure, he enjoyed almost unprecedented popularity.

To revitalize the Japanese economy, Koizumi initiated economic reforms to promote deregulation and privatization. The enactment of the Dispatch Worker Law (2004) allowed labor brokers to send temporary workers to fill job needs. The measure reduced the protection of the regular employees and provided labor market flexibility. He also reduced agricultural subsidies. Although the goal was to enhance market competition, Koizumi's neoliberal economic deregulations amid prolonged economic recession created anxiety and insecurity for these economic groups.

Another important piece of Koizumi's reforms was the privatization of the postal service, which, since the Meiji era, had provided a system of secure savings accounts and life insurance to millions of people. The massive assets under its control (about $3 trillion) had offered cheap capital to the government's Fiscal Investment and Loan Program (FILP), also called the "second budget," for public investments. Patronage and nepotism, however, made the system grossly inefficient.

In August 2005, Koizumi's privatization plan was defeated in the Diet due to considerable defection from the LDP. He responded by calling a snap election in September, appealing directly to voters for support. He recruited a group of newcomers, called by the media "Koizumi's assassins," to run against the Diet members who had opposed privatization. Though disliked and distrusted by many LDP political figures, Koizumi successfully appealed to the public over the LDP machine. Koizumi and his "assassins" won a landslide victory. The postal reform bill passed the Diet a month later.

Koizumi strongly supported the United States in the wake of the September 11, 2001, terrorist attacks. He sent Japanese SDF to Afghanistan and subsequently Iraq, promoting a more assertive role for Japan as a U.S. military ally. In 2001, two Japanese destroyers and a supply ship were sent to the Indian Ocean, providing logistical support to UN troops. In 2004, Japanese soldiers were sent to southern Iraq to rebuild the infrastructure and water supply in that region. He argued that because Japan was not sending armed troops abroad, the actions did not violate Article 9 of the Constitution.

In Asia, however, his neonationalist stand drew strong protests from South Korea and China. Koizumi visited the Yasukuni Shrine every year when he was in office, despite the fact that some war criminals were also enshrined there. No other prime ministers had so consistently emphasized the importance of visiting the shrine as the way to honor the dead from the war. He also allowed neoconservatives within the LDP to try to revise school textbooks.

Koizumi voluntarily stepped down in September 2006 and was succeeded by his protégé, Abe Shinzo, the grandson of former Prime Minister Kishi Nobusuke. Abe continued Koizumi's neonationalist ideas. As the first prime minister born after the war, he took minimal responsibility for Japan's wartime atrocities such as the "comfort women" and campaigned on revising Article 9 of the Constitution. Under the Abe administration, the Defense Agency was upgraded to the Defense Ministry and the Self-Defense Forces Law was revised, making participation in UN peacekeeping operations one of the SDF's primary activities.

The Abe administration was beleaguered by a report of missing pension records. An estimated 50 million public pension records had gone missing or were falsified while Abe was in office. The pension records of 20 million people nearing retirement were thus invalidated, and the government had made attempts to cover up the mistake. The public was outraged by the LDP and the elite bureaucracy. Several cabinet members had to resign because of scandals or controversial remarks.

Before the July 2007 upper-house elections, Ozawa (who joined the DPJ in 2003) traveled throughout Japan to win support from groups such as farmers and wage earners who had been negatively affected by Koizumi's neoliberal reforms. Striking a populist tone, Ozawa blamed the LDP for causing the widening gap between rich and poor. In the July 2007 upper-house elections, the DPJ won a plurality and became the largest party in the House of Councillors. Abe initially stayed in power even after the defeat but announced his resignation in September for health reasons. The next two cabinets were short-lived. Prime Minister Fukuda Yasuo (the son of Fukuda Takeo) resigned a year in office, unable to overcome the political battle with the DPJ in the House of Councillors. His successor, Aso Taro (the grandson of Yoshida Shigeru), lasted less than one year and resigned after the loss of the August 2009 general election.

Governance under the DPJ Administration

The DPJ put forward a comprehensive manifesto, a 23-page document that made specific promises to voters, such as exercising greater control of the bureaucracy, eliminating highway tolls, giving parents childcare subsidies, providing new income support for farmers, and offering incentives for small businesses. These campaign promises served to project the DPJ's image as the champion of social justice and supporter of welfare capitalism. In comparison, the LDP campaign emphasized its progrowth tradition.

Against the backdrop of the 2008 global financial crisis, and the long economic contraction since the early 1990s, the DPJ promises were particularly attractive to the Japanese voters. Before the bubble economy, sustained, robust economic growth was accompanied by equitable income distribution, as the majority of people thought of themselves as middle class. From the mid-1980s to 2000, Japan's Gini coefficient indicated a widening income gap (Arase 2009), rising from 27.8 (below the OECD average) to 31.4 (above the OECD average). Income inequality worsened during the protracted economic recession. Among the OECD countries, Japan ranked fourth in the prevalence of poverty, according to a 2006 OECD report.

In foreign relations, the DPJ in its manifesto pledged to engineer a more equal relationship with the United States to achieve a more autonomous foreign policy strategy and to build closer relations with Asian neighbors. The DPJ was firmly opposed to nuclear weapons and a stronger overseas military role for the SDF.

In the August 2009 general election, the DPJ won 308 out of 480 seats, compared with the LDP's 119. With its coalition partners (the Social Democratic Party and the New People's Party), the DPJ controlled two-thirds of lower-house seats. The DPJ's historic victory gave the party a tremendous opportunity to translate its policy proposals into concrete programs. Yet, for the next three-and-a-half years, the DPJ suffered from the same LDP problem of having rapid turnover of party leaders (Hatoyama Yukio, followed by Kan Naota and Noda Yoshihiko). All held the prime minister position for about a year before leaving the office. Each faced specific problems, but none were able to exercise effective leadership to overcome the challenges.

Hatoyama (the grandson of former Prime Minister Hatoyama Ichiro) campaigned on the pledge to move the Futenma airbase outside of Okinawa altogether if elected. Futenma is a U.S. Marine Corps training base, with about 4,000 American pilots and aircrew. Residents nearby have complained for years about the noise level, and many Okinawans have demanded U.S. troops leave Okinawa altogether. The Futenma issue reflected a broader policy direction of the DPJ leadership, who tried to steer Japan to a more independent foreign policy from the United States. Nevertheless, Hatoyama was unable to convince the United States to renegotiate the relocation of the Futenma base. Various proposals made by cabinet ministers were unacceptable to Americans or Okinawans. Throughout the process, Hatoyama appeared unrealistic and indecisive in international negotiations. The mishandling of the U.S.-Japan alliance over Futenma raised doubts about his leadership. At the same time, he and DPJ Secretary General Ozawa were implicated in financial scandals. After just nine months in office, Hatoyama stepped down. So did Ozawa.

Kan succeeded Hatoyama to become the second DPJ prime minister. Within a year, his administration encountered the crisis of a triple catastrophe—an earthquake, tsunami, and nuclear accident. On March 11, 2011, a massive earthquake measured at magnitude 9.0 struck off the coast of the remote northeastern region of Japan. It was the largest earthquake ever recorded in Japan and triggered a tsunami that killed 20,000 people and reduced dozens of coastal communities to rubble. Compounding the disaster, the earthquake destroyed the cooling system of a nuclear power facility in the Fukushima Daiichi (Fukushima Number One) plant, causing explosions, a meltdown of fuel rods, and the release of massive radioactive substances into the air and water that decimated the economic basis of a wide area for years to come. The direct damage by the earthquake and tsunami was estimated to be \$210 billion, making it the most expensive calamity ever for Japan.

As the crisis unfolded, the miscommunication and distrust between the government and the Tokyo Electric Power Co. (TEPCO) led to Kan's frequent intervention in details of the emergency rescue that created further confusion and chaos. In reaction to the lax government supervision and aging nuclear facilities in Japan, Kan advocated replacing nuclear energy with renewable energy. The government, however, did not have a firm plan on how to meet Japan's energy needs with the new option. By focusing exclusively on the nuclear accident in Fukushima, Kan failed to address other aspects of crisis management, such as relief work, cleanup, and recovery. The public dissatisfaction over the nuclear accident and the pace of relief and recovery forced him to step down in August 2011.

Noda, the third prime minister, attempted to focus on recovery from the 2011 disasters. He decided to restart the nuclear reactor that had been shut down since the earthquake, which drew massive antinuclear demonstrations and protests, organized by environmentalists and pacifists. The magnitude of demonstrations reached a level not seen for several decades. To pay for the national budget deficit, particularly the expenditures related to recovery efforts and the DPJ's election promises over social spending, Noda proposed raising the national consumption tax from 5 percent to 8 percent in 2014 and to 10 percent in 2015. After the tax legislation went through in August 2012, Noda's popularity steadily declined.

On December 16, 2012, the DPJ suffered a crushing defeat in the general election. It won only 57 seats, compared to 308 in 2009. In contrast, the LDP won an overwhelming majority of 294 seats, a significant gain from 119. Prior to the election, many of the DPJ Diet members left the party to form new small parties, knowing that the DPJ label meant sure defeat.

Governance under the Second Abe Administration

After the 2012 election, Abe Shinzo won the LDP presidency contest and became the prime minister for a second time. He was the first politician to return to the position of prime minister in the post-occupation era. Since then, he has led the LDP to four electoral victories in the House of Representatives elections (2014 and 2017) and House of Councillors elections (2013 and 2016). While Abe's success came at a time of continued disarray of the opposition parties, he has also demonstrated strong vision and remarkable leadership in governing the country. On November 20, 2019, Abe became the longest-serving prime minister in Japan's parliamentary history.

Abe's Economic Agenda. Abe seemed to have a clear sense of what he would like to accomplish when taking on the prime minister position for the second time. In the realm of economics, Abe aimed to revitalize the Japanese economy with policy measures in sharp departure from the orthodox approaches adopted since the early 1990s. After the burst of the bubble, the Japanese government was unable to find an effective policy mix to take the economy out of the prolonged recession. Knowing the general public's resistance to tax hikes, the government relied on government bonds to cover budget deficits. The extremely large government deficits made it difficult to use fiscal policy to stimulate the economy; furthermore, monetary policy was out of the question, given that interest rates had already been kept very low (close to 0 percent). Thus, from 1991 to 2012, with the exception of the period from 2001 to 2003, the Japanese government adopted an austerity policy emphasizing price stability with low interest rates. Koizumi tried an approach of quantitative easing of money from 2001 to 2003 without much success.

Abe called his economic strategy "Abenomics," which initially comprised three pillars (or "three arrows"): monetary easing, fiscal stimulus, and structural reforms. The monetary policy targeted a 2 percent inflation rate with qualitative and quantitative easing; the fiscal policy involved large-scale increases in public spending; the structural reforms included regulatory and corporate governance reforms.

The initiatives so far have had mixed results. While Japan has had modest growth with falling unemployment, inflation (under 1 percent) has remained below target, and the ratio of outstanding debt to GDP has continued to rise. Progress in structural reforms has been slow, largely due to resistance by certain domestic interests.

Abe's Political Agenda. Abe promoted patriotism and nationalism, arguing that Japan should strengthen the SDF and defend its honor and territory as a full-fledged sovereign country. He questioned the postwar narrative that had portrayed Japan as an aggressor and supported paying tributes to Japan's Yasukuni Shrine, dedicated to those killed in war.

Abe endeavored to build closer relations with the United States, making the U.S.-Japan alliance the core of the Japan security strategy. He took a hard-line policy against China on the Senkaku/Diaoyu Islands in the East China Sea and against South Korea on the Takeshima/Dokdo Islands. He also actively engaged in diplomacy, visiting over 90 countries throughout the world in his first four years since returning as prime minister to help project Japan's image as a contemporary great power.

Abe has accomplished two agenda items that he failed to achieve the first time he was the prime minister: the establishment of a U.S.-style National Security Council (NSC) and the reinterpretation of the Constitution to allow Japan to exercise the right of collective security.

In 2013, Abe's cabinet established the NSC with the goal of strengthening the capability of the prime minister's office for security policy coordination and crisis management. Under the principle of "proactive contribution to peace," the cabinet in July 2014 overturned previous interpretations of

Article 9 and decided that collective self-defense would be permissible under some conditions, one of them being "when an armed attack against a foreign country that is in a close relationship with Japan" poses a clear danger to Japan's own survival.

In September 2015, with the support of the LDP-Komeito majority, the Diet passed the security legislation to expand the role of the SDF abroad. During debates in the Diet, massive demonstrations not seen since the extension of the U.S.-Japan Security Treaty in 1960 gathered in Tokyo and across the nation, even though the government insisted that overseas deployment of the SDF constituted no change in constitutional interpretation of Article 9.

Abe's ultimate goal may be to revise the Constitution. With the supermajority in the Diet, Abe would have met the first requirement of a constitutional amendment: over two-thirds of votes of approval in both houses of the Diet. It is not clear, however, whether Abe can secure a majority of voter support for the constitutional amendment in a national referendum, as stipulated in Article 96 of the Japanese constitution. Over the years, public polls have shown consistently that over 60 percent of voters have been opposed to such revision. It remains to be seen whether the Abe Doctrine will replace the Yoshida Doctrine as the new guiding principle of Japanese foreign and security policy.

GOVERNING INSTITUTIONS

The Japanese Constitution

In early 1946, at the request of SCAP, the Japanese government produced a draft Constitution. Unhappy with the draft, General MacArthur had his staff prepare a more liberal model within a week. After the draft was circulated and debated in the wider political arena, the Diet overwhelmingly approved the new Constitution in October 1946. The new Constitution went into effect in May 1947 and remains in force in Japan today.

The 1947 Constitution was technically an amendment to the Meiji Constitution, since it observed the amendment procedure of the Meiji Constitution. In reality, guided by the twin goals of demilitarization and democratization, it differs in fundamental ways from the Meiji Constitution. First, sovereignty rests with the people rather than the emperor. The emperor is now only the symbol of state, having no powers related to government. His functions are limited to ceremonial ones. The Diet, the popularly elected bicameral parliament, is now the highest organ of state power and the sole lawmaking organ. The Diet selects the prime minister, who in turn forms the cabinet, in which the executive power resides. The prime minister and the cabinet are responsible to the Diet and ultimately to the people.

Second, the 1947 Constitution is more liberal than the U.S. Constitution in terms of its protection of fundamental human rights and individual freedoms. For example, the "freedom of thought and conscience" is guaranteed in the 1947 Constitution—a conception broader in scope than freedom of speech. Similarly, the wide range of rights specified in the Constitution, such as the rights to collective bargaining, full employment, free choice of residence and occupation, academic freedom, sexual equality, and the right to maintain the minimum standard of wholesome and cultured living, reflects the thinking to protect citizens' social and economic rights.

Finally, the 1947 Constitution is pacifist, denouncing Japan's right to war. No other countries have made such declarations. Article 9, known as the Peace Clause, states that "the Japanese people forever renounce war as a sovereign right of the nation and the threat or use of force as means of settling international disputes. In order to accomplish the aim of the preceding paragraph, land, sea, and air forces, as well as other war potential, will never be maintained. The right of belligerency of the state will not be recognized."

The Liberal Democratic Party

The LDP Executives. The LDP has a complicated party organization in part due to the extensive connections it established with interest groups and government bureaucrats. Of all the positions, the most important post is the party president. Given the LDP's ruling party status, whoever holds that position usually serves as the prime minister.

The tenure of the president used to be two three-year terms but was extended to three terms in 2017. The presidential selection, however, has not followed a uniform procedure. Over the years, a variety of methods has been used, including designation by the sitting prime minister, selection by party elders, election by party convention of LDP Diet members and local LDP party representatives, or a primary by rank-and-file party members plus LDP Diet members (Nakamura and Hrebenar 2015). It seems to be based on the special circumstances of each case.

The secretary-general, the second most important post, is responsible for the daily operation of the party as well as fund-raising and candidate selection. The chair of the Executive Council helps formulate the party's basic policies, while the chair of the Policy Affairs Research Council (PARC) is closely involved in policy research and development, making extensive contacts with all the interest groups connected to the LDP. All three positions are important stepping-stones for career advancement to the prime ministership.

The Policy Affairs Research Council. PARC is an important organization within the LDP, where interest groups and bureaucrats meet to negotiate with LDP leaders on policy proposals. Policies approved by the PARC are then sent to the Executive Council for review and approval before final deliberations in the legislative session of the Diet. The PARC was organized in divisions parallel to jurisdictions of cabinet ministries and standing committees of the Diet, with special committees and subcommittees under each division. Attending PARC meetings helps the LDP Diet members accumulate knowledge and experience in specific areas. By virtue of their long tenure, some Diet members who distinguish themselves by developing policy expertise in specific areas are identified as *zoku*, or policy tribes. Those who earn the *zoku* label gain credibility and influence in dealing with bureaucrats in the same policy field. It becomes another venue for politicians to rise to executive positions and exercise influence in policy sectors such as small business, agriculture, foreign policy, and education.

LDP Factions. Factions (*habatsu*) are semi-institutionalized informal organizations within the LDP. These subgroups coalesce around senior politicians and provide practical benefits and career advancement for their members. Factions developed in the aftermath of the 1955 merger that heightened rivalries among leaders between and within the two parties. To improve their chances of being elected LDP president and thus prime minister, senior party leaders began to organize their supporters in the Diet into exclusive factions.

Throughout the history of the LDP, there have been five to 13 different factions at any given time, varying in size from a handful of Diet members to over a hundred. As discussed earlier, faction leaders raise money from business groups and disperse the funds among members to finance their election campaigns and their personal support associations. They also provide members the opportunities to connect with influential bureaucrats and business people. Using their factions as a political base, senior party figures can bargain with other factions for a slate of top government and party appointments.

For followers, besides networking and financial support, joining a faction helps secure their committee assignments, party posts, and government positions. Altogether, the personal ties between LDP Diet members and their faction leaders, along with the extensive connections between LDP Diet members and their constituents, create a powerful, multilayered matrix in which a multitude of people share the common interest in preserving the LDP's political dominance.

Under the 1955 system, every LDP Diet member was typically associated with one of these factions. The percentage of the Diet members affiliated with a faction has declined since the 1993 reforms, but sizable percentages of them (about 60 percent to 70 percent) remain part of a faction. While distribution of factional strength was less of a factor in cabinet selection under Koizumi and Abe, factions are still relevant, particularly in party presidential elections. Securing support from the factions is critical for a candidate to win the LDP presidency.

Koenkai. Of all the democracies, Japanese politics has been considered the most candidate-centered (Reed and Thies 2000). Providing personal favors and services to constituencies and obtaining pork-barrel projects for the local communities were common vote-gathering tactics used by Japanese candidates (Hirano 2006).

Under the 1955 system of multimember districts, LDP candidates often had to run against other LDP candidates in the same district. This added another layer of complexity for campaigning, as the same-party candidates had to differentiate themselves without disagreeing with one another.

To deal with this dilemma, Japanese candidates frequently resorted to personal and parochial mobilization strategies to win voter support. To maintain a core of loyal voters whom they can depend on at election time, party politicians in the latter part of the 1950s gradually developed the personal support association (*koenkai*) and enlisted both ordinary voters and local elites as members. Hosting dinner parties, sponsoring sports tournaments, and subsidizing entertainment and trips helped to cultivate and nurture personal ties with members. Politicians were expected to attend weddings, funerals, and birthday parties of the *koenkai* members and their families and to arrange for generous gifts for the sake of congratulations or condolences. Providing these services to the constituencies usually required *koenkai* to maintain large permanent staffs. Of course, these support networks were two-way streets. For citizens, the *koenkai* also served as a vehicle for contact with the politicians in hopes of receiving service and assistance in times of need.

The 1993 reform package did very little to change this practice. As discussed earlier, the Public Offices Election Law imposes strict rules on campaign activities, hence preventing candidates from making general appeals to voters. They continued to rely on traditional *koenkai* to maintain voter support.

The personal bonds developed from these political networks were so strong and stable that in many cases the electoral base was inherited from the first generation of politicians to the next (Curtis 1971; Ramseyer and Rosenbluth 1993).

The phenomenon of the "hereditary parliamentarians" is an important characteristic of Japanese politics. Many LDP Diet members have been second-, third-, or fourth-generation Diet members. Since the founding of the LDP in 1955, 10 of the 25 LDP prime ministers had fathers or grandfathers as Diet members (Hrebenar and Itoh 2015). Since 1989, eight of the nine LDP prime ministers have been legatees: Miyazawa Kiichi, Hashimoto Ryutaro, Obuchi Keizo, Koizumi Junichiro, Abe Shinzo (twice as prime minister), Fukuda Yasuo, and Aso Taro.

The National Government

The Diet. The Constitution embodies the principle of popular sovereignty by making the Diet the "highest organ of the state power" and the "sole lawmaking organ of the state" (Article 41). Unlike the prewar era when imperial or ministerial ordinances could be prepared and promulgated by the Privy Council and the cabinet, the Constitution vests the whole legislative power in the Diet.

The prime minister and the cabinet are responsible to the Diet. The prime minister and the majority of ministers of the cabinet must be selected from among Diet members. If there is disagreement between the legislative and the executive branches, the prime minister resigns or calls for a general election.

The upper house (the House of Councillors) is slightly less powerful than the lower house (the House of Representatives). It is designed to provide a safety valve to prevent the lower house from moving too quickly or forcefully on legislative matters, interjecting a more reflective and sober perspective. A bill becomes law when it is passed by both houses of the Diet. If the House of Councillors initially rejects a bill, it can still become law if it is subsequently passed by two-thirds of the members of the House of Representatives. If the two houses disagree on treaties, government budget, or the selection of the prime minister, the decision of the lower house is final. Through a nonconfidence vote, the House of Representatives can force the cabinet to resign or call a general election. The House of Councillors can only pass nonbinding resolutions to express its dissatisfaction over the cabinet. To expedite legislative business, each house has 17 standing committees, largely parallel to the various ministries.

The term of office for members of the House of Representatives is four years, but it can be terminated before the full term is up in case the House of Representatives is dissolved. As discussed earlier, the overhaul of the electoral system in 1994 created a mixed electoral system that combines SMDs and PR. As of 2017, the House of Representatives has 465 members, including 289 SMD seats elected by a plurality first-past-the-post system and 176 PR seats elected from 11 multimember regional districts.

The House of Councillors, with no dissolution, has a fixed six-year term. The upper house election is held every three years to elect half of its members (i.e., 121 of the 242 members). Members are elected from different constituencies. For each election, 24 politicians are elected from single-seat constituencies, 49 from multiseat constituencies, and 48 by proportional representation from a single national list. Represented by broader constituencies, members of the House of Councillors are presumed to be above day-to-day politicking, although in practice its composition closely reflects that of the House of Representatives.

The Prime Minister and the Cabinet. According to the Constitution, the prime minister is the head of the cabinet (Article 66), with the power to appoint and remove cabinet members (Article 68). The extent of the prime minister's real power, however, has evolved over the years. Under the 1955 system, the Cabinet Law divided the executive authority among cabinet members and defined the role of the prime minister as a representative of the cabinet, unable to act independently of the cabinet (Shinoda 2013). Constrained by the collective decision of the cabinet, the prime minister could not instruct ministries without the unanimous consent of the entire cabinet. Each minister assumed direct authority over their own ministry, heeding no directives from the prime minister. Without the ability to directly control or supervise each minister, the prime minister had to be a consensus-builder to avoid resistance from his own cabinet.

LDP factions further weakened the position of the prime minister. Although in theory the party leader, the prime minister had very little influence over elections, political appointments, and policy formation—all were presumably key functions of a political party. Campaigning and vote mobilization during elections were conducted at the candidate level through *koenkai*.

Political appointments to party positions and government posts were largely determined by negotiations among factions. Ministerial posts were generally rotated among the factions, irrespective of the backgrounds, credentials, and abilities of the appointees. Policies were decided through extensive prior consultations among bureaucrats, LDP *zoku* members, and organized interests (i.e., the "iron triangle") before being submitted to the cabinet.

Thus, compared with their counterparts in other industrial democracies, Japanese prime ministers, in fact, had very little power. Their tenure in office in large part depended on whether they could keep the coalition of the factions satisfied. As such, they were more inclined to take a conservative, reactive approach rather than a proactive style in policy initiatives. Despite this risk-averse attitude, the turnover rate of the Japanese prime ministers was relatively high. Power struggles between LDP factions frequently lead to the prime minister's downfall and the reshuffling of the cabinet. As pointed out by Shinoda (2013), in the periods of 1955 to 1993 and 1996 to 2009, 22 LDP prime ministers held the office for only 2.3 years on average. It remains to be seen whether Abe's long tenure as prime minister is an aberration or a new trend.

While executive power presumably resided in the cabinet, rarely were important policy decisions made in cabinet meetings. The day before the cabinet meeting, administrative vice ministers, top bureaucrats at the ministries, would hold a subcabinet meeting to prepare and approve the cabinet agenda, which had never been reversed by the cabinet. Therefore, cabinet meetings have only limited effect on policy making.

In recent years, there have been attempts to enhance the powers of the prime minister. The single-member districts implemented by the 1994 electoral reforms eliminated factional competition in the general election, hence weakening the influence of the LDP factions. Furthermore, the 2001 administrative reforms revised the Cabinet Law to give the prime minister clear authority to initiate important, basic policies independent of the relevant ministry. Staffed by experts recruited from the private sector, the newly created Cabinet Office provides administrative support to the prime minister as a source of policy ideas without relying on the bureaucracy. The Council on Economic and Fiscal Policy was instituted as a special cabinet committee chaired by the prime minister to increase the control over economic and fiscal policy.

Evidence so far is mixed as to whether the prime ministership has been strengthened with all the reforms. While Koizumi (2001–2006) and Abe (2012–Present) stayed on as strong leaders for lengthy periods of time, the ones in between (2006–2011) all had short tenures in office.

Ministries and Bureaucracy. Unlike China and Korea, where examination-based bureaucracy has long been part of the dynastic tradition, Japanese bureaucracy was not created until the Meiji era (1868–1912) to modernize Japanese society. Bureaucrats were entrusted with broad regulatory power and administrative discretion in order to rapidly and effectively transform a backward island country into a modern power.

In the postwar era, the occupation authorities undertook a large-scale purge to remove a significant number of politicians from public office. Only 19 percent of the candidates who won the lower house seats in the first postwar election in 1946 had served in that body previously. But the bureaucracy was largely spared by the purge. Although some high officials in the Ministry of Home Affairs and Ministry of Foreign Affairs were removed, the purge was not as intense in other ministries. In fact, the occupation authorities helped open an opportunity for bureaucrats to strengthen their institutional power, as other power contenders, such as senior conservative politicians, were banned from politics. New, younger officials were promoted in the system, giving advice to inexperienced legislators and administering programs for the occupation authorities.

Bureaucratic prominence can be seen by the fact that several of Japan's postwar prime ministers were formerly bureaucrats: Yoshida (1946–1947; 1948–1954), Kishi (1957–1960), Ikeda (1960–1964), Sato Eisaku (1964–1972; Kishi's younger brother; Kishi was born into the Sato family but adopted by an uncle), Fukuda Takeo (1976–1978), and Ohira Masayoshi (1978–1980).

Under the 1955 system, bureaucracy was considered a partner of the LDP in the running of the government. The Diet members rarely introduced legislation. Most bills were advanced by the Cabinet, and the bureaucrats played a pivotal role in planning and drafting them. Nevertheless, the bureaucratic control over policy knowledge was not absolute.

The development of policies and legislation went through an extensive and time-consuming process. Bureaucrats sought approval from the relevant *zoku* members and organized interests before submitting policy or budget proposals to the cabinet. As compromises were made and consensus built, the legislative proposals then went up through bureaucratic channels. By the time they reached the Diet for deliberations, they had gathered enough support and momentum along the way to make it difficult to reverse the policies. This bottom-up policy-making process empowered bureaucrats to play a central role in the political system. At the same time, bureaucrats had wide discretionary power in interpreting and implementing laws.

There has been significant debate as to who has the upper hand in governing Japan—politicians or bureaucrats. The conventional wisdom of Japan's "developmental state" (Johnson 1982) emphasized the autonomy of bureaucrats, whose insulation from political influence gave them the superior ability to plan rationally. From this perspective, the ruling LDP is accorded a subordinate status in political governance.

Ramsayer and Rosenbluth (1993) proposed an opposite view. They argued that LDP politicians, not bureaucrats, were in control of setting national policies. Politicians simply delegated the power of drafting and enforcement to bureaucrats, but they would intervene if and when the bureaucracy neglected their legislative preferences. Politicians had effective instruments with which to control the bureaucracy; they could overturn policy proposals and control bureaucrats' career paths. Bureaucrats usually depended on the practice of *amakudari* ("descent from heaven") to secure lucrative postretirement jobs in public and private sectors, a practice that relied on the influence of politicians. Thus, for their own self-interest, bureaucrats had to act in accordance with politicians' politico-electoral interest. Bureaucratic dominance was simply an illusion.

The "bureaucratic dominance" and "politician dominance" models both made sweeping generalizations, irrespective of the policy and temporal factors. A more nuanced analysis would suggest that politico-bureaucratic influence could vary by time and policy areas. From the 1970s onward, as the Japanese economy became increasingly globalized, economic bureaucrats gradually lost their policy-making power as a result of their diminishing control over credit and foreign currency allocation. At the same time, the *zoku* politicians began to gain more influence, particularly in cases that involved competing bureaucratic interests and policy stalemates.

LDP politicians have shown different levels of interest in different policy areas. Policymaking in areas related to agriculture and small and medium-sized enterprises was especially politicized (Calder 1988). To guarantee their electoral advantages, the LDP Diet members often intervened to provide compensatory benefits to their constituencies but were less interested in other policies.

Overall, the strong political power and influence enjoyed by the bureaucracy was considered antidemocratic because they were not held accountable to the public through election. The image of the traditionally competent, efficient bureaucracy was further damaged by policy missteps and scandals during and after the bubble economy. For example, the powerful Ministry of Finance was aware of the huge pyramids of debt accumulated by highly leveraged financial institutions but did nothing to regulate such practices. Instead, it proposed to bail out these institutions with public funds. Additionally, it was discovered that the Ministry of Health and Welfare had knowingly allowed the use of HIV-tainted blood for transfusions, resulting in a number of HIV infections.

The confluence of prolonged economic stagnation and the high-profile scandals led to the enactment of a number of laws related to administrative reforms in 1999 (implemented in 2001) with the largest restructuring of the central government's ministries and agencies since the occupation years of the late 1940s. The reforms reduced the number of central government agencies and ministries for purposes of streamlining operations and generating efficiency.

In the 2009 election, the DPJ campaigned on the promise to establish a "people-centered government," as opposed to what was deemed as the "bureaucracy-controlled government" under the LDP. After the election, DPJ Prime Minister Hatoyama announced the Basic Policy to differentiate the responsibility between politicians and bureaucrats. According to the Basic Policy, only the political appointees within the ministries (i.e., the minister, senior vice minister, and parliamentary secretaries) would be allowed to make policy decisions. Bureaucrats were prohibited from making policy decisions or contacting other ministry officials and Diet members for policy coordination. Additionally, the Hatoyama government abolished the administrative vice ministers meeting that previewed and approved the cabinet agenda prior to the cabinet meeting. The intent was to foster substantive open policy debates in the Diet, following the model of a liberal democratic parliamentary system.

Centralizing policy-making power in the hands of the politicians, however, proved to be dysfunctional in operation, because political leaders could not possibly anticipate or effectively handle every single administrative detail required for policy coordination.

The Futenma Base issue was an example of this failed system. When Hatoyama promised to move the Futenma Base out of Okinawa during the election campaign in 2009, he did not have a clear vision on how to do so. Subsequently, bureaucrats in the defense and foreign ministries were excluded from the policy-making process, which hindered the development of workable alternative plans and contributed to the political fiasco.

THE STATE-CIVIL SOCIETY RELATIONS

Studies of the Japanese civil society generally follow two distinct theoretical models. The statist model (Sugimoto 1997; van Wolferen 1989) focuses on the state intervention through a strict regulatory environment to monitor and sanction those civil society organizations (CSOs). While Article 21 of the Constitution guarantees freedom of assembly and association, it does not mean that any group can automatically obtain legal status. Historically, the Japanese government applied the Civil Code (written in 1896) to regulate the establishment of those foundations and associations. Compared with other industrial democracies, Japan is a laggard in terms of the strength of its voluntary sector.

The pluralist model (Bestor 1999; Takao 2007), nevertheless, emphasizes the emerging social activism and citizens movements since the mid-1970s and their autonomy from the state. The evolving nature of civil society and different profiles of CSOs may explain the difference between the two models. The statist model usually focuses on the state-monitored public-interest corporations, to which the restrictive regulations tend to apply, whereas the pluralist perspective is primarily interested in the rise of advocacy groups or voluntary associations that have not been the target of those regulatory policies (Tsujinaka 2003).

Civil Society in the 1955 System

Civil society activities take many forms in Japan, with a variety of actors engaged in a diverse range of activities. Volunteerism at the local level reflected an important feature of the postwar Japanese society. Examples included neighborhood associations (*chonaikai*), public safety committees, and police support groups. Of them, the neighborhood associations had probably the longest tradition in functioning as a basic unit of social and political engagement for most Japanese. All households maintained active membership in local neighborhood associations and, in collaboration with the local government, worked on tasks such as recycling, community cleanup, seasonal festivals, national census, and disaster relief distribution. Many Japanese women, given the limitation of their career choices, were actively involved as "networkers" in these community organizations. Politicians also built their campaign organizations and support groups (*koenkai*) through these community networks.

At the national level, economic organizations such as business associations and labor unions were predominant in the early decades of the postwar era. Nevertheless, there were very few large, professionalized advocacy groups. The limited scope of civic activism on a national scale was caused in part by the strict regulatory environment imposed on those public-interest corporations. They must obtain "legal person" status to have legal standing to sign contracts or open bank accounts. To obtain legal status, nongovernmental organizations are required to go through formal approval by bureaucratic ministries or agencies, which by itself is a lengthy, demanding process for applicants to demonstrate "sound financial basis." Bureaucratic agencies that granted the permission have the power to exercise continued supervision and guidance. The government can investigate the organizations and dissolve them if they engage in activities outside the approved purposes or violate directives. These severe constraints made it difficult for Japan's civil society to play an active role in policy debates or policy making.

Civic activism in the 1950s and 1960s took the form of protest movements, as manifested in the U.S.-Japan Security Treaty (1960) protests and the anti-Vietnam War protests. When quality-of-life issues such as industrial pollution, public housing, welfare, and consumer rights emerged in the late 1960s and early 1970s, a new form of political activism, loosely called the "citizen movements," began to develop in Japan.

Beginning in the 1970s, the state's attitude toward voluntary associations gradually shifted from outright management to active engagement and empowerment, trying to tap into civic energies in support of its strategic policy interest in targeted areas. In response to issues of pollution and an aging society, the state began to promote public involvement in local governance. For example, the Ministry of Health and Welfare provided funding to establish local centers for welfare volunteers to provide paid services for childcare and home visits and meal delivery and house cleaning for the disabled and elderly. The state–civil society affiliation was institutionalized to help lighten the state's service load on social welfare provisions in an aging society. In the 1980s, similar projects were extended to environmental cleanup, park beautification, adult education, and lifelong learning. Volunteer groups become complementary to the state, providing services it will not offer.

Civil Society in the 1993 System

Several trends converged in the 1990s to open more space for CSOs. First, the international norm promoting stronger state-CSO cooperation in the 1980s and 1990s in the global society began to spill over to Japan, pressuring

Japanese officials to recognize CSOs' role in governance (Reimann 2003). The large number of active nongovernmental organizations dealing with women, human rights, and environmental issues in international conferences made Japanese bureaucrats aware of the fact that they needed to catch up on this standard practice.

Second, as discussed earlier, the image of the bureaucracy was damaged in a series of policy missteps and scandals in the 1990s. Previously, the bureaucrats were seen as a group of the best and brightest who considered national interest above their self-interest. With the reliability of the Japanese bureaucracy in question, CSOs gained some leverage in dealing with them.

Finally, in the aftermath of the devastating Kobe earthquake in 1995 that claimed over 6,000 lives with massive property damage, government crisis responses and relief efforts, mired in jurisdictional disputes, were slow and ineffective. In contrast, volunteer groups moved quickly to participate in the rescue efforts to aid the victims. The unprecedented level of public volunteering helped galvanize the spirit of volunteerism. In the process, the media reported that most of the volunteer groups in the relief mission had no legal status, and the volunteers were not properly insured, because of the overwhelming legal restrictions imposed by the bureaucracy, as described previously.

In response to the public outcry for a change in the regulatory environment for CSOs, the Diet passed the 1998 Law to Promote Specified Nonprofit Activities (commonly known as the "NPO Law") to change the regulatory environment for CSOs and lay the foundation for a more robust civil society.

The legislation created a new category of "specified nonprofit corporations" and allowed them to incorporate easily and operate without intrusive bureaucratic oversight if they meet certain objective organizational criteria. Organizations engaged in various public benefits activities needed to merely register with local government organs. The NPO law not only legitimized the status of these groups but also signaled a shift in state–civil society power balance (Pekkanen 2000). Since then, the legal environment for NPOs has continued to improve. Public interest corporations could now be established through registration at the Legal Affairs Bureau without the requirement of permission or approval by central or local government (Ogawa 2014).

Despite the liberalization of the nonprofit sector, fundamental differences still exist in the CSOs' view of the state. Many of the new civil society organizations, known as "citizens groups" or NPOs, prefer to maintain their autonomy from the bureaucracy, rather than operate under the traditional mode of institutionalized association with the state. They are growing in number and influence. The massive antinuclear protests against DPJ's Noda in 2012 and the peace demonstrations against Abe's security legislation in 2015 reflected the rise of the once weak advocacy sector to challenge government decisions.

Nevertheless, a significant number of civil society groups continue to pride themselves in the "proposal-style" civic engagement. Unlike the social protest movements, they prefer to offer concrete initiatives within local communities to engineer social change. They believe it to be more fruitful to engage with the bureaucrats or business executives in proposing alternatives to established practices (Avenell 2009). The debates and dialogues between these perspectives will undoubtedly continue in the foreseeable future, and they are a healthy indication that Japan's civil society is alive and well.

DISCUSSION QUESTIONS

1. The occupation authorities initiated various kinds of reforms in postwar Japan. Describe the guiding principles of these reforms and the specific policies implemented. Evaluate their impacts on modern Japan.

2. The Liberal Democratic Party (LDP) dominated the so-called 1955 system in Japan. Describe the LDP's political ideology, and discuss the various factors contributing to its success under the 1955 system.

3. The 1955 system suffered from the heavy influence of money politics. The critics believed that the multimember electoral district was the main cause of corruption. Explain their reasoning, and discuss whether changes in the electoral system in 1994 addressed their concerns.

4. Postwar Japanese prime ministers generally have had short tenure in office, a sign of the weakness of the position. Explain the factors that contribute to the executive weakness, and discuss the reform measures in recent years to strengthen the office.

5. The strong influence of bureaucracy has affected state–civil society relations in Japan. Discuss the change in the regulatory environment in the 1990s and the varying responses from the civil society organizations.

7

Japan's Pursuit of Economic Prosperity

FROM RUINS TO BUBBLE: 1945–1989

Postwar Economic Reconstruction: 1945–1952

Land Reforms. The occupation authorities placed a ceiling on land holdings and transferred a vast majority of previously tenanted land to its cultivators. Before 1946, 46 percent of farmland was cultivated by tenant farmers who paid 75 percent of their rents in kind to landlords. Under the reform measure, farmers could keep 7.5 acres to farm, plus another 2.5 acres that could remain uncultivated. Thus, landlords were forced to sell all land in excess of the ceiling to the government, which in turn resold the land to tenant farmers. Rents were lowered to half or less of prewar levels. This reform program practically destroyed the economic power of the landlord class and allowed tenants to buy land at bargain prices. Land reforms helped increase agricultural production and stabilize food supplies, which led to the creation of a middle class of small-scale farmers in rural Japan.

Labor and Business Relations. To eliminate excessive concentration of economic power and to encourage market competition immediately after the war, the occupation authorities proposed to dissolve *zaibatsu*, the family-owned conglomerates that altogether held about 40 percent of overall equity (paid-in capital) at the end of the war. An antimonopoly law was passed in April 1947 and a deconcentration law in December 1947 to break up cartels and monopolies by auctioning off the shares owned by their holding companies. In the meantime, the occupation authorities vigorously promoted a labor movement. Labor laws were introduced in 1946 and 1947 to grant workers the right to organize in unions and engage in collective bargaining.

After 1947, with the rising tension of the Cold War, the occupation authorities implemented the "reverse course" to modify some of the reform measures. Increasingly concerned with labor's political affiliation with the left-wing

Japan Socialist Party (JSP) and the Japan Communist Party (JCP), the occupation authorities intervened to prohibit a planned general strike in February 1947 and revised major labor laws to restrict collective bargaining and strikes by public sector unions. Key labor leaders were removed from their positions.

Furthermore, the occupation authorities brought back prewar conservative politicians and lent support to their political and economic agendas, including the continuation of land reforms. Large corporations, whose political allegiance was with conservative elites, also saw a change in their political standing. By 1949, the deconcentration program was abandoned, and antimonopoly laws were revised. Manufacturing corporations and financial institutions were allowed to hold the shares of other firms; the previous *zaibatsu* was rebuilt into various horizontal and vertical *keiretsu*—interlocking business alliances.

The Dodge Plan and the Korean War. In order to contain global Communist expansionism, the United States began to take an interest in building up a strong capitalist democracy in Japan. Joseph Dodge, chairman of the Detroit Bank, went to Japan in 1948 as an economic adviser to devise an austerity program for Japan to tackle postwar hyperinflation and achieve financial stability. He achieved a balanced budget by reducing government expenditures and by cutting back the size of the bureaucracy. In 1949, he took actions to control wages and prices and established a fixed exchange rate regime (1 U.S. dollar equal to 360 yen) to restore order in foreign currency markets.

The Dodge Plan was successful in taming inflation, yet it stalled production and generated fear of job losses. It stabilized the business environment for long-term growth, but in the short run, it led to massive layoffs in both private and public sectors. The economy would have entered into a recession if not for the boom provided by the Korean War.

Huge orders for supplies and equipment needed in the Korean War helped jumpstart the Japanese economy at a critical moment, providing a much-needed boost to expand domestic employment and generate domestic consumer demand. Truck orders worth nearly $13 million from July 1950 to February 1951 helped revive the Japanese automobile industry. The inflow of U.S. dollars helped Japan pay for its imports and re-equip its industries with the latest technologies, especially plants and factories destroyed by Allied bombing. By the time the Korean War ended in 1953, Japanese industrial production was nearly restored to prewar levels.

The Dodge Plan profoundly influenced the direction of the Japanese government's macroeconomic policies for decades. First, to support the yen-dollar exchange rate and to maintain the current account balance, the Japanese government began to implement strict capital controls. Foreign transactions such as trade and foreign investment were closely monitored and tightly regulated. To preserve foreign currencies, the government imposed limits on imports with high tariffs and import quotas. To earn foreign reserve through exports, capital and resources were steered to areas deemed most efficient and productive.

The Ministry of International Trade and Industry (MITI) was responsible for rationalizing the use of capital for industrial production.

Second, cognizant of the negative effect of financial contraction produced by the Dodge Plan, the Japanese government decided to pursue an expansionary monetary policy. It deliberately kept interest rates at low levels so that corporations could borrow sufficient investment funds to expand their businesses. At the same time, to lessen the pressure of potential inflation, the government kept its spending relatively small to balance the total monetary supply. This meant that the government took a deflationary fiscal policy to minimize public spending, including social welfare expenditures. The responsibility of social spending fell on to families and the private sector. Thus, the combination of an expansionary monetary policy and a deflationary fiscal policy created a favorable environment for economic growth and expansion, while keeping inflation under control.

Growth Strategies

From the supply-side perspective, three growth engines facilitated postwar Japanese economic reconstruction and development: investment, technological improvement, and increased labor input. From the demand side, domestic consumption and export markets fueled the call for production. Altogether, Japanese economic growth during the catch-up era was marked by virtuous cycles of positive feedback: demand expansion, production expansion, income increase, consumption expansion, and investment growth.

Investment and Technology Transfer. Japanese households preferred to keep the bulk of their savings in bank deposits rather than equities or bonds. Japan's household savings rate gradually moved up during the postwar era and peaked in the mid-1970s at 23.2 percent, first among the OECD countries. The high savings rate, in both absolute and comparative terms, provided much-needed resources for capital accumulation to fund investment in factories, equipment, housing, and infrastructures to propel economic growth.

The Ministry of Finance and the Bank of Japan were in charge of mobilizing national saving for investment purposes to ensure a stable supply of industrial capital for economic growth. Funds from the national postal savings system, government annuity, and pension plans were transferred to a special account called the Fiscal Investment and Loan Program (FILP) in the Ministry of Finance. The FILP allowed the government to invest in infrastructure and public works without increasing taxes directly. It also supported various industrial development projects in the form of subsidized loans for heavy and export industries. In the 1950s and 1960s, the priority for funding was for industrial infrastructure; it shifted to housing and other home-related projects in the 1970s and 1980s.

The Industrial Bank of Japan (IBJ), though not a public institution, was established with a public function. In the 1950s, it provided roughly 24 percent of the total capital for strategic industries in coal, steel, shipbuilding, and electricity. It, too, shifted its funding allocation to infrastructure and agriculture after the mid-1960s.

MITI, entrusted with the task to promote industrial growth, channeled resources to industries deemed with the potential for export expansion, technological advancement, and significant employment (Argy and Stein 1997; Okuno-Fujiwara 1991). Johnson's (1982) pioneering study on MITI was the foundation of the "developmental state" model. According to Johnson, MITI planned and steered Japan's economic growth through direct and indirect forms of administrative guidance. Staffed by the best managerial talent from a small, elite bureaucracy, the developmental state intervened in the economy through industrial policies such as strategic targeting and resource allocation and pushed for economic growth by coordinating investment and production activities with the private sector.

Heavy industries such as metal, chemicals, and machinery all benefited from MITI's allocation of scarce funds to expand their production capacities. MITI also assisted domestic industries in acquiring technological knowledge from other industrial economies. Japan, as a late industrializer, was behind advanced economies in technological inventions. Virtually all of Japan's modern industries were built on technologies transferred from the United States and Western Europe. From 1951 to early 1984, Japanese companies signed nearly 42,000 contracts to import foreign technology, including DuPont's nylon patent, Bell Laboratories' transistor technology, and Corning's TV glass tube technology (Abegglen and Stalk 1985). The cumulative cost was a small fraction of the annual U.S. research and development budget.

During the catch-up process, Japan definitely gained from the advantage of "economic backwardness," as described by Gerschenkron (1962). Late developers, such as Japan, could absorb and adopt well-established technology through emulating and improving. Following developed business models and practices helped them find the right path and avoid costly mistakes.

Labor Supply. A massive migration of young, motivated, and educated workers from rural to urban areas fueled industrialization with abundant skilled labor forces. Urban centers in *Kanto* (Tokyo-Yokohama-Kawasaki), *Chubu* (Nagoya), and *Kansai* (Osaka-Kyoto-Kobe) experienced the highest rate of migration. The shift of labor from agriculture to manufacturing helped stabilize the wage level, making Japanese products competitive internationally.

Internal and External Demands. Economic growth increased income and wealth and stimulated demands for housing and consumer goods to induce further economic production. The desire to own televisions, refrigerators, and washing machines, known as the "three sacred treasures" for each family, was a powerful drive for industrial output and expansion. By the mid-1960s, after 90 percent of the households in Japan were equipped with all three items (Horsley and Buckley 1990), consumers turned their interest to other durable goods such as color televisions, air conditioning, and cars.

Increased exports also contributed to economic growth. In the 1950s, labor-intensive manufacturing, such as textiles, constituted the bulk of Japanese exports. Absorption of imported technologies helped shift Japanese manufacturing to capital- and technology-intensive products. In the 1960s, Japan's exports expanded to capital goods in electronics and heavy industries. By the end of that decade, one-third of all Japan's exports went to the United States, making it America's single most important trading partner.

Economic Institutions: The 1940 System

The notion of "Japan, Inc." (Kaplan 1972) painted a picture of Japan as a well-oiled growth machine in single-minded pursuit of economic development. Politicians, bureaucrats, and businesses formed an "iron triangle" to work collaboratively to plan and guide Japan's economic policy. Bureaucracy created a highly competitive and dynamic economy by regulating trade, capital flow, foreign exchange, technological development, and human capital through decrees and directives (known as administrative guidance). Big corporations and their employees in turn harmonized their business operations and strategies with the government plan.

Conventional wisdom argues that postwar economic restructuring in land, labor, and antitrust reforms, as initiated by the occupation authorities, fundamentally changed the Japanese economic structure by interjecting more competition and greater equality into the system, consequently enhancing investor confidence. However, it seems that prewar economic institutions, or the 1940 system, survived and became an integral part of the modern Japanese economy.

The 1940 system did not necessarily result from any unique aspect of the Japanese culture, for it did not come into existence until after the 1930s and 1940s when the Japanese government was in preparation for the wartime economy. To mobilize scarce materials and resources for warfare, the government passed legislation and took administrative measures to coordinate policy actions. The 1940 system not only shaped relations between public and private sectors but also influenced corporate structures and employment practices such as lifetime employment, seniority pay, and company unions.

The emphasis on long-term cooperation between economic actors can be reviewed in three key areas: the relationship between government and business, between business and business, and between labor and management.

Government-Business Relations. The early notion of "Japan, Inc." conveyed a monolithic image of unified public and private sectors in pursuit of economic growth. The consensus and informal coordination of the "iron triangle" underscore the cohesiveness in the politico-economic system. Similarly, the "developmental state" model (Johnson 1982), "state-led capitalism" (Pempel 1982), "managed market economy" (Hamada 1998), and "cooperative capitalism" (Schaede 2001) all pointed to the special symbiotic relationship between government and business in Japan.

Beneath the broad consensus, however, there have been vigorous debates on the relative importance of government guidance versus the function of market mechanism, as well as how this relationship has evolved over time.

Industrial Policy. Proponents of the "developmental state" model emphasized strong coordination between the government and business community in rational resource allocation and strategic economic planning. Proponents believed that government agencies had full knowledge of rising industries and would allocate resources to the fastest growing firms and sectors accordingly. The overall performance of the Japanese economy in general and the success of targeted industries such as shipbuilding, steel, and computing technology were often cited as proof of industrial policy effectiveness.

Yet critics pointed out that numerous postwar sunrise industries (e.g., consumer electronics, petrochemicals, and aluminum) were never on the government's target list. The government's inability to identify those growth industries suggested the irrelevancy of industrial policy. Another example often used by critics was the automotive industry. To avoid "excessive competition," MITI attempted but failed to merge several automobile companies into two groups of firms in the early 1960s. Honda, as a successful automobile manufacturer, would not exist in present strength if MITI had succeeded in its plan; it remains doubtful that the Japanese automobile industry would be as strong and dominant as it is today without strong domestic competition.

Beyond anecdotal examples, there was very little empirical support for the benefit of the industrial policy, based on a review of studies that analyzed the effect of industrial policy intervention on productivity growth and welfare (Nolan 2007).

Deliberation Councils. Johnson's technocratic "developmental state" model may have been generally correct in the 1950s and 1960s, but it has evolved since then. According to Calder (1993), the scope and intensity of state intervention in Japan scaled back significantly after the 1973 oil shock, because economic globalization had reduced the state's capacity to act. Rather than leading the process of economic development, the Japanese state took into account private sector initiatives and preferences in structuring its market-conforming strategies in response to market mechanisms.

Even during the heyday of government intervention, despite widespread consensus over the priority of economic growth in the conservative coalition, there were different views on how much growth was achievable and at what price. During 1962 to 1963, when MITI sought power to encourage mergers and reduce competition, its attempts were blocked by other ministries and numerous industrial and trade associations.

Thus, the traditional image of the "iron triangle" failed to capture pluralist dynamics within the bureaucracy and between bureaucrats and private interests. Scholars have since turned to deliberation councils (*shingikai*), which bring politicians and bureaucrats together with business associations or individual firms for policy deliberations, to observe how the government and business interact to make policies (Schaede 2001; Schwartz 1998).

Through accounts of how policy making was conducted in deliberation councils on issues of labor standards, financial market reforms, and rice prices during the 1980s, Schwartz (1998) found that bureaucrats rarely dominated the policy-making process with their own agendas. Instead, business groups were consistently successful in amending or delaying policy proposals of far-reaching importance. Decisions were not driven by overarching principles or blueprints. Rather, practical consideration was often the basis for policy making: the least controversial and most attainable policies were often adopted (Okuno-Fujiwara 1991). Therefore, small businesses were able to have employees work longer hours than international norms, financial interests were able to delay the creation of derivative markets, and farmers were able to protect the rice price. The information exchange in formal and informal settings positively clarified intentions and commitments, solidifying trust (Maxfield and Schneider 1997); on a negative front, bureaucratic corruption and policy opaqueness arose from these closed-door consultations.

Interbusiness Relations. Extensive coordination also existed between industrial and corporate entities. As discussed earlier, in the postwar era, large family-owned *zaibatsu* developed into various forms of business alliances known as *keiretsu*. Horizontal *keiretsu* evolved directly from *zaibatsu* and were organized across different industries. Each group had its own bank plus 20 to 40 large companies in different areas such as financial, trading, and manufacturing. The diversity of the group helped create business synergy and maximize economies of scale. Although firms within the same group were not subject to central control, they held each other's stocks, monitored each other's performance, and promoted each other's business interests by ordering products and services from one another. Cross-shareholding of stocks served to block potential takeover by foreign companies.

A vertical *keiretsu* organized networks of manufacturers, suppliers, and distributors within the same industries. Various core suppliers and distributors in the network may have their own groups of secondary and tertiary subcontractors—many of them were small firms. Repeated transactions and long-term relationships between firms built confidence and created reliable partnership on quality control and timely delivery of orders. For outsiders, however, the maintenance of this long, trusting relationship between firms may exhibit an anticompetitive, protectionist behavior, since other more efficient producers could be excluded or ignored.

Main Bank System. Before the war, Japanese firms relied on stock markets to finance investment, much like the market-based financial system in the United States and United Kingdom. As war became imminent, the Japanese authority, concerned with the speculative and decentralized nature of the capital market, established a bank-centered financing structure—the origin of the main bank system—to control and stabilize funds that flowed to military-related industries.

A main bank for a company was usually the leading lender to the company or the largest holder of company shares. Most *keiretsu* had main banks who supplied funds and loans for investment projects. They developed a special relationship with the companies by holding their stocks and monitoring their corporate finance and governance systems. In times of financial distress, the main bank would dispatch representatives to troubled firms to take over boards or implement restructuring efforts.

Stability in banking relations gave management more freedom to focus on long-term performance without the distraction of short-term market fluctuations. Japanese firms faced fewer cash-flow constraints because the main bank-firm relations allowed these companies to continue investing and growing even when facing a cash flow shortage (Hoshi, Kashyap, and Scharfstein 1991). The close interactions between main banks and firms also mitigated asymmetrical information problems between lenders and borrowers in a market-based financial system, as long-term relations helped overcome borrowers' unwillingness to fully disclose financial information to lenders. However, the main bank system and the cross shareholding structure meant that Japanese corporate management was usually not subject to the scrutiny of the capital market. Effective supervision and monitoring from the main bank became the only effective ways to hold companies accountable.

Labor-Management Relations. Under the wartime regime, industry-wide unions were dissolved and replaced by company unions that comprised both white-collar and blue-collar workers within the same company. Partnerships of white- and blue-collar workers in the same union were supposed to induce cooperative behavior, as shared success in the growth of the company would benefit everyone. Efforts to increase wages and expand employment benefits and retirement plans would then be directed at the company itself, instead of being negotiated through national labor organizations. As a result, enterprise consciousness, the psychological attachment to the company, prevailed over class consciousness and significantly undermined the appeal of any class-based labor movement.

Lifetime employment and seniority-based pay were first introduced in large corporations around the time of World War I to keep skilled textile workers from leaving their jobs. The practices then spread to other sectors before World War II. Lifetime employment guaranteed job security for regular, core workers, mostly male and white-collar employees in large companies, until around the age of 55. The practice traditionally did not apply to women, part-timers, and seasonal laborers. Most employees of smaller enterprises did not have the same level of job security either. Only a quarter of Japan's workforce received such benefits.

Salaries were largely based on seniority within the organization rather than performance. As people accumulated more experience, their salaries gradually increased. The arrangement worked to retain workers' loyalty. Knowing that the worker was unlikely to quit, the company would be more willing to spend resources for on-the-job training. Employees, though having guaranteed employment, could be asked to take a different job assignment or transfer to a subsidiary or a related company based on production needs. During economic crisis, such as the oil shock of 1973, questions were raised about the long-term feasibility of such practice, but big corporations were forced to continue the practice in exchange for cooperation from labor unions in slowing wage growth. By the time of the Plaza Accord (1985), as rapid appreciation of the Japanese yen brought renewed pressure on Japanese corporations to adjust labor costs, permanent employment had become a deeply institutionalized ideology in the Japanese corporate structure.

The Conservative Coalition

As discussed in Chapter 6, the conservative coalition led by the LDP has dominated postwar Japanese politics since the 1950s. Conservative politicians, bureaucrats, and big businesses are the principal groups of this coalition, with farmers and small and medium-sized enterprises (SMEs) being junior partners. The coalition has succeeded not only in occupying political offices but also in translating the economic interest of its constituents into a growth model. The political alignment between political parties and organized interests helps explain the subsequent choice of economic and social policies.

At the national level, two major peak business organizations speak for big business. The Japan Business Federation (*Keidanren*), founded in 1947, is the most well-known and important alliance of industry associations and leading firms. *Keidanren* coordinates financial contributions to the LDP based on a firm's capital base and profitability, while industries and firms also give generously to faction leaders and individual politicians (Ramseyer and Rosenbluth 1993). The Japan Association of Corporate Executives (*Keizai Doyukai*), the second most influential business group, is joined by top corporate executives who participate as individuals, not as members of the corporation. Although these organizations are not without their internal disagreements and divisions, they are a major vehicle for coordination and articulation of business interests.

The Japan Agricultural Cooperatives Association (JA) is the comprehensive organization that represents organized agriculture. Agricultural cooperatives performed multiple functions in rural Japan: operating banks, insurance companies, and small credit bureaus; allocating credit; promoting new crops and technology; providing agricultural education; and purchasing crops. Their wide-ranging financial and functional powers, coupled with their organizational strength, make them formidable actors in rural Japan. To win rural support through the cooperatives in the late 1940s, conservative politicians earmarked government-subsidized loans and projects for the cooperatives to manage and incorporated personnel of these cooperatives into their own political support groups. To solidify the political support of rice farmers (considered the backbone of Japanese agriculture), the conservative government implemented import restrictions and purchased rice at higher prices to raise farmers' income levels. Since then, agricultural cooperatives have mobilized votes exclusively for the LDP. In return, farmers receive policy benefits such as subsidies, price supports, import restrictions, and rural work projects.

SMEs—firms with fewer than 300 employees or with less than $3.7 million in capital—are another pillar of the conservative coalition. Although the general impression of Japan's economy involves mega banks and big businesses, the SMEs accounted for over 99 percent of Japanese firms. As early as 1953, 73.5 percent of Japan's manufacturing workforce was employed by SMEs (Calder 1988). Many SMEs were integrated into *keiretsu* as suppliers or subcontractors, meeting the demand of boss companies in exchange for a stable, longer-term relationship in the supply chain. Facing disparities in technology and productivity with large firms, SMEs relied on cheap labor to survive in business competition.

Given their diverse backgrounds and operations, the needs and economic interests of the SMEs were not as cohesive as those of farmers. Nevertheless, many conservative politicians, recognizing the sheer number of voters they could potentially mobilize, pressed for legislation to allow small businesses to form protective cartels similar to those of larger firms. The enactment of the Medium and Small-Sized Companies Stabilization Law in 1953 marked the beginning of long-term collaboration between SMEs and conservatives. Over decades of LDP rule, many regulations were created to help SMEs maintain high prices and excess employment. Lax rules also encouraged widespread tax evasion by SMEs.

The postwar conservative coalition in charge of the growth machine had clear economic goals in mind: industrial development, gross national product growth, and promotion for exports (Pempel 1982). Conservative elites, who shared the sense of Japan's economic vulnerability, as seen by its heavy dependence on imported raw materials, actively pursued mercantilism to promote the macroeconomic interests of the state. As a later industrializer that had struggled to keep up with other well-established industrial economies, the Japanese government sought to nurture and protect domestic industries. It developed strong coordination with business communities to ensure that limited resources would be used in the most efficient, strategic way to expedite the catch-up process. However, this narrative—pursuing economic efficiency and productivity—did not tell the whole story about the postwar Japanese economy.

This coalition, in fact, had other goals in mind: a social contract of shared growth and total employment (Calder 1988; Gao 2001; Pempel 1998; Schaede 2004), which conformed to the conservative, risk-adverse orientation of the LDP in maintaining social stability and income equality. In 1960, in response to riots and demonstrations following the Diet's vote to renew the Mutual Security Treaty, Prime Minister Ikeda Hayato announced a goal for Japan to double the national income in a decade. The vision of shared growth channeled talent and energy toward economic growth, rather than ideological debates. The conservative coalition was largely successful in achieving these goals, as seen in consistently low unemployment rates in the postwar era and in the fact that the overwhelming majority of Japanese (80 percent to 90 percent) considered themselves "middle class."

Nevertheless, the simultaneous pursuit of economic efficiency and total employment led to conflicting objectives. On the one hand, the industrial policy sought to allocate resources efficiently in strategic sectors for growth purposes. On the other hand, total employment called for the use of subsidies or preferential treatment to protect the businesses that were weak and inefficient. For the sake of full employment and shared growth, the government provided subsidies and protectionist measures to maintain income levels in less competitive sectors. The coexistence of both productive and less productive groups within the conservative coalition necessitated these conflicting policies.

The manufacturing sector, though protected by tariff and nontariff barriers in the domestic market, steadily built a comparative advantage because of the need to compete in foreign markets. In contrast, productivity growth in agriculture, SMEs, and nonmanufacturing sectors such as construction, distribution, finance, and services trailed, relying heavily on trade barriers and government subsidies to survive. Many construction companies were supported by government projects, and numerous retailers were propped up by loose tax codes. Few foreign companies were active in Japan due to policy-induced high entry costs and public assistance to local competitors. Protectionist measures helped retain surplus workers in those sectors, perpetuating inefficiency. Thus, the interplay of economic and political factors sustained a dual structure within the Japanese economy. The efficient and inefficient sectors coexisted, with a huge difference in productivity and competitiveness between them.

Additionally, such a broad-based coalition meant that a large number of actors had to be consulted in the economic decision-making process. Over the years, the coalition became so entrenched in economic governance that it discouraged any significant departure from established norms, despite changes in the economic environment. Economic decision making became so highly consensual and coordinated that it impeded swift and decisive actions in response to external pressure and domestic crises. How did the coalition maintain a policy mix to satisfy both productive and unproductive groups?

Dual Economic Structure and Social Policy

Within this dual economic structure, the coexistence of the efficient and inefficient sectors helped the government accomplish both economic growth and social distribution at the same time. In light of the legacy of the Dodge Plan to limit public spending, the government placed the burden of welfare programs in the hands of the companies through lifetime employment practices and seniority-based wage scales. During the early 1960s, Japan's public social expenditure accounted for only 7 percent of the GDP, lower than all the other industrial economies, which were in the range of 10 percent to 17 percent (Pempel 2002).

The government used tax and regulatory policies to achieve social protection for the weak and the inefficient. From the early 1950s to the early 1980s, direct subsidies in the form of government budget expenditures went to agriculture, mining, and SMEs—all known for their low productivity (Nolan 2007). These subsidies were financed by taxes from Japanese manufacturing. Therefore, in the dual structure, the efficient sectors shouldered the financial burden to support the less efficient ones. The LDP government preferred a particular social policy to benefit specific groups in its coalition, rather than a universal welfare program applicable to all citizens, unless it was needed to ensure the party's electoral advantage.

In the late 1960s and early 1970s, the LDP was slow to respond to quality-of-life issues such as industrial pollution, environmental protection, social welfare, and consumer interest, as proposed by progressive candidates. At that time, wages, benefits, and company-based pension programs showed widening gaps between big corporations and SMEs. The progressive forces were able to gain ground in local elections by promoting these issues and won governorships in Tokyo, Osaka, and Kyoto.

The LDP finally decided to co-opt those policies promoted by social movements and by leftist mayors and governors. Under Prime Minister Tanaka, the Japanese government declared 1973 as the "First Year of the Welfare Era" to institute major expansions in elderly care, medical programs, and pension systems. The recession triggered by the oil crisis of 1973, however, led to a significant shortfall in state revenue, and critics blamed the subsequent rise in the national debt on increased welfare spending.

The subsequent electoral setback for progressive forces after the oil crisis emboldened LDP politicians and business leaders to engage in the discourse of the "Japanese-style Welfare Society" that emphasized a society of self-help and mutual help with only a limited degree of state intervention. Conservative groups put forth proposals in 1982, seeking to roll back social welfare benefits introduced in the early 1970s, including free medical care for the elderly, the child allowance, and the special allowance for single mothers. In so doing, they intended to place social welfare obligations back on the family, particularly in the hands of women. The reforms drew strong reactions from women's groups, who bore the heaviest burden in elderly care in a rapidly aging society.

THE POST-BUBBLE ERA: 1990–PRESENT

Economic Challenges

After the burst of the economic bubble in the early 1990s, unemployment rates climbed and corporate profits declined. Japanese banks, which were at the center of the financial and real estate speculation during the bubble years, initially backed away from calling off nonperforming loans for fear that the write-off of bad loans would reduce existing capital. Rather, to dress up their balance sheets, they continued to lend to insolvent borrowers. By supplying additional funding to an unprofitable borrower to meet the capital require-ment on paper, banks rewarded firms of low productivity while impairing their ability to support healthy companies. Following the bankruptcy of several large financial institutions in November 1997 and the Asian Financial Crisis of 1997–1998, most large banks had difficulty maintaining the 8 percent capital adequacy ratio recommended by the Basel Accord to ensure enough capital to meet obligations. The subsequent massive bailouts by the government in the amount of $90 billion raised questions about the main-bank system that was part of the Japanese growth strategy in the 1940 system.

At the same time, Japanese manufacturing, the central pillar of postwar economic growth, was losing its cost advantage in exporting consumer prod-ucts. After the Plaza Accord of 1985, the yen was on a sustained trajectory of appreciation for 20 years, as the nominal exchange rate moved from 240 yen/dollar to 80 yen/dollar at its peak for a 300 percent appreciation. Other things being equal, an appreciated yen reduced the international competitiveness of Japan's manufacturing industries and made exportation difficult, leading to a yen-induced recession (Hamada and Okada 2009). In response to its lost cost advantages, Japanese companies relocated production through foreign direct investment to China and Southeast Asian countries.

Amid political and economic uncertainty, the demographic trend of aging further complicated the policy environment in the post-bubble era. For about 50 years between 1945 and 1996, Japan's labor force increased by 37 million. The added workforce combined with rising productivity spurred its growth. The trend began to reverse. In 1975, the age group of 65 and older accounted for 8 percent of the population. The number went up to 26 percent in 2015 and is expected to reach 40 percent in 2050—the highest in the OECD (OECD 2017b). Japan's population reached its peak in 2010 at 128.1 million and will likely fall below 100 million by 2050.

Population aging, caused by low fertility and increased longevity, will have long-term economic implications. The aging population in Japan is probably the single most important factor in contributing to the decline of its savings rate, as the elderly draw on personal savings to finance their living expenses (Horioka 2008). In addition, aging adds more burden to Japan's social security system, raising the cost for pensions. The aging factor affects business by increasing the demand for human capital investment to replace lost labor, while decreasing its incentive for investment in new factories. In fact, facing a shrinking consumer base, many Japanese companies have cut back investments at home. The guiding principle for companies has changed from profit maximization to debt minimization. Consequently, solvent but heavily indebted companies forgo profitable investment opportunities to repair balance sheets, causing "balance sheet recession" (Koo 2009). Unless Japan's productivity increases faster than its decline in the labor force, which is unlikely, economic output will shrink, and the Japanese economy will natu-rally become smaller.

Reforms and Economic Policies

It seems that the Japanese economy, once projected to dominate the world, is at a crossroads in the post-bubble era. Japan is in search of the next growth engine along with the optimal institutions for economic development. The fundamental issue is about the relationship between government and business, or between the state and the market. Many of the post-bubble reforms emphasized marketization and competition, in the direction of liberalizing government control.

Reform Measures. After the LDP lost its majority in the House of Representatives in the summer of 1993, multiple crises and scandals involving the Ministry of Finance and financial institutions further undermined public confidence in the close relationship between government and business, the cornerstone of the LDP conservative coalition. Upon returning to power in January 1996, LDP Prime Minister Hashimoto Ryutaro initiated reforms to restore public trust and regain electoral advantage. The LDP leadership deliberately excluded bureaucrats, business lobbyists, and LDP politicians specializing in financial affairs (the financial *zoku*, or tribe politicians) from the deliberation process to exercise full control over the reform agenda, which included liberalization of foreign investment in the financial sector, improved marketization and transparency, and reorganization of government administrative structures. Foreign companies quickly took advantage of these opportunities and transformed the business landscape in the financial sector.

Elite ministries plagued by scandal and incompetence went through reorganization. The all-powerful Ministry of Finance (MOF) no longer oversaw the Bank of Japan. The newly created Financial Services Agency (FSA) took over supervision of the financial industry, and MOF had to share part of its budget-making power with the new Cabinet Office for Economic and Fiscal Policy. MITI was restructured as the Ministry of Economy, Trade, and Industry (METI) to accommodate a broader definition of national economic interest in a neoliberal environment.

Liberalization continued in 1998 when the new Foreign Exchange Law removed the remaining restrictions on international investment. Leading foreign multinational corporations (MNCs) are now prominent in many of the sectors previously closed to foreign investors, such as pharmaceuticals, automobiles, telecommunications, and finance (Kushida 2013). These MNCs brought with them new business models and practices with different expectations for government-business coordination. The focus of the new entrants was on profitability and competitive advantage, much different from the traditional *keiretsu* structure's emphasis on stability and reciprocity.

Following Hashimoto's reforms, Koizumi introduced additional reforms to the public sector to reduce government intervention. Along with spending cuts on public works and the FILP (i.e., the "second budget"), he proposed to privatize the postal savings system and reorganize public corporations. Most of Koizumi's neoliberal reforms were supported by his allies in business and by academics but ran against the interests of other constituents in the "old" conservative coalition, such as farmers, small business owners, and construction workers (Noble 2013).

Toward the end of Koizumi's tenure, there was a vigorous debate about whether these neoliberal reforms had created an "unequal and unjust" society. Cuts in public works and government expenditures in Koizumi's reforms fueled the perception of increased inequality and may have contributed to the LDP's downfall in 2009.

It seems that there is a deeper conviction for the value of the 1940 system, whose existence is reinforced by strong vested interests as well as the broad social norms and expectations of the Japanese society (Lincoln 2001). While many of the LDP leaders acknowledged the value of greater market competition, they also qualified their support of reforms on the grounds that unrestrained competition would undermine the fabric of Japanese society. The perceived incompatibility of the concept of competition with the Japanese value of coordination and cooperation explained why there had not been fundamental changes in Japanese economic institutions (von Staden 2012).

Economic Policies. Prime Minister Abe Shinzo in 2013 proposed a three-pronged strategy to revitalize the economy after two decades of sluggish growth. Popularly called Abenomics, or Abe's "three arrows," it included a bold, expansionary monetary easing, increased public spending, and structural and regulatory reforms. The immediate effect was the increase in real output growth to 1.1 percent, matching the OECD average (OECD 2017b).

Implementation of the third arrow—structural reform—was highly anticipated but has not produced any concrete results yet. Agriculture has long been considered the sector in need of structural reform. Agriculture's share in the Japanese economy has steadily declined in the last 50 years, dropping from 9 percent of GDP to 1 percent, while agricultural employment shrank from 28 percent of the total workforce to less than 3 percent. Farmland, mostly small and fragmented, has been cultivated by a workforce that is increasingly part-time and aging. Over 60 percent of workers are now part-time farmers receiving more than half of their income from nonfarm sources. The average age of farmers was 66 in 2015. Agriculture is a sector that is inefficient and low in productivity; yet, against these economic trends, farm lobbying remains powerful in sustaining an agricultural policy that supports farm household income at a level comparable to that in other sectors.

The subsidy and price support for agricultural goods place burdens on consumers and taxpayers. In fact, farm household income, on a per capita basis, has consistently exceeded that of nonfarm households since 1980 (Jones and Kimura 2013). In recent years, Japan has attempted to expand its economic growth potential by negotiating comprehensive regional or bilateral free trade agreements with its trading partners. However, under the influence of agricultural lobbying, Japan has been reluctant to reduce its tariff rate or lift its import restriction for agricultural goods, a core issue complicating its participation in these arrangements and limiting integration into the world economy. Although there has been speculation that the political influence of agriculture is declining, given the electoral reforms discussed in Chapter 6, it seems that the farm lobby continues to be a formidable force in resisting the trend toward marketization and liberalization. Whether agriculture is included in Abe's structural reform list will be a good indication as to how much the LDP coalition has changed.

Economic Institutions and Growth

During the catch-up phase of economic growth, Japan followed the path and pattern of development of advanced economies, enjoying the benefits of "economic backwardness." Technological acquisition from abroad played an important role in stimulating Japan's productivity growth during the catch-up phase. After its economy matured in the mid-1970s, Japan faced competition with other major industrial economies in developing advanced, innovative technologies. The opportunity to import and imitate well-established technologies is diminishing. As Japan approaches the technological frontier, innovation, not imitation, becomes the key to future success.

Many analysts argued that the well-entrenched economic institutions and practices of the 1940 system, though performing well to achieve economic growth during the catch-up phase, would hinder Japan's ability to respond to the new economic environment.

As stated earlier, postwar Japanese economic institutions emphasized the value of long-term cooperation between economic actors, as seen in the ties between government and business, business and business, and labor and management. Cooperation forms converging expectations and eventually reduces uncertainty and transaction costs.

Those routinized and institutionalized cooperative ties embodied in the *keiretsu* corporate structure help strengthen coordination between production units. When the technology is relatively mature and well established, the competitive edge lies in the production process. The cooperative ties in Japanese economic institutions provide an advantage in production coordination and promote effective competition, especially for manufacturing industries such as automobiles and electronics that depend on timely, reliable delivery of parts.

The negative aspect of inward-looking relationships, however, began to appear as the economic environment changed. Institutions built on relationalism limit the circulation of information, especially new sources of information from the outside. Economic actors, bound by strong ties and connections, may be less responsive to market signals than reciprocal relations in economic decision making. The institution is particularly deficient in the new knowledge economy where advanced information must be constantly introduced from outside.

Furthermore, large businesses prefer to hire from top Japanese universities. They routinely treat Japanese graduates with advanced degrees from foreign universities as "overqualified." In so doing, Japanese corporate recruiters may miss the opportunity to hire competent, foreign-trained scientists, engineers, and managers with a global perspective in graduate training who may be risk-takers or nonconformists working on radical innovation.

The practice of lifetime employment offered by major companies implicitly encourages teamwork and versatility, rather than independent thinking or specialization. These are skills valued in a business environment oriented toward coordination and cooperation. Nevertheless, this kind of recruitment and employment practice may be ill-suited for the risk-taking and creative thinking that are essential for technological innovation.

The influx of foreign MNCs has certainly added a new dimension in business competition in the post-bubble era. There is no denying that changes in business practices are happening at various levels, allowing large corporations to stay competitive (Schaede 2008, 2013; Vogel 2006). The roles of cross shareholdings and the main bank have diminished, and shareholders take a more active stance on demanding better performance from management. Venture capital is expanding as companies take more initiatives at their own risk. Price competition now features more prominently than the old subcontracting relationship. There is growing literature to indicate that private firms are increasingly taking additional responsibilities and risks, de-emphasizing government relations (Schaede 2008; Vogel 2006). Questions remain on the real meaning and implication of these changes. The scope of change is still quite selective and differentiated, with wide variations across companies.

Recalibration of Social Policy

Despite efforts by the Koizumi administration to control government spending, the budget continues to grow. The confluence of economic stagnation and an aging society contributes significantly to the burden of balancing the government budget. Social security outlays have significantly increased, as the population over age 65 nearly doubled from 1992 to 2012. Currently, Japan has the oldest population in OECD economies, with a quarter of the population being over 65 years old. The 2008 global economic and financial crisis and the reconstruction programs after the 2011 Great East Japan Earthquake—the worst natural disaster in Japan's postwar history—further contributed to Japan's fiscal problem. Budget deficits of more than 20 years have driven up public sector debt from 68 percent of GDP in 1992 to 219 percent in 2016, making Japan the highest among the industrialized economies (OECD 2017b). Nearly a quarter of the annual government budget was tied to interest payments (Pempel 2017).

Fortunately, unlike the debt crisis of the Eurozone, where the national debt is largely held by foreign entities, most of Japan's national debt is purchased and held by domestic entities (i.e., Japanese banks, insurers, and public pension funds), which are unlikely to cause a sudden increase to the Japanese national debt.

Many of the changes to social welfare programs were made while the LDP was out of power, but the LDP was reluctant to totally reverse them when it returned to power. In 1993, the non-LDP coalition government promoted social policy reforms to show its prosocial welfare stance (Peng 2003). Political realignments, along with support from the Ministry of Health and Welfare in the context of favorable public opinion, made it possible for the Long-Term-Care Insurance Act (LTCI) to pass the Diet in 1997, for implementation in 2000. As the first new social insurance program since the 1960s, LTCI transfers much of the responsibility for taking care of the elderly from family to society and the government, in the "socialization of care" scheme. It was a sharp departure from the LDP's long-standing practice to privatize social responsibility into the hands of families or corporations.

LTCI covers both home-based care and institutional care services with joint funding from social insurance, taxes, and a user fee. Against the same political background, the Angel Plan, a new childcare policy, was introduced in 1994 as part of a large child welfare reform to expand public childcare provisions for families with dependent children. Additionally, the parental leave policy allows flexibility and replacement income for parents to take childcare leave up to one year.

In recent years, economic stagnation and the rising public deficit led to rollbacks in these programs. By 2005, LTCI expenditures exceeded the projected expenditure by 1 billion yen. Within the context of Japan's rapidly aging population and economic uncertainty, the government scaled back the program in 2005 by imposing stricter rationing, tightening service eligibility, and assessing new fees. Similarly, public childcare facilities were cut back due to funding shortages at national and local levels. Under the slogan of "from public to private," the idea of a universal childcare policy was abandoned. Instead, more public, licensed childcare centers are being converted through outsourcing or privatization, which will not reduce the burden on the family for caregiving or the cost for these services. It is clear that Japan is still struggling to maintain a balance between growth and distributive policies.

DISCUSSION QUESTIONS

1. According to the developmental state perspective, Japanese bureaucracy plays an active role in engineering Japan's postwar economic miracle. Describe what various government actors did to promote investment and technology transfer and evaluate their efforts within the overall framework of the supply-side and demand-side economies.

2. Some economists describes the Japanese postwar economic institutions as the 1940 system, a system in support of the Japanese wartime economy. What are the expectations for the government and business in

the 1940 system? Discuss whether the postwar Japanese institutions and practices fit the model.

3. The postwar conservative coalition provides electoral support to the LDP in exchange for favorable economic policies. Who are the principal groups of this coalition? What are their economic agendas?

4. The Japanese economy has experienced sustained stagnation for most of the post-bubble era, despite repeated economic stimulations. Describe the reform measures taken by various administrations, and discuss their intentions and targeted interests.

5. The aging population in Japan will have a negative effect on the country's economic growth while adding to the cost for social and health care policies. Discuss the efforts of the Japanese government in supporting welfare policy while maintaining budget balance.

8

Japan's Pursuit of National Security

Due to defeat in World War II, Japan lost its prewar colonial possessions. The United States and the Soviet Union received surrenders in the Korean peninsula, and the Nationalist China took back Taiwan and Manchuria.

At the time, anti-Japanese feeling was prevalent in China, the Korean Peninsula, and various parts of Southeast Asia; all were leery of any attempt to rearm Japan. Inside Japan, there was strong antimilitarism as well (Berger 1998; Izumikawa 2010; Katzenstein 1996, 2008). Japanese wartime military and political leaders were totally discredited for their roles in leading the country to disastrous defeat, and the public was skeptical of the colonialism and militarism that had driven the country from the Meiji era. The confluence of these internal and external factors thus built a broad support for the Japanese constitutional prohibition of the armed forces (Article 9 of the 1947 Constitution), relegating the role of the Japanese military to the minimum.

Against this backdrop, the United States used the hub-and-spoke model to build the security framework in postwar Asia, which was quite different from the multilateral regional security organization of the North Atlantic Treaty Organization (NATO) that it created in Europe. A series of bilateral military alliances were concluded separately between the United States and its allies to contain Communist expansionism: Japan, Taiwan, South Korea, the Philippines, Australia, and New Zealand. These parallel, discrete security arrangements were anchored to the United States, whose hegemonic position offered a security guarantee for peace and stability in the region.

The U.S. dominance in the U.S.-Japan alliance provided a double guarantee. On the one hand, it protected Japan from external threat; on the other hand, it helped constrain the revival of militarism and expansionism in Japan. In retrospect, the approach worked remarkably well in the postwar era by containing Communist expansion; the resulting peace and stability facilitated economic modernization in Japan and the newly industrialized economies such as South Korea, Taiwan, Singapore, and Hong Kong.

Nevertheless, there were critics of this security approach (Johnson 1986). Many conservatives in Japan disapproved of Article 9 of the Constitution and advocated constitutional revision to restore Japan's power and international status. Additionally, many Americans believed that Japan was a free rider of the U.S. defense protection and demanded the country take more responsibility in sharing the burden.

In recent years, the rise of China and the nuclear brinksmanship of North Korea raise security stakes in East Asia and reignite the debate about Japan's role in regional security. Will Japan repeal the peace clause in the constitution? Will Japan reorient its security posture and rebuild its military? This chapter examines the competing views of Japan's security strategies and defense policies and discusses factors that shape the security policy making.

SECURITY GOALS AND STRATEGIES

Security Goals

According to Article 9 of the Japanese Constitution, the Japanese people would "forever renounce war as a sovereign right of the nation and the threat or use of force as means of settling international disputes" and "land, sea, and air forces, as well as other war potential, will never be maintained." As discussed further, successive Japanese administrations have interpreted the Constitution to support the country's inherent right of self-defense and the maintenance of military forces for that purpose.

To clarify the nature and scope of Japan's self-defense, the 1957 Basic Policy on National Defense defines the goal of Japan's defense as to prevent "direct and indirect aggression." While Japan-U.S. security arrangements is the basis for defense against foreign aggression, it is also necessary to develop Japan's own "effective defense capability" toward this end. Subsequent revisions of the Basic Policy expand national security to include international cooperation under the United Nations for world peace. The broadened conception of security reflects the gradual evolution from economic security to comprehensive security (Hughes 2004; Llewelyn 2010).

Economic Security. Historically, the sense of economic vulnerability significantly shaped Japan's threat perception and its security strategy. Japanese leaders since the Meiji Restoration have recognized their country's heavy dependence on foreign resources and markets for economic growth. The colonization of Taiwan, Korea, and Manchuria reflected the drive to achieve economic security in the prewar era.

International economic and political instability in the early 1970s, such as the Nixon Shock in 1971 (i.e., the implementation of the New Economic Policy to impose an extra 10 percent tariff on U.S. imports and to abandon dollar-gold convertibility) and the 1973 oil embargo, further confirmed Japan's vulnerability, despite its sustained economic success in the postwar era.

A number of international conflicts in the late 1970s, such as the 1979 Sino-Vietnamese War, the Soviet invasion of Afghanistan, and the 1980 Iran-Iraq war, further raised concerns in Japan. In light of the relative decline in U.S. hegemony, and the increasing assertiveness of the developing world, the concept of multidimensional "comprehensive security" began to emerge to guide Japan's security thinking.

Comprehensive Security. The 1980 *Report on Comprehensive National Security,* commissioned by Prime Minister Ohira Masayoshi (1978–1980) and adopted by Prime Minister Suzuki Zenko (1980–1982) became the national policy. The report called for Japan to adopt a security strategy across multiple dimensions and levels. In the military dimension, it advocated the strengthening of Japan's defense capabilities and increased cooperation with the United States through the bilateral security treaty. In the economic dimension, it emphasized the importance for Japan to secure food and energy supplies and to maintain economic competitiveness in a liberal trading order. In the environmental dimension, it stressed the need to improve crisis management capabilities to respond to natural disasters.

The concept has gained influence and traction since it was first proposed. Prime Minister Nakasone Yasuhiro (1983–1987), Suzuki's successor, embraced the idea, taking steps to build up Japan's military capabilities and enhance cooperation with the United States. The concept was reiterated in subsequent security policy reports. Within the framework of comprehensive security, Japan has taken a greater degree of autonomy in its security and foreign policy making and employed a multifaceted approach to regional security in East Asia. Using an array of economic, political, and military tools to maintain its security, Japan deployed official development assistance (ODA) strategically to maintain friendly relations with its allies, economic partners, and even potential adversaries.

The Evolution of Security Strategies

As discussed in Chapter 6, under the twin goals of democratization and demilitarization, the occupation authorities engaged in broad social, economic, and political reforms in Japan that had significant impacts on Japan's postwar security identity and policy.

The pacifist idea underlying the 1947 Japanese Constitution did not come out of a vacuum. It can be traced back to idealism embedded in Article 1 of the 1928 Kellogg-Briand Pact, which declared the intention of the signatory states to "condemn recourse to war for the solution of international controversies, and renounce it, as an instrument of national policy in their relations with one another."

At the time of drafting the Constitution, Article 9 reflected the prevailing belief that the elimination of militarists in Japan, Germany, and Italy would lead to world peace and security. The mounting threat of the Communist movement, however, changed the U.S. strategic priority in Japan from reform (1945–1947) to recovery (1947–1952). The strategic value of Japan as a frontline state in regional security was further enhanced after the establishment of Communist China (October 1949) and the outbreak of the Korean War (June 1950). As the tension intensified in Asia, the United States began to pressure Japan to remilitarize in order to support the U.S. war efforts.

Competing Ideas and the Yoshida Doctrine. While the Allied forces played a significant role in influencing the direction of Japan's postwar security policies, the Japanese were ultimately the ones that decided on the course of action. Several key ideas emerged to shape the postwar security debates and discourses (Glosserman and Snyder 2015; Hirata 2008; Mochizuki 1983–1984; Pyle 1982; Samuels 2007).

On the left, the pacifists/progressives supported the postwar pacifist constitution and advocated the position of unarmed neutrality to make Japan the "Switzerland of the Far East," as once suggested by General MacArthur. Proponents of this position included intellectuals, labor activists, and leftist politicians from the Japan Socialist Party (JSP). For them, Japan should achieve security through diplomacy and economic cooperation, not through military alliance. They believed that neutralism could enable Japan to focus on economic recovery, while easing East Asian states' concerns over Japan's militarism.

At the opposite end of the ideological spectrum on the right were conservative nationalists (or revisionists) who called for full remilitarization to regain Japan's autonomy and security. Hatoyama Ichiro (prime minister 1954–1956), Kishi Nobusuke (Abe Shinzo's grandfather; prime minister 1957–1960), and, later, Nakasone Yasuhiro (prime minister 1982–1987) were the major proponents of this kind of aggressive rearmament. They advocated revision of Article 9 and removal of foreign troops from Japanese territory to restore Japan' rightful place as a military and economic power. They exercised formidable power as a group within the Liberal Democratic Party (LDP).

In the middle was the centrist position advocated by Prime Minster Yoshida Shigeru, who emphasized the reconstruction of the war-torn economy as a means to rebuild national security and autonomy. Yoshida argued that Japan should separate politics from economics and devote its energy to economic development. He suggested that Japan keep a low diplomatic profile and follow the U.S. foreign policy to enjoy not only the protection of the U.S. security umbrella but also the U.S. market and technology for economic development.

Yoshida viewed the nationalist/revisionist stance of constitutional revision and large-scale rearmament as untenable, for it would increase the defense burden for Japan while causing strong reactions from other Asian states. He believed that Japan could have a small self-defense force under the pacifist constitution but should rely mainly on the United States for protection against the Soviet and Chinese military threats.

With these contending ideas and interests, Japan's security orientation became a subject for intense debates and negotiations during the 1950s. Not a single group was able to dominate the process. It took more than 10 years to forge a consensus. While the pacifists/progressives found common ground with the nationalists/revisionists in their dislike of the continued presence of U.S. forces in Japan, they were suspicious of the latter's idea of rearmament. In the end, they drew closer to Yoshida's moderate position, due to his support of the pacifist Constitution. Their opposition to the nationalist/revisionist position led to Kishi's resignation over the controversy related to the renewal of the U.S.-Japan Security Treaty in 1960 (Chapter 6).

From 1960 onward, the Yoshida line, later known as the Yoshida Doctrine, was accepted by the LDP mainstream as the grand strategy (Sugita 2016). Yoshida's protégés such as Ikeda Hayato (prime minister 1960–1964), Sato Eisaku (Kishi's younger brother—Kishi had been adopted by an uncle; prime minister 1964–1972), and Ohira Masayoshi (prime minister 1978–1980) altogether held the LDP leadership for almost two decades, providing continued political support to the position.

Relying on the United States to provide defense for Japan, however, was not entirely based on pacifism. Instead, it was a realist calculation on Yoshida's part to capitalize on the opportunity of the Cold War and maximize Japanese strategic influence and standing. The pacifist Constitution was a convenient excuse for Yoshida. Whenever pressured by the United States to increase Japan's military capabilities or to support U.S. military operations, Yoshida would invoke the constitutional constraint to deflect the request. During the Korean War, Yoshida refused to send troops to Korea, even though Japan had benefited economically from the war.

The Yoshida Doctrine was a deliberate effort to navigate through the competing economic-security ideas and interests on both the international and domestic fronts. Throughout the Cold War years, it was flexible enough to accommodate internal and external stakeholders, while curtailing political and ideological clashes. By focusing on economic reconstruction, alignment with the United States, and limited rearmament, Japanese leaders maintained a delicate balance between constitutional constraints and military commitments, while gradually and incrementally building up Japan's military capabilities.

While the Yoshida Doctrine succeeded in distancing Japan from American Cold War planning, it paid the price of a long-term strategic loss for Japan, as Tokyo was unable to become a "normal" state to assert itself independently in international affairs. Distancing itself from controversial security issues in international affairs while pursuing exclusively economic interests, Japan acted more like a trading firm than a nation-state (Pyle 1982).

The Formulation of the Abe Doctrine? As discussed in Chapter 6, since Abe Shinzo's return as prime minister in December 2012, Japan has undertaken several security policy initiatives. In December 2013, the Abe cabinet approved the first-ever National Security Strategy (NSS), whose basic formulation calls for "proactive contribution to peace" in taking proactive efforts such as enhanced capabilities and strengthened cooperation with allies and partners to deal with an increasingly severe security environment. The Abe administration created the National Security Council (2013) to centralize policy responsibility, reinterpreted the Constitution to allow Japan's involvement in collective self-defense (2014), and moved the security legislation through the Diet to provide guidelines for the Self-Defense Forces (SDF) to engage in collective defense (2015).

Scholars differ in their assessments of whether these new initiatives constituted a new security doctrine or whether they fell within a stretched interpretation of the old Yoshida Doctrine (Kim 2015; Liff 2015; Nakanishi 2015). What is clear, however, is that gradual and incremental reforms have been implemented by previous administrations, including the Democratic Party of Japan (DPJ) government (2009–2012), since the end of the Cold War. Some of the actions and policies initiated by the second Abe administration are built on those foundations. To shed more light on the change and continuity in the Japanese security institutions and practices, the next section provides a comprehensive review of the baseline established after World War II and discusses recent changes in the context of policy evolution since the post–Cold War era.

SECURITY INSTITUTIONS AND POLICY MAKING

Establishment of Self-Defense

After the Korean War broke out in 1950, most occupation troops were transferred to the Korean Peninsula, leaving Japan defenseless. With the encouragement of the Supreme Commander of the Allied Powers, Japan established a National Police Reserve with 75,000 personnel to maintain domestic security and to guard U.S. bases in Japan. In January and February 1951, U.S. Secretary of State John Foster Dulles met with Prime Minister Yoshida, requesting that Japan rebuild its troops up to 350,000. Yoshida rejected the request on the grounds that other Asian countries would not want Japan to rearm, which was also a line of argument supported by General Douglas MacArthur.

Before the end of the U.S. occupation in 1952, steps were taken to reconstitute Japan's security forces. The National Police Reserve and the minesweeping unit of the Japan Coast Guard were combined into the National Safety Forces, which expanded to be SDF in July 1954 under the newly created Japan Defense Agency (JDA).

Prior to the formal establishment of the SDF, Yoshida requested a legal opinion from the Cabinet Legislation Bureau (CLB), an office advising the government on legal and constitutional issues of prospective legislation. He closely supervised the process.

The CLB issued the opinion in May 1954. According to the CLB, the verbiage of Article 9 supports the view that Japan as a sovereign state can maintain the SDF and exercise the right of individual self-defense (Samuels 2004). Article 9 states:

Aspiring sincerely to an international peace based on justice and order, the Japanese people forever renounce war as a sovereign right of the nation and the threat or use of force as means of settling international disputes.

To accomplish the aim of the preceding paragraph, land, sea, and air forces, as well as other war potential, will never be maintained. The right of belligerency of the state will not be recognized

The CLB argues that the second paragraph of Article 9, which forbids the maintaining of military forces and "war potential," must be understood in the context of the first paragraph, as illustrated by the connecting phrase at the beginning of the second paragraph (i.e., "To accomplish the aim of the preceding paragraph . . . "). In their view, the Constitution prohibits Japan from maintaining military forces only if they are used "as means for settling international disputes," as discussed in the first paragraph. It is not incompatible with the Constitution if Japan maintains military forces for other purposes, such as self-defense. In other words, Japan renounces "war" and "the threat or use of force" as a way to settle international disputes but does not renounce the right to self-defense.

The JSP, the main opposition, challenged this interpretation. Staking out the position as defender of the pacifist Constitution, it viewed the creation of the SDF as unconstitutional on the grounds that Article 9 of the constitution clearly and specifically prohibits the maintenance of "war potential." The JSP held this view until July 1994, when it reversed its position under Socialist Prime Minister Murayama Tomiichi (1994–1996), declaring in the Diet that the SDF was constitutional.

During the Cold War, Japanese courts, including the lower courts and the Supreme Court, had not opposed the position of the LDP government. The Supreme Court deferred to the Diet and evaded the constitutionality issue by treating the issue as a political question, hence outside the scope of its jurisdiction.

Establishment of Defense Constraints

While permitting self-defense, the CLB nevertheless imposes self-constraints to uphold the spirit of Article 9: nonaggression and exclusive defense. The CLB limits the use of force by the SDF to three conditions: in response to the threat of imminent direct attack, in the absence of alternative means of dealing with the threat, and the use of force is set to the minimum extent necessary.

In light of the CLB interpretation, the Diet passed the Ban on Overseas Dispatch in June 1954. It reaffirmed that the U.S.-Japan Security Treaty would serve as the basis of Japan's defense against foreign aggression and that the SDF was merely a supplement to the U.S. forces based in Japan.

In 1956, Japan became a member of the United Nations. The government concluded that collective self-defense under the United Nations, such as sending troops abroad or participating in collective arrangements to defend another country, would exceed the minimum necessary threshold and therefore did not fall under the scope of self-defense permitted by the Constitution.

Other self-imposed constraints were developed subsequently in the form of laws, Diet resolutions, or government declaration (Keddell 1993). First, the JDA was established at a sub-Cabinet level, not as an independent ministry, and housed within the prime minister's office to ensure civilian control of the SDF. Second, to ensure that the SDF was exclusively defense-oriented, Japan pledged not to acquire offensive weapons such as ballistic missiles, intercontinental ballistic missiles (ICBMs), long-range bombers, in-flight refueling capabilities, and aircraft carriers. Third, to prevent weapons produced in Japan from being used for aggression, a ban on arms exports was established in 1967 and expanded in 1976. In particular, Japan chose not to transfer arms to communist countries, to countries under UN arms embargo, or to countries involved in international conflicts. Fourth, to reduce controversy over nuclear weapons, Prime Minister Sato declared in 1967 the three non-nuclear principles: Japan will not produce, possess, or permit deployment of nuclear weapons in Japan. Finally, Prime Minister Miki Takeo (1974–1976) announced in 1976 that Japanese defense expenditures would be limited to a ceiling of 1 percent of gross national product.

By the mid-1970s, it appeared that a greater degree of consensus over Japan's defense and military buildup had been achieved, as security debates shifted from ideological and constitutional conflicts to budgetary considerations.

Developments in the Post–Cold War Era

Japan became a global economic powerhouse during the Cold War era. The end of the Cold War, however, brought rapid changes in the domestic and international politico-economic environment (Oros 2008). Initially, some pacifists viewed the dissolution of the Soviet Union as an opportunity for Japan to become a neutral player in Asia, as the United States lost the reason to keep its forward-based forces in Japan. Nevertheless, subsequent developments, including the outbreak of the Gulf War (1990–1991) and the development of nuclear programs in North Korea, created a volatile security environment that necessitated reevaluation of some of the defense constraints already in place. Japan, however, was unable to move quickly and decisively to address all the issues holistically because of the economic uncertainty from the financial meltdown in the early 1990s and the political instability from the collapse of the 1955 political system. Since then, there have been gradual but consistent efforts to modify and relax these core constraints.

Overseas Deployment. After Iraq invaded Kuwait in 1990, the United States asked Japan to take part in Operation Desert Storm. The request to send the SDF overseas triggered a national debate in Japan over its long-standing pledge not to participate in conflict abroad or to use force to settle international disputes. Prime Minster Kaifu Toshiki attempted to introduce legislation to permit Japan to make a military contribution to the crisis. Nevertheless, it failed to pass the Diet because of the dominant view of the constitutional prohibition. In the end, Japan decided to support the war effort with a significant monetary contribution, an action that was heavily criticized by international community as "checkbook diplomacy."

The expectation for Japan to play a more active role in global affairs became the catalyst for Japan to reassess its security institutions in the post–Cold War era. The International Peace Cooperation Law of 1992 provides a legal framework for the SDF to participate in UN peacekeeping operations, although the scope is limited to humanitarian relief and economic assistance such as medical service and infrastructure construction. The law marks the beginning of a gradual evolution of the SDF roles and missions from territorial defense to regional and global operations.

In the wake of the 9/11 terrorist attacks in the United States, and subsequent American military actions in Afghanistan (2001) and Iraq (2003), the SDF's foreign involvement was further expanded. The Diet passed the Anti-Terrorism Special Measures Law in October 2001 and the Iraqi Reconstruction Law in July 2003 to allow the SDF to engage in noncombat logistical and reconstruction support in conflict zones that were clearly beyond Japan's surrounding areas. Under the Koizumi administration (2001–2006), Japan deployed the SDF for postconflict reconstruction in Iraq and refueling operations in support of the coalition forces in Afghanistan. Since 2009, with the passage of the Anti-Piracy Measures Law, the SDF has joined a multilateral antipiracy operation in the Gulf of Aden and off the coast of Somalia to escort and protect foreign vessels.

Collective Self-Defense. In July 2014, the Abe cabinet overturned the official constitutional interpretation that had forbidden Japan's exercise of collective self-defense for 60 years (Liff 2017). In light of the security threats from potential nuclear, missile, and cyber-attacks in the region, the Abe administration deemed Japan's participation in collective security as necessary for its self-defense.

In the lead-up to the reinterpretation, many LDP members sought an unconditional mandate to exercise the right collective self-defense. Nevertheless, the Buddhist New Komeito Party, a junior partner of the LDP coalition, insisted on having explicit, restrictive conditions for the use of force in collective self-defense. In the end, Komeito was able to attain concessions from Abe. The use of force in collective security must meet three conditions: Japan's survival threatened by a "clear danger," an absence of alternative means of dealing with the threat, and the use of force limited to minimum necessary. Thus, while the 2014 reinterpretation loosened the constitutional constraint on SDF activities, Japan's exercise of collective self-defense is still subject to restrictive conditions. Nevertheless, the reinterpretation opened new opportunities for the SDF to participate in bilateral or multilateral military training and exercises.

Arms Exports. In view of the surging costs of modern defense technology and the need for defense research collaboration with allies, the DPJ government in 2011 practically abolished the 1967 ban on arms exports. In 2014, the Abe government adopted "Three Principles on Transfer of Defense Equipment and Technology" to open up opportunities for defense cooperation agreements with allies and partners as a means to build up indigenous defense capabilities.

Offensive Weapons. During the Cold War era, to emphasize the defense purpose of the SDF, Japan refrained from possessing offensive weapons such as ICBMs and aircraft carriers, even though it was difficult to draw the line between defensive and offensive technology.

In 1993, the test launch of a North Korean medium-range ballistic missile Nodong-1 (up to 900 miles) in the Sea of Japan revealed Japan's vulnerability. The test launch of a Taepodong-1 missile in August 1998 further escalated the tension.

The threat from North Korea prompted Japan to invest in American anti-missile technology. In 1999, Japan and the United States signed a Memorandum of Understanding to collaborate in ballistic missile defense research. In terms of the technology, the development of an interceptor missile is similar to that of an attack missile, hence making the distinction of offensive versus defensive weapons meaningless.

The Ministry of Defense and National Security Council. In 2007, the first Abe administration upgraded the JDA to the full cabinet-ranked Ministry of Defense (MOD) that enjoyed the same legal and organizational status as other ministries. Abe explained the upgrade on the grounds of making "a clean break with the post-war regime" and protecting "the lives and bodies of the people of Japan."

In 2013, the second Abe administration created the National Security Council (NSC), aimed at providing strong leadership for regular discussions of diplomatic and security affairs and for rapid responses. Its "four minister meeting" brings together the prime minister, chief cabinet secretary, foreign minister, and defense minister for interagency coordination and strategic deliberations centered on the prime minister. The creation and operation of the NSC reflects a long-term attempt exemplified in the 2001 administrative reforms (Chapter 6) to strengthen the office of the prime minister in initiating and making foreign and domestic policies.

An Overview of the Defense Budget and the SDF. Japan's defense expenditure in 2018 was about $47.3 billion, which is roughly commensurate with its 1997 spending in nominal yen terms. In comparative terms, Japan's 2018 defense spending is less than one-third of China's expenditure ($168.2 billion) and ranks the eighth in the world.

Japan's defense spending has more or less adhered to the 1 percent ceiling for more than four decades since its establishment in 1976. It seems that the number has proven to be large enough to provide strong capabilities in defending Japan but small enough to raise no fears among the neighbors about its remilitarization. In fact, Japan has been able to find budgetary flexibility through the practice of deferred payments, which spread the expenses of large-scale weapon acquisitions over a number of years against future budgets. The practice enables Japan to engage in significant military upgrades while maintaining on paper the formal 1 percent limit.

The pacifist constitution created a widespread impression that Japan lacks a military or has only a token defense force. In fact, Japan's armed forces—with nearly a quarter million in personnel—are formidable. It has some of the most modern military equipment in Asia. Its army, called the Ground Self-Defense Force (GSDF), is larger than that of the United Kingdom or France. Its navy, the Maritime Self-Defense Force (MSDF), has a large fleet of destroyers, frigates, and submarines and ranks as the best navy in Asia. Similarly, the Air Self-Defense Force (ASDF), its air force, also has the most advanced capabilities in the region. With its order of F-35 Joint Strike Fighters from Lockheed Martin, it will have stealth capabilities to penetrate enemy air defense.

Security Policy Making

Many actors are involved in security discourses and discussions. Besides governmental agencies such as the prime minister's office (*kantei*), the cabinet, the bureaucracy, and the Diet, nongovernmental actors such as political parties, businesses, and the media also take part in the process. During the Cold War era, pacifist public opinions, mass media, and opposition parties formed the political constraints on security policies. At the inner circle of the decision making were the cabinet and the Ministry of Foreign Affairs (MOFA). The Ministry of Finance also exercised significant influence over the size of defense spending, because of its authority to review all budget requests. In the post–Cold War era and prior to the establishment of the MOD in 2007, the MOFA continued to be a dominant player in all foreign and security policies, because the JDA, as a subministry agency, did not have the same legal and organizational status to compete with the MOFA.

After 2007, the newly created MOD began to assume the responsibility for security policy making. Its role became increasingly important, eclipsing that of the MOFA. The MOD's impact on security discourse can be seen in the change of Japan's official view of national threat before and after its creation (Schulze 2018). From the mid-1990s to the mid-2000s, even as Japan began to strengthen its alliance with the United States to counter Chinese expansion, the Defense White Papers, which were shaped primarily by the view of the MOFA, did not specifically identify China as a security concern. In fact, they often portrayed China's rise as an economic opportunity for Japan. That changed quickly after the MOD's creation. In the 2007 Defense White Paper, China was, for the first time, categorized as a "concern," the highest perceived potential threat for Japan. The lack of transparency in China's double-digit military expenditure, national defense policies, and military activities was considered a destabilizing force for Japan and the region. The change in the security characterization of China reflected the MOD's influence in the inner circle. After the creation of the NSC in 2013, the role of the MOD was further enhanced as one of the four members in the regular security consultations.

In recent years, weakened opposition parties and shifting public opinions gave the Japanese policy makers greater leeway in expanding Japan's defense posture (Hughes 2017). A 2015 opinion survey conducted by the Cabinet Office showed an increased interest among the Japanese people in defense affairs— from 56.8 percent in 1994 to 71.5 percent in 2015, driven mainly by "problems relating to Japanese peace and independence." China's military modernization and maritime activities were identified as the top concern by 60.5 percent of the people, followed by situations on the Korean peninsula (52.7 percent) and international terrorist activities (42.6 percent).

JAPAN-U.S. SECURITY RELATIONS

In September 1951, immediately following the signing of the San Francisco Peace Treaty between Japan and the Allied powers, the United States and Japan signed the Mutual Security Treaty, in which Japan agreed to give the United States the right to station troops on Japanese soil. The bilateral defense treaty was significant in two ways: first, it transformed wartime enemies into allies, and second, it incorporated Japan into the U.S. containment strategy against the Soviet Union and China.

While relying on the U.S. security guarantee, Japan was careful in hedging against the possibility of being either abandoned or entrapped by this bilateral alliance (Hughes 2009). Abandonment referred to a situation where the United States might try to achieve its own global strategic goal by compromising Japan's security interest, whereas entrapment meant that the United States might enlist Japan as a proxy to support Washington's global or regional operations, placing Japan in harm's way.

The Cold War Era

At the height of the Cold War, Japan was less concerned about abandonment because of its strategic value in the global bipolar structure. Rather, its paramount concern was about entrapment, as Japan tried to stay out of the U.S. military actions in Korea and Vietnam.

During the Korean War, Japan played its strategic role by providing supplies to the U.S. forces while reaping economic benefits from the wartime procurement. It was a staging ground for the U.S. defense of South Korea. The United States, however, expected more from Japan, asking Japan to rearm and to play an active role in regional defense, to free the United States for other global responsibilities. Nevertheless, the public distrust of the military in Japan, along with the strong concerns of its neighboring countries, formed formidable external and internal constraints on Japan's rearmament.

In the 1950s, defense cooperation with the United States was highly controversial and often generated heated debates in Japan. Domestic opposition was the main reason for Japan to take a cautious attitude toward rearmament and foreign deployment. In the face of strong domestic pressure, the U.S.-Japan Security Treaty was revised in 1960, removing U.S. forces from any role in Japanese internal security and increasing Japan's role in its self-defense. Nevertheless, during deliberations of the Treaty renewal at the Diet, students and union members gathered in massive demonstrations around the Diet building against the Treaty. The strong backlash from the public forced Prime Minister Kishi to resign.

Controversy flared up again in the mid-1960s, as the United States intensified its involvement in Vietnam. Opposition parties in Japan contended that Japanese businesses were selling rifles, machine guns rockets, and ammunitions to the United States, who then used the weapons in Vietnam. Under pressure from the opposition parties, Japan established more defense constraints. The ban on arms exports and the three nonnuclear principles were announced in 1967 against this background.

In 1969, President Nixon announced in Guam that the United States would not commit ground troops on the Asian mainland anymore, and would expect greater burden sharing by America's Asian allies. The statement, known as the Nixon Doctrine, signaled that the United States might be gradually disengaged from Asia. The potential policy shift alarmed Japanese officials, who began to fear the possibility of U.S. abandonment. The fear deepened in 1970 as the United States announced the plan to reduce military forces in South Korea.

Nakasone Yasuhiro, then director-general of the JDA (1970–1971) and later the prime minister (1982–1987), responded to the emerging trend by proposing the notion of "autonomous defense" for Japan. He advocated building up Japan's own defense capabilities to cope with conventional local wars of aggression. While the idea was met with resistance from officials in the JDA, it showed the apprehension about the U.S. security commitments.

The oil crisis of 1973 further heightened the need for Japan to protect its economic interests. As the external strategic environment evolved, Japan sought to recalibrate its security commitments and adjust its security responsibilities. Discussions on strengthening bilateral security cooperation led to the development of the 1978 Guidelines for Japan-U.S. Defense Cooperation, which established the cooperation framework by outlining how the U.S. and Japanese militaries interact in peacetime and war. Most importantly, the Guidelines institutionalized the U.S. military commitment to Japanese defense, while defining Japan's roles and responsibilities (Satake 2016). For Japanese leaders, the Guidelines made the alliance commitment more credible and helped ease their fear of U.S. abandonment. For American policy makers, the Guidelines formalized the Japanese responsibility in sharing the defense burden.

Under the 1978 Guidelines, the United States promised to maintain a sufficient military presence in Japan and in Northeast Asia for Japan's defense, and Japan agreed to expand its military operations beyond the home islands. Prime Minister Suzuki Zenko (1980–1982) announced in May 1981 that the MSDF would be responsible for patrolling sea lanes up to 1,000 nautical miles from Japan's coastline.

The Post–Cold War Era

As discussed earlier, international criticism of Japan's "checkbook diplomacy" during the Gulf War (1990–1991) led to the 1992 International Peace Cooperation Law enabling the SDF to participate in UN peacekeeping operations. Subsequently, external security threats, including North Korea's nuclear and missile programs, and China's rise and maritime assertiveness, made Japan more inclined to align its security interest with that of the United States.

From the mid-1990s onward, Japan showed a greater willingness to undertake a more robust role in regional peace and stability. In 1995, Japan revised the National Defense Program Outline, emphasizing the necessity of a harmonious and effective Japan-U.S. alliance in dealing with situations that may emerge "in the areas surrounding Japan." In the same year, to ease international concerns about the U.S. withdrawal from Asia, the Clinton administration published the East Asia Strategy Report to make clear the U.S. intention of maintaining robust troop presence in Asia and Europe.

From 1995 to 1996, tensions across the Taiwan Strait (Chapter 4) brought Japan closer to the United States. In April 1996, Prime Minister Hashimoto and President Clinton signed the Japan-U.S. Joint Declaration on Security to reaffirm both countries' determination to increase their security and political cooperation to ensure peace and stability in the region. The Japan-U.S. security relationship was transformed from a bilateral military defense cooperation into a partnership for global security. The scope of the security cooperation expanded from protecting Japan to countering aggression and maintaining peace and stability throughout the entire Asia-Pacific theater, as threats had shifted from the former Soviet Union to China and North Korea.

Following the Joint Declaration, both sides developed the 1997 Guidelines for Japan-U.S. Defense Cooperation. Under the 1997 Guidelines, the SDF took on additional responsibilities in refugee assistance, search and rescue operations, and noncombatant evacuation. Japan agreed to provide "rear area" support to the U.S. forces in "areas surrounding Japan where situations have a direct impact on Japan's peace and security."

After the 9/11 terrorist attacks, Japan actively supported the U.S. War on Terror in Afghanistan and Iraq. Japan's counterterrorism efforts were driven primarily by its need for security reassurance from Washington, as the security environment in East Asia became volatile and unpredictable. Supporting the American priority would foster trust with Washington and strengthen bilateral security ties to ensure the continued protection of Japan.

In the 2010s, in the face of rapid rise of China, the vicious circle of low growth and high debt levels has heightened the sense of strategic vulnerability in Japan. President Obama's "pivot to Asia" policy and Abe's proactive pacifism laid the foundation for further strengthening the Japan and U.S. alliance, which was one of the pillars of Japan's 2013 NSS. The 2015 Guidelines for Japan-U.S. Defense Cooperation reflected the latest effort in solidifying defense commitments from both sides.

The 2015 Guidelines expanded bilateral cooperation into three areas not mentioned in the 1997 Guidelines: cybersecurity, the use of space for defense, and ballistic missile defense. Rather than separating the role of the SDF from that of the U.S. military, the 2015 Guidelines integrate the American and Japanese forces in all phases during peacetime, wartime, and "gray-zone" contingency of low-intensity conflicts. An Alliance Coordination Mechanism was established to facilitate frequent, real-time communication between civilian and uniformed staff from all the relevant agencies the both governments.

The broad scope of the Japan-U.S. collaboration, including intelligence sharing, contingency planning, and crisis management across all domains and scenarios, has transformed the Japan-U.S. alliance from the traditional threat-centered alliance to an order-centered alliance, as envisioned in the Joint Declaration signed by Hashimoto and Clinton.

JAPAN-CHINA SECURITY RELATIONS

After regaining its sovereignty in 1952, Japan aligned with U.S. foreign policy and took part in containing the People's Republic of China (PRC). At the behest of the United States, Japan in April 1952 signed a separate peace treaty with Taiwan, recognizing its status as the legitimate government of China. In exchange, Taiwan renounced its right to claim reparations from Japan.

In the 1950s and 1960s, Japan's relations with the PRC were carried out in the form of "people diplomacy" through nongovernmental exchanges. Some LDP lawmakers formed the Council on the Normalization of the Japan-China Diplomatic Relationship to promote Japan-PRC relations in semi-official campaigns.

A fundamental shift in Japan's relations with China came after the U.S.-China rapprochement. In July 1971, President Nixon announced his upcoming visit to China. Japan was not consulted prior to the announcement. Totally unprepared for the move, Japan had to scramble to reset its China policy.

In September 1972, seven months after President Nixon's February 1972 visit to China, Japanese Prime Minister Tanaka Kakuei visited Beijing to normalize diplomatic relation with the PRC and sever relations with Taiwan. In the Joint Communique, Japan recognized the government of the PRC as the sole legal government of China and expressed its understanding of PRC's stance that Taiwan was "an inalienable part" of the PRC. Japan also indicated that it was "keenly conscious of the serious damage that Japan caused in the past to the Chinese people through war, and deeply reproaches itself."

In 1978, Deng Xiaoping visited Japan and concluded the Treaty of Peace and Friendship with Japan. At the time, bilateral relations were friendly and cooperative. Japan was willing to engage China economically as part of its comprehensive security strategy, promoting mutual understanding through interactions and exchanges. China considered Japan a peaceful neighbor that could contribute to China's economic growth. Beijing took comfort in the fact that Japan's militarism would be constrained by the U.S.-Japan security alliance.

In 1979, Japanese Prime Minister Ohira Masayoshi visited China and provided China economic cooperation and official development assistance (ODA). For the next three decades, Japan became the primary provider of ODA to China, until the program was terminated in 2008. From 1979 to 2005, Japan disbursed more than $26.6 billion in loans, $1.23 billion in grants, and $1.23 billion in technical aid to the PRC. Bilateral trade grew, and China overtook the United States in 2004 as Japan's largest trading partner.

Nevertheless, economic cooperation failed to spill over to political and security relations (Bush 2010; Dreyer 2014). Beneath the increased economic and cultural interactions between China and Japan were strong undercurrents of mutual antipathy, particularly along the lines of historical issues and maritime disputes (Kawashima 2015; Lam 2017).

Controversy over Historical Issues

Controversy over history revolves around two issues: the high-level visit to the Yasukuni Shrine and the revision of Japanese textbooks. At the core of the problem is that history can be constructed and construed differently in these two countries.

The Yasukuni Shrine. The Yasukuni Shrine in Tokyo was founded by Emperor Meiji in 1879 to honor soldiers who died protecting the emperor. During World War II, it became an emblem of militarism. As part of the demilitarization effort, the occupation authorities inhibited ceremonies for honoring the war dead. In 1946, the Shrine was "privatized" to sever its official relationship with the government. In the postwar era, prime ministers usually visited the shrine during autumn or spring festivals. In 1975, Prime Minister Miki became the first one to visit the Yasukuni on August 15, the anniversary of Japan's surrender, although in a "private" capacity.

In 1979, at the Shrine's 100th anniversary, names of 14 Class A war criminals were quietly enshrined as deities. In 1985, Prime Minister Nakasone, along with 18 of his cabinet ministers, paid an official visit to the Yasukuni Shrine on the 40th anniversary of Japan's surrender. The visit resulted in a strong protest from the Chinese government and massive demonstrations and boycotts of Japanese products throughout China. The diplomatic storms led to a hiatus in prime ministerial visits for more than 10 years.

China responded by building the Memorial Hall of the Victims in Nanjing Massacre in 1985. The Museum of the Chinese People's War of Resistance against Japanese Aggression was opened in 1987, at the 50th anniversary of the outbreak of the second Sino-Japanese War. Throughout the 1990s and the 2000s, China promoted the patriotic education campaign to emphasize China's humiliation and suffering in modern history.

In July 1996, Prime Minister Hashimoto, as a nationalist and a former chair of the Japan War Bereaved Families Association, visited the Yasukuni Shrine on his birthday. Other nationalist prime ministers such as Koizumi and Abe followed his act, although they sometimes chose a different date from the more contentious August 15th.

For many Chinese who had experienced and remembered the warfare and atrocities during the Japanese invasion, they viewed these visits by high-ranking officials as a sign of revived militarism. For the Japanese officials, they explained the visits as simply paying homage to Japan's fallen soldiers.

The Textbook Issue. Under the U.S. occupation, new textbooks were written to describe Japan's invasion of its neighbors and its wartime atrocities. In the early 1950s, the government's attempt to tone down the textbook criticisms of Japan's wartime activities was unsuccessful. In 1982, the Ministry of Education revised some textbooks to describe Japan's prewar actions in Northern China as "advance," not "invasion." The new language was seen by the Chinese as glossing over Japanese aggression. This attempted censorship drew vigorous protests from China and South Korea.

The revision of textbooks reflected a broader attempt by the Japanese nationalists to reinterpret wartime history. The Japanese nationalists challenged the dominant narrative about Japan being an aggressor. Rather, they contended that the reason Japan went to war was to free Asians from European colonialism and racism, hence the act was defensive and just. Their views were marginalized during the Cold War but gained new popularity in light of the growing public concern over the perceived threats from China and North Korea. They founded the Japanese Society for History Textbook Reform in 1996 and published a revisionist history textbook in 2001 to downplay Japan's wartime aggression. Demands from China and South Korea to make corrections to the controversial textbook were refused by Japan.

In China, historical issues with Japan became an important piece of the curriculum in the patriotic education. The narrative emphasized the atrocities committed by the Japanese Imperial Army since its occupation of Manchuria in 1931 and subsequent invasion of the rest of China. The focus was on the Chinese Community Party's (CCP) leadership role in leading heroic resistance to Japanese invasion. In February 2014, the Chinese National People's Congress designated two national days to commemorate the country's victory in the anti-Japanese war (September 3) and the victims of the Nanjing Massacre (December 13).

While patriotism became another source of CCP legitimacy, it also cultivated strong nationalistic sentiments against Japan. Popular nationalism forced the PRC government to take a hardline approach toward Japan in official discourse, making it difficult to maintain stable trade and economic relations with Japan.

The Senkaku/Diaoyu Islands Dispute

Located in the East China Sea between Okinawa and Taiwan, the uninhabited Senkaku (or Diaoyu, as called by the Chinese) Islands are claimed by Japan, China, and Taiwan. After World War II, they were placed under U.S. control but were returned along with Okinawa to Japan in 1972.

China argues that its ownership of the islands dates back to the Sino-Japanese War, when Japan annexed the islands illegally from China in 1895. The area around the islands is reportedly rich in oil reserves and fishing grounds. The disputed territorial claims have implications for legal control of the nearby fishing grounds, as well as oil and gas deposits. Securing rights to this area means establishing an exclusive economic zone so that the country would then have access to these valuable resources. Additionally, the islands hold strategic value. China has been following a naval strategy to obtain control over the first island chain in the East China Sea by 2010 and the second island chain by 2020 in order to increase its access to the Western Pacific. The Senkaku/Diaoyu Islands fall in the first chain.

In June 2008, setting aside the territorial disputes, China and Japan reached an agreement to explore and develop the area. In September 2010, Japanese seizure of a Chinese trawler and its captain near the islands sparked fierce reactions from China, including large-scale public demonstrations.

In April 2012, then nationalist Tokyo Governor Ishihara Shintaro revealed his plan to purchase from the owner of three islands of the Senkaku/Diaoyu chain. His plan immediately drew strong reactions from China. To preempt Ishihara's move, the Noda administration of the DPJ declared nationalization of the islands. The action, however, did little to mitigate the crisis. The Chinese public reacted negatively with massive anti-Japanese protests. Events planned for the 40th anniversary of the China-Japan diplomatic normalization (1972) were canceled.

Both sides intensified their activities in the area, deploying patrol ships and surveillance planes, and even military assets, to bolster their respective claims. Japan deployed new ships to its Coast Guard and established a dedicated 12-vessel fleet to patrol the area at all times. In November 2013, China declared an Air Defense Identification Zone in the region to challenge Japan's territorial claims. In 2014, President Obama affirmed that the U.S.-Japan Security Treaty would extend to an armed attack situation over the

Senkaku/Diaoyu Islands. The 2015 Guidelines formalized the U.S. commitment to the defense of the islands, and President Trump reaffirmed the commitment in 2017.

Hot Economics, Cold Politics

Japan-China relations are often described as "hot economics, cold politics." The term reflects the duality of China-Japan relations and the coexistence of engagement and contention. As discussed earlier, Japan has strengthened the Japan-U.S. alliance. Under Abe, it proposed an Indo-Pacific strategy to upgrade its relations with other U.S. allies such as India, Australia, and South Korea. Its interest in building a "ring of encirclement" against China has caused serious concerns in China and strained the bilateral relations.

China is also concerned about Japanese military buildup. Tokyo's acquisition of new military capabilities, including ballistic missile defense systems, is seen by China as power expansion. The recent increase in military spending under Abe took place amid rising public debt and economic stagnation, reversing more than a decade of downward trend.

Despite confrontation on the security front, recently there have been efforts to cooperate. Abe and Xi Jinping held a summit meeting during the Asia-Pacific Economic Cooperation (APEC) forum in December 2017, paving the way for mutual visits, after long gaps in such exchanges. Chinese Premier Li Keqiang visited Japan in May 2018, eight years after the 2010 visit by Premier Wen Jiabao. Abe visited China in October 2018, seven years after Noda's visit in 2011. Abe proposed to coordinate with China in developing a free and fair trade system and to convert mutual relations from threat to partnership.

The "America First" policy under the Trump administration may have opened up the opportunity for Japan-China cooperation on the economic front. After the U.S. withdrawal from the Trans-Pacific Partnership (TPP), Japan has been committed to safeguarding the rule-based international economic order. It led the effort in reviving the TPP without U.S. participation, reaching an agreement with the other 10 remaining TPP members in November 2017 on the Comprehensive Progressive Trans-Pacific Partnership (CPTPP). CPTPP retains many of the trade rules in the original TPP agreement. Japan and the European Union (EU) signed the Japan-EU Economic Partnership Agreement in July 2018. Thus, Japan is working with like-minded countries to sustain the free trade regime without the participation of the United States.

Against this backdrop, Japan is contemplating integrating its own Partnership for Quality Infrastructure with China's Belt and Road Initiative (BRI). Working with China's BRI on the western Pacific front, Japan can expand its presence in the infrastructure development sector through the CPTPP countries on the eastern Pacific front. If Japan and China can cooperate on these important economic projects, it would be interesting to see whether hot economics spills into hot politics in the future.

DISCUSSION QUESTIONS

1. What were the competing ideas and interests in the security debate of postwar Japan? Why do you think the Yoshida Doctrine emerged in the end as the chosen strategy?

2. How did the interpretation of Article 9 of the 1947 Constitution change over time? What are the internal and external reasons for the change?

3. Describe the self-imposed constraints on Japan's defense in the postwar era and how they have evolved after the end of the Cold War.

4. Compare Deng Xiaoping's strategy of "keeping a low profile" with the proposition of the Yoshida Doctrine. How are they similar, and how are they different?

5. What are the factors that shaped Japan-China security relations since the 1980s? Discuss whether the imbalance between economic relations ("hot economics") and politico-security relations ("cold politics") can be sustained.

9

Korea

THE FOUNDATIONS

PEOPLE AND GEOGRAPHY

Located at the northeastern rim of the Asian continent, the Korean peninsula extends 680 miles southward from continental Asia into the Pacific Ocean, with a total land area of 85,000 square miles, about the size of the state of Utah. The peninsula is enclosed by the East Sea (or Sea of Japan) and the West Sea (or Yellow Sea), with the Korea Strait (or Tsushima Strait in Japan) connecting the two bodies of water in the south.

The land is largely mountainous, with small valleys and narrow coastal plains. Mountains and hills account for approximately 70 percent of the peninsula;areas of higher elevation are in the northern and eastern parts of the peninsula. Most of the rivers flow westward or southward into either the Yellow Sea or the East China Sea. Only 15 percent of the land is arable. Population concentrates in the lowlands and river valleys in the south and west. Lowland plains are separated by mountains and hills that, in the past, created communication barriers between various parts of the country and caused regional rivalry.

The Korean Demilitarized Zone (DMZ), established in 1953 after the Korean War, formed the boundary between North and South Korea. South Korea controls 45 percent of the peninsula (or 38,000 square miles), making it slightly larger than Hungary or the state of Indiana, but its population (over 51.3 million in 2018) far exceeds that of the North (estimated 25.4 millions). The southern part of the peninsula has historically been the base for agricultural production, particularly rice. The peninsula is moderately endowed with natural resources mostly located in the mountain ranges in the north, including coal, gold, silver, aluminum, iron ore, and so on.

China and Japan are only 110 miles and 129 miles away to its west and east coasts. In the north, the Yalu (Amnok) and the Tumen (Tuman) rivers formed the borders with China (about 640 miles long) and Russia (roughly 10 miles). Historically, Korea served as a land bridge between China and Japan, transmitting Buddhism and Confucianism from China to Japan. Nevertheless, it was also at the strategic center of the conflict between the continental powers and the maritime forces, having been invaded by Chinese (in the 7th century), Mongols (in the 13th century), Japanese (in the 16th century), and Manchus (in the 17th century). Its ability to survive foreign interventions and invasions testifies to the strength and resilience of its people and civilization.

THE HISTORICAL ROOTS

In 194 BCE, Wi Man invaded the Korean peninsula from northern China and founded the kingdom of Choson. Within a century, Choson was conquered by the Han Dynasty, which subsequently established four administrative units (commanderies) and ruled the northwestern part of the Korean peninsula for the next four centuries.

Around the 4th century, three Korean kingdoms emerged to challenge the Chinese: Koguryo (located in the northernmost region), Paekche (in the center and southwest), and Silla (in the southeast) were centralized indigenous states ruled by kings with the assistance of administrative officials. Battling with China and one another, they began to adopt Buddhism, Confucianism, and the Chinese governance structure for reform or restoration.

Silla Dynasty: 668–935

In 676, Silla allied with the Chinese Tang army and conquered the other two kingdoms to unify the Korean peninsula. It was a pivotal event in Korean history. Silla's centralized framework facilitated the development of a homogeneous Korean nation with a common identity and shared values.

Ruling from the southeastern capital of Kyongju, Silla embraced Buddhism as the predominant religion. During this period, Buddhism strongly influenced the Korean culture, including poetry, music, and painting. For political governance, Silla kings turned to Confucianism. To consolidate royal power, they promoted its teachings on loyalty to the ruler and respect for authority. A national academy was established to teach Confucian ethics and literature.

Silla kings participated in the Chinese tributary system to gain legitimacy and prestige at home. Additionally, tributary missions helped promote trade and cultural exchanges. Silla modeled itself on Tang China by adopting the Chinese calendar, laws, and governing institutions. As was the case in Japan, the introduction of the Tang-style civil service exam system encountered strong resistance from the entrenched aristocracy. The aristocrats in Silla possessed enormous wealth and private armies, which were the sources of their economic and military power. They had been given special privileges by Silla kings for their contributions. Closely guarding their monopolized control over the upper echelon of the bureaucracy, they were unwilling to share power with Confucian scholar-bureaucrats. Thus, while in Tang China the hereditary aristocracy was significantly weakened by the civil service exams, the aristocratic families in Silla retained their power and authority.

Silla was a class-based society with little opportunity for social mobility. Ranks and status, as shown in clothing, footwear, and the size of houses, were strictly regulated to maintain the hereditary class lines. The royal family, aristocrats, and government officials stood atop the social structure. The authority of the monarchs, however, was limited by the alliance of powerful aristocratic families in the capital and provinces.

Beneath the aristocratic class was a mass of commoners such as farmers and workers who provided taxes and labor for the government. Merchants were active in maritime trade with China and Japan. Through trade, Silla narrowed the technology gap with China in silk and ceramics.

Silla gradually entered a period of decline in the 9th century and disintegrated in the early 10th century. Wang Kon, who was a maritime lord, founded the Koryo state in 918 as a successor to Koguryo. Wang invoked the Chinese concept of the Mandate of Heaven and formed alliances with old Silla aristocrats and powerful warlords to consolidate his power. The dynasty ruled the entire peninsula for the next four centuries (935–1392) from Kaesong. It is from the name Koryo that the Western name Korea is derived.

Koryo Dynasty: 935–1392

An important institutional innovation during Koryo was the implementation of the civil service examination in 958. Modeled on Tang China, the Korean exam system included required knowledge in subjects such as Chinese literature and Confucian classics. The exam system was used more as a means to train the aristocratic elite and validate their status, less as a method of recruiting officials. Nevertheless, it helped establish the structure of bureaucracy to support the monarchs and promote education and literacy among the elites.

Beginning in the 12th century, Koryo entered a turbulent period plagued by rebellions, factional infighting, and military coup. Military leaders eventually controlled the government between 1170 and 1270, establishing a military regime that resembled the Japanese shogunate. In the 13th century, the country suffered from a series of invasions by the Mongols, who looked to expand their military campaigns into the Korean peninsula, before accomplishing their ultimate mission of conquering Japan and the Southern Song Dynasty in China. In 1232, hoping to take advantage of the Mongol military weakness at sea, the military regime moved its capital to Kanghwa Island off the west coast of the central peninsula. Although Koryo successfully defended its island capital for four decades, the Mongol forces brought devastation to much of the peninsula.

In 1270, the Koryo monarch ended the long military rule, returned the capital to Kaesong, and surrendered completely to the Mongols. Under the Mongols' Yuan Dynasty (1271–1368), Koryo was forced to take part in the two invasions of Japan. The Yuan Dynasty imposed enormous economic burdens on Korea, demanding tributes such as gold, silver, ginseng, and medicinal herbs. Nonetheless, Korea benefited from the global reach of the Yuan empire, whose contact with the Islamic world brought new trading opportunities. During this time, new agricultural technology in rice farming such as irrigation and deep plowing was introduced to Korea from Yuan China, supporting population growth in Korea. Although the reign of the Mongols faded rather quickly, decades of military struggle with the Mongols weakened the political grip of the Koryo royal family. In 1392, General Yi Song-gye overthrew the regime and founded the Choson Dynasty (or Yi Dynasty, 1392–1910), moving the capital to Seoul.

Choson Dynasty: 1392–1910

While the transition from Koryo to Choson was justified on the grounds of the Mandate of Heaven, the process was relatively smooth without a significant war or conflict. The smooth transition meant that most of the Koryo institutional structure and the elite personnel were retained by the new regime.

Political Governance. As the longest of Korea's dynasties, the Choson court governed Korea for more than 500 years. During its long rule, it consistently sought to establish the political and social order based on Confucian ideals and beliefs. Confucianism became the state philosophy and the foundation for political and social authority. It laid down the standard of proper behaviors and attitudes in family and society and provided the tenets for political and social institutions. Choson's long-lasting embrace of Confucian doctrines had a profound impact on the attitudes and behaviors of modern Koreans (Kim 2012; Seith 2011).

Although Choson's effort in adopting Chinese civilization earned it the recognition of "Little China," it also engaged in creative adaptation to turn transplanted norms and institutions into indigenous traditions and heritage. An independent writing system (the *hangul* alphabet) was invented in the 15th century under the fourth king of Choson, Sejong the Great, though the Chinese characters remained popular for several more centuries. The revived use of the script in the 19th century inspired the Korean national consciousness, and it became the official script in both the North and South after 1945.

Choson built a highly stratified society based on inheritance. Administrative apparatus was organized from central to local levels. At the apex of the Choson state was the king, assisted by a complex set of bureaucratic institutions to carry out his rule. The officials, or *yangban* (meaning two orders of officials), consisted of civil and military officials. Of the two, the civil officials commanded more respect and prestige, because Confucian scholars were less interested in military affairs and generally viewed the military with contempt. By the 16th century, the term came to mean the entire elite aristocratic class of Korea, who comprised less than 10 percent of the population.

The continuity of the aristocratic elite in Korea was remarkable. Many of the same families consistently maintained their economic and social dominance for over a thousand years, from Koryo to Choson. It was quite uncommon to see such a stable social order elsewhere.

Yangban were granted land and stipends and were tax-exempted until the late 19th century reform. To maintain their privileges, their families needed to produce officials through civil service exams. While the civil service exam was instituted by Koryo, Choson placed even greater importance on it, making it virtually the only venue to obtain a high-level official position. Unlike the equalitarian system in China where civil service exams offered commoners the opportunity for upward mobility, the Korean civil service exam was confined to members of the elite and therefore reinforced their status and privilege.

As in Confucian tradition, learned scholars served as censors to criticize the actions of the king and his officials. The expectation was for the king and his officials to govern wisely and adhere to the moral expectations of the teaching of Confucianism.

Political power gradually moved into the hands of a small segment of the hereditary aristocracy who could significantly limit the royal authority. A small number of powerful clans, divided into factions, maneuvered for political advantages in fierce competition for power, prestige, and positions.

Below *yangban*, the "middle people" (*chungin*) served as the lower-ranking technical specialists and clerks such as scribes, medical officials, interpreters, or translators. They played an important role in the functioning of the local government. Because of their expertise in foreign languages, many of them helped introduce Western culture into Korea in the late 19th century.

Commoners, who constituted the majority of the population, carried the burden of taxes, labor duties, and military services but were barred from civil service exams. The vast majority lived in villages and engaged in farming, with a small number of craftsmen and merchants. Agriculture was the basis of the economy, and commercial activity centered around ginseng and rice became more significant in the 17th century. There was hardly any violent, large-scale farmer rebellion until the 19th century. Below commoners were the outcast (*chonmin*), including slaves and various outcasts such as innkeepers, prostitutes, entertainers, and butchers.

Foreign Relations before the 19th Century. Korea had the most enduring tributary relationship with China, while maintaining its political independence. Korean kings regularly dispatched tributary missions to China for trade and scholarship purposes, but the nature of the interactions was more cultural and diplomatic than economic. The Chinese also benefited from the interactions, for it enabled them to secure peaceful borders and reaffirm their pretenses as universal rulers. While Korea viewed China as the central civilization, it viewed itself as nearly coequal with China.

From a cultural perspective, Koreans considered Japan small and insignificant in the Sinitic world order. They historically did not display the same kind of interest in and respect for Japan as they did for China. Korea refused to acknowledge the Japanese ruler as emperor, unwilling to place itself at an inferior position.

Toyotomi Hideyoshi's (1536–1598) invasions into Korea in 1592 and 1597, particularly his scorched-earth policy to overcome resistance, devastated the Korean economy and left an enduring hostility toward Japan. Korea-Japan diplomatic relations were restored after Tokugawa shogunate was established, but the Japanese were not permitted to go beyond Pusan.

Korea enjoyed extended peace, given the self-contained geography of the peninsula within the Sino-centric regional order. Its political boundaries had been quite stable since the 10th century, despite brief invasions by the Mongols, the Japanese, and the Manchus.

All the states of East Asia practiced isolationist policy from the 17th century onward. Of them, Korea was perhaps the most isolated, referred to by Westerners in the 19th century as "the hermit kingdom." Since the Japanese invasions of the late 16th century, Korea had placed severe restrictions on foreign contacts. Foreigners were not allowed to enter the country, and Koreans were forbidden to travel abroad, except for the official diplomatic missions to China. Trade with Japan, conducted by authorized Koreans, was limited to the southern port of Pusan.

Korea in the Age of Imperialism. Beginning in the 1830s, as Western imperialism expanded to East Asia, Korea received sporadic trade requests from the European states. Through their diplomatic missions in Beijing, Koreans were mindful of the growing threat posed by the Westerners.

The Western states intensified their pressure in the 1860s but encountered fierce resistance from Koreans, who met military challenges from the United States and France without making any political concessions. The temporary retreat by the Westerners reinforced Korea's uncompromising stance. In the end, it was Japan that pried open the country. Unlike Western powers who did not value the significance of Korea as a trading partner, Japan had its own plan to expand into the country.

After the Meiji Restoration, Korean officials refused to receive the Japanese notification of the restoration of the imperial rule, as they were unwilling to recognize the "emperor" status of the Japanese ruler. The action greatly offended the Meiji oligarchs. In 1874, they returned with a letter to the Choson court, demanding to trade. The Choson court rejected the demand, for the letter followed the format of new diplomatic protocol based on international law, rather than the traditional form. Determined to open Korea, the Japanese resorted to gunboat diplomacy, the same strategy used by Western powers to open their country.

By 1876, the demonstration of Japan's superior naval power was sufficiently intimidating for the Koreans to sign the Treaty of Kanghwa, which was Korea's first modern treaty with a foreign country. The treaty granted the Japanese the right of extraterritoriality and opened ports to Japanese trade. Another purpose of the Treaty was to undermine China's traditional suzerainty claims over Korea. Hence, Article 1 of the treaty affirmed Korea's sovereign rights as an independent state to justify Japanese expansion of political and economic influence over Korea without Chinese interference. With their advantage in capital, technology, and geographic proximity, Japanese businesses gradually took control of the Korean economy, particularly in timber, fishing, shipping, and rice export. Other colonial powers soon followed Japan's example and concluded unequal treaties with Korea.

In response to these external challenges, Korean leaders adopted the policy of "Eastern Ways, Western Machines" to achieve economic prosperity and military strength. Similar to the Self-Strengthening Movement in China, they sought to modernize the country by selectively accepting Western technology while maintaining their traditional cultural values. Along this line, the Choson government launched reforms, creating new administrative structures to manage foreign affairs and modernize troops. Observation groups were sent to foreign countries to learn about their administrative institutions, military training, and industrial facilities.

The conservatives, who favored the Chinese model of gradual changes, had the dominant influence in the 1880s. Impatient with the slow pace of reform, a small group of pro-Japan aristocrats looked to follow Japan's rapid-reform model. In 1884, they launched a coup to remove the royal family and initiate reform programs. The coup was soon put down by Chinese troops, along with Chinese-trained Korean troops.

After the failed coup attempt, Japan resorted to strong-arm tactics against the Choson court. In 1894, the Korean government sought help from China to put down a rebellion. Japanese troops, however, arrived at Seoul first and refused to withdraw. They provoked another coup and installed a pro-Japanese government. In July 1894, Japanese warships launched a preemptive attack against the Chinese fleet, leading to the Sino-Japanese War (1894–1895). On both land and sea, the rising Meiji Japan decisively defeated the Qing China.

The postwar Treaty of Shimonoseki (Chapter 5) recognized Korea's "independence," implicitly granting Japan uncontested suzerainty over Korea. Under the guidance of Japanese advisors, a series of reforms were introduced to modernize Korea on the Meiji model. Collectively known as the Kabo reforms, they touched all aspects of Korean society, from administrative, judicial, economic, and social to educational. Although the reforms appeared to transform Korea into a modern country, Japan was in fact the chief beneficiary as it tightened its grip on Korea.

As Japanese influence in Korea grew, Russia became alarmed at Japan's potential threat to its sphere of influence in Manchuria and the nearby port of Vladivostok. To counterbalance the Japanese intervention, the antireform factions in the Choson court turned to the Russians for help. King Kojong in February 1896 secretly took refuge in the Russian legation. With the protection of Russia, Kojong nullified some of the reform measures. Russians replaced the Japanese as economic advisors and military instructors.

Wary that Choson was under ruthless aggression by foreign powers, a group of intellectuals in 1896 formed a political organization called the Independence Club to promote Western liberalism. With its enlightenment mission, it introduced modern science and Western perspectives through publications printed entirely in Korean *hangul*. In 1898, the Independence Club presented a reform proposal to Kojong, calling for the establishment of a constitutional monarchy and the rule of law. The activism led to a confrontation between the Club and the conservatives in the government. The Club was banned in November 1898, and many of its leaders were arrested and jailed. Nevertheless, it inspired Korean nationalism and ushered in an enlightenment movement, leaving a long-lasting effect on the country.

The Russo-Japanese War (1904–1905) finally settled the competition between Russia and Japan over Korea. The Treaty of Portsmouth recognized Japan's interest in Korea (Chapter 5). In November 1905, with Japanese troops in Seoul, Korea was forced to sign the Protectorate Treaty, transferring all Korean foreign relations to Japan. The Korean army was disbanded in 1907, reinforcing the need for Japanese "protection." By 1910, Korea was occupied by two Japanese army divisions, making the country totally dependent on Japan for security. Korean insurgents organized smaller guerrilla bands to fight the Japanese. Although supporters of Korean independence did manage to assassinate Ito Hirobumi in 1909, one of the Meiji oligarchs and first resident-general in Korea, many of them were defeated or driven across the border to Manchuria or Siberia. In August 1910, Japan concluded the Treaty of Annexation with the Choson government, making Korea a colony of Japan.

COLONIAL KOREA: 1910–1945

The 35-year Japanese colonial rule profoundly affected the development of modern Korea. While there are debates over whether Japan contributed to the modernization of the Korean society, there is little doubt that contemporary Koreans almost universally view the Japanese rule as harsh and brutal, which made anti-Japanese sentiment an important pillar of patriotism in both North and South Korea.

Political Governance

The governing institutions that the Japanese colonial government built in Korea were highly centralized and authoritarian, aimed to promote efficiency. After annexation, the office of resident-general was replaced with the governor-general, who stood at the apex of the colonial governing system. The governor-general was granted extensive legislative and executive authority, including the power to command the occupying army and navy. Therefore, the post was usually taken by military officers. Appointed by the Japanese emperor from among the highest-ranked officers of the Imperial Japanese Army, the governor-general possessed enormous power to appoint officials, including those at the provincial and county levels. He also enjoyed the power to issue laws and regulations. Under his command was a vast administrative apparatus supported by military and police forces consisting of the Japanese and Korean collaborators, who together exercised tight control of Korea's civil and judicial affairs. The police enjoyed broad power, authorized to arrest and imprison individuals without trial.

Compared with Western counterparts, the Japanese colonial bureaucracy was unusually large, which allowed for expansive and intrusive control of the cultural and political life of the Koreans. Besides exercising control, Japan intended to influence the Korean people to voluntarily accept its leadership. It began by revising school curriculum to instill Japanese values in Koreans. Many books on Korean history and geography were confiscated and destroyed. In 1911, the colonial government issued a decree to discourage Koreans from receiving a higher education. The educational system was reorganized to move most of the Koreans into vocational schools and to learn the Japanese language in preparation for work in the Japanese system.

The heavy-handed colonial policy placed tight control and rigid censorship over the Korean-language press. Public gatherings required police permit, and political organizations and meetings were prohibited. At the beginning of the era of Taisho democracy, some restrictions were eased, including the ban on Korean newspapers and the control over political organizations. The trend toward liberalization, however, was short-lived. In 1925, the Peace Preservation Law passed by the Japanese Diet was extended to Korea to suppress pro-independence Korean leaders. Subsequent deployment of "thought police" and "thought prosecutors" in the 1930s reflected an intensified effort to prosecute political offences.

In 1936, under the proposed policy of "Japan and Korea as One Body," the colonial government attempted to abolish the Korean culture, religion, and tradition to achieve total assimilation of the Korean people by the Japanese. Koreans were forced to visit Shinto shrines to worship Japanese gods. In 1938, it was decreed that all classes be conducted in Japanese and that all students speak only Japanese, even at home. In 1939, the colonial government pressured Koreans to adopt Japanese names, which was a humiliation for a society that prized family lineage. Korean-language newspapers were ordered to shut down in 1940.

Despite the colonial government's efforts, assimilation largely failed. The two groups of people rarely mixed socially. Japanese citizens, as businessmen, bureaucrats, teachers, and soldiers, enjoyed privileges in Japanese communities in large Korean cities such as Seoul, Pyongyang, Pusan, and Taegu. All key positions, whether in government or in business, were staffed by the Japanese. Koreans became second-class citizens. They were restricted to clerical positions, working longer hours and receiving half the wages of their Japanese counterparts. Korean entrepreneurs could only take part in light industries such as leather, ceramics, and food processing.

Economic Transformation

At the time of annexation, Korea was an agrarian economy. Following the classic pattern of colonial trade, Japan was an exclusive trading partner for Korea. Korea supplied foodstuffs, mainly rice, to Japan and, in exchange, imported manufactured goods from Japan.

The colonial government conducted land surveys in 1912 to establish modern ownership of farmland. It confiscated land that did not have proper registration or legal documentation, which eventually amounted to one-third of the entire land in Korea. The confiscated land was then sold to Japanese immigrants and land companies at a reduced price. The colonial government also used ordinances to gain control over forest, fishery, and mineral resources and transferred ownership to Japanese citizens or companies.

Japanese corporations and conglomerates monopolized key industries such as electricity and finance. Roads, railways, and ports were constructed to facilitate the transportation of goods and materials.

As the Japanese imperialist ambition expanded in the late 1920s, particularly after its occupation of Manchuria in 1931, it began to redefine Korea's role in the Japanese empire. In light of the need for massive supplies to sustain its war effort on the Asian mainland to realize its empire ambition, Japan began to make a concerted effort to industrialize Korea and improve its manufacturing capabilities. Japanese conglomerates such as Mitsui and Mitsubishi were invited to Korea to produce military supplies. Northern Korea, with its abundant mineral resources and hydroelectric power potential, received most of the industrial investment, making it a bridge to link Japan with industrial centers in Manchuria. A large number of Koreans came to work as laborers in the mines and factories in northern Korea and Manchuria.

After the Sino-Japanese War broke out in 1937, the Japanese government began a big push for Korean industrialization, particularly in areas of machinery, chemicals, and metals. The purpose was to transform the colony into a supply base to support its military actions. By 1939, nearly half of the Korean exports to Japan were manufactures.

The National Mobilization Law (1938) enacted by the Japanese Diet was applied to Korea, too. The mobilization effort was intensive and intrusive. Koreans were conscripted to work in mines, factories, and transportation and construction work sites during the last decade of the colonial period. The demand for labor in mines and factories further escalated after the outbreak of the Pacific War in 1941. Millions of Koreans were uprooted from their homes to move to urban and industrial centers for wartime production, not only in Korea but also in Japan and Manchuria. Many young Korean women became "comfort women," sent to the front lines and forced into sexual servitude for the Japanese troops. At its peak, an estimated 4 million Koreans, or 16 percent of the Korean population, had been deported outside Korea to support Japanese wartime efforts.

Beginning in the late 1930s, the Japanese army began to accept Koreans into the military academies. Although the total number was small, they became the core of the officer corps of the postwar South Korean army. For example, Park Chung-hee, the president of South Korea from 1963 to 1979, enrolled in the Manzhouguo Military Academy and was commissioned a second lieutenant in the Japanese Guandong Army in 1944.

Korean Nationalism

As discussed earlier, Koreans had held strong beliefs about their cultural superiority in the Sinicized world order. Even before the annexation, Koreans had long resisted Japanese control of their country. Political coercion and cultural assimilation by the colonial government only served to heighten the Korean national consciousness. Many Korean nationalists, unable to launch overt protests at home, fled the country and organized exile communities in China, Russia, and the United States.

As the Versailles Peace Conference took place in January 1919 after World War I ended, U.S. President Woodrow Wilson's call for self-determination raised hopes for colonies throughout the world. Inspired by the idea, many intellectual leaders in Korea began to campaign for national Korean independence.

Korean nationalism came to the forefront in massive demonstrations against Japan's colonial rule on March 1, 1919. A group of 33 religious leaders had secretly drafted and signed the Korean Declaration of Independence as "representatives of all the Korean people." After the public reading of the document on March 1 in Pagoda Park in Seoul, a crowd of people, many of whom were students, began to gather on the streets, demanding Korean independence. More and more Koreans spontaneously joined in the non-violent demonstrations that spread to cities throughout the peninsula. The colonial government in panic called in the military and resorted to bloody suppression to dissipate the crowds. The armed forces and police opened fire on peaceful demonstrators, killing thousands and wounding many more. The event, known as the March First Movement (or *Sam-il* Movement, referring to its occurrence on the date of March 1), was a major turning point in Korean history. Although all 33 leaders were arrested, approximately 2 million Koreans were involved in 1,500 demonstrations nationwide. It gave rise to modern Korean nationalism and sustained the momentum for Korean independence. The ensuing crackdown forced many activists to flee the country.

In the aftermath of the March First Movement, the Japanese reassessed their colonial policy and made some changes. The colonial government also showed more tolerance of the Korean culture. The change was only temporary; the harsher, more repressive rule soon returned. In May 1925, the colonial government promulgated the Peace Preservation Law, aimed at ending any anti-Japanese newspapers and political associations.

Several provisional governments were organized at home and abroad, and they were eventually consolidated into one in Shanghai in November 1919: the Provisional Government of the Republic of Korea. The U.S.-educated Syngman Rhee (or Yi Sungman, 1875–1965), a former member of the Independence Club, became its first acting president. Rhee was imprisoned and tortured after the dissolution of the Club. Released in 1904, he went to the United States and earned his PhD. He returned to Japan-occupied Korea in 1910 but was driven out by the Japanese in 1913. He then went to Hawaii to campaign for Korean independence.

During this period, a division among Korean nationalists began to emerge, foreshadowing the left-right split in postwar Korea. On the one hand, the more moderate, Western-educated cultural nationalists such as Rhee, who looked to the West as a model to transform their country, believed that education held the key to transform Korea's cultural backwardness into modern standards. They were pragmatic and were willing to achieve the goal of independence through peaceful, diplomatic means.

On the other hand, the more radical nationalists advocated direct confrontation with the colonial authority. Inspired by Socialist and Communist ideas after the Bolshevik Revolution of 1917, they organized Communist groups in Korea in support of tenant farmers and industrial workers but encountered harsh repression by the Japanese.

The division in the resistance movement turned into factional feuding in the Provisional Government, resulting in Rhee's impeachment in 1925, an act he refused to recognize. He moved from Hawaii to Washington, DC, in 1940 to lead the effort in lobbying for Korean independence and became a well-known figure in the overseas community. After the surrender of Japan in 1945, Rhee returned to Korea and was elected the first president of South Korea in 1948.

In the Communist camps, some engaged in guerrilla warfare against the Japanese, others employed terrorist tactics. Kim Il-sung (1912–1994), the founder of the North Korean regime, was one of the guerilla leaders who fought in small units along the Korean-Manchurian border.

Kim was a member of a Korean guerrilla army organized by the Chinese Communist Party in Manchuria and became a well-known anti-Japanese guerrilla leader in the 1930s. In June 1937, he led a small guerrilla group to attack Pochonbo on the northern border of Korea, killing Japanese police officers and burning down the police station. Pursued by the Japanese, Kim and his followers retreated to the Soviet Union, where they were trained and protected by the Soviet army. At the end of World War II, Kim returned to Korea with the Soviets.

DISCUSSION QUESTIONS

1. Koreans often modified foreign ideas and institutions through creative adaptation. Compare the civil service exam systems in China and Korea, and explain how one contributed to social mobility and the other solidified social hierarchy.

2. In China and Korea, students historically have played an active role in social protests and reforms. What explains this kind of student activism?

3. In the 19th century, the Qing and Choson courts shared similar views about foreign technology and adopted similar modernization strategies. Discuss their similarities, and explain why they did not choose the strategy of the Meiji government.

4. The March First Movement (Korea) and the May Fourth Movement (China) both took place in 1919. Compare their backgrounds and evaluate their impacts on the modern history of these two countries.

5. Review Japan's colonial policies in Korea, and discuss how they, in various ways, affected the postwar development in the Korean peninsula.

10

Political Governance in South Korea

Japan's defeat in 1945 ended its 35 years of imperial rule over Korea (1910–1945). The abrupt collapse of Japanese colonialism led to joy on the streets and high hopes that an independent state would be established soon. Celebration for Korean nationalists, however, was short-lived. The division of Korea along the 38th parallel by the United States and the Soviet Union, without the consent of the Korean people, dashed hopes of creating a unified independent state in the postliberation era. Moscow supported the communist Democratic People's Republic of Korea (DPRK) in the north, while Washington helped establish the Republic of Korea (ROK) in the south. The escalation of the Cold War and the ensuing military standoff reinforced the division.

The outbreak of the Korean War in 1950 turned the peninsula into a field of destruction. Over one million lives and two-thirds of South Korea's industrial capacity were destroyed. By the end of the Korean War, with a gross domestic product (GDP) per capita of only $70, the ROK was considered one of the poorest countries in the world. Politically, the early years of its domestic politics followed the path of many developing states: underneath what appeared to be a multiparty constitutional democracy was actually autocratic leadership plagued by patronage and corruption. The military intervened in 1960 and established control for the next three decades. Political and economic situations at that time did not point to a bright future.

Yet, beginning in the 1960s, the government implemented a series of five-year economic plans to develop the economy. The export-led growth strategy achieved, on average, a remarkable 8.45 percent GDP growth rate from 1960 to 1971 and transformed the ROK into an industrial economy. Starting in the late 1980s, democratic transition and consolidation has taken place and turned the country into a flourishing, vibrant democracy.

How did the ROK manage to transform itself economically and politically, particularly in the face of a formidable security threat from the north? What were the challenges, and how did the government respond to them? This chapter will review the history of political governance in the ROK and the evolution of its governing institutions.

THE U.S. MILITARY GOVERNMENT: 1945–1948

The United States Army Military Government in Korea (USAMGIK) ruled South Korea from 1945 to 1948 and played a major role in shaping the political and economic orders in South Korea. Its strategic direction was to establish an anti-Communist regime with a capitalist economy and a parliamentary democracy. As it did similarly in Japan, the American military government in South Korea initially welcomed the trade union movement. The development of the Cold War on the Korean peninsula, however, meant that global security interests would trump democratic ideals. In 1947, the American military authority declared left-wing trade unions illegal, containing leftist and socialist forces to ensure the establishment of a capitalist economy in South Korea.

General John R. Hodge, the head of USAMGIK, collaborated with conservative leaders and right-leaning moderates in South Korea to restore order. Korean bureaucrats who had served in the Japanese colonial government (called "collaborators" by Korean nationalists) were recruited by USAMGIK to ensure continuity between the colonial government and the new Korean administration. They expanded the National Police to enhance the government's coercive capacity, taking swift actions to root out union activists and suppress perceived communist activities.

The collaborators were not only spared; they were given the opportunity to purchase state-vested properties. Shops and factories previously owned by Japanese investors were handed over to Koreans who had worked for Japanese colonists as submanagers and skilled workers. Many of them became entrepreneurs and helped solidify capitalist development in South Korea. This was a stark contrast to the practice in North Korea, where collaborators were thoroughly purged.

USAMGIK also engaged in economic and social reforms. With over 70 percent of the South Korean population directly and indirectly involved in agricultural production in 1948, the military government initiated land reforms to sell farmland formerly held by the Japanese to tenant farmers, who could purchase the land with the principal crop over a 15-year time span without interest. The measure brought significant changes to landholding patterns in South Korea: from 1947 to 1949, land ownership of the farming population increased from 19 percent to 37 percent, while tenant households declined from 42 percent to 21 percent (J. Kim 2012). USAMGIK expanded enrollments in elementary and secondary education, laying the foundation for future economic and industrial development.

Under the auspices of the United States, South Korea held its constitutional assembly election in May 1948. The newly formed National Assembly drafted a constitution in July 1948 and elected Syngman Rhee, who was educated in the United States and spent nearly 40 years there, as the country's first president.

GOVERNANCE UNDER THE AUTHORITARIAN REGIME: 1948–1987

In the postliberation era, the division of the country into two Korean states created a deep and long-lasting fissure in the Korean peninsula. Within the global security structure, the outbreak of the Korean War perpetuated the separation and division between the two states with the establishment of a demilitarized zone (DMZ) roughly along the 38th parallel.

Against this backdrop, government programs and policy actions in South Korea were shaped by political actors' attitudes and beliefs toward three distinct yet interrelated ideas: democracy, development, and unification. For conservatives, survival and national security were the ROK's top priorities. They believed that, in the face of hostilities from the DPRK, the ROK-U.S. alliance would help defend the country's political and territorial integrity; democracy was a luxury that had to wait until the country was safe from subversive forces instigated by communists. The ROK should thus mobilize economic resources for industrialization and modernization. Economic modernization and development would build up national power and strength and ultimately help unify the country.

The liberal/progressive camp, however, had a very different view. They contended that conservatives had used national security as an excuse to delay democratization and that economic modernization occurred at the cost of increased economic disparities. Issues of wealth distribution and social justice had been ignored in a growth model that emphasized collusion between politicians and big businesses. The radical wing of the liberal camp would further argue that division of North and South Koreas was the result of the Cold War structure and the global security competition between the United States and the Soviet Union. An alliance with the United States would perpetuate the division of the north and south rather than promote national unification.

The sharp division between the two camps over these issues helps explain much of the political dynamics in the ROK during the authoritarian era as well as the policies advocated by different political actors.

The First and Second Republics: 1948–1961

The First Republic (1948–1960). Despite the proclaimed idea of liberal democracy, democratic principles steadily eroded under Rhee. He was antagonistic toward the National Assembly, where his supporters were significantly outnumbered. He consolidated political power through a patronage system based on personal exchanges, with loyalties built on regional, familial, and other personal ties (Haggard 1990; Mo and Weingast 2013). Through the patron-client network, he distributed policy favors and economic resources in exchange for political support and illicit political contributions. Materials, bank loans, government contracts, import licenses, and properties formerly owned by the Japanese were subject to political bidding by industrialists and capitalists.

To maintain his authority, Rhee relied heavily on the police. National security provided the Rhee administration with a legitimate reason to centralize state power and eliminate any nonstate organizations with the potential for violence, including leftist guerrilla soldiers. The 1948 National Security Law enacted by the National Assembly gave broad authority to the police to arrest those engaged in antistate activities, which were vaguely defined to include all kinds of real and perceived threats. Within a year, more than 30,000 were detained and prosecuted under the law.

Land reform had been an important economic initiative before the war as the United States had implemented reforms on lands previously possessed by the Japanese. In 1949, the National Assembly extended reforms to lands owned by Korean landlords. From March to May 1950, immediately before the Korean War, the government was able to distribute 70 percent to 80 percent of the farmland to tenants, elevating their status to small landowners. Having received their own land, tenant farmers became loyal supporters of the ROK, even when North Korea later promoted land reform in the occupied areas of the south during the war. This first implementation of land reforms took away the most appealing call of the Communist North and helped solidify the national identity of the ROK.

The outbreak of the Korean War in 1950 gave Rhee an opportunity to expand his power. Carrying out his duties from the temporary capital of Pusan, Rhee founded the Liberal Party in 1951 to prepare for the 1952 presidential election. The party was the creation of his personal networks, based on patronage and personal appeals. In fact, other Korean political parties were essentially the same—formed by party leaders and held together by their charisma and social networks.

Concerned that he did not have enough support in the National Assembly, Rhee proposed a constitutional amendment to elect the president directly through a popular election, rather than indirectly through the National Assembly, as was done previously. When the National Assembly rejected the proposal, he declared martial law in Pusan and began to arrest its members. Intimidated, the National Assembly complied, and Rhee won his second term handily with 74.6 percent of the votes.

At the request of Rhee, the United States and the ROK signed the Mutual Defense Treaty in October 1953. A significant number of U.S. troops were stationed in South Korea to help defend its political and territorial integrity. Between 1954 and 1960, approximately $4 billion of U.S. economic and military aid was delivered to the ROK to assist its postwar economic recovery.

For the Rhee administration, rebuilding war-destroyed infrastructure and industrial facilities was the top priority. With the help of huge inflows of American aid, which accounted for as much as 60 percent of the government's budget, the government launched extensive reconstruction plans to rebuild roads, communications networks, and primary and secondary schools. Notwithstanding the emphasis on education and infrastructure rebuilding, economic policy making under the Rhee government still lacked a clear vision for policy goals. Demands from the patron-client networks and interference by politicians often distorted economic policies and decisions, resulting in financial mismanagement and stymied growth.

In 1954, Rhee's supporters in the National Assembly passed a constitutional amendment to remove the two-term limit on the presidency, paving the way for Rhee to win the 1956 presidential election for a third term.

While Rhee received strong support in rural areas, he was unable to form a broad governing coalition. In fact, he deliberately excluded from this government the most efficient and powerful organization that emerged from the Korean War—the military (Mo and Weingast 2013). Rhee used a divide-and-conquer tactic to control the military, creating divisions among senior military officers.

The Second Republic (1960–1961). By the time of the March 1960 election, Rhee and his Liberal Party had regularly used intimidation, bribery, and massive election fraud to stay in power. In protest, tens of thousands of middle school, high school, and university students throughout the country took to the streets from February to April 1960 to call for Rhee's resignation. Rhee imposed martial law to stop the demonstrations but to no avail. Demonstrations turned violent, and Rhee eventually sought asylum in the United States after resigning.

The "April Revolution" of 1960 was the first clash between student activism and the authoritarian regime in postcolonial Korea. For the next several decades, students became increasingly active in political and social issues, setting the stage for South Korea's youth-driven democratization struggles.

Following Rhee's ouster, the opposition party, the Democratic Party, cruised to victory in the May 1960 National Assembly election and passed a new constitution in June to build a parliamentary cabinet system with the president as a mere figurehead, hence creating the Second Republic (1960–1961). The political system, however, was plagued by unending street demonstrations and political gridlock. Factions in the Democratic Party fought over political appointments, nominations, and party control. Student and labor groups, empowered by their success in overthrowing the Rhee regime, began to make demands on the new government. Some advocated leftist agendas and promoted immediate unification with North Korea. The government was ineffective and the country in disorder.

The Third and Fourth Republics: 1963–1981

The Coup of 1961. On May 16, 1961, the military, led by General Park Chung-hee, seized power through a bloodless coup to overthrow the civilian government. The military junta—the Supreme Council for National Reconstruction (SCNR)—disbanded all political organizations and banned all political activity. It launched a large purge to dismiss approximately 40,000 civilian and military officials from office. The SCNR established the Korean Central Intelligence

Agency (KCIA; now the National Intelligence Service) to coordinate intelligence activities and criminal investigation, but it soon became a security apparatus to suppress political dissidents. An estimated 3,000 students, union leaders, and progressive politicians were arrested under the newly enacted Anticommunist Law, a part of the National Security Law.

In August, Park announced that he would establish a civilian government by the summer of 1963. Assured that the coup was not Communist-inspired and that a representative civilian government would be restored soon, U.S. Secretary of State Dean Rusk visited Seoul in November 1961 to meet Park, signaling recognition of the regime. Subsequently, when Park wavered in his commitment to restore civilian rule, the United States applied diplomatic pressure to ensure the power transfer.

The Third Republic (1963–1972). Military leaders drafted a new constitution in December 1962 to establish the Third Republic, featuring a strong executive presidency, a unicameral legislature, and broad national emergency power for the president. A national referendum soon approved the new constitution with a wide margin of support (79 percent). To support his presidential bid, Park in February 1963 created the Democratic Republican Party (DRP). It had a hierarchical, single-command structure with a large staff, core leaders primarily being military officers.

Park retired from the military and ran as a candidate of the DRP. He received overwhelming support in the rural areas and narrowly won the presidency against his opponent (46.6 percent to 45.1 percent).

Economic Development. The Park government focused on industrialization and modernization and installed economic and political institutions conducive to economic growth in two major ways. First, the First Five-Year Economic Development Plan (1962–1966) aimed to provide a long-range, multiyear direction for development. Industries such as electricity, fertilizers, synthetic fiber, and cement were emphasized to develop a self-sufficient, industrial structure. Having served in the Japanese colonial army before, Park had experience with the Japanese wartime model that used state guidance to organize capitalism. Politicians and political parties would no longer have control over economic decision making; instead, bureaucrats, particularly the economic technocrats in the Economic Planning Board (EPB), would provide rational economic strategies to guide the country forward.

Second, Park strengthened business-government relations by linking government support to business performance. Park adopted the Japanese economic model and facilitated the establishment of large business conglomerates, the *chaebol*, based on the old prewar Japanese *zaibatsu*. The government then allocated economic resources such as rewards, subsidies, licenses, and tax refunds to business organizations based on merit-based objective criteria. Firms that failed to meet export targets received diminished subsidies, while firms that did perform benefited from greater allocations.

To attract foreign investment, Park normalized relations with Japan in 1965, 20 years after Korean independence. Japan offered an assistance package of $800 million in the form of grants and loans. The opposition considered the act a betrayal of Korean nationalism. The National Assembly, without the presence of these opposition party members, approved the normalization treaty.

Using the country's cheap labor force in manufacturing industries for export expansion, Park and his developmental state set the economy on a path for sustained growth and ultimately transformed the country into an economic powerhouse (Chapter 11). The real average annual growth rate of gross national product (GNP) was 7.8 percent during the first five-year economic development plan (1962–1966) and accelerated to 10.5 percent during the second five-year economic development plan (1967–1971). Continued economic growth increased tax revenue to support the government expansion, which helped strengthen the governing ability of the Park administration.

Political Governance. In May 1967, Park won a second four-year term with a comfortable margin over his opponent (52 percent to 41 percent), and the DRP won the National Assembly elections in June 1967 with a two-thirds majority. The supermajority in the National Assembly gave Park a clear path to pass a constitutional amendment. Encouraged by popular support, he decided to seek a third term. Massive student demonstrations erupted in protest. The ruling DRP met in an annex to the National Assembly to pass the amendment without the presence of the opposition members. In October 1969, 68 percent of the voters approved the constitutional amendment to authorize a third term for the presidency.

The political coalition assembled by Park consisted of the military, the *chaebol*, and the rural population. Much like Rhee did, Park drew his political support from the older and more conservative rural populations and had less support in urban centers. A regional divide (east vs. west, or more precisely, southeast vs. southwest) began to emerge in Park's era. Conservatives drew support mainly from the southeastern provinces, while progressives had their strongholds in southwest. Uneven distribution of economic resources, in part, accounted for the political regionalism.

Key leaders of the Park regime, mainly from the North Kyongsang and South Kyongsang provinces in the southeastern region, frequently rewarded their hometowns and supporters with government spending and development projects. In contrast, North Cholla and South Cholla provinces in the southwestern region, traditionally agricultural economies, were neglected. Economic discrimination led to widespread resentment toward the Park government in these regions and drove the voters toward the progressive camp.

Kim Dae-jung, a young, charismatic politician from the South Cholla province, ran an effective campaign against Park in the presidential election of April 1971. Although Park won his third term with 53 percent of the vote against Kim's 45 percent, the opposition party significantly increased its seats in the National Assembly elections a month later in May 1971, making it difficult for Park to manipulate the legislature. Anti-Park social protests and political demonstrations continued even after the election. The Park government frequently invoked the National Security Law to suppress dissidents.

National Security. Since the late 1960s, the changing international environment had heightened national security concerns for the ROK. North and South were engaged in a series of skirmishes along the DMZ, leading to casualties on both sides. In 1968, North Korea commandos raided the Blue House (the official residence of the president) and nearly succeeded in killing Park. Later that year, North Korean commandos landed on the northeast shore of South Korea, trying to establish a base for guerrilla warfare against the South Korean government. Against this backdrop, President Nixon announced his plan in 1970 to withdraw 20,000 U.S. troops from South Korea and reached out to China in 1971 to improve the U.S.-China bilateral relationship. These diplomatic actions raised questions about the United States' commitment to East Asia and to the Korean peninsula. In December 1971, Park declared a national state of emergency. Soon after, the National Assembly, under violent resistance from the opposition, passed special measures to grant Park extraordinary emergency power to regulate and control all activities in the country. Park claimed that these measures were necessary to prevent a second Korean War.

The Fourth Republic (1972–1981). On October 17, 1972, Park imposed martial law on the country, suspended the constitution, dissolved the National Assembly and the political parties, and outlawed all political activities. He proposed the *Yushin* (i.e., "revitalizing") Constitution, which was approved by an overwhelming majority in a national referendum in November 1972.

The *Yushin* regime eliminated the electoral democracy and centralized the president's power. It gave the president almost total power, allowing him to appoint one-third of the National Assembly and almost all levels of administrative officers, from top posts down to the lowest level. Under the *Yushin* Constitution, the president was to be elected indirectly by a National Conference for Reunification (NCR) for an unlimited number of six-year terms. Park was elected president of the Fourth Republic by the NCR delegates without one dissenting vote in December 1972 and was later reelected in 1978.

Park justified the establishment of the *Yushin* system on the grounds of promoting efficiency and eliminating waste to build national strength. The North and South Koreas engaged in dialogues in 1972, but the exchanges broke down in 1973, especially as discovery of the infiltration tunnel built by the North Koreans under the DMZ further amplified the distrust. In August 1974, an assassination attempt nearly missed Park but killed his wife. The serious threat from North Korea made people more willing to tolerate political restrictions.

To strengthen the ROK's long-term military capabilities, the Park government raised the military budget for defense buildup. It also launched a massive economic project to develop heavy and petrochemical industries (HPI) in

1973. The HPI drive required rapid capital accumulation in targeted industries, made possible only by favorable government industrial policies, including tax incentives and policy loans. Nearly 70 percent of the National Investment Fund and 80 percent of the Korean Industrial Bank's loans between 1974 and 1980 were allocated to HPI (S.-y. Kim 2008). The concentration of capital investment ultimately led to an accelerated expansion of *chaebol*. In the 1970s, the top five conglomerates grew at an annual rate of 30 percent (Kim, Han, and Jang 2008).

The harsh working conditions endured by Korean workers became a national issue after a garment worker, Chun Tae-il, committed suicide by setting himself on fire in November 1970. The incident highlighted the social justice issues resulting from the drive for economic growth. Labor issues became another rallying point for dissident groups, paving the way for political alliance between workers, students, and urban inllectuals.

The harsh repressive tactics used by Park since the *Yushin* regime helped radicalize the dissident groups. In August 1973, Kim Dae-jung, who had been involved in anti-Park campaigns in the United States and Japan, was abducted by KCIA agents from Tokyo and put under strict house arrest in Seoul. Students, labor organizations, and a radical wing of the Korean church began to organize petition drives and street demonstrations in opposition of Park's authoritarianism. Many of the dissidents, embracing the *minjung* (the masses, or the people) ideology viewing Korean history as the struggle by the ordinary people against political repression and social injustice, turned against not just the military regime but also the entire political and economic system. Some demanded the destruction of the military-capitalist regime, advocating U.S. troop withdrawal and Korean unification.

Tension between the government and the opposition escalated in October 1979, after Kim Young-sam, another opposition leader, was expelled from the National Assembly for making anti-Park comments in a *New York Times* interview. Riots broke out in Pusan, Kim's home area, and spread to nearby cities. Park declared martial law in the area to suppress the demonstrators. In a dispute over the best course of action in dealing with the popular unrest, Park was killed by KCIA Chief Kim Jae-kyu.

The Fifth Republic: 1981–1987

The Coup of 1979. After Park's death, a brief period of political openness followed. Choi Kyu-hah, a prime minister under Park, was elected president by the NCU under the *Yushin* Constitution on December 6, 1979. He moved quickly to free hundreds of political prisoners, including Kim Dae-jung, and promised a referendum within a year for a new constitution.

A small clique of generals, however, had a different plan. Chun Doo-hwan, Roh Tae-woo, and others of the 11th class of the Korean Military Academy (graduated in 1955) began to seize power through two coups, the first in December 1979, when they took over the military, and the second in May 1980, when they took control of the government. They came from the same region as Park, the Taegu-Kyongsang province.

Prodemocracy groups and students organized a series of prodemocracy demonstrations that turned into full-scale riots in May 1980. The widespread demonstrations and protests gave the military an excuse to declare martial law, close universities, control news media, ban political activities, and arrest opposition leaders, including Kim Dae-jung.

The Kwangju Incident. Students and residents in Kwangju, the largest city in South Cholla that had long been resentful of military dominance and economic neglect, demanded the release of Kim Dae-jung, the local hero. In response, Chun sent in tanks and helicopters to retake the city, leading to hundreds of civilian casualties. The Kwangju Incident left a stain on the Chun regime from which it could never recover. The suppression radicalized the prodemocracy groups, especially student activists, as they began to embrace more radical ideologies such as Marxism and the concept of *juche* (or self-reliance) developed by Kim Il-sung that combined Socialist and nationalist ideas into a state ideology in North Korea.

The prodemocracy groups now opposed not only the Chun regime but also the United States for perceived inaction in reining in Chun. The convergence of the student activism, labor movement, and radical nationalism (anti–United States and pro–North Korea) brought the opposition forces together throughout the 1980s.

The Fifth Republic (1981–1988). In August 1980, Choi resigned from the presidency and the NCU elected Chun. He then revised the constitution to create the Fifth Republic. To boost the legitimacy of his government, Chun kept the indirect election of the *Yushin* Constitution but amended it in two ways. First, unlike the *Yushin* system that allowed unlimited terms for the presidency, the new constitution restricted the presidency to a single seven-year term, and he promised to retire in 1988 after one term. Second, different from the *Yushin* system in which one-third of the seats in the National Assembly were appointed by the president, the new constitution abolished the appointment system, making all National Assembly members elected. The constitution was approved by a referendum in October 1980. All political parties, including Park's DRP, were dissolved. In January 1981, Chun formed his own party, the Democratic Justice Party (DJP), which was essentially DRP under a different name.

Chun's revisions were critical for the opposition parties, who gained sufficient seats in the National Assembly under the more liberal electoral system to block important legislation or constitutional amendments that required a two-thirds majority. After 1985, midway through Chun's presidency, his one-term promise became the focus of politics. While the prodemocracy activists mobilized to pressure Chun to honor his promise, succession politics also began and gradually intensified within the ruling party.

Democratic Transition. Political jockeying for power in anticipation of Chun's departure began with constitutional debates. The opposition New Korea Democracy Party (NKDP), led by Kim Dae-jung and Kim Young-sam with the support of prodemocracy activists, began a nationwide campaign in 1986 for constitutional revision. Playing a pivotal role in steering the prodemocracy movement in the mid- to late 1980s, NKDP demanded the return of a directly elected executive presidency, in hopes that they could win the presidential election behind a single candidate. Instead, the ruling DJP insisted on a parliamentary system, believing that they could retain a majority of the seats through their financial advantage. Amid the deadlock, Chun announced in April 1987 that a new president would be decided by the NCU, which meant that his hand-picked successor, Roh Tae-woo, would be elected in an indirect election.

The announcement led to massive uprisings and demonstrations. Amid escalating clashes between riot police and protesters, a college student was tortured to death. The discovery of the student's body sparked public outrage, leading to widespread support for the opposition movement. The authoritarian regime had to reopen negotiations with the opposition that ultimately resulted in the June 29 Declaration for constitutionally amending the direct election of the president in 1987. Also accepted were the opposition's demands for political amnesty and restoration of civil rights for Kim Dae-jung, protection of human rights and freedom of the press, and promotion of local authority and self-governance.

What accounted for such a dramatic turnaround within such a short time? A complete account of the events would have to consider the bargaining and negotiation between political leaders, as well as the confluence of internal and international factors leading to democratic transition.

Internationally, the International Olympic Committee, which had awarded the 1988 Summer Olympics to Seoul in 1981, threatened to relocate the games if there was further political unrest. Chun, and particularly Roh, who was the chair of the ROK Olympic Committee, had hoped to showcase the country's spectacular rise from the devastation of the Korean War to a modern industrial economy through the Olympics Games. The repercussions of losing the games would be too great to bear for either of them. Additionally, the United States was for political reform and against further military intervention. The assistant secretary of state was sent to South Korea by President Reagan to deliver the message.

Domestically, South Korean society had experienced enormous change since Park's military coup. Economic growth since the 1960s produced a population that was more educated and affluent. The growing middle class may have supported political order and stability for purposes of national security but not necessarily military rule. Many were proud of the country's economic success but disappointed by the lack of progress in political development as the country was still mired in the politics of military coups and strongmen. They were inspired by the previous year's People Power uprising in the Philippines, a far less developed economy in Asia, that had overthrown the Marcos dictatorship for a peaceful transition to electoral democracy. For many South Koreans, it was unthinkable not to be able to participate in a direct election to decide the next president.

Protests and demonstrations continued to gain momentum. After DJP announced Roh as its candidate in June 1987, thousands of white-collar professionals and sympathetic citizens from all walks of life in major urban areas began to join students and activists on the streets, which had become a battle zone between the riot police and the massive demonstrators. On June 26, a peace protest march in Seoul attracted over 100,000 people, many of whom were government bureaucrats as well as media and economic elites who could potentially lose their privileged status in democratic transition.

The growing strength of the prodemocracy movements affected the relative bargaining power between the ruling party and the opposition. While the opposition parties were divided on other issues, they were united behind the demand for the direct election of the president. In contrast, there was no consensus in the ruling DJP on what the best position should be. The hard-liners, primarily those of the military background, were in favor of the status quo or reversion to the *Yushin*-type authoritarian system and would use force if necessary. The soft-liners, however, were interested in working with the opposition to negotiate a transition. They were also more optimistic about the direct presidential election, believing that the administration's strong economic record could keep the DJP in power. The moderates, including Roh, were closer to the hard-liners in their position but were unwilling to use force. The internal division of the ruling party undercut its ability to control the process, reflective of a weakened resolve to hold on to the authoritarian system.

Establishing the Sixth Republic (1988–Present). The June 29 Declaration launched the process of democratic transition. The transition leaders (i.e., Roh Tae-woo, Kim Young-sam, and Kim Dae-jung) took a minimalist approach to constitutional revision by focusing exclusively on the issue of presidential election without touching more controversial issues such as military neutrality, workers' rights, and human rights. The National Assembly quickly passed a new constitution in August 1987 that stipulated a direct election of president for a single five-year term and legislators for four-year terms. The new Constitution was formally approved in October 1987 in a national referendum, ushering in the Sixth Republic.

GOVERNANCE IN THE DEMOCRATIC ERA: 1987–PRESENT

As mentioned earlier, political contention during the authoritarian era had been driven by political actors' different positions and attitudes toward three main ideas—democracy, economic development, and national unification. Democratic transition, however, did not fully resolve the issue of democracy, as the legacy of authoritarianism was rooted deeply in the political and economic institutions that had existed for decades. Thus, democratic consolidation in the postdemocracy era has involved continual struggle to institutionalize democratic values.

At the same time, the conservative and progressive camps continued to differ in their positions on economic issues and inter-Korean relations. The conservative camp anchored its foreign policy on the basis of a close alliance with the United States, and promoted market-oriented, probusiness policies for economic growth. The conservatives often took a hawkish attitude toward North Korea, particularly as Pyongyang accelerated the development of its missile and nuclear programs. In contrast, the progressive camp's economic policy advocated structural reforms for *chaebol* governance and welfare reforms for equitable income distribution. As for North Korea, the progressive camp sought to engage Pyongyang by promoting bilateral economic and social interactions.

The changing geopolitical environment in East Asia has further complicated these policy decisions. The normalization of diplomatic relations between the ROK and the PRC in 1992 broadened the policy options for South Korea, yet brought new challenges, too. China, arguably the closest ally of North Korea, has surpassed the United States as South Korea's largest trading partner since 2003, accounting for approximately 25 percent of South Korean exports. Competition and cooperation between the United States and China in the region adds a layer of complexity to the ROK's economic and security strategies. The analysis of the attitudes and actions of the South Korean leaders and political groups in handling these policy issues can help us understand the opportunities and challenges they face in governing the democratic Korea.

Democratic Consolidation

The 1987 Presidential Election. In December 1987, Roh was elected president with 37 percent of the popular votes. The opposition votes were split among the three Kims, with Kim Young-sam receiving 28 percent of the votes, Kim Dae-jung 27 percent, and Kim Jong-pil 8 percent. Four regional voting blocs emerged in the election. The industrial Ryongnam region (in southeast Korea, including the North and South Kyongsang provinces and the cities of Pusan, Taegu, and Ulsan) was split between Roh and Kim Young-sam. Roh drew strong support from his home base in north Kyongsang province and Taegu, whereas Kim Young-sam's stronghold was in south Kyongsang province and the metropolitan cities of Pusan and Ulsan. The agricultural Honam region (in southwest Korea, including North and South Cholla provinces and the metropolitan city of Kwangju) voted heavily for Kim Dae-jung. Finally, Kim Jong-pil received support from his home base in the Chungchong region (to the north of Honam, including North and South Chungchong provinces and the metropolitan city of Taejon).

Presidential Elections since 1987. Before 1987, each new ROK president or prime minister would modify constitutional procedures before taking power, a sign of weak constitutionalism. Since the founding of the Sixth Republic in 1987, the constitution has been upheld despite rotation of power between different administrations. Presidential and parliamentary elections have been free, fair, and held regularly. Throughout these years, the military has exercised restraint. The country has not had another military coup.

Some of the presidential elections marked important milestones in the country's journey toward democracy. In 1992, Kim Young-sam (1993–1998) became the first popularly elected civilian president after Rhee. Kim Dae-jung (1998–2003) in 1997 won the presidential election in his fourth bid for power, which witnessed the first peaceful power transfer from the ruling party to an opposition party in the history. For many, Kim Dae-jung's election to presidency was more than a power transition; it marked the dismantling of the developmental coalition and a transfer from conservative dominance to a pluralist democracy. Roh Moo-hyun (2003–2008) from the liberal camp succeeded Kim Dae-jung, indicating the consolidation of the progressive forces. In 2008, the election of Lee Myun-bak (2008–2013) marked the second peaceful transfer of power, with the conservatives back in office after being in opposition for 10 years. This transition implies that South Korea has successfully passed Huntington's (1991) "two turnover" test for democratic consolidation in nascent democracies (i.e., if the democratic order remains intact after the loss of power by an incumbent party, followed by the loss of its successor). In 2012, South Korea elected its first woman president, Park Geun-hye (2013–2017), the daughter of former president Park Chung-hee. Nevertheless, Park was impeached by the National Assembly in December 2016 for influence peddling and power abuse, and the Constitutional Court upheld the decision in March 2017. In May 2017, Moon Jae-in (2017–Present) was elected president.

Governance under Roh Tae-woo (1988–1993). Rho Tae-woo's victory preserved the structure and interest of the old authoritarian regime, sustained by the close ties between the politicians, the bureaucracy, and the *chaebol*. The *chaebol* received subsidized loans from state-owned banks with the approval of the bureaucracy under the support of the politicians and, in exchange, provided political contributions to politicians. In fact, the *chaebol* expanded their power in the democratic system, as their campaign contributions to politicians became more important in a political environment with intensified competition. The *chaebol* were not only able to thwart corporate reform attempts; they actually demanded more bank loans to expand their business. The increased financial leverage gave large conglomerates a false sense of security that they were too big to fail. As many of them were already heavily leveraged, increased borrowing significantly amplified the risk of bankruptcy.

After democratic transition, union membership quickly increased along with labor strikes, some of which turned violent. From 1987 to 1989, labor wages rose at a pace of 15 percent per year. For conservatives, wage hikes were a cause of concern for the international competitiveness of Korean products. For progressives, the increase simply made up for the sacrifices workers made in the past. The Roh government initially refrained from intervening in labor disputes. After 1990, the Roh government began to restrict wage growth and detain major labor leaders, leading to tension in government-labor relations.

Though elected president, Roh faced serious constraints. Competition between four political parties prevented the ruling DJP from winning the majority in the National Assembly in April 1988. With opposition parties holding a majority for the first time in the National Assembly, the legislators became more assertive, exercising their investigative and oversight power. Demands for judicial independence were also voiced by judges, and a new chief justice with no government ties was appointed.

In January 1990, Kim Young-sam engineered a deal to merge his party (Reunification Democratic Party) with the ruling DJP and Kim Jong-pil's New Democratic Republican Party to form the Democratic Liberal Party (DLP). Kim Dae-jung's Peace Democratic Party became the lone opposition party. Although the DLP had a commanding majority in the National Assembly (219 out of 299 seats), the mix of conservative and liberal politicians in the same party created ideological confusion, leading to constant internal strife. Thus, the DLP could not be an effective vehicle to carry out any reforms or policy initiatives. Instead, it relied on regionalism and charismatic leaders to attract support. The DLP lost one-third of its seats in the 1992 legislative election. As part of the deal, Kim Young-sam was to be the DLP candidate in the 1992 presidential election, which he won with 42 percent to Kim Dae-jung's 37 percent.

Governance under Kim Young-sam (1993–1998). Kim Young-sam was the first democratically elected civilian president in more than three decades. Although he was elected as the candidate of the ruling DLP, whose political base included many allied with the Fifth Republic, he initiated reforms that deeply affected civilian-military relations. Once in office, Kim Young-sam purged generals and colonels of the *Hanahoe* ("The Society of One"), a major pillar of Chun's support group, and filled the military leadership with officers previously excluded by *Hanahoe* generals to cultivate new discipline and professionalism in the armed forces.

He publicly disclosed his financial assets and demanded cabinet members do the same, leading to several resignations. In 1993, Kim Young-sam launched a "real name" reform in hopes of cutting down corruption. For years, banks in Korea had allowed customers to open bank accounts under pseudonyms, providing a channel for tax evasion, money laundering, and bribery. This reform aimed to eliminate these illicit financial activities to make business practices more transparent. Nevertheless, he was unsuccessful in pushing for more reforms against the *chaebol* that continued to expand and extend their business operations with excessive borrowing.

In 1995, Kim Young-sam brought charges against former presidents Chun and Roh, the spiritual leaders of the dominant faction of the DLP, for rebellion, subversion, and corruption. The trial laid a foundation for new political norms, indicating that even successful coup leaders could eventually be punished. Both were found to have kept vast sums of money as political contributions from all the leading *chaebol*. A group of top business executives were also indicted. Chun was sentenced to death and Roh to life imprisonment, although both were later pardoned. Kim Young-sam's approval ratings rose due to these anticorruption actions; however, his associates' involvement in bribery scandals tainted his anticorruption record. Most damaging to his reputation was the conviction of his second son for bribery and tax evasion.

Economically, Kim Young-sam promoted economic liberalization through the *Segyehwa* (globalization) initiative to further South Korea's integration into the global economic system. The liberalization drive aimed to liberalize the country's financial markets, reduce state intervention in the economy, and ultimately qualify South Korea for membership in the Organisation for Economic Co-operation and Development (OECD). In 1996, the OECD accepted South Korea as its 12th member, recognizing its economic success and accomplishments.

The financial liberalization lifted the limitation on foreign currency loans and allowed *chaebol* to increase their short-term foreign borrowing, which had lower interest rates. Excessive borrowing for business expansion by *chaebol* significantly increased their risk exposure. Rising labor costs and stiff competition from Chinese businesses further reduced the profitability of the South Korean *chaebol*. Several large companies started to go bankrupt in early 1997. As financial institutions tried to tighten their short-term loans, the trouble spread to the whole economy.

A financial meltdown in Thailand, where currency collapsed and the stock market plummeted, exacerbated the situation. Worried about the prospect of Asian economies, foreign investors began to take their money out of Asian markets, eventually triggering the 1997 Asian Financial Crisis. The Hong Kong stock market collapsed in October 1997, and Seoul soon followed. The Korean won lost nearly two-thirds of its value. Without sufficient foreign currency in reserve, the South Korean government in November 1997 had no choice but to call upon the International Monetary Fund (IMF) for help.

In December 1997, Kim Dae-jung was elected president amid the financial crisis. Earlier, Kim Jong-pil had broken off from the ruling party to create the United Liberal Democratic Party and subsequently formed an electoral alliance with Kim Dae-jung's National Congress for New Politics (NCNP). A popular governor, Lee In-jae, also split off from the conservative party in 1997 to run for president. Kim Dae-jung narrowly won the three-way race with 40.3 percent of the votes to Lee Hoi-chang's 38.7 percent and Lee In-jae's 19.2 percent. This election marked the first power transition from the conservative regime to the opposition. Kim Dae-jung appointed Kim Jong-pil as acting prime minister, bypassing the confirmation process of the National Assembly that was solidly controlled by the conservatives.

Economic Reforms and Engagement with the North

Governance under Kim Dae-jung (1998–2003). Kim Dae-jung began negotiating with IMF representatives and working out a recovery plan before his inauguration. Reforms recommended by the IMF were along the line of economic liberalization: enhancing labor market flexibility, privatizing the public sector, opening financial markets to foreign investors, and restructuring corporate governance of the *chaebol.*

These neoliberal policies faced strong opposition from workers, farmers, and the urban poor. Kim Dae-jung formed a tripartite presidential Commission of Labor, Business, and Government to seek consensus for economic reforms and restructuring under the principle of "fair burden-sharing." In February 1998, government, business, and labor reached a labor-market agreement to legalize immediate layoffs in case of "urgent managerial need." Additionally, temporary help agencies were allowed to dispatch temporary workers to firms for up to two years in all occupations. Labor market flexibility, however, undermined job security, as many Korean firms began to fire permanent workers to hire cheaper temporary workers, which further drove up the unemployment rate.

The Kim administration promised to carry out social welfare reforms to ease concerns about economic insecurity—an area long neglected under the growth model pursued by the authoritarian and conservative regimes. The intent was to increase social expenditure and expand national social insurance programs, such as pensions, unemployment benefits, and health insurance. Nevertheless, it was difficult to increase funding for social security systems while the government was implementing the IMF adjustment programs. Regulatory reforms were instituted to ensure transparency and accountability in corporate management, leading to the closure or merger of a number of banks.

The economy contracted 5.8 percent in 1998, and unemployment rose from 2 percent to 8 percent. The devalued won, however, made Korean exports more competitive, and the economy soon recovered. South Korea was able to repay the IMF loans within two years. Ironically, because of the quick recovery, attempts for further reforms such as setting ceilings on the debt-capital ratio to contain corporate debt lost momentum.

In February 1998, Kim Dae-jung initiated the "Sunshine Policy" to engage North Korea by expanding economic interactions and cultural exchanges. In January 2000, Kim proposed a summit with the North to discuss issues of mutual cooperation and peaceful unification. He traveled to Pyongyang in June 2000 to meet with North Korean leader Kim Jong-il for a three-day summit, the first conference between leaders of the two Koreas after the Korean War. In the joint declaration issued after the meeting, the two leaders stated their intention to achieve reunification based on the Korean people's initiative, build confidence by promoting economic cooperation, and promote inter-Korean dialogue.

The unprecedented summit caused great excitement and raised high expectations, and Kim Dae-jung was awarded the Nobel Peace Prize in the fall of 2000. The summit produced some tangible results, such as visits by separated family members and relatives and construction of a massive industrial complex at Kaesong, where North Korean workers could work for South Korean companies. Nevertheless, there was little substantive policy change.

North Korea did not reciprocate with concrete concessions. Polls in Korea reflected the public's initial excitement and subsequent disillusionment of the process. About 87 percent of South Koreans supported the policy immediately after the June 2000 summit, but the number fell to 34 percent just a year later.

As Kim promoted reforms, he also launched investigations against opposition politicians, leading to massive defections from the opposition to the ruling coalition. The ruling coalition, however, faltered in 2001, as Kim Jong-pil terminated political support to Kim Dae-jung on the grounds that the president failed to honor their earlier agreement to adopt the parliamentary system. Weakened by his sons' involvement in financial irregularities, Kim Dae-jung ceased using prosecutorial tactics to deter the opposition.

Kim Dae-jung's Millennium Democratic Party (MDP; renamed from NCNP) instituted an open primary system for candidate nomination. Roh Moo-hyun won the primary with strong public support, even though he was not popular within the party itself. As a maverick with no political faction of his own, Roh pulled off a surprise victory in 2002. The 2002 presidential election was viewed as a generational change in South Korean politics. For the first time in 15 years, none of the three Kims appeared on the ballot. However, it was another close election. The center-left Roh won with 48.9 percent of the vote compared with the conservative candidate Lee Hoi-chang's 46.6 percent.

Governance under Roh Moo-hyun (2003–2008). Roh Moo-hyun took a populist approach to political and economic, reforms. Identifying five strongholds of Korean political, economic, and cultural elites—Samsung Electronics (*chaebol*), *Chosun Ilbo* (*Chosun Daily*; conservative media), Seoul National University (elite educational system), Gangnam (the wealthiest district of Seoul), and the Supreme Court (conservative judicial elites)—Roh formulated policies to equalize economic and education opportunities and democratize information flow.

He sought to address economic inequality through distributive policies by increasing taxes, expanding social welfare expenditures, and rebalancing regional economic disparities. He tried, but failed, to move the capital from Seoul to Chungchong (about 100 miles away) to close the economic gap between Seoul and the rest of the country.

Roh appointed political activists to his administration and devolved powers to local governments. Additionally, he introduced campaign contribution reforms to increase transparency and promote free and fair competition, trying to sever cozy business-government relations. Nevertheless, his administration was plagued by corruption scandals involving his aides as well as revelations of illegal campaign funds used in the presidential election.

Roh's outspoken leadership style and antiestablishment policies encountered vigorous resistance. A pro-Roh faction broke away from the MDP and formed the Uri Party (Our Open Party), and Roh publicly expressed his support for the new party. The MDP together with the main opposition party, the Grand National Party (GNP; renamed from the New Korea Party, the successor to Kim Young-sam's DLP), voted to impeach him in March 2004 for violating the code of presidential political neutrality. Massive demonstrations erupted in support of Roh, as people viewed the impeachment proceeding as politically motivated to undermine reforms. Voters supported Roh's Uri Party in the April 2004 National Assembly election, helping the party gain a slim majority. In May, he was reinstated as president after the Constitutional Court overturned the impeachment.

Roh continued Kim Dae-jung's engagement policy with North Korea. The Kaesong Industrial Complex opened in December 2004. South Korean companies in search of cheap labor employed thousands of North Korean workers there, using utility services from South Korea. Trade between North and South Koreas surpassed $1 billion for the first time in 2005. Despite North Korea's repeated missile tests, Roh maintained an optimistic view about the inter-Korean relations. After North Korea's first underground nuclear test in 2006, the ROK government pleaded with the United States not to take punitive action. In October 2007, Roh traveled to Pyongyang and met with Kim Jong-il in a three-day summit. Both sides issued a joint declaration to focus on more economic cooperation but did little to address the DPRK's nuclear program.

While Roh's conciliatory policy toward North Korea created tension with the United States, he also took the initiative to pursue a free trade agreement with the United States, a move well received by the conservatives. Both governments signed the agreement in June 2007, despite strong opposition from ROK farmers and various citizen groups.

Overall, Roh was unsuccessful in delivering robust economic growth or improving economic inequalities. In the December 2007 election, Lee Myung-bak, the conservative candidate of the GNP, labeled the decade ruled by Kim Dae-jung and Roh Moo-hyun as the "lost decade of diminished economic growth." Lee, a former chief executive officer of Hyundai Construction and mayor of Seoul, pledged to "Revitalize the Economy" by cutting taxes, trimming public spending, and easing regulations on *chaebol* that were introduced by the two progressive presidents. Lee won the election with 48.7 percent of the vote, defeating Roh's chosen successor, Chung Dong-young (26.1 percent), and the independent candidate, Lee Hoi-chang (15.1 percent).

Roh was targeted by the prosecutor's office for bribery investigations after he left office. Roh vehemently denied the allegations and committed suicide in May 2009 by jumping off a cliff near his home. Over half a million people bid a final farewell at Roh's funeral.

Restoration of the Conservative Rule

Governance under Lee Myung-bak (2008–2013). Despite Lee's landslide victory, his approval rating dropped to the teens within six months of his inauguration. His trouble began with the formation of the cabinet, as many of the nominees were accused of real estate speculation, tax evasion, or plagiarism. In the end, three had to withdraw their nominations.

His popularity plunged again after the United States and South Korea reached an agreement in April 2008 to remove the ban on U.S. beef imports, imposed after the discovery of a case of mad cow disease in the United States in 2003. The action triggered huge demonstrations throughout the country for more than three months; nearly one million people gathered in Seoul for a candlelight vigil in June 2008. Although the beef fiasco finally ended with the United States making some concessions, the event seriously damaged the Lee administration's reputation.

The third challenge came from the overseas markets when the country's economy was hammered by the 2008 global financial crisis. Prompted by the investment bank Lehman Brothers filing for Chapter 11 bankruptcy in September 2008, the financial market meltdown soon spread from the United States to the rest of the world. The Lee government initially tried to devaluate the Korean won to promote export growth, but the weakened currency caused price spikes in imported oil and commodities. The government then intervened to raise the value of the won. The policy confusion contributed to a worsening economic situation.

Lee took active, interventionist policy measures to reverse the liberalization effort taken by Kim Dae-jung and Roh Moo-hyun. He used heavy-handed actions to streamline bureaucracies, privatize state enterprises, and launch major infrastructure projects.

In terms of Lee's foreign policy, the top priority was to repair and restore relations with the United States, which had been damaged by his predecessor's pro–North Korea policies and the U.S. beef incident. The June 2009 summit between Presidents Lee and Obama reaffirmed the strategic partnership between the two countries against nuclear threats or attacks from North Korea. To overcome resistance to the trade deal by Congress and President Obama, Lee renegotiated the agreement with the United States in December 2010 to expand concessions in automobile trades, which led to a strong boycott by the opposition parties. With the support of the ruling GNP, the National Assembly ratified the pact in November 2011.

The Lee government's U.S.-centered foreign policy caused strained relations with China. Recognizing China's status as an important player in regional and global politics, the Lee government decided to launch free trade agreement negotiations with China in April 2011 as a balancing attempt to improve Korea-China bilateral relations. Nevertheless, Korea-Japan relations soured under Lee after he visited the disputed Dokdo Islands in August 2012.

Lee took a hard-line policy toward North Korea. His policy of "principled engagement" was based on North Korea's concrete moves toward denuclearization. In May 2009, North Korea successfully conducted the second underground nuclear test, after the first one failed in 2006. The UN Security Council adopted a resolution in June 2009 to impose tougher economic sanctions on North Korea. The UN sanctions nearly eliminated all inter-Korean economic activities. In March 2010, the unexplained explosion of the South Korean patrol boat *Cheonan* caused the death of 46 seamen. The study of the wreckage by an international investigative team concluded that the boat was sunk by a North Korean torpedo, but the North strongly denied it. After the report was released, the Lee administration suspended nearly all its trade with the North. In November 2010, North Korea launched an artillery attack on Yonpyongdo, a South Korean island, and killed four people. The inter-Korean relations reached a low point.

At the end of his term, Lee was perceived as favoring *chaebol* at the expense of small businesses and increasing income disparity. Some of his close aides and one of his brothers were implicated in corruption scandals.

Park Geun-hye, the eldest daughter of Park Chung-hee, took over the conservative party leadership in December 2011 and rebranded the party as the *Saenuri* (New Frontier) Party in 2012. She advocated "economic democratization" during her 2012 presidential campaign, vowing to restore economic growth and to fight against social disparity with more social safety nets. Park received 50.6 percent of the vote and became South Korea's first woman president, defeating the liberal candidate Moon Jae-in (48 percent).

Governance under Park Geun-hye (2013–2017). Park campaigned on the promise of better, more extensive welfare services to address the problems of economic disparity and an aging population, but she scaled back her pledges after election. The plans to introduce a basic pension plan and to have full government support for people with long-term care needs were both delayed. The *chaebol* reforms met strong resistance from the owners of the conglomerates. The "creative economy" proposed in her campaign did not contain specific measures to support start-ups. Under Park, economic growth mostly came through government fiscal stimulus, which increased long-term public debt.

North Korea conducted its third nuclear test in February 2013, right before Park's inauguration, and did so twice more during her administration (the fourth in January 2016 and fifth in September 2016), along with numerous missile tests. Amid heightened inter-Korean tensions, in July 2016, the United States and the Park administration agreed to deploy in South Korea the U.S. Terminal High Altitude Area Defense system (THAAD), which could protect the country from missile attacks by intercepting missiles at high altitude. The move caused enormous domestic and international controversies. Supported by the progressives and opposition leaders, residents near the announced missile site expressed concerns about the environmental impact of the system. China protested strongly against the deployment, arguing the THAAD radar system would undermine China's national security. To pressure the ROK government, it began to launch unofficial sanctions against the South. The Chinese boycotted key South Korean exports to China like automobiles, electronics, and cosmetics, and the number of Chinese tourists visiting South Korea fell sharply.

Amid the controversies, news came out in October 2016 that Park's longtime friend Choi Soon-sil, holder of no public office, had been illegally influencing government policy and personnel decisions. It was reported that Park relied heavily on her to make key domestic and foreign policy decisions. Infuriated by the scandal, the Korean public held massive candlelight protests. A special prosecutor, authorized by the National Assembly, launched an independent investigation and found that Park had abused her power. She pressured *chaebol*, including Hyundai Motor and Samsung, to donate funds to foundations run by Choi, and blacklisted some people from receiving government funding because of their progressive ideology. While presidential families and relatives had been involved in corruption scandals before, this was the first time a sitting president was directly implicated.

In December 2016, the National Assembly passed the impeachment bill in secret ballot, clearing the two-thirds majority required for the procedure. Over 50 lawmakers of the ruling *Saenuri* Party might have joined the opposition to vote for the impeachment. Following the vote, Prime Minister Hwang Kyo-ahn immediately became the acting president. In March 2017, the Constitutional Court issued a unanimous 8–0 ruling to uphold the impeachment vote.

A special presidential election was held in May 2017. Moon Jae-in, a liberal leader from the Democratic Party and a former chief of staff to Roh Moo-hyun, won the election with 41 percent of the vote in a five-way race and immediately assumed the duties of the presidency.

Return of the Liberal Administration

Governance under Moon Jae-in (2017–Present). Moon has advocated for dialogue with North Korea and balanced diplomacy between the United States and China, given the important role China might play in dealing with North Korea. In June 2017, Moon suspended the deployment of the controversial THAAD system, citing his concerns about its environmental impact. In November 2017, South Korea and China agreed to "normalize exchanges" and end the conflict over THAAD. In exchange for Beijing's lifting of sanctions, South Korea pledged that it will not deploy additional THAAD launchers, will not use other U.S. missile defense systems, and will not join an alliance with the United States and Japan.

Notwithstanding the sixth nuclear test conducted by North Korea in September 2017, Moon was determined to engage North Korea early in his tenure as president. The opportunity came in 2018. In his 2018 New Year's Message, Kim Jong-un offered to send a delegation to participate in the 2018 Winter Olympics hosted by South Korea. The Moon administration seized the overture and initiated diplomatic talks. Moon met with Kim Jong-un on April 27, 2018, at the Panmunjom Truce Village. This was the third South-North summit, following the previous ones in 2000 and 2007. Moon and Kim agreed to complete denuclearization, which laid the groundwork for President Trump's meeting with Kim in Singapore in June 2018. Nearly 90 percent of South Koreans approved of the inter-Korean summit in public polls, reflecting strong support of Moon's rapprochement strategy.

Former President Lee Myung-bak was arrested in March 2018, under allegations of embezzlement and misappropriation of more than $32 million, as well as receiving illicit business contributions. Lee's arrest sparked political debates on whether it was really an issue of corruption or an act of political retribution.

GOVERNING INSTITUTIONS

The 1987 ROK Constitution

The 1987 Constitution for the Sixth Republic stipulates that the ROK shall be a democratic republic, with sovereignty residing in the people. According to the Constitution, its territory shall consist of the Korean peninsula, and the process of unification shall be peaceful and based on the basic free and democratic order.

Consistent with all the constitutional traditions since 1948 (except for the parliamentary system of the short-lived Second Republic), the 1987 Constitution adopts the presidential system. The president is directly elected under a first-past-the-post system in a single round of voting in which the candidate receiving the highest number of popular votes is elected. The president serves a single five-year term and cannot be reelected. As the head of state, the president appoints public officials and performs executive functions through the State Council. The legislative power is exercised by the unicameral National Assembly, whose members are directly elected for a four-year term.

From the perspective of institutional stability and peaceful transfer of political regimes, South Korea as a young democracy seems to perform quite well. Competitive elections for the presidency and legislators have been held regularly, and power transitions between the ruling and opposition parties have met the "two-turnover test." It appears that democracy in South Korea has stood the test of time.

Many citizens and politicians, however, believe that the current constitution is flawed. The high frequency of corruption scandals associated with former presidents and their families raises questions about whether power is overconcentrated in the hands of the president and whether the single-term presidency is counterproductive, as elected presidents face no pressure of reelection. An overwhelming majority of the people believe that the current political system does not properly respond to their voices (Sohn and Kang 2013).

While there are plenty of discussions on constitutional revision, there has been no consensus on how the constitution should be revised. Some suggest a parliamentary system in which the executive power is in the majority party of the legislature, while others propose a semipresidential system with the president handling diplomatic and military affairs, leaving internal affairs to the prime minister. Still others believe that a four-year presidency that allows for reelection will solve the problem. It remains to be seen whether a broad consensus can emerge from such discussions.

The National Government

Presidency. Standing at the apex of the executive branch, the president is the head of state, representing the entire country in government affairs and foreign relations. There is no vice president in the current structure.

As chief executive of the South Korean government, the president enforces legislation and appoints the prime minister (with the consent of the National Assembly), along with members of the State Council (i.e., the cabinet), based on the recommendation of the prime minster. The president is commander-in-chief of the armed forces, has the duty to safeguard the independence and territorial integrity of the state, and is trusted with the task of pursuing the peaceful reunification of Korea.

The president chairs the State Council, and the prime minister serves as the vice chair. Members of the State Council lead and supervise their administrative ministries, participating in the deliberation of major state affairs. In reality, cabinet meetings are rarely used to discuss policies or exchange ideas. Presidents usually dominate the meeting by giving directives while cabinet members quietly take notes.

The single-term provision prevents any individual from holding government power for an extended period of time, a safeguard measure aimed to avert dictatorship, which was an issue in the recent history of the country. Critics, however, point out that the one-term limit for the South Korean presidency reduces incentives for legislative-presidential collaboration, because a president becomes a lame duck midway through the third year, having little time to implement his or her campaign platforms.

Even though tenure of certain positions such as commissioner of the National Tax Service, prosecutor general, and chairman of the Board of Audit and Inspection are protected by the constitution to ensure their political independence, most office holders resign from their posts after presidential election to make room for new appointments. This practice undermines the constitutional design of political neutrality but reflects the tradition of a strong presidency.

Cabinet appointments do not require legislative approval. This is another feature of strong presidential power. Legislative ratification is required for prime minister, Supreme Court Justices and Chief Justice, the head of the Constitutional Court, and chairman of the Board of Audit and Inspection but not for cabinet members. Although the National Assembly holds confirmation hearings for ministerial candidates, the legislature does not have the power to reject a specific nominee, because its reports are only advisory.

Traditionally, the president has mostly turned to career bureaucrats for ministerial appointments, followed by outside experts such as university professors and medical doctors (Hahm, Jung, and Lee 2013). After South Korea's democratic transition, politicians, including members of the National Assembly, have become the third most popular group for ministerial selection. The heavy reliance on policy experts reflects the expectation to have individuals with qualified credentials manage departments effectively.

Nevertheless, the turnover rate for South Korean ministers is relatively high, with the average tenure being only one year. Presidents often reorganize the cabinet strategically to break out of political deadlock or boost approval ratings. The rapid turnover provides very little time for the ministers to become familiar with the department affairs, much less serve as effective leaders.

Bureaucracy. As discussed earlier, economic development was an important source of political legitimacy for Park Chung-hee. To ensure that the state had the managerial capacity to sustain economic success, he built a cadre of skilled bureaucrats for policy formulation and implementation. These economic technocrats, many of them trained at prestigious universities in the United States, took over core economic institutions in economic planning and research. Extensive regulatory power was granted to Korean bureaucrats so that they could employ incentives and sanctions on private industry to promote economic success. It should also be noted, however, that the meritocratic bureaucracy coexisted with a patronage network based on regional ties, family connections, and school affiliations. Buying off supporters with government posts helped Park consolidate his political control.

Beginning in the early 1980s, succeeding presidents have implemented administrative reforms for political purposes. Promoting a clean and efficient government helps garner public support and gives the president an opportunity to exercise control over the bureaucracy (Moon and Ingraham 1998). After the 1979 coup, to win over business support, Chun promised to reduce government intervention in the banking and financial sectors. Thus, the Chun government downsized the central government and sold its stake in commercial banks to reduce the state's control over personnel appointment and loan allocation.

After democratization, bureaucrats, who were unelected but had policy-making authority, were under increasing pressure to be more accountable. To reduce the regulatory power of the bureaucracy, the first civilian president, Kim Young-sam, proposed to develop a "clean, small and strong government," underscoring the importance of transparency, democracy, and efficiency. His other initiative, *Segyehwa* (globalization), though aimed to promote economic liberalization and marketization, also had the effect of minimizing bureaucrats' discretionary power through deregulation and privatization. To make policy making more transparent and more democratic, the administrative procedure reforms promoted by Kim Young-sam mandated public notice and comment for all proposed regulations. Public hearings and notice of draft rules empowered citizens and organized interests to voice their opinions about every government decision but added an obstacle to bureaucrats' discretion, reducing their capacity to control policy outcomes.

Despite these reform measures, bureaucracy remains a powerful actor in policy making. Under the one-term limit for presidents, bureaucrats have an incentive to resist presidential initiatives, knowing that a president will not be around for long.

The National Assembly. The legislative power of the government in the Sixth Republic resides in the unicameral National Assembly, whose 300 members serve four-year terms. The National Assembly enacts and amends laws; proposes amendments to the Constitution; inspects and investigates state administration; and has the power to impeach the president, the prime minister, and members of the Cabinet, among others. Additionally, it decides upon budget bills submitted by the executive and consents to the conclusion and ratification of treaties.

The relationship between the president and the National Assembly usually follows one of two patterns: executive dominance or institutional gridlock (Croissant 2002). When the president's party controls a majority of the seats in the National Assembly, the executive-legislative relationship usually takes the path of executive dominance. Under authoritarian rule (1972–1986), the National Assembly passed about 90 percent of the executive branch's legislative proposals (i.e., government bills) without any revision, suggesting the image of a rubber stamp (Jang and Shin 2008). The ratio fell below 50 percent in the aftermath of the democratic transition, indicating a more assertive legislative body. Nevertheless, government bills still had an average 80 percent success rate in the National Assembly (compared with 90 percent prior to democratic transition), reflecting the continued pattern of executive dominance.

This was particularly the case in economic legislation. Most of the National Assembly members in charge of finance and economic affairs acknowledged the lack of power on their part, as the Office of the President and the economic staff under the president continued to exercise leadership in economic policy making.

When the president's party is a minority party in the National Assembly—a phenomenon known as "divided government"—it creates gridlock. Both sides can claim a mandate from the people, with neither side thus willing to compromise. In the end, the president might have to build political coalitions or use political tactics to break the stalemate.

When Kim Dae-jung was elected president, the opposition-controlled legislature refused to confirm his nominee, Kim Jong-pil, as prime minister. In the end, Kim Dae-jung appointed him as acting prime minister to bypass the confirmation process of the National Assembly. Kim also launched investigations against opposition politicians, wielding the president's control over prosecutors. To avoid the investigation, a large number of politicians defected to join his ruling coalition, hence solidifying his control.

The electoral system adopted for the National Assembly elections since democratic transition has involved different experiments with different combinations of local districts and national (party) lists. In 1988 and 1992, South Korea used a single-vote mixed system. Each voter was allowed to cast only one vote, and the vote was counted at the single member district (SMD) to determine the winner. The vote would then be aggregated to the national level to allocate seats to parties. The distribution, however, was not proportional. The party that won the most districts would automatically receive one-half to two-thirds of the party-list seats, assuring it an overall majority in the Assembly. In 1996 and 2000, this system was slightly modified to distribute national-list seats on the basis of each party's vote share at the district level. In 2001, the Constitutional Court ruled it unconstitutional to allocate the party list by district votes.

The current two-vote, mixed-member electoral system was adopted in March 2004. Similar to the electoral system used in Japan since its 1994 reforms (Chapter 6), the South Korean system combines SMDs with proportional representation (PR), electing a majority of the legislators through local districts and the rest from PR at the national level. Each voter has two ballots: one for a candidate in the SMD and the other for a party in PR. Of the 300 seats in the National Assembly, 253 of them (246 before 2016) are elected from single-member constituencies, while the remaining 47 seats (54 before 2016) are distributed to a political party in proportion to the number of votes earned. Political parties that gained 3 percent or more of all valid votes, or had five or more elected Assembly representatives, are eligible for party-list distribution. Unlike the Japanese system, the South Korean model does not allow candidates to run in both the district and on the party list at the same time.

Economic development in South Korea has led to rapid urbanization and population migration from rural areas to cities. As the case in Japan, it created an urban-rural imbalance in representation (or malapportionment). In October 2014, the Constitutional Court of Korea ruled that population ratio between the smallest to largest districts be raised to 1:2 to better match the current population distribution. The National Assembly made the adjustment in 2016, rebalancing the SMD and PR seats.

The purpose behind South Korea's 2004 mixed-member system, much like Japan's 1994 electoral reform, was to discourage pork-barrel politics and to reduce party fragmentation, in hopes of moving in the direction of a two-party system. It also aimed to reduce the effects of regionalism. As discussed earlier, the regional voting blocs of the 1987 presidential election played a significant role in subsequent elections at all levels. Most parties drew support from distinct territorial strongholds. The candidate's home district or place of origin heavily influenced voters' decisions (Park 2002; Sonn 2003). Politicians were welcome as the favorite sons or daughters by their regions and were expected to advocate for the region. As a result, political parties tended to promote regional interests, not necessarily national interests. Adding the nationally elected party list presumably would encourage political parties to deliver their policy messages to a national audience rather than a regional one (Reilly 2007). So far, the results have been mixed (Rich 2014). The implementation of the 2004 electoral system has led to a gradual decrease in the number of candidates at the district level, but regional voting remained noticeable.

POLITICAL PARTIES

The Party System

Party splits and mergers, along with member defections, have been quite common in South Korean politics. Between 1988 and 2012, 28 different political parties that had received at least 5 percent of national votes existed, but their average longevity was only 4.6 years (Lee 2014). Political leaders formed or disbanded political parties as part of legislative or campaign strategies. The rise and fall of the parties frequently reflected the political fortune of their leaders. Politicians of iconic stature (such as the three Kims) created, dismissed, and recreated political parties for the sake of their political aspirations and interests.

In the 1987 presidential election, Kim Dae-jung and Kim Young-sam both decided to run, and both expected the other to pull out of the race. Unable to compromise, Kim Dae-jung broke from the Unification Democratic Party and its leader Kim Young-sam and formed his own Party for Peace and Democracy, leading to the split of the opposition camp and the election of Roh Tae-woo.

In 1990, Kim Young-sam made a deal with two politicians who previously supported the authoritarian regime—Roh Tae-woo and Kim Jong-pil—to run as the next presidential candidate for the conservative camp. They created the DLP by combining the Democratic Justice Party (Roh Tae-woo), the Reunification Democratic Party (Kim Young-sam), and the New Democratic Republic Party (Kim Jong-pil).

In 1995, when Kim Jong-pil was denied the candidacy by the conservative camp, he founded the United Liberal Democratic Party and formed an electoral alliance with Kim Dae-jung. Kim Dae-jung promised, if elected, to change South Korea's political structure to a parliamentary system and to make Kim Jong-pil the prime minister to wield the real power. Kim Dae-jung did not keep his promise, and Kim Jong-pil broke from the coalition in 2000.

As political expediency becomes the dominant value in party politics, there is widespread distrust of political parties. More than 70 percent of the voters view political parties as "corrupt," and 25 percent to 30 percent show absolutely no trust in political parties (Hellmann 2014; Lee 2014). Another indicator is the continued increase of nonpartisans who do not support any political parties.

Interestingly, despite all the mergers, splits, and name changes, there has been remarkable continuity in the principal actors and their political networks, along the conservative versus progressive camps.

The DLP, formed after the 1990 super merger engineered by Kim Young-sam, was the base of the conservative camp. Subsequently, it has rebranded as the New Korea Party (1995), Grand National Party (1997), *Saenuri* (2012), and Liberty Korea Party (2017).

In the progressive camp, a faction of Kim Young-sam's Reunification Democratic Party joined forces with Kim Dae-jung's Party for Peace and Democracy to form the Democratic Party in 1991. It then evolved into the National Congress for New Politics (1995) and the MDP (2000). After Roh Moo-hyun left the MDP to form the Uri Party (2003), the MDP was renamed the Democratic Party (2005) and reorganized into the New Politics Alliance for Democracy (2014) and then the Democratic Party of Korea (2016).

The Organization and Procedure of the Political Parties

Notwithstanding their ideological continuity, South Korean political parties have not developed strong organizations and procedures; party organizations are inchoate and unstable, trapped in a vicious cycle of organizational instability. Political leaders anticipate frequent party realignment and therefore do not invest in building a party base. The lack of continuity and stability significantly undermines the ability of political parties to develop a consistent, credible brand.

South Korean parties tend to operate in a highly factionalized and personalistic manner, with no clear rules on intraparty matters and procedures. The three Kims enjoyed enormous influence and exercised complete control over their own parties, making decisions on all aspects of party affairs, including nominating candidates, appointing party officials, and designating chairs for National Assembly standing committees (Im 2004). Loyalty and allegiance pledged by followers were to an individual leader, rather than a particular party.

In the post-Kims era, decisions for candidate selection, party finance, and appointments to party posts continue to be conducted in an ad hoc manner. Party leaders and the dominant faction in the parties usually control candidate selection in a "winner-take-all" manner, and nominations for parliamentary elections have often been determined on the politicians' personal ties to presidential hopefuls. For example, President Lee Myung-bak and his faction in the Grand National Party would not nominate a large number of Park Geun-hye's supporters, Lee's chief rival for the 2008 parliamentary elections. After Park controlled the party, she returned the favor by not renominating Lee's loyalists for the 2012 parliamentary elections. Without well-established procedures and organizations, underinstitutionalized parties can be easily captured by politicians for their own interests.

At the district level, parties are organized on the basis of patron-client ties between a political boss and followers. Legislators maintain their own informal groups (*sajojik*) that are similar to the Japanese *koenkai* (Chapter 6) in that they help cultivate personal networks to mobilize votes for the candidate during elections. The *sajojik*, however, are rather short-lived, rarely passed down through generations as are *koenkai*.

Since 2002, major parties have adopted some democratic procedures using a mix of primaries and public opinion surveys to nominate presidential candidates, who would then assume positions as party leaders. These nomination procedures, however, have not been formalized, as they are changed before every election to accommodate the demands and preferences of new contenders.

Reasons for Underinstitutionalized Parties. What accounts for the underinstitutionalized nature of South Korean parties? Some (Park and Shin 2006; Shin

1999; Steinberg and Shin 2006) take the cultural approach and argue that personalized parties are the manifestation of the Confucian legacy of paternalism and hierarchical social structure. Given the South Korean political culture of entrusting preponderant authority to individuals at the leadership position, they argue that it is natural that political parties operate on a personal basis.

Others (Croissant and Volkel 2012; Lee 2014) point to the authoritarian legacy by Park and Chun. Both of them relied primarily on the security apparatus, not political parties, to control the populace, even though each created his own political party (i.e., the Democratic Republican Party by Park and the Democratic Justice Party by Chun). Neither used political parties to develop organizational infrastructures to reach out to social groups, coopt opposition forces, or manage elite conflicts. In fact, their regimes placed restrictive regulations and severe constraints on the development of stable political parties and party systems. As such, the authoritarian legacy of underinstitutionalized parties persists in the postauthoritarian era.

Consequences of Underinstitutionalized Parties. After democratization, there has been a relatively high level of strikes, sit-ins, and protests in South Korea; many have turned violent and disruptive. The main streets of Seoul near the National Assembly Hall are often congested with demonstration crowds. In a consolidated democracy, party politics or other forms of institutionalized, conventional participation normally replace popular protests and social movements. Thus, the persistence of massive demonstrations, and their intensity in confrontation, raises questions as to why political parties have failed to channel social movements into meaningful policy debates in the National Assembly for productive consultation and compromise.

Generally, parties have not maintained close or substantive links to social organizations. The dominant effect of regionalism means that regional identities, not policy issues, shape South Korean party politics and electoral outcomes. Political parties have very little incentive to cultivate close ties with civil society organizations (CSOs) and address their policy concerns. Presidents Kim Dae-jung (1998–2003) and Roh Moo-hyun (2003–2008) reached out to civic organizations because of their personal ties to some of these groups. But the collaborative relations were temporary and short-lived, far from being institutionalized.

From the perspective of the CSOs, given the volatility of the party system, there is no reason to invest their political capital in existing political parties and to develop long-term alliance relationships with them. This is particularly true given the fact that South Korean citizens have little trust and confidence in the politcal parties. A large share of civil society groups remains unaffiliated with political parties. For example, labor unions would rather resort to strikes or take to the streets than channel their demands through political parties when dealing with labor issues.

Because of the weak linkage between political parties and social groups, no proper channels have been established to incorporate the voice of civil society in the policy-making process. CSOs feel compelled to confront the state publicly to exert direct pressure on the government. The reliance of CSOs on street demonstrations is an indication of the dysfunctional party politics in South Korea.

THE STATE-CIVIL SOCIETY RELATIONS

Under the Authoritarian Regime

Under the authoritarian regime, autonomous organizations were suppressed. The state incorporated social groups as quasi-governmental organizations and mobilized them to support state ideologies and implement state policies. For example, the national labor umbrella organization, the Federation of Korean Trade Unions (FKTU), and business associations such as Federation of Korean Industries (FKI) and Korea Employers' Federation (KEF) were the groups endorsed by the state. They acted under the supervision and guidance of the state.

The 1970 New Village Movement (NVM; *Saemaul Undong*), along with the organizations created by the movement, was another example of state dominance over the civil society. In the 1960s, industrialization was an important policy goal of the Park administration. Allocating resources mainly to industries, however, created an imbalanced economic structure, causing growth stagnation and relative poverty in the rural area, the major support base of the Park's regime. By promoting traditional values of hard work and self-help and organizing the countryside into mutual support teams, the NVM aimed to prevent the rise of social movements against the regime.

Local communities and workplaces became the basic units of NVM organization. Farmers were organized into a *Saemaul* farming association, as were women, youth, and the elderly into their respective associations. Local authorities operated neighborhood groups (with 20–30 households) at the grassroots level and oversaw political monitoring and ideological indoctrination through mandatory monthly meetings (Seo and Kim 2015).

The revolt against authoritarian regime on April 19, 1960, was the first significant prodemocratic movement against the ruling regime in postcolonial Korea. The state suppression since the 1971 *Yushin* era helped radicalize the dissident movement to embrace the *minjung* (i.e., the people or the masses) ideology in its attempt to liberate marginalized groups such as industrial workers, urban poor, and farmers through radical, violent resistance campaigns. Ultimately, escalating clashes between riot police and protesters in 1987 galvanized the conservative middle class into support of the opposition, leading to the democratic transition.

In the Democratic Era

The Rise of the CSOs. After the democratic transition, a great number of labor unions, industry associations, and civil organizations were created.

The number of organizations tripled from 1991 to 1996, with explosive growth occurring in the citizens-led associations and labor organizations (Tsujinaka 2003). The upward trend of registered nonprofit civic groups continued in the 2000s. Nevertheless, despite the increase in the number of registered civic groups, membership in voluntary associations has been in decline since the mid-1990s (Oh 2012).

A new type of CSOs, commonly called "citizens' organizations" or "citizens' movement organizations," began to emerge. Different from the radicalized dissident groups, their main purpose is to engage in social change through legal and policy reforms. Unlike previous democratization movements aimed to transform or reorganize state power, they recognized the existing political institutions but sought to monitor and challenge their arbitrary actions and illegal operations. With active participation by educated urban elites such as scholars, lawyers, and professionals, the new civic groups moved away from the class-based *minjung* ideology and instead promoted an encompassing concept of *simin* (i.e., citizens; Choi 2000; Moon 2010).

Out of these citizens' organizations, the development of comprehensive citizens' organizations is a unique feature for South Korea. Since 1989, three major citizens' organizations have taken the lead in civil society (Cho 2006): the Citizens' Coalition for Economic Justice (CCEJ; founded in 1989), the Korean Federation for Environmental Movement (KFEM; created in 1993), and the People's Solidarity for Participatory Democracy (PSPD; founded in 1994). Each began with a specific area of concern. The CCEJ aimed to promote economic fairness and justice through regulation of real estate speculation, expansion of public housing, and maintaining the independent status of the Bank of Korea. The KFEM promoted environmental protection, and the PSPD campaigned for a social safety net, anticorruption reform, and *chaebol* reforms.

Over the years, these citizens' groups have grown to be comprehensive organizations that deal with a wide variety of political, economic, social, and cultural issues such as education, human rights, consumer rights, eradication of corruption, gender equality, and media freedom. Linking various specialists and consultants in loosely connected policy networks, they act as umbrella organizations involved in an array of policy reforms. Bringing heterogeneous issues under their wings, these organizations have been the driving force behind massive movements such as the 2004 anti-impeachment vigils, the 2008 anti-U.S. beef imports candlelight vigils, and the 2016–2017 vigils demanding the immediate resignation of President Park Geun-hye. Interest groups in other countries tend to focus on a specific function area, or even a single issue, rather than act as catch-all movement associations. The emergence of the comprehensive citizens' organizations serves to bridge the representation gap for the dysfunctional political parties.

Relations with the State. In the democratic era, the state–civil society relationship has not followed a consistent pattern of either antagonism or collaboration.

The relationship is more nuanced, based on each side's strategic goal for a policy area. While CSOs are much more empowered because of democratization, they also face competition with others such as business or labor for policy makers' attention. Sometimes, the state finds it useful to ally with civic groups to balance the interest group; other times, it may make concessions to organized interests. Similarly, civic groups may collaborate with the state in policy reforms or may challenge the state by taking the issue to the street.

The case of *chaebol* reforms illustrates the state's strategy of selective alliance with civil society (Kim, Han, and Jang 2008). Comprehensive organizations such as the CCEJ and PSPD have long advocated for *chaebol* reforms to achieve economic democratization. In particular, they sought to eradicate unfair and unsavory business practices such as insider trading, real estate speculation, excessive diversification, unfair trading with subsidiaries, and mutual debt guarantees among affiliates. After the 1997 Asian Financial Crisis, the scope of their reform efforts expanded to corporate governance and business structure, with particular interest in managerial malpractices and exclusive control of *chaebol* by the owners' families. As such, the CCEJ and PSPD proposed to restructure *chaebol*, including limiting the decision-making rights of *chaebol* owners/chairman, appointing outside directors, and strengthening the voice of minority shareholders.

These efforts, however, encountered strong resistance from the pro-*chaebol* groups such as FKI, the Korea Chamber of Commerce and Industry (KCCI), and the Korea International Trade Association (KITA), which raised concern about these measures' long-term implications for the country's economic growth. As such, each of the administrations since the democratic transition has had to navigate carefully between these competing camps. On some occasions, the government would incorporate civic groups' demands into reform measures; on others, it would bypass their suggestions or limit their scope of implementation, for fear of destabilizing the economy or inhibiting investment confidence.

The strategic alignment with different civic and economic groups at various points of time reflects the strength of the South Korean state that maintains an autonomous status to attain its policy goals, rather than being captured by a particular set of social groups. Unlike the authoritarian regime that derived autonomy through coercion and repression, the democratic government positions itself between conflicting interests and demands of various social forces to achieve balance.

The ideological orientation of the civic groups can complicate the state–civil society relations. Many of the CSOs advocated democratic reforms, economic equality, and peaceful engagement with North Korea, which were in tune with the policy agenda of the liberal governments of Kim Dae-jung and Roh Moo-hyun. Hence, both Kim and Roh administrations actively supported civil society under the slogan of "participatory democracy" or "participatory government" in an attempt to strengthen political coalitions of the anti-establishment, anticonservatism forces. While nonprofit civil organizations received financial support from the government through the Non-Profit

Private Organizations Support Act, funding was allocated more generously to civil organizations that supported the liberal government's reform agenda.

During the Roh administration, conservative social groups such as the Free Citizens' Alliance of Korea and the Korea Forum for Progress began to emerge. To counteract liberal, or populist, tendencies, they advocated renewal of South Korea's economic competitiveness, cutbacks on welfare programs, and a hard-line policy toward North Korea.

The election of Lee Myong-bak ended his predecessors' cordial and collaborative relations with progressive civil organizations. The Lee administration reduced government funding to the organizations previously supported by the Kim and Roh administrations. Instead, conservative CSOs began to work closely with the government. Ideological pluralization has been an interesting development in South Korean civil society. It remains to be seen how tensions between progressive and conservative groups may play out in the long term. For now, it appears that cooptation of the CSOs by the state could, in the long run, undermine their integrity and moral authority in the eyes of the public.

DISCUSSION QUESTIONS

1. Describe the negotiations at the elite level that ultimately led to the democratic transition in South Korea in the 1980s. Discuss how the confluence of various domestic and international factors resulted in its democratization.

2. What are the policy divisions between the conservatives and progressives in South Korea? Identify the key areas of difference between the two, and compare their policy positions.

3. The military played a dominant role in South Korean politics for three decades from the early 1960s to the late 1980s. How did President Park and President Chun exercise control over the military? In the democratic era, what actions were taken to help restore the civilian control of the military?

4. Describe the relationship between the president and the National Assembly in the Sixth Republic. Are there any patterns of interactions? What are the implications for policy making?

5. South Korean political parties are said to be underinstitutionalized. Explain what that means and provide some examples. What may explain the phenomenon? What is its impact on political governance?

11

South Korea's Pursuit of Economic Prosperity

GROWTH UNDER THE AUTHORITARIAN REGIME: 1948–1987

Economic Challenges in the Early Days of Independence

Following Japan's defeat in World War II and the repatriation of 700,000 Japanese bureaucrats, managers, and workers from Korea, as well as the hasty withdrawal of Japanese capital (roughly 90 percent of total capital in Korea), a huge economic void was left in the former colony. Soon afterward, the partition of Korea into two zones along the 38th parallel (Chapter 4) created another economic nightmare for the South. While the South possessed rich agricultural lands and light manufacturing industries, power plants, chemical factories, and heavy industries had been located in the North. The partition left the South largely without electricity, fertilizer, and other raw materials and intermediate goods. Total industrial output fell to only one-fifth of the 1940 level. Widespread unemployment, food shortages, and hyperinflation, along with strikes and demonstrations, created social tension in the postliberation South.

In the early days of the postliberation era, U.S. military forces played a significant role in shaping the political and economic orders in South Korea. Amid rising tension between the United States and the Soviet Union, the American military authority in 1947 declared left-wing trade unions illegal, suppressing leftist and socialist forces to ensure establishment of a capitalist economy in South Korea.

The U.S. military government seized properties previously owned by Japanese investors and handed them over to Korean managers. Many of them had worked for Japanese colonists as submanagers or workers and were considered "collaborators" by Korean nationalists. The newly established entrepreneurial group helped solidify capitalist development in South Korea.

After the Korean War, the South Korean state in the 1950s continued the U.S. policy to support the capitalist class, suppress the working class, and weaken the landlord class. Syngman Rhee's administration expanded the land reforms initiated under the U.S. occupation. Redistribution of land to tenants created a sizable rural population with small holdings (averaging one hectare) that were incentivized to increase agricultural productivity. With reduced rural poverty, farmers were able to send their children to school. Subsequently, the abundant supply of young, educated rural workers helped fuel the industrialization programs.

The anti-Communist atmosphere resulting from the war lent legitimacy to the state apparatus and helped justify its suppression of the collective power of the working class. The labor laws adopted in 1953 imposed various state controls on labor movements. The government had extensive power to mediate labor disputes and monitor the financial operations of trade unions. Although workers' rights to association and collective action were guaranteed, collective bargaining was confined to company (enterprise) unions, similar to the union structure in Japan. By the end of the 1950s, the South Korean political economy was firmly placed in the U.S.-led international capitalist system.

Growth Strategies

The Rhee government's main goals after the Korean War were to rebuild industrial facilities and infrastructure and to stabilize macroeconomic conditions to curb hyperinflation. It launched extensive reconstruction plans to channel foreign aid toward building roads, schools, and communication networks. By the end of the decade, South Korea had achieved universal primary education and rapidly expanding enrollment rates at all levels above the primary level (Westphal, Kim, and Dahlman 1984). The effort laid a solid foundation for economic growth in the following decades. Nevertheless, pulled in different directions by the demands of the private sector and political interference from politicians, the Rhee administration was unable to formulate a consistent, systematic strategy for economic growth.

Park Chung-hee's aspiration to transform South Korea into a "wealthy nation with a strong army" was similar to that of the Meiji oligarchs, but he later referenced Bismarck and Ataturk as influences in his 1962 autobiography, *Our Nation's Path*. Under Park's leadership, industrialization and economic growth were the top priorities. The political legitimacy of Park's regime was built on its commitment to economic modernization and its ability to deliver that promise.

Export-led Growth. The Park regime formulated a development plan based on an outward-looking, export-oriented industrialization strategy to address the adverse environment faced by the South Korean economy: diminishing U.S. aid, the small domestic market, and the limited endowment of natural resources. Central to the strategy was production of labor-intensive, light consumer goods for export, all guided by centralized economic planning and policy making. Beginning in 1962, the economic bureaucracy launched and completed a series of five-year economic development plans, outlining goals and actions to create and enhance domestic capabilities in industry, technology, and trade. The government developed industrial complexes and made them available at bargain prices to firms entering the complex.

Exports were identified as the "engine of growth" (Collins and Park 1988). To make South Korean products more competitive in the international markets, the government initiated comprehensive financial reforms and devaluated its currency in 1964 (the first of several subsequent times). Under the slogan of "Export First," officials in the Ministry of Trade and Industry assigned annual "export targets" to large firms as "orders" or "missions." Businesses meeting or exceeding those targets were rewarded by the government in the form of more export subsidies, fewer profit taxes, and more low-interest loans.

The pursuit of labor-intensive industrialization in South Korea in the 1960s came at a time when Japan began to shift its production from labor-intensive industries to machinery and heavy industry. Korean exporters seized the opportunity and moved into labor-intensive exports vacated by the Japanese producers. The move reflected the observation made by Akamatsu (1962) about the "flying geese pattern" in East Asia—to migrate manufacturing from low-cost to lower-cost economies in the region. At a time when the U.S. economic aid to South Korea was phasing out, the United States was willing to open its markets to the country. In 1967, South Korea became a contracting party of the General Agreement on Tariffs and Trade (GATT), and its exports were granted most-favored-nation status in the global trading system. Altogether, the export-led growth turned out to be a timely and effective strategy, as the Korean economy was connected to the upswing in global economic expansion in the 1960s and subsequently to the Vietnam War boom (Moon and Lim 2001).

Saving and Foreign Direct Investment. The foreign exchange earned from exports helped to cover external debt accumulated from foreign borrowing, due to the shortfall in domestic saving. Unlike Japan, the South Korean savings rate was relatively low in the early 1960s, accounting for 1 percent to 2 percent of gross domestic product (GDP). To encourage more saving in the state-owned banking system, the Park administration doubled interest rates in 1965 (Haggard, Kim, and Moon 1991). For the purpose of economic development, the government allowed the use of pseudonyms for bank accounts to stimulate savings, though the practice was commonly abused in cases of corruption and tax evasion. The system was not abolished until 1993 under Kim Young-sam's financial reforms (Chapter 10).

To encourage an inflow of foreign capital to supplement low domestic savings during the initial stage, Park normalized South Korea's diplomatic relationship with Japan in 1965 after a 20-year break. In turn, Japan guaranteed over $800 million of financial support in the form of public and commercial loans and grants. Japanese investments gradually flowed in. The opposition, however, considered the move to be a sellout of Korean nationalism.

Wary of foreign control of, and competition with, domestic firms, the South Korean government exerted strong control over the pattern of foreign investment with detailed and, sometimes, conflicting regulations to contain foreign investment within the export sector of the manufacturing industries. Foreign ownership was allowed but limited to free export zones. Outside of these enclaves, ownership of the industrial base of the economy was to remain in South Korean hands. The amount of foreign direct investment (FDI), compared with the magnitude of foreign borrowing, was very small. Between 1964 and 1973, FDI accounted for only 1 percent of total gross domestic capital formation (Minns 2001). Foreign borrowing in the form of public and commercial loans, not FDI, constituted the main source of capital formation for the South Korean economy.

As industrialization progressed, principal sectors for FDI changed from fertilizer, textiles, and apparel to chemicals, machinery, and electronics (Koo 1985). For industrial upgrades, South Korean manufacturers actively absorbed and adapted technologies from advanced states such as the United States and Japan. Technological transfers took the form of formal licensing and technical assistance, as well as informal contact with foreign suppliers or buyers for training and quality control. After gaining experience in basic production processes, South Korean engineers and technicians quickly expanded their roles to assimilate the know-how to South Korean environments. Learning-by-doing enhanced technological proficiency in production engineering. The human capital formation, marked by a high enrollment rate in secondary education and a high percentage of engineering students among the postsecondary student population, was considered an important reason to facilitate the learning process (Westphal et al. 1984).

Heavy and Petrochemical Industries. In 1973, President Park announced the Heavy and Petrochemical Industry (HPI) Plan to promote heavy industrialization. Iron, steel, automobiles, shipbuilding, electronics, and petrochemical industries were selected as the new engine of economic growth for the next phase of the South Korean industrial policy. The ambitious "big push" was extraordinary at the time, as most other countries in the region dealt with the oil shock by pursuing contractionary policies.

Given South Korea at that time still had a comparative advantage in labor-intensive industries, some thought the shift in strategy was a security strategy in response to the withdrawal of a U.S. combat division from South Korea. Development of heavy and chemical industries could create linkages with the defense industry and promote self-reliance in national security (Moon and Lim 2001). Others noted the plan's domestic political rationale to secure political support from big business conglomerates, the *chaebol* (Cheng, Haggard, and Kang 1998).

Between 1973 and 1980, the Korean Industrial Bank allocated about 80 percent of its total loans for the manufacturing sector to firms involved in heavy industry. In addition, the state established a massive National Investment Fund in 1974 to mobilize employee pensions and certain bank deposits and channel them into designated projects and sectors at highly preferential rates.

During the period of the big push (1974–1979), the South Korean economy grew more than 10 percent a year on average and achieved its first surplus in the balance of payments in 1977 (Moon and Lim 2001). Nevertheless, HPI was blamed for leading to a surge in inflation and external debt, while slowing down exports. Most importantly, economic power was increasingly concentrated into the hands of a few business conglomerates. Only a small number of *chaebol* were allowed to enter into heavy and chemical industries, which, in essence, granted them monopoly power. Growth between *chaebol* and small and medium-sized companies became quite unbalanced.

Industrial Policy. The Economic Planning Board (EPB) was created in 1961 under the Office of the President to propose policy ideas and formulate long-term economic plans. A series of five-year economic plans have been implemented since 1962 to identify the level of investment required for the desired rate of growth and the areas of targeted investment. The EPB enjoyed a special status in the cabinet, and its minister was given the title of deputy prime minister. Besides planning, it had the authority to approve foreign loans. With the power to screen and allocate foreign borrowing, EPB could selectively promote industrial investment in areas meeting the government's development strategies, playing a key role in capital accumulation for infant industries. With its purview over government budget guidelines, and its authority over a variety of policy instruments such as foreign exchange, finance, and trade policy, the EPB enjoyed a high degree of autonomy and flexibility in setting policy priorities and formulating economic policies. The Ministry of Finance, subordinate to the EPB, was responsible for implementing government economic policies.

The effectiveness of South Korean industrial policies, however, was subject to debate. Some (Amsden 1989; Wade 1990) believed that government intervention through subsidies, trade restrictions, and credit allocation was instrumental in reshaping a comparative advantage in the desired direction; others (Lee 1996) found no empirical evidence to link industrial policies, such as tax incentives and subsidized credit, to productivity growth in the promoted sectors. In fact, trade protection was found to reduce productivity growth.

Perhaps the most helpful aspect of the industrial policy was its ability to help resolve the issue of "credible commitments." The economic plan signaled government commitment to the identified growth sectors. The authorities distributed subsidies based on objective, measurable data such as export performance. Targeted infant industries received preferential allocation of credit and imported materials as promised. Sanctions and corporate discipline were enforced if a company failed to perform. Thus, South Korean businesses involved in growth industries were rarely concerned about government policy inconsistencies or reversals. They understood the expectation and strived to perform. The plans helped coordinate government-business actions by developing an exchange relationship in which the government incentivized business for good performance with tangible support; business responded with good performance in anticipation of government rewards (Mo and Weingast 2013).

The Developmental Coalition

The ideological clashes between conservatives and progressives described in Chapter 10 have translated into differences in economic priorities and agendas. Conservatives viewed the drive for economic modernization as an important pillar of national security in the fight against North Korea. National wealth and power built by industrialization would not only solidify domestic political support but also deter potential aggression from the North.

For progressives, while the extraordinary economic dynamism under the authoritarian regime transformed the South Korean economy, it was accompanied by forceful political oppression. They considered industrialization as a capitalist-imperialist imposition to exploit South Korea's farmers and workers. They regarded the conservative regime's collaboration with the Japanese and Americans for capitalist development as a sellout to Korean nationalism. The call for political reform and democratization, an important part of the progressive platform/program, was placed on the back burner by the conservative, industrialization-first coalition. Demands from students, labor, and religious groups to advocate human rights, social justice, and democracy, though suppressed by the authoritarian regime, never disappeared. Political activism and civil movements kept these issues alive.

Big businesses and farmers allied with conservative politicians and military strongmen to form a developmental state coalition that promoted economic policies of shared growth by offering expanded economic rights and opportunities to the populace while limiting political and civil rights (Campos and Root 1996).

The South Korean military became a formidable institution in the 1950s after the Korean War. As a cohesive organization with expertise and resources, it was a powerful stakeholder. The Rhee regime, however, excluded the military from its power circle and deliberately weakened it by promoting factional competition between senior officers. Park and Chun Doo-hwan rose to power with military support but were both able to exercise control over the military. The South Korean military was not directly involved in economic policy making, though some compared the developmental state to a state mobilizing for war.

To stay in power and govern effectively to achieve economic growth, the Park government carefully built political coalitions and closely monitored and balanced social and political forces. Economic rationality and political expediency were mixed to preserve power. For example, while ministries such as the EPB and Ministry of Finance relied primarily on technical experts for reason of efficiency, military clienteles were often appointed to positions in other ministries such as transportation and construction for the purpose of patronage. This bifurcated bureaucracy allowed Park to achieve economic growth through rational planning and execution while building up patron-client networks to broaden his political support (Kang 2002).

A new commercial class emerged after the Korean War. Many of the entrepreneurs turned their businesses into big conglomerates (*chaebol*) through preferential receipt of foreign aid during the period of reconstruction (post–Korean War to late 1950s) or favorable policy loans and tax schemes during the period of growth (1960s and 1970s). Many of the Korean leaders were familiar with the model of extensive coordination between the state and *zaibatsu* during Japan's wartime effort and found it politically advantageous to have the entrepreneurial class bound to political leadership. *Chaebol* became the carriers of South Korean capitalism.

Conservatives relied on farmers for political support in rural areas. After the 1961 coup, the military regime initially took a populist, pro-rural policy stance. The government supported agricultural pricing with subsidies and abolished some of the farmers' debts deemed above the legal interest rate limit. It controlled farmers' organizations as well as seed, fertilizer, credit, and distribution channels. However, government support of the agricultural sector fluctuated over the years in response to political and economic situations.

For example, rural investment was decreased to support export-oriented industrial strategies. To maintain low wages for international competitiveness, Park's government suppressed food prices and eased inflation and wage pressure through foreign imports. The widening gaps in income between rural and urban areas led to massive population migration from the countryside to urban centers in search of jobs. Thus, the agricultural policy under Park, a policy of relative neglect, had the effect of guaranteeing continued supply of labor from rural areas to fuel the growth in the manufacturing sector. Between 1967 and 1976, about 6.7 million people (nearly 20 percent of the population) migrated from rural areas to cities. The size of the population shift was unprecedented, even greater than what took place during the Korean War (Choi 1993).

It was not until the late 1960s that policies favorable to agriculture were reinstated to solidify political support in rural areas and to enhance economic self-sufficiency in food production. The state instituted the "grain management fund" and supported dual prices to subsidize farmers while maintaining low prices for consumers. The system allowed farmers to receive, on average, a 20 percent increase in grain price during the 1970s when the country was losing its comparative advantage in agriculture.

Additionally, the New Village Movement (*Saemaul Undong*) launched in 1970 helped farmers mobilize resources to improve rural infrastructure, build roads and bridges, and renovate communities; this was accomplished by a strong motivation for self-reliance. The initiative reduced the gap in the quality of life between urban and rural populations and broadened the base of shared economic growth.

After Park's assassination, the Chun government rolled back subsidies for grains and fertilizers as part of the austerity measures to achieve fiscal stability. The ruling party's 1985 election setback, however, motivated ruling party politicians and the Ministry of Agriculture and Fisheries to reinstate price supports for farmers, despite opposition from the EPB and the Ministry of Finance (Haggard and Moon 1990).

Under the authoritarian regime, labor was excluded from the developmental state coalition. The export-led growth strategy was predicated on low wages to ensure the country's comparative advantage in international markets. The overriding concern of economic growth often superseded labor's welfare. Suppression of labor union activities was justified by the economic imperative. At the beginning of export-led growth (1960–1964), real wages declined on average by 2 percent per year, helping South Korea establish its competitive position.

The Park regime established the government-sanctioned Federation of Korean Trade Unions (FKTU). Union leaders were under constant surveillance by the police and national security agencies so that government could directly intervene, if necessary. The government limited strikes while inserting itself in dispute settlement. These tactics worked effectively in reducing the number of industrial conflicts during the 1960s.

In the early 1970s, reports of harsh working conditions in the textile industry sparked nationwide demonstrations and protests. Throughout the 1970s, as surges in oil prices increased production costs, employers squeezed profit and productivity with unfair labor practices, late wage payments, and harsh working conditions, causing widespread labor unrest and protests. In the meantime, the Park regime suspended the labor law for security reasons and further heightened labor-management tensions. The Special Decrees for National Security (1971) gave the Park government the authority to ban union activities if they were deemed contradictory to the public interest. Unions had to ask for arbitration from the government and follow the results of arbitration before exercising the right to collective bargaining and collective action. Even though the government sometimes acted as an arbitrator between labor and management, its interventions were usually delayed and insufficient.

Labor, though politically suppressed, did take part in the shared growth after the initial decline in real wages at the beginning of the export-led expansion. From 1965 to 1972, real wages rose 9 percent per year on average and accelerated to an annual growth rate of 12.5 percent between 1973 and 1979 (Collins and Park 1988). The trend continued in the 1980s. South Korea was able to maintain its export competitiveness because the growth in labor productivity outpaced rising wages at the same time.

Economic Institutions

Chaebol. Following the template of the Japanese *zaibatsu*, South Korean entrepreneurs strived to expand their companies into a large business organization (i.e., *chaebol*), having multiple companies operating in different markets but with common financial and management control.

For the government, the preference for large *chaebol* was based on the assumption that large enterprises could exploit the economies of scale more effectively than small and medium-sized enterprises (SMEs). Nationalization of banks in the early 1960s gave the government full control of credit lines to channel resources to strategic sectors through low-interest-rate, policy-based lending. *Chaebol* were encouraged to respond to the government's economic initiatives accordingly. With limited capital accumulation, *chaebol* depended on a credit-based system of industrial finance. The availability of heavily subsidized credits gave *chaebol* strong incentives for highly leveraged debt-financing, leading to excessive growth and expansion of their businesses.

The implementation of the HPI programs in the early 1970s further deepened *chaebol's* involvement in the HPI sectors. A small number of *chaebol* were granted licenses to participate in HPI projects, receiving a large portion of national investment funds and bank credits. Because of extensive protection and guaranteed government procurement, *chaebol* were able to grow into conglomerates with monopolistic or oligopolistic positions in the domestic market. By 1980, the top 50 *chaebol* accounted for 49 percent of GDP (Mo and Weingast 2013).

The growing size of the *chaebol* gave the impression that they were too big to fail, further emboldening them to take on more risk. During periods of financial downturn, their potential for bankruptcy created social and economic instability, forcing the government to bail them out. Unfortunately, bailouts only encouraged more aggressive risk-taking behavior.

Government assistance to *chaebol* contributed to their fast growth, which occurred at the expense of thousands of SMEs in the South Korean economy. Lack of investment funds for innovation and technological upgrades made it difficult for SMEs to keep up with big business in technical know-how and labor productivity. The problem of this dual structure was particularly evident during the transition from light to heavy industry, as it was difficult to reorient and enhance the technological capabilities of the SMEs that supplied inputs and materials to exporting manufacturers.

For progressives, the concentration of economic resources within a few big *chaebol*, and the concentration of wealth in the hands of the *chaebol* owner or the owner's family, raised serious questions about economic equality and social justice.

Government-Business Relations. Under different presidents, the state and business exhibited different relational patterns. Rhee forged alliances with businessmen to finance his election campaigns and party activities. Companies allegedly received special favors from the government in return for kickbacks and other payments. Some purchased machinery and real estate from the state at low prices, while others were favored for bank loans, government contracts, and import licensing that provided windfalls for them (Haggard and Moon 1993).

Park's Supreme Council on National Reconstruction (SCNR) eliminated Rhee's political networks and centralized authority in political and economic decision making. Prominent businessmen and leading industrialists were arrested and accused of corruption and illicit accumulation of wealth. The government, however, soon realized that to modernize the economy, entrepreneurs should be coopted, not punished. A compromise was reached, under which many of the accused corporate leaders paid fines to the government. Notwithstanding the compromise, the event marked a new phase of business-government relations. Under Park's regime, rent-seeking was significantly reduced, and policy instruments were generally used for developmental purposes.

Businesses emerged as a powerful force in the formulation of economic policy in Park's government, although they generally worked within the broad confines set by the government. Government provided the blueprints for industrial expansion, while businesses converted the plans to reality with their organizational ability and competitive strategies. Even under Park's authoritarian regime of a "strong state," the government was not in a position of complete command and control. The relationship was never authoritarian or top-down; it involved continuous consultations, negotiations, and compromises between both sides. The economic governance structure was more of a symbiotic partnership.

The Association of Korean Industries (AKI) was the main vehicle for business leaders to lobby for beneficial concessions from the government within the bounds of government industrial strategy. Created in August 1961 in response to the arrest and release of business leaders, AKI submitted a plan to SCNR to identify 14 industrial plants that they would be interested in investing in, including cement, steel, and fertilizer. AKI also organized an overseas mission to solicit foreign investment. In 1968, AKI was reorganized as the Federation of Korean Industries (FKI) in order to be more broadly representative.

AKI/FKI lobbied successfully for government guarantees of foreign loans as well as simplified legal and administrative procedures on foreign loans. It was instrumental in the construction of integrated industrial complexes to facilitate manufacturing and export processing (Kang 2002). FKI continues to be an integral part of the government-business policy network.

Under Chun, the government enacted the Monopoly Regulation and Fair Trade Law in 1981 to regulate business concentration, trying to curb cross-investment, reciprocal buying, and cross-subsidization among *chaebol* subsidiaries. The Chun administration also initiated financial reforms to privatize state-owned commercial banks, reduce policy loans, and grant more autonomy to banks for credit allocation.

Financial reforms, however, weakened the state's ability to control business. Liberalization in the financial sector gave *chaebol* the opportunity to establish their own financial institutions and enhance their financial independence. Previously, they depended on credit lines offered through the government-controlled banking system. Their businesses were at grave risk if they failed to consider government macroeconomic policies or industrial strategies; compliance with those directives, in contrast, helped them link up to the next growth opportunity. Financial reforms shifted the balance of power between government and business in favor of the latter. Businesses became more autonomous and more vocal in challenging government intervention as they depended less on government for credit support.

Labor-Management Relations. Labor demonstrations in the late 1960s and the early 1970s were largely localized protests concerning harsh working conditions in small garment and textile industry sweatshops. In November 1970, a young worker named Chun Tae-il set himself on fire in a desperate attempt to raise public awareness of the horrific conditions in garment factories. Chun's death was a turning point for labor movements in South Korea. It mobilized student activism and church involvement and helped develop labor consciousness and identity (Koo 1993).

The Labor Standards Act, which stipulated the employer's obligation to provide good working conditions for employees, was revised several times under the Park regime in reaction to growing labor discontent. The law, however, was rarely enforced. The Trade Union Act, revised in 1973, bypassed the company unions and placed issues such as production, job training, grievances, and working conditions in the hands of firm-based Labor Management Councils. Unions did not regain their priority status over the council until November 1987, when democratization finally eased restrictions on union activities.

While large corporations controlled the majority of industrial capital, the majority of industrial workers were employed by SMEs, which served as suppliers to big businesses. Employees of SMEs did not receive the same pensions and employment benefits as the workers in *chaebol,* and they had to endure less desirable working conditions and environments. Industrial conflicts and disputes often arose from these smaller companies.

Although the authoritarian regime suppressed labor movements and trade unions, it adopted other measures to ensure industrial stability and worker productivity. Workplace-based benefits and nontransferrable occupational welfare at the company level were established to encourage worker loyalty and retain the required workforce. Against the backdrop of low wages and weak trade unions, the arrangement of lifetime employment and a seniority-based compensation system was implicit in the contractual agreement between the large corporations and their core workers. Nevertheless, differential benefits and treatments between production workers and managerial staff were often a bone of contention. Production workers had to endure army-barracks discipline imposed by the company but received inferior bonus and welfare packages.

GROWTH IN THE DEMOCRATIC ERA: 1987–PRESENT

Developmental Coalition in Transition

Progressive forces continually challenged the developmental coalition under the authoritarian regime. Democratic transition unleashed new political dynamics and reshaped the balance of power between the state and the society. The economic groups previously repressed or disadvantaged under the authoritarian regime were empowered in the new political landscape. Labor could no longer be excluded from the policy-making process. The wage adjustment demanded by newly empowered labor unions amounted to a raise of more than 46 percent from 1987 to 1989. Farmers and SMEs also benefited from the new political dynamics. Income subsidies were raised for farmers and SMEs. More policy loans and credit lines went to SMEs, as the government limited credits and loans extended to the country's top 30 *chaebol*. Yet labor movements in the democratic era did not lead to radical demands for sweeping redistribution of wealth. It seemed that the shared-growth strategy in the era of authoritarianism was successful in generating relative equity between economic groups, hence reducing the appeal of radical populism.

After democratic transition, government increased its spending on universalistic welfare programs, sustaining the trend since the mid-1980s. While some (Ahn and Lee 2012; Takegawa 2009) explained the expansion of the South Korean welfare state as a natural result of economic development and demographic changes, others (Kwon 2005; Ringen et al. 2011) emphasized the importance of political and ideational factors in the aftermath of democratic transition and regime change.

The South Korean economy experienced some decline in growth in the late 1980s. Did democratization have any adverse effect on the country's economic performance? Some (Lee and Lee 1992) believed so, arguing that the demand for income growth from every social group to compensate for their past "sacrifices" (the so-called democratization cost) created inflationary pressure and reduced international competitiveness. Others (Cheng and Krause 1991) acknowledged the immediate cost of the democratic transition but found that the longer term impact of democratization on economic performance was inconclusive. The record of South Korea was consistent with the conclusion from a growing body of literature that democracy would not necessarily generate slower growth (Przeworski and Limongi 1993).

Chaebol and the 1997 Asian Financial Crisis. Of all the economic groups, *chaebol* gained the most political influence in the newly democratized environment. Previously, government was the only institution that could counterbalance business interests with sanctions and regulations. After democratic transition, the government lost leverage over big business, as politicians came to rely on campaign contributions from large companies. The breakdown of government supervision at the time when no other social institutions were strong enough to balance the *chaebol* created a power vacuum for big businesses.

Riding on the global trend toward liberalization and deregulation, *chaebol* actively pushed for less government restriction and intervention. They successfully blocked a series of corporate reforms that would have banned risky borrowing and nontransparent business practices, while allowing new entrants to fair trade and greater market competition. These institutional and structural developments formed the backdrop for the 1997–1998 Asian Financial Crisis.

The immediate cause of the crisis, however, was the corporate bankruptcy of several major conglomerates, which had taken advantage of cheaper foreign credit and had borrowed aggressively to finance business expansion. From 1994 to 1996, the South Korean economy experienced an investment boom. Large *chaebol* in the sectors of automobiles, petrochemicals, steel, and electronics borrowed aggressively to expand their production lines to cope with rising labor costs from wage hikes and to contend with Japanese exporters whose competitiveness suffered from the appreciated Japanese yen. In the meantime, banks and financial institutions battled for lending opportunities without conducting due diligence and monitoring, particularly for loans extended to their *chaebol* parents. Altogether, the supply of (and demand for) easy credit led to excessive risk taking by many conglomerates.

In 1996, the average debt-to-equity ratio for the top 30 Korean conglomerates was 386 percent, far more than that in Japan (206 percent). A large portion of the private debt involved short-term loans. At the beginning of 1997, South Korea's foreign exchange reserves were less than half of its short-term liabilities. The total profit return for the top 49 largest *chaebol* was just over 0.01 percent (Hwang 2012), which could not sustain the large amount of accumulated debt. Excessive loans, coupled with declining profitability, led to bankruptcies of several major *chaebol*. As the country's international credit rating plunged and the Korean won went into free fall, foreign investors quickly withdrew their money from the Korean stock market, prompting a full-scale financial crisis, not only in South Korea but also in other parts of Asia.

In the postcrisis reform, *chaebol* lost their ability and credibility to drive the reform agenda. Kim Dae-jung's electoral victory gave him the mandate to modify the economic system previously shaped by the conservative coalition, which, weakened by the crisis, was unable to mount serious resistance to reforms.

The financial reforms and corporate restructuring initiated by Kim changed the rules and helped lay the institutional foundation for market-based corporate discipline. The crisis provided him a window of opportunity to leverage social support with swift action to curb *chaebol's* economic and political influence and reclaim government's role in economic policy making.

Insolvent financial institutions were closed or consolidated, while the viable ones were strengthened. Regulatory systems were put in place to ensure transparency, accountability, and sound management in *chaebol* and in financial institutions. Internal financial transactions between subsidiaries of the *chaebol*, including their cross-holdings and mutual-payment guarantees, had to be disclosed for external audits. *Chaebol* were asked to streamline their business areas, and the owners were held accountable for their business decision making. Top conglomerates such as Hyundai, Samsung, Daewoo, SK, and LG were required to downsize their subsidiaries and sell their marginal and unprofitable businesses. To discourage corporate borrowing, the government revised the tax code to disallow interest-payment deductions on "excessive" borrowing.

Kim's progressive background probably gave him more latitude and credibility in instituting changes and imposing stringent regulations on *chaebol* than other conservative politicians. Kim's successor, Roh Moo-hyun, also from the progressive camp, continued to favor an arm's-length relationship with business. He vowed not to accept political contributions from *chaebol* and continued to restrain their expansion by restricting their equity investment in subsidiary companies.

Roh pursued economic liberalization and openness by entering into formal free-trade agreement (FTA) negotiations with the United States. The scope of the U.S.-Korea FTA extended beyond the traditional issues of tariff reduction and market access. More importantly, it had the effect of bringing South Korean economic norms and institutions closer to international standards for good governance structure. By the time Roh left office in 2008, the concept of economic openness was deeply embedded in political rhetoric, making it difficult to reverse.

Labor before and after the 1997 Crisis. In the democratic era, as organized labor became a legitimate social force, *chaebol* were concerned that undisciplined labor movements could deprive the Korean economy of its global competitiveness. Union leaders sought to abolish the restrictions concerning multiple trade unions (i.e., to form new unions independent of the government-sanctioned FKTU), third-party intervention in collective bargaining, and union participation in party politics. Big business, however, attempted to keep all restrictions while pursuing greater labor market flexibility (i.e., the right to lay off workers or to replace striking workers).

In May 1996, President Kim Young-sam convened the Presidential Commission on Industrial Relations to reconcile the divergent interests of business and labor. Labor representatives were from FKTU and the yet-to-be-officially-legalized Korean Confederation of Trade Unions (KCTU), while business was represented by the Korea Federation of Employers. The mediation was unsuccessful. KCTU withdrew from the Commission, claiming that government priorities on globalization and economic growth represented a reconfigured government-*chaebol* alliance. Soon afterward, the ruling party tried to force through a probusiness bill in favor of labor market flexibility in the early hours of the morning of December 26, 1996. The action backfired. Trade unions were outraged and launched nationwide protests; tensions between labor and business escalated. Under public pressure, the National Assembly struck a new compromise in March 1997, making concessions to both business and labor. The compromise, however, did not survive the 1997 Asian Financial Crisis.

After the Financial Crisis, the International Monetary Fund, the United States, and other creditors pressured the newly elected Kim Dae-jung government to pursue neoliberal measures to revitalize the economy, but Kim also had to honor his lifelong prolabor and prodemocracy commitments. In January 1998, he formed a tripartite commission comprising labor, business, and government to seek agreement for reforms. In the face of economic hardship, the committee was instrumental in fostering social consensus for reforms. Greater labor market flexibility was linked to a broader social safety net to limit the negative effect of unemployment. The new labor law allowed layoffs for "urgent managerial reasons" in exchange for recognition of basic labor rights such as legalized political activities by labor. The government promised expanded efforts in social security, poverty eradication, and worker retraining, to be discussed later.

Economic Challenges

From 1960 to 1997, the South Korean economy grew by more than 8 percent per year. After the 1997 Asian Financial Crisis, the economic growth rate slowed down to 5 percent per year and further declined to 3 percent in the 2010s. The slowdown of economic growth, in part, reflected the challenge of a mature economy approaching the end of the catch-up phase, and, in part, resulted from slower growth in exports, which dropped from an annual rate of 11.4 percent (2001–2011) to 2.6 percent (2011–2017) OECD 2018. The traditional export-led growth model seemed to lose momentum. The rise of the Chinese economy posed a challenge to South Korea in low- and medium-end markets, as Korean manufacturers tried to make inroads into high-end markets competing with advanced economies. It was increasingly difficult for South Korea to expand its global market share, unless new sources of growth were found.

Another problem with the export-led model was the bifurcated economic structure it created. *Chaebol*-centered industrial sectors, which accounted for 25 percent of employment, have significantly increased their productivity because of their international and technology-intensive focus. Sales revenue from the top five *chaebol*—Hyundai, LG, Lotte, Samsung, and SK Group—accounted for more than half of the nation's entire economy. In contrast, SME-dominated service sectors, accounting for 70 percent of total employment, have lagged behind in productivity and wage increases. One-third of the total workforce was comprised of part-time or irregular workers, and they earned only two-thirds the salaries of the full-time employees. The wage differential in the bifurcated economic structure contributed to rising relative poverty and income inequality. Income ratio between the top 20 percent and bottom 20 percent increased from 6.7 percent in 2006 to 9.3 percent in 2016. Relative poverty rate rose from 16.6 percent in 2006 to 19.5 percent in 2016.

Like China and Japan, the long-term demographic trend in South Korea added to economic uncertainty. Currently, it has a low birth rate of 1.19 births per woman. In 2016, the population aged 65 or older reached 6.8 million, accounting for 13 percent of the total population. By 2030, the figure is projected to be 24 percent. The aging trend will accelerate thereafter and is projected to surpass Japan by 2060.

Growth Strategies and Industrial Policy

The South Korean developmental state has evolved because of the changing political landscape since the democratic transition, but it continues to provide economic leadership in search of new growth engines. Over the years, the South Korean industrial policy gradually switched from individual sectors to technology-based R&D and innovation (OECD 2014a). Different administrations proposed different growth plans in response to the emergence of the information and knowledge economy. Notwithstanding differences in policy slogans and platforms, the main thrust was to transform the country into an innovation-driven economy.

The Kim government (1998–2003) formulated Vision 2025, in 1999, to support information and communication technology. The Roh administration (2003–2008) created the five-year Basic Plan of Science and Technology (2003–2007) and identified 10 technologies as priorities. The Lee government (2008–2013) chose green technology as a new growth engine, while the Park government (2013–2017) proposed the Creative Economy to strengthen R&D ties to economic growth.

In contrast to his predecessors who believed economic growth led to job creation, Moon Jae-in (2017–Present) emphasized "fair economy" and income-driven growth. He hoped to boost wages to stimulate domestic consumption, which in turn would promote investment, productivity, and employment. To that aim, he raised the minimum wage and requested funds to create public sector jobs untied to exports. It remains to be seen whether these measures will produce long-term economic growth.

To transform from an effective innovation-follower to an innovation-front-runner, the South Korean economy needs to create growth based on creativity, which in turn depends on its investment in science and technology. To that end, the government has taken the initiative to promote R&D. Korea's R&D investment was 4.23 percent of GDP in 2015, the second highest in OECD economies, behind Israel, and much higher than the 2.4 percent OECD average.

Nevertheless, a closer analysis of its R&D pattern reveals some imbalances (Connell 2013). First, its R&D is heavily weighted toward applied research with particular emphasis on the categories of radio, television, and communication. In areas requiring basic research, such as biotechnology, nanotechnology, and environmental sciences, which South Korean policy makers have identified as future growth engines, its track record of patents is relatively weak.

Second, much of Korea's R&D has been conducted by *chaebol*, with little contribution from universities or SMEs. This reflects the nature of the country's corporate structure, in which SMEs served as suppliers and subcontractors for large conglomerates, rather than partners of innovation. The *chaebol* prefer to rely on their in-house knowledge and resources for R&D, rather than seeking to partner with SMEs for innovation. Being excluded from the *chaebol's* business arrangements, SMEs have had difficulties with overcoming gaps in wages and productivity. With SMEs comprising 99 percent of South Korean business and 87 percent of employment, addressing the technological and productivity gaps of SMEs could be a potential source of growth. Altogether, these imbalances in R&D efforts reflect the legacies of past economic development priorities—a strategy centered on *chaebol* and manufacturing, which, if not addressed, could hinder South Korea's capability for comprehensive technological innovation.

Social Policies

The South Korean government spends singificantly less than other OECD economies on social welfare programs. Public social spending was at 10.4 percent of GDP in 2016, compared with the OECD average of 21.6 percent. Neverthelss, it represents a significant increase from its position in 1990 (2.8 percent) or 1995 (3.2 percent). For the first several decades since independence, government played the role of a regulator, instead of a provider, in the realm of social service (Ringen et al. 2011). As a regulator, it set the standards for others such as companies and social service organizations to be the welfare provider. Resources usually came from insurance contributions, not tax revenues, so as to reduce the financial burden on the state budget.

Under the authoritarian regime, social spending generally followed the policy priority of the developmental coalition. The provision of social security extended only to groups deemed strategically important to the government for political support, rather than to groups that were economically vulnerable. Pension systems were implemented for selected groups, such as civil servants, military personnel, and school teachers. The implementation of the 1973 National Pension Act, which had an implicit policy goal of mobilizing capital for industrial investment, was postponed by the 1973 oil crisis. The National Health Insurance was established in 1977 with initial coverage extended only to government employees, teachers, and big-corporation workers (with 500 employees or more).

After the democratic transition, health insurance was extended to the rural and urban self-employed. Before then, health insurance had been considered a middle-class privilege. Through subsequent reform and expansion, more than 300 health funds were pooled into a national system to extend coverage to the entire population. Nevertheless, the out-of-pocket payment was significantly higher than the OECD average, and the government subsidy has declined substantially (Hwang 2012).

A new pension law—the National Pension Scheme (NPS)—was passed in 1988, expanding coverage to all firms with 10 or more workers (five workers since 1992), and subsequently to farmers and fishermen in 1995, to compensate the agricultural sector for the policy to open the rice market. The deficiency of the South Korean welfare system became clear during the Asian Financial Crisis of 1997–1998. Built on the assumption of full employment with minimal support for the unemployed, the program could not adequately deal with the sudden rise in unemployment. In response to the Asian Financial Crisis, the South Korean government launched various public works projects.

In the aftermath of the crisis, Kim Dae-jung's campaign catchword of "productive welfare state" was used to guide welfare reform. To balance the pursuit of democracy and the market economy, the government drastically increased social expenditures to expand social insurance (i.e., pensions, health insurance, and unemployment insurance) and social assistance programs while retaining a strong emphasis on work ethics.

In the past, the welfare rationale was based on discretionary relief of the poor. The 1999 National Basic Livelihood Security Act, which set minimum standards of living as a universal right, reflected the new belief that entitlement to benefits is a basic social right. The Basic Livelihood Security Program (BLSP) provided a cash benefit and in-kind support (such as health care and education) to eligible people in absolute poverty—currently defined as an income below 40 percent of the national median income. Yet the scope of welfare expansion remains limited in its coverage. The eligibility criteria of BLSP, for example, were quite strict. Those with the possibility for family assistance were excluded from BLSP under the "family support obligation rule," making the actual benefits coverage less than universal.

The new public assistance system introduced the self-support program in which able-bodied recipients had to participate in self-reliance measures to preserve their eligibility for support. To avoid "welfare dependence," a guaranteed social minimum was combined with workfare measures to enhance employability and self-support ability.

As in the case of Japan, the South Korean government began to be involved in long-term care. The real purpose, according to the Ministry of Health and Welfare, was not simply to ease the burden of family-based care and rising medical expenses; it was to allow more women and other informal caregivers to participate in economic activities. Expanding employment for women may help offset the negative effect of a rapidly aging society.

DISCUSSION QUESTIONS

1. President Park initiated the First Five-Year Economic Development Plan and laid the foundation for South Korean economic growth. Describe the economic strategies pursued by the Park government during the Third and Fourth Republics, and analyze these efforts based on supply-side and demand-side economics.

2. What was the origin of *chaebol?* How did they grow and expand during the time of South Korean economic development? What was their role in the 1997–1998 Asian Financial Crisis? How have the conservative and progressive leaders approached *chaebol* reforms?

3. Under the authoritarian regime, the developmental coalition provided critical support to the authoritarian leaders. Discuss the principal groups in the coalition, and analyze their economic and political agendas.

4. Democratization in South Korea empowered the previously disadvantaged economic groups. The change in their political status brought forth new demands. Identify the economic groups that were empowered by democratic transition, and discuss whether their demands led to economic slowdown.

5. Describe the authoritarian government's attitude toward social welfare. Did policy change after the democratic transition? Discuss the internal and external factors that could contribute to, or hinder, higher public spending on social welfare and health care in South Korea.

12

South Korea's Pursuit of National Security

After Japan's defeat, the United States and the Soviet Union agreed to occupy Korea as a temporary trusteeship with the zone of control divided along the 38th parallel, without ever consulting the Koreans. While the U.S. military strategists considered South Korea an important buffer to prevent the spread of Communism to Japan, the land itself was only of peripheral concern to the United States. Thus, at the end of the U.S. military rule in South Korea, the U.S. troops withdrew in June 1949. Although the U.S. forces had handed over their weapons and equipment to the Koreans prior to the withdrawal, the resources were hardly enough to support the Republic of Korea (ROK) troops, which functioned more as a police force.

The outbreak of the Korean War in 1950 changed the security landscape on the Korean peninsula. The war represented a forceful move by North Korea to achieve national unification on its own terms, but it only resulted in perpetuating the separation and division between the North and South. The war ended in 1953 by an armistice, not a peace treaty. Hence, the two Koreas officially are still at war.

After the Korean War, South Korea joined the U.S. alliance system for security protection. Over the last several decades, the Republic of Korea's remarkable achievement in economic development and democratic governance has had a significant effect on its pursuit of foreign and security policies (Kim and Cohen 2017; Snyder and Easley 2014). Economic growth has enhanced not only the standard of living for its people but also its defense capability, which requires a strong industrial base.

These achievements, however, have not resulted in cooperation between the two Koreas. Although the Cold War ended two decades ago, the Korean peninsula retains the vestige of the Cold War, and South Korea continues to face a formidable security threat from the North. With 1.28 million personnel (2018), the military of the Democratic People's Republic of Korea (DPRK) is the fourth largest in the world, behind China, the United States, and India. In recent years, the development of its nuclear and missile programs has posed security threats not only to South Korea but also to regional peace and stability.

Repeated diplomatic and economic efforts by the international community since the 1990s have not succeeded in persuading the DPRK to terminate these programs (Roehrig 2017).

How has South Korea dealt with North Korea? What are South Korea's security strategies? What is likely to happen to Pyongyang's weapons of mass destruction? This chapter reviews the security challenges faced by South Korea in the postwar era and discusses the security strategies employed by South Korea in dealing with these challenges.

SECURITY GOALS AND STRATEGIES

Security Goals

After Japanese colonialism ended in 1945, conflicts between Communists and anti-Communists led to social and political unrest and heightened the sense of urgency to maintain internal security. In December 1948, less than four months after the ROK was established, the National Assembly enacted the National Security Law to target the "anti-state groups," who were defined as "domestic or foreign organizations or groups whose intentions are to conduct or assist infiltration of the government or to cause national disturbances."

Subsequently, the tragedy of the Korean War (1950–1953) further shaped South Korea's sense of threat, making the state's survival the top national priority. Located only 30 miles south of the Demilitarized Zone (DMZ), the greater area of Seoul had to be under constant alert for potential military attacks from the North, which necessitated a standing military capability at a high level of readiness.

After the failed attempt at conventional war, Pyongyang switched tactics to special warfare, sending infiltration units across the DMZ for sabotage, subversion, bombing, and espionage in the South. The infiltration operations intensified in the 1960s, when North Korea tried to duplicate the model of guerrilla missions used by North Vietnam. These operations gave the authoritarian governments more reasons to impose strict law and order and to safeguard internal security. Beginning in the 1990s, North Korea's development of missile and nuclear programs took the military threat to a new level. The combined effect of these programs (i.e., missiles capable of carrying miniaturized nuclear warheads) could possibly put South Korea at a strategic disadvantage.

Besides the paramount concern for internal and external security, another important goal for South Korea is national unification. Internationally, the situation of a divided Korea compelled the ROK to compete with the DPRK for diplomatic recognition and legitimacy, until both of them joined the UN in September 1991. Domestically, all the postwar administrations in South Korea have embraced the vision of a unified Korea, although they often politicize the goal to serve their respective agendas. For the authoritarian governments, with their deep distrust of the Communist regime, the quest for unification is meant to prevail over Communism. Thus, the mission of unification justified internal political repression to counter Communist subversion.

In the democratic era, beginning with President Roh Tae-woo's (1988–1993) initiative of *Nordpolitik* (or Northern Policy; discussed below), North Korea has been treated as an equal partner, rather than an adversary, in building the Korean "national community." While all the administrations since have supported unification by consensus, not by absorption, there exist policy differences. For progressives, reconciliation and peaceful coexistence with North Korea should come first; for conservatives, unification can only be accomplished under the values and ideals embodied in the South Korean system.

The Evolution of Security Strategies

During the Cold War, South Korea took a realist approach to its national security. To deter future attacks from North Korea, it devised a two-pronged strategy: alliance with the United States and development of strong and advanced military capabilities. Its vigorous pursuit of economic development to eradicate poverty and reduce social instability was also part of the security strategy.

Sustained economic growth since the 1960s gradually elevated South Korea's international standing and expanded the range of policy instruments at its disposal. As North Korea experienced diplomatic isolation and economic stagnation in the post–Cold War era, South Korea began to engage North Korea confidently, using economic statecraft to confront the security challenge (Bae 2010; Haggard and Noland 2011).

ROK-U.S. Alliance. In the wake of the Korean War, President Rhee requested that Washington provide $1 billion in economic aid over three years plus equipment for an army of 700,000 soldiers to ensure the ROK's security. Additionally, Rhee asked the United States to sign a mutual defense treaty with South Korea. President Eisenhower initially declined Rhee's requests. Rhee then threatened to undermine the armistice negotiation and to take unilateral military action against North Korea. In the end, the Eisenhower administration gave in, and both countries signed the ROK-U.S. Mutual Defense Treaty in October 1953. The aid accounted for a significant part of South Korea's budget and provided much-needed raw materials and consumer goods for the country.

Security partnership with the United States helped provided a full range of military options for South Korea, including conventional strike, nuclear umbrella, and missile defense capabilities. To complement U.S. troops stationed in South Korea, the United States deployed nuclear weapons in South Korea from 1958 to 1991 (Kristensen and Norris 2017). The U.S. arsenal in South Korea reached its peak in 1967 with over 900 nuclear warheads but gradually declined due to improvement of the ROK's conventional capabilities. Since the 1991 withdrawal, the United States continues to use nuclear bombers and submarines based elsewhere to protect South Korea under the nuclear umbrella. The recent deployment of the Terminal High Altitude Area Defense system (THAAD) in South Korea is intended to intercept missiles at high altitude to prevent missile attacks.

ROK Military Buildup. Alliance with the United States also helped strengthen South Korea's defense capability through military modernization. By 1955, the Rhee administration reinforced the ROK armed forces to 600,000, with most of the weapons, equipment, and supplies from the United States. The purpose of South Korea's defense buildup was to prepare for another ground war with North Korea. It did not focus on expanding its power projection resources; instead, it concentrated on the ground and air forces, including ground-to-ground missiles.

Defense expenditures in South Korea have been on the upward trend since the Korean War, irrespective of economic conditions. For most of the Cold War era, South Korea spent an average 5 percent to 6 percent of gross national product (GNP), or approximately 30 percent of its annual budget, on defense (Moon and Hyun 1992).

Like South Korea, North Korea significantly expanded its military strength after the Korean War. In December 1955, Kim Il-sung proclaimed the ideology of *juche* (or self-reliance), which combines socialist and nationalist elements as governance philosophy to solidify his control of the North Korean government and political system. The self-reliance principle led to the development of an independent military strategy. In December 1962, Pyongyang announced a massive military buildup, with the twin goals of "arming the entire population" and "fortifying the entire country." The self-reliance military doctrine prepared not only for regular warfare but also for irregular warfare like mountain combat and guerrilla tactics (Hamm 1999).

After the fall of Vietnam in 1975, in response to the growth of the DPRK capabilities and the perceived decline of the U.S. military commitment to Asia, the ROK government undertook military modernization. The Park government initiated the Force Improvement Plan, financed by a national defense surtax. President Park also considered the possibility of the ROK developing its own nuclear weapons but had to abandon the idea due to the U.S. pressure (T. Kim 2016).

Sustained economic growth provided a strong base for ROK defense buildup. By the late 1980s, defense expenditures declined to 4 percent of the GNP but were sufficient to achieve superiority in conventional military strength vis-à-vis North Korea. The overwhelming advantage in conventional forces enjoyed by combined U.S. and ROK forces achieved effective deterrence at the strategic level to prevent large-scale conflict. Nevertheless, it also compelled North Korea to accelerate its nuclear and missile programs. In response, South Korea and the United States decided to use economic incentives to dissuade Pyongyang from pursuing nuclear and missile options.

Economic Statecraft. President Kim Young-sam (1993–1998) strongly opposed the Clinton administration's plan for a preemptive attack on the nuclear facilities at Yongbyon. Instead, he supported continued negotiations that resulted in the 1994 Agreed Framework, which promised North Korea economic incentives of light water reactors and regular shipments of heavy fuel oil (HFO) in exchange for freezing the operations at the Yongbyon complex. The engagement strategy gained more momentum after Kim Dae-jung (1998–2004) was elected president. President Kim Dae-jung's Sunshine Policy brought a drastic change in South Korean policy toward North Korea. Kim reached out to North Korea, significantly expanding trade with the North and facilitating South Korean investments in the North. Through aggressive engagement, Kim shifted from a security-oriented strategy to a peace-oriented initiative to make North Korea a less belligerent, less isolated country to achieve peace on the peninsula.

The George W. Bush administration, skeptical of engagement, suspended HFO shipments in November 2002 in response to intelligence that North Korea had a clandestine highly enriched uranium (HEU) program. President Roh Moo-hyun (2004–2009), operating under another progressive government, continued to expand North-South economic interactions. The Kaesong Industrial Complex was opened, and further development was achieved under Roh, who believed that inter-Korean economic cooperation would expose the North to capitalism and induce broader social and economic changes in North Korea.

Subsequently, several rounds of escalation and de-escalation of tensions surrounding the North Korean nuclear and missile programs in the 2000s and 2010s were often accompanied by mixed use of imposing and lifting of economic sanctions.

SECURITY INSTITUTIONS AND POLICY MAKING

Security Institutions

In the name of national security, the ROK military intervened in domestic politics through military coups, as seen in the rule of Park Chung-hee and Chun Doo-hwan. Under the authoritarian regime, the military enjoyed autonomy and political privileges. Ranking positions in the presidential secretariat and intelligence services were almost exclusively recruited from the military. Staffed mainly by active and retired military officers, the Ministry of National Defense (MND) enjoyed absolute authority and influence in matters of defense and external security policy (K. -J. Kim 2014; Kuehn 2016). Public debates on defense and security matters were severely restricted. Nonmilitary agencies had no meaningful oversight over the defense budget and the development and planning of security policy. Furthermore, the military was heavily involved in internal security, monitoring political parties, universities, and the media.

Since democratic transition in the late 1980s, particularly after the first civilian president, Kim Young-sam, the military gradually lost its political influence, and its role was limited to national defense. Several institutional innovations initiated by Kim Dae-jung and Roh Moo-hyun aimed to strengthen civilian and legislative oversight of the military. For example, Kim Dae-jung in 1998 established the National Security Council (NSC) to facilitate and coordinate his reform agendas in foreign and security policies. To make defense and military policy more transparent, Kim asked the MND to publish defense white papers. Roh further expanded the power of the NSC and established the Defense Acquisition Program Administration to oversee the military's arms procurement programs. Under Roh, the National Defense Committee (NDC) of the National Assembly was empowered to approve the president's nominee for the chairman of the Joint Chiefs of Staff.

The MND provides leadership for the military and is responsible for major issues related to defense and security. Notwithstanding the recent progress in civilian control of the military, true civilians in the MND remain the minority. Most of the MND leadership (defense ministers and vice ministers) are "quasi-civilians," who retired from their active duty before being appointed to the civilian position. The slow process of the MND civilianization is in part due to the immense threat from North Korea, as the government and the public are more willing to trust military personnel for their professional knowledge and skill in defense matters.

Legislative oversight over the defense and security policies is exercised by the NDC of the National Assembly. It deliberates and approves the defense budget, conducts annual inspection of the military, and can discharge the defense minister if wrongdoing is found. After democratic transition, the decline in NDC members with military background has helped strengthen the legislative oversight of the MND and the military.

Security Policy Making

South Korean presidents since the First Republic have enjoyed broad control over foreign and domestic policies. For Presidents Park and Chun, their military backgrounds and contacts gave them advantages in defense and security policy making during the Cold War. In the democratic era, the 1987 Constitution grants the president special power in foreign and security affairs. For example, Article 66 of the 1987 Constitution states that the president "shall be the Head of State and represent the State vis-à-vis foreign states." The president has "the responsibility and duty to safeguard the independence, territorial integrity and continuity of the Sate and the Constitution" and "the duty to pursue sincerely the peaceful unification of the homeland." Substantive powers to "conclude and ratify treaties; accredit, receive or dispatch diplomatic envoys; and declare war and conclude peace" are vested in the president (Art. 73), who is also "Commander-in-Chief of the Armed Forces" (Art. 74).

While security policy making often falls in the exclusive domain of the chief executive, the MND and the NDC are also key government actors in security policy making. As discussed earlier, institutional innovations under

Kim Dae-jung and Roh Moo-hyun broke the conventional decision-making pattern to empower new actors (such as the NSC) in policy planning and implementation.

Besides government actors, the diffusion of democratic norms in the democratic era encourages participation by outside interests and civil society groups such as business organizations, labor unions, student groups, and citizen groups. On issues relating to U.S.-ROK alliance, the anti-Americanism promoted by some of the groups is particularly notable.

Furthermore, South Korean political leaders have to deal with the geostrategic constraints in international politics. The fact that the Korean peninsula remains divided in the post–Cold War era reflects the delicate balance among the major powers such as China, Russia, and the United States. The preferences of the major powers create the parameters and boundaries of South Korea's foreign and security policies, hence limiting the president's policy options.

The superstructure imposed by the U.S.-ROK alliance is particularly important in framing the ROK's policy restraints. The United States expects mutual consultations relating to North Korea, because the security alliance with South Korea is an important pillar of its security policy in East Asia. Differences in ideas and interests between allies can translate into policy disagreements and result in an extra layer of complexity in security policy making.

INTER-KOREAN SECURITY RELATIONS

Under the Authoritarian Regime

During the Cold War, the two Koreas were locked in fierce competition for legitimacy and recognition on multiple fronts with different levels of intensity. Mutual antagonism and hostility were the characteristics of their relationship, except for brief periods of dialogues in the early 1970s and the 1980s.

The Korean War (1950–1953). The Korean War represented a failed attempt by the DPRK to settle the legitimacy issue. On June 25, 1950, North Korea launched a full-scale offensive along the border. Its army, which was better equipped, better trained, and superior in size (a 135,000-person force compared to the South's 98,000), soon captured Seoul and steadily advanced south.

Surprised by the attack, the Truman administration asked the UN for intervention, while directing General MacArthur to support the South Korean army with U.S. armed forces. At the time, the Soviet Union was boycotting the UN, for the UN had not granted the China seat to the Communist government in Beijing in the place of the Nationalist government in Taipei. In the absence of the Soviets, the UN Security Council passed a resolution on July 7 to establish a unified military command. Fifteen states, in addition to the United States and South Korea, contributed troops to the UN forces.

By early August, the North Korean troops pushed the South Korean troops to a small area in the southeast corner of the peninsula around Pusan; however, they ultimately failed to punctuate the defensive perimeter. The tide turned by mid-September as MacArthur launched a surprise landing at Inchon, the second largest port of Korea and only 15 miles from Seoul. The move outflanked North Korean troops and cut off their main supply line. By the end of September, the North Korean forces were in total disarray, and UN forces recovered Seoul.

On October 7, the UN General Assembly passed a resolution that approved the advance of UN forces beyond the 38th parallel to establish a unified, democratic Korea. UN forces crossed the parallel and moved swiftly northward on October 9. By October 19, they captured Pyongyang, forcing Kim Il-sung to establish a new capital at Sinuiju on the Yalu River. On October 20, Chinese forces, under the name of the Chinese People's Volunteer Army, crossed the Yalu River into North Korea. The massive intervention by the Chinese forces drove UN troops into a full retreat. On December 6, Pyongyang was back under Communist control. The Chinese forces continued their advances and captured Seoul on January 4, 1951.

On February 1, the UN General Assembly voted to condemn the Chinese aggression in Korea. UN forces regrouped, stopped the Chinese advances, and pressed north. On March 14, they retook Seoul—the fourth time that the city changed hands in less than a year. By the end of March 1951, UN forces were back at the 38th parallel. The war essentially settled into a stalemate.

The war aimed to unify the country turned out to perpetuate its division. Both sides paid high costs in human casualties and property losses and were driven further apart. Both political regimes survived and consolidated their power for more confrontations and competition.

Provocations. After the Korean War, North Korea tried to destabilize the South from within by using lower-level provocations. In January 1968, North Korea sent a 31-man commando squad to Seoul to assassinate President Park at his Blue House residence. The mission failed as the commandos were discovered within one mile of the presidential mansion.

Two days after the failed assassination attempt, North Korea seized the U.S. intelligence ship the USS *Pueblo* and took 82 crewmembers as prisoners. After the incident, the United States deployed the Seventh Fleet and some 600 aircraft in or near Korea for several months in a show of force to pressure Pyongyang to release the *Pueblo* crew.

The issue was finally resolved through U.S.-initiated secret negotiations with North Korea. The United States issued an apology in December 1968, pledging that no U.S. ships would enter North Korea's territorial waters in the future in exchange for North Korea's return of the *Pueblo* crew. Viewing this as a great diplomatic victory, North Korea was emboldened. In April 1969, it shot down an unarmed U.S. Navy EC-121 reconnaissance plane and killed all 31 aboard.

In August 1974, another assassination attempt missed President Park but killed his wife. In August 1976, a group of North Korean soldiers wielded axes to attack a U.S.–South Korean tree-trimming work team in a neutral area of the DMZ, killing two U.S. Army officers and wounding nine American and South Korean soldiers.

Two infiltration tunnels dug by North Korea into the southern part of the DMZ were discovered in the mid-1970s, with a third found in 1978. Designed for surprise attacks on the South, they could accommodate moving great numbers of personnel and small vehicles through.

In 1983, during President Chun's state visit to Burma (Myanmar), DPRK agents exploded a bomb in the capital city of Rangoon. Chun escaped the assassination attempt, but 17 South Koreans were killed, including several cabinet members. In November 1987, to stir instability in South Korea before the presidential election and the 1988 Seoul Olympics, North Korean agents planted a bomb on Korean Air Flight 858, killing all 115 persons onboard.

At the same time, the South also conducted raids and incursions into North Korea, destroying its facilities. While these incidents did not lead to major military clashes, they heightened tensions on the peninsula and destabilized regional security.

To bolster national defense against these infiltration attempts, South Korea in April 1968 organized the 2.5 million-strong Homeland Reserve Force, including all discharged soldiers under age 35. It also fortified Seoul, constructing shelters that could accommodate 300,000 to 400,000 people in case of an emergency.

Diplomatic Competition. Trying to secure as many states as possible for de jure recognition as the sole, legitimate government of Korea, South Korea and North Korea were engaged in a battle for diplomatic recognition (Koh 2001). The contest in the 1950s was an even-split in the number of countries with ambassadorial-level relations: Seoul had 14 countries, and Pyongyang had 13. Seoul then had the edge in the 1960s, but Pyongyang closed the gap in the 1970s.

Initially, no state would simultaneously recognize both Seoul and Pyongyang. Neither the North nor the South would accept the arrangement of dual recognition, for their goal was to discredit the legitimacy of the other. The situation, however, changed in the 1970s because of the East-West detente, as nearly 50 countries extended recognition to both countries.

North Korea gained some ground in the diplomatic battle in the 1970s. It joined the World Health Organization and obtained observer status in the UN (South Korea was granted observer status in 1948). North Korea's diplomatic efforts, however, faltered in the 1980s, because of its involvement in state-sponsored terrorism, as seen in its assassination attempt of President Chun in Burma and its bombing of Korean Air Flight 858. Burma derecognized the DPRK after the assassination attempt and expelled its officials.

Economic Competition. Economic development, which could enhance national wealth and capabilities, was an integral part of the security strategy in South Korea. In the early 1960s, to reduce its economic assistance to South Korea, the United States began to ask Japan to share the financial burden to finance South Korean development projects (S. Kim 2017). At the behest of the United States, the Park administration negotiated with Japan to normalize bilateral relations. In June 1965, South Korea and Japan signed the Treaty on Basic Relations to establish formal diplomatic relations, despite strong objections from the opposition politicians and dissident activists. The $800 million assistance package was instrumental for the initial phase of South Korean economic development.

Similar to South Korea, postwar reconstruction of North Korea depended heavily on foreign aid. In the wake of the Korean War, North Korea actively sought foreign aid to rebuild its economy. Besides China and the Soviet Union, many of the Eastern European communist states provided economic assistance to North Korea. In a highly centralized command economy, Kim Il-sung mobilized resources to collectivize agriculture and promote industrialization. The big push toward heavy industries achieved impressive results and outperformed the South in the late 1950s.

Nevertheless, North Korea's high-performing economy started to lose its luster in the 1960s. The guiding principle of *juche* emphasized the development of a self-sufficient economy that was inward looking, isolated from the rest of the world. The lack of competition in self-imposed seclusion made the economy increasingly inefficient with outdated technology. Furthermore, the heavy burden of military spending, close to 30 percent of its GNP, diverted resources away from economic development.

Meanwhile, South Korea began to show dynamic growth after the First Five-Year Economic Development Plan (1962–1966). The export expansion policy adopted by the Park government put the country on track for sustained economic growth. By the late 1960s and early 1970s, South Korea's economic capability overtook that of the North.

Inter-Korean Dialogues. Amid hostile competitions, two inter-Korean dialogues took place during the brief periods of 1972–1973 and 1984–1985. Both episodes showed a similar pattern. Initial progress in negotiations generated positive momentum and produced agreements. The success, however, soon hit an impasse with increasing conflict and hostility. Talks were suspended and agreements abandoned.

Changes in the international environment were the catalyst for the 1972–1973 talks. In the wake of the U.S.-China rapprochement resulting from President Nixon's 1972 visit to China, both Koreas shared the fear that their great power patrons might begin to abandon them. Trying to resolve their differences on their own, North and South Korea held secret talks, resulting in a Joint Communique in July 1972 about the basic principles of reunification. Both sides reaffirmed the principle of national unity and pledged to achieve reunification without foreign interference and without the use of military forces. They agreed to create a North-South Coordination Commission, support exchanges, and promote cooperation between the two Koreas' Red Cross societies.

The optimism and excitement produced by the reunification dialogues turned out to be the leaders' political tactics to gain political capital for power consolidation. In October 1972, three months after the Joint Communique, Park dissolved the National Assembly, terminated the Third Republic, and established the *Yushin* regime. In December 1972, Kim Il-sung promulgated a new constitution and became the newly created permanent president of North Korea. North Korea called off the talks in August 1973 after Korean Central Intelligence Agency agents abducted Kim Dae-jung in Tokyo (Chapter 10).

President Chun, in an attempt to overcome his legitimacy deficit at the beginning of the Fifth Republic, proposed in January 1981 an exchange of visits by leaders of the two Koreas, but North Korea quickly rejected the idea. In June 1981, the North again turned down Chun's second proposal for a summit meeting.

The inter-Korean dialogue of 1984–1985 was launched after South Korea was hit by a devastating typhoon. In September 1984, North Korea, which had attempted to assassinate President Chun in Burma just a year prior, delivered relief supplies, including rice and medicine, to South Korea through the Red Cross. Bilateral relations improved as a result of DPRK's humanitarian actions, opening the door to Red Cross–arranged reunions in September 1985 between family members separated for more than 35 years because of the Korean War. Exchanges between legislators and economic officials ensued. In January 1986, however, North Korea suspended all dialogues with South Korea on the grounds of the annual U.S.-ROK military exercise.

In the Democratic Era

Nordpolitik (Northern Policy). President Roh launched *Nordpolitik* in 1988 prior to the Seoul Olympics to develop closer ties with all the Communist nations except Cuba. The objectives of *Nordpolitik* were to improve relations with Eastern Europe, Russia, and China and to reduce tension with North Korea. Between 1989 and 1990, the Roh administration established diplomatic relations with the Socialist states of Eastern Europe, such as Hungary, Poland, Yugoslavia, Czechoslovakia, and Romania. Direct trade with the Soviet Union began in November 1988, and formal diplomatic relations were established in October 1990. Efforts to establish ties with China were briefly disrupted following the June 1989 Tiananmen Square crackdown, but both countries were able to establish full diplomatic relations in 1992.

By now, South Korea has won the competition with North Korea for international recognition and reputation. South Korea's normalization of diplomatic relations with China and the Soviet Union put North Korea on the defensive in inter-Korean confrontations. These diplomatic initiatives not only raised South Korea's profile in the world stage but also improved its security standing.

In contrast, North Korea faced increasing economic and diplomatic challenges. The collapse of the Communist bloc, coupled with Moscow's and Beijing's normalization of diplomatic relations with Seoul, made North Korea quite isolated. Declines in food and petroleum subsidies from Russia and China created further economic hardship for North Korea.

Inter-Korean Reconciliation. From July 1990 to December 1991, the two Koreas engaged in high-level official talks, with the prime ministers alternating their meetings in Seoul and Pyongyang. In September 1991, the ROK and DPRK formally joined the UN, making it an obligation for both sides to abide by the UN Charter.

In December 1991, they signed the Basic Agreement Concerning the North-South Reconciliation, Nonaggression, Exchange and Cooperation, reaffirming the principle of peaceful unification embodied in the July 1972 ROK-DPRK Joint Communique. Under the Basic Agreement, they renounced the use of armed force or acts of terrorism against each other and recognized each other's right to exist as a legitimate government. They pledged to remove all military equipment from the DMZ and install hotlines between military commands. In February 1992, North and South signed a Joint Declaration of the Denuclearization of the Korean Peninsula.

Provocations. Although North Korea in the post–Cold War era was open to rapprochement with South Korea, it continued the provocation strategies. A fourth infiltration tunnel was discovered in 1990; there may be many more undetected.

From the mid-1990s, North Korea was increasingly involved in naval clashes with the South over the Northern Limit Line (NLL), a maritime border in the West Sea between North and South Korea. The NLL was established in August 1953 by the UN Command to protect South Korean ships from straying northward. Nevertheless, North Korea would not recognize the line; instead, it proclaimed its own version of the maritime border, leading to a number of armed maritime engagements. The dispute was in part economic in nature, because of the large concentration of valuable blue crab south of the NLL.

In September 1996, 26 North Korean military personnel from a disabled North Korean submarine on an espionage mission landed on the east coast of the South. Ensuing exchange of fire led to military and civilian casualties. In June 1999, several North Korean naval boats provoked a nine-day naval confrontation near the ROK-controlled Yonpyong Island, causing severe losses on the North Korean side, including an estimated 80 deaths and one sunk torpedo boat. The second battle of Yonpyong occurred in June 2002, resulting in the death of six South Korean sailors and 13 North Koreans. In November 2009, a

North Korean patrol boat crossed the NLL and entered waters near Taechong Island. The boat was damaged in the short exchange of fire.

In March 2010, a 1,200-ton South Korean patrol boat, the *Cheonan*, was severed in half and sank in the waters off Paengnyong Island near the NLL after an explosion. Forty-six South Korean sailors died in the incident. After nearly two months of investigation, a multinational commission concluded that it was sunk by a North Korean torpedo, although North Korea denied responsibility. Months later, in November 2010, the North Korean army shelled Yonpyong Island with their artillery, killing two South Korean marines and two civilians.

In response to these provocations, the ROK built up its military assets on these islands. It developed a new defense plan in March 2011 to authorize the military to move beyond self-defense and take prompt, proportional actions in retaliating against these small-scale attacks.

DPRK's Nuclear and Missile Programs. Despite the fact that North and South Korean representatives signed the Joint Denuclearization Declaration in 1991, North Korea has since accelerated its nuclear and missile programs. The move can be explained from military, economic, and political perspectives. First, after the South's military modernization in the 1980s, North Korea could no longer match the ROK's conventional capability. Pyongyang thus resorted to the nuclear option for a robust and efficient deterrent shield to offset its inferiority in conventional military forces.

Second, with the dwindling economic support from Beijing and Moscow, Pyongyang needed fresh resources to sustain its stagnant economy and to support its political elites. Missile sales to countries in the Middle East and Africa have brought in hard currency and alleviated some of North Korea's trade deficit. During the course of nuclear development, North Korea has also found a way to extract economic concessions from foreign governments, using the nuclear program as a bargaining tool. Conducting coercive diplomacy for economic benefits opened up nuclear bargaining as an opportunity for North Korea.

Finally, and most importantly, the ultimate goal for North Korean leaders is regime survival, which takes precedence over other considerations such as its economy and citizens' well-being. Its self-imposed isolation embodied in the ideology of *juche*, along with the negative responses from the international community about its weapons programs, reinforces the siege mentality of the leaders. For them, the pursuit of nuclear and missile programs is not only for deterrence and defense but also for self-protection of the regime and its dictatorial power (B. Kim 2016).

Historical Background. Kim Il-sung initiated the nuclear project in the late 1950s to counter the U.S. nuclear deployment in South Korea. Several nuclear research centers and industrial complexes were created, led by the Atomic Research Center in Yongbyon (about 56 miles north of Pyongyang).

Even though China and the Soviet Union repeatedly rebuffed its requests for technical assistance, North Korea managed to obtain a small, experimental plutonium reactor in the 1980s.

Pyongyang's missile program started in the 1960s and 1970s, as it purchased several types of cruise missiles and artillery rockets from China and the Soviet Union. In the 1980s, it acquired more advanced Soviet technology from Egypt and reverse engineered the production to provide the platform for its subsequent missiles.

First Nuclear Crisis, 1993–1994. North Korea had signed the Treaty on the Non-Proliferation of Nuclear Weapons (NPT) in 1985 but delayed the signing of the related safeguard agreement to authorize inspections of its nuclear facilities by the International Atomic Energy Agency (IAEA). In 1989, a report that North Korea had constructed a nuclear processing facility in Yongbyon raised international concerns. This facility would have allowed the North to process the nuclear waste from its reactor and extract small amounts of plutonium to make nuclear weapons.

As discussed earlier, the United States withdrew nuclear weapons from South Korea in 1991. The move was in part to persuade North Korea to allow inspection. In January 1992, North Korea signed the nuclear safeguard agreement to allow IAEA inspections. In six separate inspections, IAEA inspectors confirmed violations by North Korea, which had removed spent fuel from its nuclear research reactor.

Subsequently, North Korea issued a series of ultimatums, including the announcement in March 1993 to withdraw from the NPT, resulting in the first North Korean nuclear crisis. At the same time, it test-launched the medium-range ballistic missile Nodong-1 (up to 900 miles in estimated range), showing its ability to strike all of South Korea and Japan.

Agreed Framework of 1994. Beginning in June 1993, the United States and North Korea held high-level talks to search for a solution. The U.S. intelligence sources estimated that North Korea might have obtained enough materials for one or two nuclear weapons. During negotiations, Pyongyang threatened to increase fissile material production if demands were not met. Tensions deescalated after former U.S. President Jimmy Carter had a meeting with Kim Il-sung in Pyongyang. Talks resumed after the meeting but were temporarily disrupted by Kim Il-sung's death in July 1994.

In October 1994, the United States and North Korea adopted the Agreed Framework in Geneva. North Korea agreed to freeze its nuclear program and place declared nuclear sites (i.e., Yongbyon and Taechon) under IAEA supervision, in exchange for annual HFO shipments and the construction of two 1,000-megawatt, light-water nuclear reactors, whose fuel rods are more difficult to use to produce weapons-grade plutonium. A multinational consortium (the Korean Peninsula Energy Development Organization, or KEDO) was created to finance this project and to provide North Korea with alternative energy resources. The United States promised to move toward normalized economic and diplomatic relations with North Korea. Critics of the agreement believed that, with compliance limited to declared facilities and materials, and freezing but not dismantling of the facilities, the loopholes in the agreement would allow North Korea to pursue a clandestine nuclear program on undeclared facilities.

In 1997, Kim Jong-il assumed the leadership position in North Korea and continued defense buildup under the principle of Military First (*songun*). In August 1998, North Korea test-fired the intermediate-range ballistic missile Taepodong-I rocket that traveled over Japanese airspace, raising concerns that its missiles could reach Alaska and Guam. Although the Clinton administration sought to engage a grand bargain with North Korea, offering to lift U.S. economic sanctions for North Korean concessions on its nuclear and missile programs, the negotiations yielded no concrete results.

Second Nuclear Crisis, 2002–2003. The George W. Bush administration was skeptical of the North Korean regime as well as the engagement strategy. It demanded reduction of North Korea's conventional forces along the DMZ, as well as verification of its nuclear and missile programs.

Relations between the United States and North Korea further deteriorated after the 9/11 terrorist attacks. President Bush named North Korea part of the Axis of Evil in his January 2002 State of the Union address, condemning its development of weapons of mass destruction. In October 2002, the United States announced that North Korea had admitted to having a secret HEU nuclear weaponization program during U.S. Assistant Secretary of State James Kelly's visit to Pyongyang, which Pyongyang denied. In response to this development, KEDO announced suspension of HFO deliveries to North Korea, and the IAEA adopted a resolution calling upon North Korea to clarify this report. In the meantime, the construction of the light-water reactors was seriously behind schedule, pushing the completion date from 2003 to 2008. Alleged violations from both sides led to the collapse of the Agreed Framework. North Korea expelled the IAEA inspectors in December 2002 and announced its withdrawal from the NPT in January 2003.

Six-Party Talks. With North Korea declaring the Agreed Framework "null and void," the United States proposed in early 2003 a multilateral approach to include South Korea, Japan, Russia, and China in six-party talks (Liang 2018). From August 2003 to September 2005, four rounds of negotiations took place. The joint statement by six parties on September 19, 2005, outlined steps toward the denuclearization of the Korean peninsula. North Korea pledged to abandon all nuclear weapons and return to NPT and IAEA inspections. In return, the other parties promised to supply Pyongyang with energy aid. The United States and Japan agreed to work on normalization of relations with North Korea.

A few days prior to the joint statement, the U.S. Treasury Department on September 15, 2005, took actions against Banco Delta Asia in Macau for its role in laundering North Korean funds derived from illicit activities such as drug trafficking, arms sales, and counterfeiting U.S. currency. Banks around the world followed the U.S. lead, freezing or closing North Korean accounts.

Pyongyang reacted strongly to the actions, suspending its participation in the six-party talks until these sanctions were lifted. In July 2006, North Korea conducted seven missile tests. The launch of the medium-range Nodong was a success, but the long-range Taepodong-2 failed. In October 9, 2006, North Korea conducted its first nuclear weapons test at an underground facility.

International reaction to the nuclear test was swift and harsh. The United States immediately condemned the test and called for UN sanctions. On October 14, 2006, the UN Security Council passed Resolution 1718 calling for North Korea to abandon its nuclear and missile programs and rejoin the six-party talks. Under domestic pressure, the Roh administration also suspended humanitarian aid to North Korea, until it agreed to return to the six-party talks.

The six-party talks concluded the fifth round in February 2007 with an agreed plan to implement the joint statement announced on September 19, 2005. In October 2007, following the sixth round, the six-party talks issued a joint statement to implement the February agreement. North Korea agreed to disable the Yongbyon nuclear facilities in exchange for HFO shipment. The United States also agreed to remove North Korea from the list of state sponsors of terrorism and end the U.S. Treasury sanctions. Nevertheless, negotiations broke down in 2008 over the verification system.

Pyongyang test-fired a three-stage modified version of the long-range Taepodong-2 rocket on April 5, 2009. The UN Security Council called the test a violation of Resolution 1718 and expanded sanctions on North Korea. North Korea withdrew from the six-party talks on April 14, 2009, and declared that it would no longer observe any of the previous agreements. On May 25, 2009, Pyongyang conducted a second nuclear test.

Missile and Nuclear Tests under Kim Jong-un. After Kim Jong-il's death in December 2011, Kim Jong-un was declared North Korea's new leader and the supreme commander of the military. In February 2012, North Korea announced the Leap Day Agreement with the United States to suspend operations at Yongbyon and freeze the nuclear and missile tests, in exchange for 240,000 metric tons of U.S. food aid. The United States quickly abandoned food aid after North Korea launched a three-stage rocket in April 2012.

North Korea amended its constitution in April 2012, declaring itself a nuclear weapon state in the preamble. On March 31, 2013, Kim Jong-un declared the so-called *byeongjin* strategy, aiming to achieve both economic development and nuclear buildup simultaneously. In December 2015, Kim declared the country's status as a nuclear power. Since his takeover, North Korea has conducted four more nuclear tests: February 12, 2013; January 6, 2016; September 9, 2016; and September 3, 2017. There were doubts about whether the test in January 2016 was thermonuclear; the test in September 2017 dispelled any lingering doubts.

Besides nuclear tests, North Korea has invested in efforts to miniaturize the warheads carried by various types of missiles and to enhance the accuracy of the delivery systems. In July 2017, North Korea tested an intercontinental ballistic missile (ICBM), with an estimated range (i.e., 6,500 miles) that technically could reach a large part of the mainland United States. In August, the UN Security Council passed Resolution 2371 to impose additional sanctions on North Korea, including a complete ban on the export of coal, iron, and lead.

Opportunities for Rapprochement? In April 2018, Kim Jong-un announced a policy change, shifting from the simultaneous pursuit of nuclear and economic development (*byeongjin*) to sole focus on economic development. Since then, he has participated in a series of summits with Chinese President Xi Jinping, South Korean President Moon Jae-in, and U.S. President Donald Trump to create an international environment favorable for North Korea's economy.

The Moon-Kim summits in April and May 2018 laid the foundation for the June 2018 Trump-Kim summit in Singapore, the first ever meeting between U.S. and North Korean leaders. Both sides pledged their efforts to improve the U.S.–North Korea relationship, establish peace on the Korean peninsula, work toward denuclearization, and resume recovery of Korean War solders' remains.

In September 2018, Moon and Kim met in Pyongyang and signed a Comprehensive Military Agreement (CMA), which was the first security and confidence-building measure since the conclusion of the Basic Agreement (1991) and the Joint Declaration of the Denuclearization (1992). Aimed to reduce the risk of accidental military clash, the CMA created a no-fly zone, as well as maritime and ground buffer zones around the DMZ, halted military drills targeting each other near the military demarcation line that runs within the DMZ, and removed guard posts inside the DMZ.

While the CMA represented a tangible effort toward inter-Korean peace, the long-term sustainability of the agreement will depend on future progress on North Korea's denuclearization. The February 2019 summit between Trump and Kim in Hanoi, Vietnam, ended without a signed agreement. Although follow-up negotiations have continued, it is unclear how the divergent goals and ideas would be reconciled.

For the last three decades, Washington and Seoul have tried to confront North Korea's nuclear and missile challenges. Different administrations have approached the issues with different ideas and plans, but none of them has succeeded in finding a durable solution. In the meantime, North Korea's nuclear and missile capabilities have grown steadily.

SOUTH KOREA–U.S. SECURITY RELATIONS

Military alliance with the United States has been an important pillar of South Korea's national security. With the signing of the 1953 ROK-U.S. Mutual Defense Treaty, the United States assumed a major responsibility to defend ROK's political and territorial integrity through economic assistance and troop deployment. At that time, there were more than 320,000 American soldiers stationed in South Korea. The inflow of the U.S. economic and military aid played an important role in South Korea's economic reconstruction and defense preparedness after the Korean War. The traumatic experience of the Korean War reinforced the alliance.

In the post–Cold War era, success in economic development and democratization has led to increased confidence and national pride in South Korea. The worldview of the younger generation does not necessarily share the threat perception of the older generation. Many of them view North Korea as a nation of common culture and heritage rather than a state of serious military threat. The generational change in the democratic era brings new dynamics to the alliance relationship at the very time when North Korea is enhancing its military capability (Steinberg 2005).

Under the Authoritarian Regime

Although South Korea was not always a compliant junior partner under the authoritarian regime during the Cold War, its dependence on American military protection created an asymmetrical alliance structure. The United States had significant power in the ROK's decision-making process. For example, it was the United States that persuaded President Rhee not to act against student demonstrations in 1960 and granted him political asylum. When General Park Chung-hee was reluctant to return power to a civilian government after the coup in 1961, the United States intervened. Under U.S. pressure, Park retired from the military and ran as a civilian candidate for the presidency of the Third Republic in 1963. Again, under strong pressure from the United States, President Park gave up the nuclear weapons program.

The asymmetrical alliance partnership was, in part, driven by South Korea's need for security assurance (i.e., its fear of U.S. abandonment), in the face of the formidable threat from North Korea. South Korea's involvement in Vietnam illustrated its willingness to show solidarity with the United States by accommodating American security priorities. From 1965 to 1972, as the second largest foreign military contributor to Vietnam (after the United States), South Korea maintained 47,000 troops in Vietnam each year. The United States, in return, funded all expenses of the South Korean troops in Vietnam and modernized the equipment of the ROK forces as a way to maintain military balance on the Korean peninsula.

The announcement of the Nixon Doctrine in 1969 for military withdrawal from Asia (Chapter 8) came as a shock to many South Koreans, who had viewed the U.S. military presence as an indispensable part of national defense. In March 1971, the United States revealed the plan to reduce the number of troops stationed in South Korea from 60,000 to 40,000. In 1972, President Nixon's visit to China and the subsequent U.S.-China rapprochement further heightened the fear that U.S.-China collusion could lead to U.S. abandonment of South Korea.

Under these circumstances, South Korea was determined to develop its military and defense independent of the United States. In the face of U.S. troop withdrawals and aid reduction, the Park administration launched the Force Improvement Plan in 1974 to modernize its weapon systems and to conduct research on the development of nuclear weapons. The funding increased from the original $1.5 billion to $5.5 billion by 1978.

Another attempt to secure the U.S. defense commitment was through the creation of the Combined Forces Command (CFC) in 1978. A combined military command could trace its origin back to the early days of the Korean War, when President Rhee transferred authority to UN Commander and placed the ROK military under the operational control of the United States (Yoon 2015). To integrate the U.S. and ROK forces for unified military operations, a combined operational planning staff was created in 1968, which further evolved into the CFC in 1978. The 1978 agreement called for a four-star American general to serve as the CFC commander, with a four-star South Korean general as the deputy commander. The commander, in charge of both the U.S. and ROK forces, would report to both presidents. Given the superiority of the U.S. forces in technology, communication, and intelligence gathering, they naturally took on a greater responsibility in a unified command. While the CFC represented a reaffirmed commitment by the United States to defend South Korea, it was also seen as solidifying the alliance in a patron-client arrangement.

In the Democratic Era

During the Cold War, Washington and Seoul had very few differences over their attitude toward Pyongyang. Policy disagreements began to appear in the post–Cold War era. During the first and second nuclear crises, while the United States considered taking military actions against the Yongbyon nuclear facilities both times, President Kim Young-sam and President Roh Moo-hyun voiced objections. As South Korean leaders sought reconciliation with North Korea through economic engagement, they were concerned about the potential negative effect of U.S. hard-line actions (Park 2011). Thus, to ease its fear of entrapment, South Korea has attempted to shape institutional practices to retain greater control over its own security relations.

The 1978 arrangement was modified in 1994, for South Korea to assume operational control of its military during peacetime, indicating a change into a partnership relationship. In 2005, President Roh asked that wartime operational control of the U.S.-ROK forces be transferred to South Korea. In 2007, both governments agreed to develop a path toward eventual ROK wartime operational control, placing the U.S. military forces under ROK command during war by 2012. Since then, consecutive conservative presidencies in South Korea (Presidents Lee Myung-bak and Park Geun-hye) decided to postpone the transfer until the mid-2020s. In November 2018, the United States and the ROK developed the Alliance Guiding Principles that outlined how the U.S.-ROK combined defense mechanisms will operate post transfer, paving the way for eventual transfer. Based on the guidelines, a South Korean four-star general will lead the combined forces, and a U.S. general will assume a deputy commander role.

In recent years, the rise of the pro–North Korean attitude and anti-American sentiment in the younger generation has led to concerns about the future of the U.S.-ROK alliance. The images of protesters burning American flags in South Korea were signs of shifting attitudes toward the United States.

Despite the strong U.S.-ROK alliance, negative views of the United States became more common and explicit among South Koreans in the 1980s (Kim 1989; Matray 2012). The continued U.S. support of the authoritarian regime in the aftermath of the Kwangju incident (May 1980) and the U.S. pressure on South Korea to open its markets to American goods, such as beef, cigarettes, and automobiles, were the main reasons for the rise of the anti-Americanism. Activists in the prodemocracy movement turned the struggle against dictatorship to struggle against the United States, calling for the withdrawal of American troops and American nuclear weapons from South Korea.

With democratization, anti-Americanism gradually changed its focus in the 1990s. Dissidents and activists began to concentrate on protesting the presence of U.S. forces. With the end of the Cold War, a growing number of South Koreans began to think that the presence of U.S. forces had made the division of Korea permanent. The emotion against the United States reflects nationalist reaction to perceived intervention by the United States to undermine Korean aspirations for unification.

It remains to be seen how Koreans will react to the recent Trump-Kim summit meetings. On one hand, the Singapore summit signaled that Washington was willing to follow the move made by President Moon Jae-in and pursue peace and reconciliation with North Korea. On the other hand, the Hanoi summit could reflect the U.S. reversion to the entrenched position toward North Korea. Whether the U.S. disappointment over the slow or limited advancement of denuclearization will lead to escalated tension in the Korean peninsula will further shape South Koreans' attitudes and perceptions of the U.S.-ROK alliance in the future.

DISCUSSION QUESTIONS

1. Describe the various kinds of provocations undertaken by North Korea after the Korean War. Why do you think North Korea engaged in such activities?

2. Discuss some of the reasons that may have led to the acceleration of the nuclear and missile programs in North Korea since the end of the Cold War. Based on these reasons, evaluate the prospect of denuclearization in the Korean peninsula in the near future.

3. How has South Korea's unification policy changed after *Nordpolitik*? What is the role of economic statecraft in South Korea's security strategies since the change?

4. Alliance with the United States has been an important pillar of the security strategy for Japan and South Korea. Discuss how the fear of abandonment and fear of entrapment have affected each country's security policies and strategies at different times.

5. Discuss why economic incentives, whether in the form of positive economic inducements or negative economic sanctions, have not significantly changed North Korean behaviors in its nuclear and missile programs. Based on those reasons, what kind of policy change would you recommend to Washington to make economic statecraft more effective?

China: TIMELINE OF MAJOR EVENTS SINCE 1945

1900

1945 Defeat of Japan and end of Sino-Japanese War

1946–1949 Outbreak of the Chinese civil war between KMT and CCP

1949 CCP wins the civil war, and KMT retreats to Taiwan

Mao Zedong declares the founding of the People's Republic of China (PRC)

1950 PRC and Soviet Union sign the Treaty of Friendship, Alliance, and Mutual Assistance

China enters Korean War to assist North Korean forces

1951 The Three-Anti-Movement

1952 The Five-Anti-Movement

1953 The First Five-Year Plan (1953–1957) is launched

1954 PRC's first formal constitution is promulgated

PRC heavy bombardment of off-shore islands controlled by Taiwan (Jinmen and Mazu)

1955 Zhou Enlai proposes five principles of peaceful coexistence at Bandung Conference (Indonesia)

1956 CCP Eighth Party Congress is convened

The Hundred Flowers Campaign is launched

1957 The Anti-Rightist Campaign

1958 Mao Zedong launches the Great Leap Forward

PRC resumes bombardment of Jinmen and Mazu

1959 Defense Minister Marshal Peng Dehuai is purged after his criticism of the Great Leap Forward at the Lushan Conference

Lin Biao is appointed to succeed Peng Dehuai

1960 Soviet Union withdraws technical advisors from China

1962 Border conflicts between the PRC and India

1964 China tests nuclear weapon

1966 Mao Zedong launches the Cultural Revolution

1967 Liu Shaoqi and Deng Xiaoping are removed from the PRC leadership

1969 Border clashes at Zhenbao island between PRC and Soviet Union in March

Mao Zedong convenes the CCP Ninth Party Congress in April

1971 PRC is admitted to the United Nations

1972 U.S. President Richard Nixon visits China

1973 Deng Xiaoping returns to power

PRC and the United States establish liaison offices

1975 A new constitution is adopted to supersede the 1954 Constitution

1976 Deaths of Zhou Enlai, Zhu De, and Mao Zedong

Deng Xiaoping is ousted

Hua Guofeng succeeds Mao and arrests the Gang of Four

1977 Deng Xiaoping returns to power the second time

1978 National People's Congress adopts a new constitution in March to supersede the 1975 Constitution

China and Japan sign the Treaty of Peace and Friendship in August

Economic reforms begin

1979 The idea of Special Economic Zones is pilot tested

PRC government introduces the one-child policy

United States and the PRC establish diplomatic relations, and United States severs diplomatic relations with Taiwan

2000

1980 China is admitted to International Monetary Fund and World Bank

1982 The National People's Congress adopts a new constitution to supersede the 1978 Constitution

1987 Organic Law of the Village Committees (Experimental) is adopted

1989 Student democracy movement and Tiananmen Square crackdown

Jiang Zemin becomes CCP general secretary and chair of the Central Military Commission

1992 Deng Xiaoping's Southern Tour and relaunch of reforms

1993 Jiang Zemin becomes PRC president

1996 PRC launches missile tests off Taiwan

1997 Deng Xiaoping dies

Hong Kong reverts to PRC as Special Administrative Region

1998 State Council issues the Regulation on the Registration and Management of Social Organizations in October

The Organic Law of Village Committees is adopted in November

2001 The Shanghai Cooperation Organization is established

PRC and Russia sign the Treaty of Good Neighborliness and Friendly Cooperation in July

China is admitted to World Trade Organization in December

2002 Hu Jintao becomes CCP general secretary

2008 Sichuan earthquake (magnitude 7.9)

Beijing Olympics

2010 PRC overtakes Japan as the second largest economy

2012 Xi Jinping becomes the CCP general secretary and chair of the Central Military Commission

2013 Xi Jinping launches anticorruption campaign

Xi Jinping proposes the Asian Investment and Infrastructural Bank and the Belt and Road Initiative

2014 The National Security Commission is created

China undertakes land reclamation projects in the Spratlys

2015 Supply-side Structural Reforms are implemented

PRC government officially repeals the one-child policy

2016 National People's Congress Standing Committee adopts Foreign Non-Governmental Organization Management Law to tighten registration of foreign nongovernmental organizations

2017 Military standoff between PRC and Indian forces in Doklam (Bhutan)

2018 National People's Congress adopts constitutional amendment to eliminate term limits on PRC president and vice president

Japan: TIMELINE OF MAJOR EVENTS SINCE 1945

1900

1945 Japan surrenders to Allies after atomic bombing of Hiroshima and Nagasaki

1946 First postwar general election is held

Yoshida Shigeru is elected prime minister

1947 The Japan Socialist Party wins the general election in April

New Constitution takes effect in May

1950 The outbreak of the Korean War

National Police Reserve is created

1951 San Francisco Peace Treaty and U.S.-Japan Mutual Security Treaty are signed

The Japan Socialist Party splits

1952 Allied occupation ends

1953 The Diet passes the Medium and Small-sized Companies Stabilization Law

1954 The Cabinet Legislation Bureau interprets Article 9 of the Constitution as permitting the right to self-defense

Self-Defense Forces (SDF) are created under the Japan Defense Agency

The Diet passes the Ban on Oversea Dispatch

1955 The Right Socialist and Left Socialist reunite to recreate the Japan Socialist Party (JSP)

The Conservative Liberal Party and Democratic Party form the Liberal Democratic Party

1956 Japan is admitted to the United Nations

1957 Basic Policy on National Defense is adopted

1960 U.S.-Japan Mutual Security Treaty is renewed

Prime Minister Ikeda Hayato announces the National Income Doubling Plan

1964 Tokyo Olympics

Komeito (Clean Government Party) is formed

1967 Ban on arms exports is established

1970 Mutual Security Treaty is revised

1972 Japan and PRC establish diplomatic relations

1973 Prime Minister Tanaka Kakuei declares the year as the "First Year of the Welfare Era"

1976 Prime Minister Miki Takeo announces the ceiling of "1% of GNP" for defense expenditure

1978 Guidelines for Japan-U.S. Defense Cooperation are developed

China and Japan sign the Treaty of Peace and Friendship

1985 The Plaza Accord among France, Germany, United Kingdom, United States, and Japan leads to the appreciation of yen relative to the dollar

1989 The LDP for the first time loses the majority in the House of Councillors election

1991 "Bubble" economy bursts

1992 The Diet passes the International Peace Cooperation Law

1993 The LDP is defeated in the general election, ending the 1955 system

1994 The Diet undertakes electoral reforms in January, adopting a mixed-member majoritarian electoral system

JSP president Murayama Tomiichi forms a coalition government with the LDP, declaring the Self-Defense Forces as constitutional

1995 Kobe earthquake

1996 The LDP regains control of the government

The Democratic Party of Japan (DPJ) is formed

2000

1997 Guidelines for Japan-U.S. Defense Cooperation are developed

The Diet passes the Long-Term Care Insurance Law to ensure the care of the elderly

1998 Komeito is rebranded as New Komeito

The Diet passes the Law to Promote Specified Non-profit Activities

1999 The Diet passes legislation for administrative reforms

The LDP forms ruling coalition with New Komeito

2001 Koizumi Junichiro becomes prime minister

The Diet passes the Anti-Terrorism Special Measures Law

2003 The Diet passes the Iraqi Reconstruction Law

2005 The Diet passes the postal reform bill to privatize the postal service

2006 Abe Shinzo succeeds Koizumi Junichiro as prime minister

2007 Defense Agency is upgraded to full cabinet-ranked Ministry of Defense

2009 The Diet passes the Anti-Piracy Measures law

The DPJ wins the general election

2011 A magnitude-9 earthquake hits northeastern Japan, unleashing a fierce tsunami

2012 The DPJ Noda administration declares nationalization of the Senkaku/Diaoyu islands

The LDP wins the general election and regains control of the government

Abe Shinzo returns as prime minister

2013 National Security Council is created to centralize security policy making

2014 The Abe cabinet overturns previous interpretations of Article 9 and decides that collective self-defense is permissible under some circumstances

2015 The Diet passes security legislation to expand the role of SDF abroad

Guidelines for Japan-U.S. Defense Cooperation are developed

2017 Japan signs the Comprehensive Progressive Trans-Pacific Partnership with other 10 members

2018 Japan and European Union sign the Japan-EU Economic Partnership Agreement

Korea: TIMELINE OF MAJOR EVENTS SINCE 1945

1900

1945 End of Japanese colonialism and the creation of a divided Korea at the 38th parallel by the United States and Soviet Union

The United States announces the creation of the U.S. Army Military Government in Korea

1947 South Korean Interim Government is established

1948 First general elections are held in South Korea in May

National Assembly adopts the new constitution and elects Syngman Rhee as president in July

The Republic of Korea (ROK) is formally established in August

The Democratic People's Republic of Korea (DPRK) is created in September, with Kim Il-sung as premier

1949 The United States withdraws troops from ROK

ROK implements land reforms

1950 DPRK forces cross the 38th parallel and invade ROK

1952 Syngman Rhee wins direct presidential election

1953 Korean armistice is signed to temporarily cease the military conflict of the Korean War

ROK and United States sign the Mutual Defense Treaty

1955 Kim Il-sung proclaims the *juche* ideology

1960 Syngman Rhee resigns after student "April Revolution"; First Republic ends

ROC Constitution is amended in June to established a parliamentary cabinet system, inaugurating Second Republic

1961 General Park Chung-hee launches a coup and establishes the Supreme Council for National Reconstruction

1962 ROK announces the First Five-Year Economic Development Plan (1962–1966)

A new constitution is drafted and approved in December

1963 Park Chung-hee is elected as president, inaugurating Third Republic

1965 ROK and Japan sign the Treaty on Basic Relations and establish formal diplomatic relations

1969 Constitutional amendment to abolish two-term limit is ratified by national referendum

1972 ROK and DPRK in July issue a joint statement to reaffirm the basic principles of reunification

Park Chung-hee proposes the *Yushin* Constitution and is elected president in December, ending Third Republic

DPRK promulgates a new constitution in December and elects Kim Il-sung president

1979 Park Chung-hee is killed in October by the chief of the Korean Central Intelligence Agency

General Chun Doo-hwan controls the ROK armed forces in December

1980 Street demonstrations by students and residents in Kwangju are suppressed by ROK armed forces in May

Chun Doo-hwan is elected president in August

New constitution is approved by national referendum in October, inaugurating Fifth Republic

1983 DPRK agents detonate bomb in Rangoon, Burma, killing 17 ROK senior officials

1987 New constitution of Sixth Republic is approved by national referendum in October

Roh Tae-woo is elected president in December

1988 Seoul Olympics

1990 ROK and Soviet Union establish diplomatic relations

1991 ROK and DPRK are admitted to the United Nations in September

ROK and DPRK adopt the Basic Agreement in December, reaffirming the principle of peaceful reunification

1992 ROK and China establish diplomatic relations in August

Kim Young-sam wins ROK presidential election in December

1993 DPRK announces intention to withdraw from Nuclear Nonproliferation Treaty

1994 DPRK leader Kim Il-sung dies in July

United States and DPRK adopt the Agreed Framework in October to freeze DPRK's nuclear activity

1996 ROK becomes a member of the Organisation for Economic Co-operation and Development (OECD)

1997 Kim Jong-il becomes general secretary of Korean Workers Party in DPRK in October

ROK receives bailout loans from International Monetary Fund amid the Asian Financial Crisis

Kim Dae-jung is elected ROK president in December

1998 DPRK test-fires an intermediate-range ballistic missile

2000

2000 Kim Dae-jung and Kim Jong-il meet in Pyongyang for North-South summit

2002 Roh Moo-hyun is elected president

2003 DPRK declares the Agreed Framework null and void

Six-party talks begin

2006 DPRK conducts multiple missile tests and announces successful completion of its first nuclear test, resulting in UN sanctions

2007 Roh Moo-hyun and Kim Jong-il hold summit in Pyongyang in October

Lee Myung-bak is elected ROK president in December

2009 DPRK withdraws from six-party talks, test-fires a three-stage long-range rocket, and completes its second nuclear test, resulting in more UN sanctions

2010 United States and ROK conclude free-trade agreement

2011 Kim Jong-il dies and is succeeded by Kim Jong-un

2012 Park Geun-hye is elected ROK's first woman president

2016 ROK National Assembly impeaches Park Geun-hye

2017 ROK Constitutional Court upholds Park Geun-hye's impeachment in March

Moon Jae-in is elected ROK president in a special election in May

2018 Moon Jae-in and Kim Jong-un meet in April at Panmunjom for the third North-South summit

U.S. President Donald Trump meets Kim Jong-un in June in Singapore summit

2019 U.S. President Donald Trump meets Kim Jong-un in February in Vietnam and in July in Panmunjom

Bibliography

Abegglen, James C., and George Stalk. 1985. *Kaisha, the Japanese Corporation.* New York, NY: Basic Books.

Ahn, Sang-Hoon, and Sophia Seung-yoon Lee. 2012. "Explaining Korean Welfare State Development with New Empirical Data and Methods." *Asian Social Work and Policy Review* 6 (2): 67–85.

Akamatsu, Kaname. 1962. "A Historical Pattern of Economic Growth in Developing Countries." *The Developing Economies* 1 (1): 3–25.

Amsden, Alice H. 1989. *Asia's Next Giant: South Korea and Late Industrialization.* New York, NY and Oxford, UK: Oxford University Press.

Ang, Yuen Yuen. 2012. "Counting Cadres: A Comparative View of the Size of China's Public Employment." *The China Quarterly* 211: 676–696.

Arase, David. 2009. "Japan in 2008: A Prelude to Change?" *Asian Survey* 49 (1): 107–119.

Argy, Victor, and Leslie Stein. 1993. *Strategic Capitalism: Private Business and Public Purpose in Japanese Industrial Finance.* Princeton, NJ: Princeton University Press.

Argy, Victor, and Leslie Stein. 1997. *The Japanese Economy.* New York, NY: New York Unviersity Press.

Atanassova-Cornelis, Elana. 2012. "Chinese Nation Building and Foreign Policy: Japan and the US as the Significant 'Others' in National Identity Construction." *East Asia* 29: 95–108.

Avenell, Simon A. 2009. "Civil Society and the New Civic Movements in Contemporary Japan: Convergence, Collaboration, and Transformation." *Journal of Japanese Studies* 35 (2): 247–283.

Bae, Jong-Yun. 2010. "South Korean Strategic Thinking toward North Korea: The Evolution of the Engagement Policy and Its Impact upon U.S.-ROK Relations." *Asian Survey* 50 (2): 335–355.

Balassa, Bella. 1982. "Development Strategies and Economic Performance." In *Development Strategies in Semi-Industrial Economies,* edited by Bela Balissa, 38–62. Baltimore, MD: Johns Hopkins University Press for World Bank.

Balassa, Bella. 1988. "The Lessons of East Asian Development: An Overview." *Economic Development and Cultural Change* 36 (3) (April, 1988 Supplement): S273-S290.

Barnett, Doak. 1974. *Uncertain Passage.* Washington, DC: Brookings Institution.

Beeson, Mark. 2018. "Geoeconomics with Chinese Characteristics: the BRI and China's Evolving Grand Strategy." *Economic and Political Studies* 6 (3): 240–256.

Berger, Thomas U. 1998. *Cultures of Antimilitarism: National Security in Germany and Japan*. Baltimore, MD: Johns Hopkins University Press.

Bestor, Victoria Lyon. 1999. "Reimaging Civil Society in Japan." *Washington-Japan Journal*: 1–10.

Burns, John P. 1993. "China's Administrative Reforms for a Market Economy." *Public Administration and Development* 13 (4): 345–360.

Burns, John P. 2003. "'Downsizing' the Chinese State: Government Retrenchment in the 1990s." *China Quarterly* 175: 775–802.

Burns, John P. 2004. "Governance and Civil Service Reform." In *Governance in China*, edited by Jude Howell, 37–57. Lanham, MD: Rowman & Littlefield.

Bush, Richard C. 2010. *The Perils of Proximity: China-Japan Security Relations*. Washington, DC: Brookings Institution Press.

Cabestan, Jean-Pierre. 2009. "China's Foreign- and Security-policy Decision-making Processes under Hu Jintao." *Journal of Current Chinese Affairs* 38 (3): 63–97.

Calder, Kent E. 1988. *Crisis and Compensation: Public Policy and Political Stability in Japan, 1949–1986*. Princeton, NJ: Princeton University Press.

Callick, Rowan. 2007. "The China Model: How Long Can Economic Freedom and Political Repression Coexist?" *AEI*. http://www.aei.org/publication/the-china-model.

Campos, Jose Edgardo, and Hilton L. Root. 1996. *The Key to the Asian Miracle: Making Shared Growth Credible*. Washington, DC: Brookings Institution.

Campos, Nauro F., and Yuko Kinoshita. 2003. *Why Does FDI Go Where It Goes? New Evidence From the Transition Economies*. Working Paper. Washington DC: International Monetary Fund.

Chan, Alfred L. 2001. *Mao's Crusade: Politics and Policy Implementation in China's Great Leap Forward*. Oxford, UK: Oxford University Press.

Chang, Ching. 2018. "The Chinese Military in National Security Policy-making." *Contemporary Chinese Political Economy and Strategic Relations: An International Journal* 4 (3): 1151–1176.

Chen, Jian. 2001. *Mao's China and the Cold War*. Chapel Hill, NC: University of North Carolina Press.

Chen, Ye, Hongbin Li, and Li-An Zhou. 2005. "Relative Performance Evaluation and the Turnover of Provincial Leaders in China." *Economics Letters* 88 (3): 421–425.

Cheng, Tun-jen, and Lawrence B. Krause. 1991. "Democracy and Development: With Special Attention to Korea." *Journal of Northeast Asian Studies* 10 (2): 3–25.

Cheng, Tun-jen, Stephan Haggard, and David Kang. 1998. "Institutions and Growth in Korea and Taiwan: The Bureaucracy." *The Journal of Development Studies* 34 (6): 87–111.

Chiang, Ting-wei. 2018. "Chinese State-Owned Enterprises and WTO's Anti-Subsidy Regime." *Georgetown Journal of International Law* 49 (2): 845–886.

China Power Team. 2017. "Does China Have An Aging Problem?" *China Power*. https://chinapower.csis.org/aging-problem.

Cho, Dae-Yop. 2006. "Korean Citizens' Movement Organizations: Their Ideologies, Resources, and Action Repertoires." *Korea Journal* 46 (2): 68–98.

Choi, Jang Jip.1993. "Political Cleavages in South Korea." In *State and Society in Contemporary Korea*, edited by Hagen Koo, 13–50. Ithaca, NY: Cornell University Press.

Choi, Jang Jip. 2000. "Democratization, Civil Society, and the Civil Social Movement in Korea: The Significance of the Citizens' Alliance for the 2000 General Elections." *Korea Journal* 40 (3): 26–57.

Christensen, Ray. 1998. "The Effect of Electoral Reforms on Campaign Practices in Japan: Putting New Wine into Old Bottles." *Asian Survey* 38: 986–1004.

Christensen, Ray, and Paul E. Johnson. 1995. "Toward a Context-Rich Analysis of Electoral Systems: The Japanese Example." *American Journal of Political Science* 39 (3): 575–598.

Collins, Susan M., and Won-Am Park. 1988. *External Debt and Macroeconomic Performance in South Korea*. Working Paper Series. Cambridge, MA: National Bureau of Economic Research. http://www.nber.org/papers/w2596.

Connell, Sean. 2013. *Building a Creative Economy in South Korea: Analyzing the Plans and Possibilities for New Economic Growth*. Academic Paper Series. Washington, DC: Korea Economic Institute of America.

Croissant, Aurel. 2002."Strong Presidents, Weak Democracy? Presidents, Parliaments and Political Parties in South Korea." *Korea Observer* 33 (1): 1–45.

Croissant, Aurel, and Philip Volkel. 2012. "Party System Types and Party System Institutionalization: Comparing New Democracies in East and Southeast Asia." *Party Politics* 18 (2): 235–265.

Curtis, Gerald L. 1971. *Campaigning, Japanese Style*. New York, NY: Columbia University Press.

Davis, Elizabeth Van Wie. 2008. "Uyghur Muslim Ethnic Separatism in Xinjiang, China." *Asian Affairs* 35 (1): 15–29.

Deng, Kent. 2014. "A Survey of Recent Research in Chinese Economic History." *Journal of Economic Surveys* 28 (4): 600–616.

Deyo, Fred, ed. 1987. *The Political Economy of the New Asian Industrialism*. Ithaca, NY: Cornell University Press.

Dittmer, Lowell. 2003. "Leadership Change and Chinese Political Development." *The China Quarterly* 176: 903–925.

Doyle, Michael W. 1986. "Liberalism and World Politics." *American Political Science Review* 80 (4): 1151–1169.

Dreyer, June Teufel. 2014. "China and Japan: 'Hot Economics, Cold Politics'." Orbis 58 (3): 326–41.

Eisenstadt, Shmuel Noah, ed. 1967. *The Decline of Empires*. Englewood Cliffs, NJ: Prentice Hall.

Fewsmith, Joseph. 2013. "Debating Constitutional Government." *China Leadership Monitor*, Hoover Institution, Stanford. http://www.hoover.org/sites/default/files/uploads/documents/CLM42JF.pdf.

Frolic, B. Michael. 1997. "State-led Civil Society." In *Civil Society in China*, edited by Timothy Brook and B. Michael Frolic, 46–67. New York, NY: M. E. Sharpe.

Gao, Bai. 2001. *Japan's Economic Dilemma: The Institutional Origins of Prosperity and Stagnation*. New York, NY: Cambridge University Press.

Garver, John W. 2002. "The Security Dilemma in Sino-Indian Relations." *India Review* 1 (4): 1–38.

Gerschenkron, Alexander. 1962. *Economic Backwardness in Historial Perspective: A Book of Essays*. Cambridge, MA: Belknap Press of Harvard University Press.

Glosserman, Brad, and Scott Snyder. 2015. *The Japan-South Korea Identity Clash: East Asian Security and the United States*. New York, NY: Columbia University Press.

Gold, Thomas. 1986. *State and Society in the Taiwan Miracle*. New York, NY: M.E. Sharpe.

Grasso, June, Jay Corrin, and Michael Kort. 1991. *Modernization and Revolution in China*. Armonk, NY: M. E. Sharpe.

Haggard, Stephan. 1990. *Pathways from the Periphery: The Politics of Growth in the Newly Industrializing Countries*. Ithaca, NY: Cornell University Press.

Haggard, Stephan, Byung-kook Kim, and Chung-in Moon. 1991. "The Transition to Export-led Growth in South Korea: 1954–1966." *The Journal of Asian Studies* 50 (4): 850–873.

Haggard, Stephan, and Chung-in Moon. 1990. "Institutions and Economic Policy: Theory and a Korean Case Study." *World Politics* 42 (2): 210–237.

Haggard, Stephan, and Chung-in Moon. 1993. "The State, Politics, and Economic Development in Postwar South Korea." In *State and Society in Contemporary Korea*, edited by Hagen Koo, 51–93. Ithaca, NY: Cornell Unviersity Press.

Haggard, Stephan, and Marcus Noland. 2011. *Engaging North Korea: The Role of Economic Statecraft. Policy Studies*. Honolulu, HI: East-West Center.

Hahm, Sung Deuk, Kwangho Jung, and Sam Youl Lee. 2013. "Exploring the Determinants of the Entry and Exit of Ministers in Korea: 1980–2008." *Governance* 26 (4): 657–675.

Hamada, Koichi. 1988. "The Incentive Structure of a 'Managed Market Economy': Can it Survive the Millennium?" *AEA Papers and Proceedings* 88 (2): 417–421.

Hamada, Koichi, and Yasushi Okada. 2009. "Monetary and International Factors behind Japan's Lost Decade." *Journal of the Japanese and International Economies* 23 (2): 200–219.

Hamm, Taik-Young. 1999. *Arming the Two Koreas: State, Capital and Military Power*. New York, NY: Routledge.

Hao, Yufan, and Zhihai Zhai. 1990. "China's Decision to Enter the Korean War: History Revisited." *China Quarterly* 121: 94–115.

Harding, Harry. 1981. *Organizing China*. Stanford, CA: Stanford University Press.

He, Baogang. 1997. *The Democratic Implications of Civil Society in China*. New York, NY: Palgrave Macmillan.

Hellmann, Olli. 2014. "Party System Institutionalization Without Parties: Evidence from Korea." *Journal of East Asian Studies* 14 (1): 53–84.

Higuchi, Yoshio. 2008. "Circumstances behind Growing Regional Disparities in Employment." *Japan Labor Review* 5 (1): 5–35.

Hirano, Shigeo. 2006. "Electoral Institutions, Hometowns, and Favored Minorities: Evidence from Japanese Electoral Reforms." *World Politics* 59 (1): 51–82.

Hirata, Keiko. 2008."Who Shapes the National Security Debate? Divergent Interpretations of Japan's Security Role." *Asian Affairs, 35* (3): 123–151.

Holslag, Jonathan. 2009. "The Persistent Military Security Dilemma between China and India." *Strategic Studies* 32 (6): 811–840.

Horioka, Charles Yuji. 2008. "The Flow of Household Funds in Japan." *Public Policy Review* 4 (1): 37–52.

Horsley, Jamie. 2010. "The Rule of Law: Pushing the Limits of Party Rule." In *China Today, China Tomorrow: Domestic Politics, Economy, and Society*, edited by Joseph Fewsmith, 51–68. Lanham, MD: Rowman & Littlefield.

Horsley, William, and Roger Buckley. 1990. *Nippon: New Superpower: Japan since 1945*. London, UK: BBC Books.

Hoshi, Takeo, Anil Kashyap, and David Scharfstein. 1991. "Corporate Structure, Liquidity, and Investment: Evidence from Japanese Industrial Groups." *Quarterly Journal of Economics* 106 (1): 33–60.

Howell, Jude. 2007. "Civil Society in China: Chipping Away at the Edges." *Development* 50 (3): 17–23.

Hrebenar, Ronald J., and Mayumi Itoh. 2015. "Japan's Changing Party System." In *Party Politics in Japan: Political Chaos and Stalemate in the Twenty-first Century*, 1–21. New York, NY: Routledge.

Hsu, Jing-Yun, and Jenn-Jaw Soong. 2014."Development of China-Russia Relations (1949–2011)." *The Chinese Economy* 47 (3): 70–87.

Hu, Weixing. 2016. "Xi Jinping's 'Big Power Diplomacy' and China's Central National Security Comission." *Journal of Contemporary China* 25 (98): 163–177.

Huang, Yasheng. 2008. *Capitalism with Chinese Characteristics: Enterpreneurship and the State*. New York, NY: Cambridge University Press.

Huang, Yasheng. 2011. "Rethinking the Beijing Consensus." *Asia Policy* 11: 1–26.

Hughes, Christopher W. 2004. *Japan's Security Agenda: Military, Economic, and Environmental Dimensions*. Boulder, CO: Lynne Rienner.

Hughes, Christopher W. 2009. "'Super-Sizing' the DPRK Threat: Japan's Evolving Military Posture and North Kora." *Asian Survey* 49 (2): 291–311.

Hughes, Christopher W. 2017. "Japan's Grand Strategic Shift: From the Yoshida Doctrine to an Abe Doctrine?" In *Strategic Asia 2017–18: Power, Ideas, and Military Strategy,* edited by Ashley J. Tellis, Alison Szalwinski, and Michael Wills, 73–105. Washington, DC.: National Bureau of Asian Research.

Hughes, Helen. 1980. "Achievements and Objectives of Industrialization." In *Policies for Industrial Progress in Developing Countries,* edited by John Cody, Helen Hughes, and David Wall, 11–37. New York, NY: Oxford University Press.

Huntington, Samuel P. 1991. *The Third Wave: Democratization in the Late Twentieth Century.* Norman, OK: University of Oklahoma Press.

Hutton, Will. 2006. *The Writing on the Wall: Why We Must Embrace China as a Partner or Face It as an Enemy.* New York, NY: Free Press.

Hwang, Gyu-Jin. 2012. "Explaining Welfare State Adaptation in East Asia: The Case of Japan, Korea and Taiwan." *Asian Journal of Social Science* 40 (2): 174–202.

Im, Hyug Baeg. 2004. "Faltering Democratic Consolidation in South Korea: Democracy at the End of the 'Three Kims' Era." *Democratization* 11 (5): 179–198.

Izumikawa, Yasuhiro. 2010. "Explaining Japanese Antimilitarism: Normative and Realist Constraints on Japan's Security Policy." *International Security* 35 (2): 123–160.

Jakobson, Linda. 2004. "Local Goverance: Village and Township Direct Elections." In *Governance in China,* edited by Jude Howell, 97–120. Lanham, MD: Rowman & Littlefield.

Jang, Jiho, and Doh Chull Shin. 2008. "Democratizing Economic Policymaking in South Korea: Painfully Slow Progress toward an Executive-Legislative Balance of Power." *International Review of Public Administration* 13 (1): 59–71.

Johnson, Chalmers. 1982. *MITI and the Japanese Miracle: The Growth of Industrial Policy, 1925–1975.* Stanford, CA: Stanford University Press.

Johnson, Chalmers. 1986. "Reflections on the Dilemma of Japanese Defense". *Asian Survey* 26 (5): 557–72.

Johnson, Chalmers. 1987. "Political Institutions and Economic Performance: The Government-Business Relationship in Japan, South Korea and Taiwan." In *The Political Economy of the New Asian Industrialism,* edited by Fred Deyo, 136–164. Ithaca, NY: Cornell University Press.

Johnson, Chalmers. 1995. *Japan: Who Governs? The Rise of the Developmental State.* New York, NY: W. W. Norton.

Jones, Randall S., and Shingo Kimura. 2013. *Reforming Agriculture and Promoting Japan's Integration in the World Economy.* OECD Economics Department Working Papers, OECD. doi:10.1787/5k46957lorf4-en.

Kang, David C. 2002. *Crony Capitalism: Corruption and Development in South Korea and the Philippines.* Cambridge, UK: Cambridge University Press.

Kang, Xiaoguang, and Heng Han. 2008. "Graduated Controls: The State-Society Relationship in Contemporary China." *Modern China* 34 (1): 36–55.

Kaplan, Eugene J. 1972. *Japan: the Government-Business Relationship.* Washington, DC: U.S. Department of Commerce.

Katzenstein, Peter J. 1996. *Cultural Norms and National Security: Police and Military in Postwar Japan.* Ithaca, NY: Cornell University Press.

Katzenstein, Peter J. 2008. *Rethinking Japanese Security: Internal and External Dimensions.* New York, NY: Routledge.

Kawashima, Shin. 2015. "Postwar Japan-China Relations: A Consideration from the Perspective of Reconciliation." *Asia-Pacific Review* 22 (2): 28–43.

Keddell, Joseph P., Jr. 1993. *The Politics of Defense in Japan: Managing Internal and External Pressures*. New York, NY: M. E. Sharpe.

Kennedy, John J., Scott Rozelle, and Yaojiang Shi. 2004. "Elected Leaders and Collective Land: Farmers' Evaluation of Village Leaders' Performance in Rural China." *Journal of Chinese Political Science* 9 (1): 1–22.

Kim, Bomi. 2016. "North Korea's Siege Mentality: A Sociopolitical Analysis of the Kim Jong-un Regime's Foreign Policies." *Asian Perspectives* 40 (2): 223–244.

Kim, Jinwung. 1989. "Recent Anti-Americanism in South Korea: The Causes." *Asian Survey* 29 (8): 749–763.

Kim, Jinwung. 2012. *A History of Korea: From "Land of the Morning Calm" to States in Conflict*. Bloomington, IN: Indiana University Press.

Kim, Ji Young. 2015. "Dismantling the Final Barrier: Transforming Japan into a 'Normal Country' in the Post-Cold-War Era." *Pacific Focus* 30 (2), 223–248.

Kim, Ki-Joo. 2014. "The Soldier and the State in South Korea: Crafting Democratic Civilian Control of the Military." *Journal of International and Area Studies* 21 (2): 119–131.

Kim, Soon-yang. 2008. "The East Asian Developmental State and Its Economic and Social Policies: The Case of Korea." *International Review of Public Administration* 12 (2): 69–87.

Kim, Sung Chull. 2017. *Partnership Within Hierarchy: The Evolving East Asian Security Triangle*. Albany, NY: SUNY Press.

Kim, Sung Chull, and Michael D. Cohen. 2017. *North Korea and Nuclear Weapons: Entering the New Era of Deterrence*. Washington, DC: Georgetown University Press.

Kim, Sunhyuk, Chonghee Han, and Jiho Jang. 2008. "State-Society Relations in South Korea after Democratization: Is the Strong State Defunct?" *Pacific Focus* 23 (2): 252–270.

Kim, Tongfi. 2016. *The Supply Side of Security: A Market Theory of Military Alliances*. Stanford, CA: Stanford University Press.

King, Gary, Jennifer Pan, and Margaret E. Roberts. 2013. "How Censorship in China Allows Government Criticism but Silences Collective Expression." *American Political Science Review* 107 (2): 326–343.

Kingston, Jeff. 2013. *Contemporary Japan: History, Politics, and Social Change since the 1980s*. Second Edition. Maden, MA: Wiley-Blackwell.

Koh, Byung Chul. 2001. "The Foreign and Unification Policies of the Republic of Korea." In *Understanding Korean Politics: An Introduction*, edited by Soong Hoom Kil and Chung-in Moon, 231–268. Albany, NY: SUNY Press.

Koo, Bohn Young. 1985. "The Role of Direct Foreign Investment in Korea's Recent Economic Growth." In *Foreign Trade and Investment: Economic Growth in the Newly Industrializing Asian Countries*, edited by Walter Galenson, 176–216. Madison, WI: University of Wisconsin Press.

Koo, Hagen. 1984. "The Political Economy of Income Distribution in South Korea: The Impact of the State's Industrialization Policies." *World Development* 12 (10): 1029–1037.

Koo, Hagen. 1993. "The State, Minjung, and the Working Class in South Korea." In *State and Society in Contemporary Korea*, edited by Hagen Koo, 131–162. Ithaca, NY: Cornell University Press.

Koo, Richard C. 2009. *The Holy Grail of Macroeconomics: Lessons from Japan's Great Recession*. Singapore: John Wiley and Sons (Asia).

Krauss, Ellis S., and Robert Pekkanen. 2008. "Reforming the Liberal Democratic Party." In *Democratic Reform in Japan: Assessing the Impact*, edited by Sherry L. Martin and Gill Steel, 11–37. Boulder, CO: Lynne Rienner.

Kristensen, Hans M. and Robert S. Norris. 2017. "A History of US Nuclear Weapons in South Korea." *Bulletin of the Atomic Scientists* 73 (6): 349–357.

Kuehn, David. 2016. *Institutionalising Civilian Control of the Military in New Democracies: Theory and Evidence from South Korea*. GIGA Working Papers. Hamburg: German Institute of Global and Area Studies.

Kuznets, Simon. 1966. *Modern Economic Growth: Rate, Structure, and Spread*. New Haven, CT: Yale University Press.

Kwon, Huck-ju. 2005. "Transforming the Developmental Welfare State in East Asia." *Development and Change* 36 (3): 477–497.

Lam, Peng Er. 2017. "China and Japan: A Clash of Two 'Anti-Status Quo' Powers?" *China: An International Journal*, 15 (1): 83–97.

Lampton, David M. 2015. "Xi Jinping and the National Security Commission: Policy Coordination and Political Power." *Journal of Contemporary China* 24 (95): 759–777.

Lee, Jong-Wha. 1996. "Government Interventions and Productivity Growth." *Journal of Economic Growth* 1 (3): 391–414.

Lee, Keun, and Chung H. Lee. 1992. "Sustaining Economic Development in South Korea: Lessons from Japan." *The Pacific Review* 5 (1): 13–24.

Lee, Yoonkyung. 2014. "Diverging Patterns of Democratic Representation in Korea and Taiwan: Political Parties and Social Movements." *Asian Survey* 5 (3): 419–444.

Li, Cheng. 1996. "The Local Factor in China's Intra-Party Democracy." In *Democratization in China, Korea and Southeast Asia? Local and National Perspectives*, edited by Kate Xiao Zhou, Shelley Rigger, and Lynn T. White III, 87–109. New York, NY: Routledge.

Li, Cheng. 2013. *A Biographical and Factional Analysis of the Post-2012 Politburo*. China Leadership Monitor, No. 41, Hoover Institution. Stanford, CA: Stanford University. http://www.hoover.org/publications/china-leadership-monitor/article/148836.

Li, David D. 1996. "A Theory of Ambiguous Property Rights in Transition Economies." *Journal of Comparative Economics* 23 (1): 1–19.

Li, Hongbin, and Li-An Zhou. 2005. "Political Turnover and Economic Performance: The Incentive Role of Personnel Control in China." *Journal of Public Economics* 89 (9–10): 1743–1762.

Li, Wei, and Dennis Tao Yang. 2005. "The Great Leap Forward: Anatomy of a Central Palnning Disaster." *Journal of Political Economy* 113 (4): 840–877.

Liang, Xiaodon. 2018. "The Six-Party Talks at a Glance." *Arms Control Association* (June 21). https://www.armscontrol.org/factsheets/6partytalks.

Lieberthal, Kenneth. 1995. *Governing China: From Revolution through Reform.* New York, NY: W. W. Norton.

Lieberthal, Kenneth, and Michael Oksenberg. 1988. *Policy Making in China: Leaders, Structure, and Processes.* Princeton, NJ: Princeton University Press.

Liff, Adam P. 2015. "Japan's Defense Policy: Abe the Evolutionary." *Washington Quarterly* 38 (2): 79–99.

Liff, Adam P. 2017. "Policy by Other Means: Collective Self-Defense and the Politics of Japan's Postwar Constitutional Reinterpretations." *Asia Policy* 24: 139–172.

Lin, Justin Yifu. 1992. "Rural Reforms and Agricultural Growth in China." *American Economic Review* 82 (1): 34–51.

Lin, Justin Yifu. 2013. "Demystifying the Chinese Economy." *The Australian Economic Review* 46 (3): 259–268.

Lincoln, Edward J. 2001. *Arthritic Japan: The Slow Pace of Economic Reform.* Washington, DC: Brookings Institution Press.

Lipset, Seymour M., and Stein Rokkan, eds. 1967. *Party Systems and Voter Alignments: Cross-National Perspectives.* New York, NY: Free Press.

Little, Ian M. D. 1982. *Economic Development: Theory, Policy, and International Relations.* New York, NY: Basic Books.

Liu, Yawei. 2010. "Local Elections: The Elusive Quest for Choice." In *China Today, China Tomorrow: Domestic Politics, Economy, and Society,* edited by Joseph Fewsmith, 165–179. Lanham, MD: Rowman & Littlefield.

Llewelyn, James. 2010. *Japan's Evolving Notion of National Security.* New York, NY: Nova Science.

Lu, Xiaobo. 2014. "Does Changing Economic Well-Being Shape Resentment about Inequality in China?" *Studies in Comparative International Development* 49 (3): 300–320.

MacFarquhar, Roderick. 1974. *The Origins of the Cultural Revolution, Volume 1: Contradictions among the People, 1956–1957.* New York, NY: Columbia University Press.

Maddison, Angus. 2001. *The World Economy: The Millennial Perspective.* Paris, France: Organisation for Economic Co-operation and Development.

Malik, Mohan. 2012. "China and India Today." *World Affairs* 175 (2): 74–84.

Manion, Melanie. 2006. "Democracy, Community, Trust: The Impact of Elections in Rural China." *Comparative Political Studies* 39 (3): 301–324.

Martinez-Bravo, Monica, Gerard Padró i Miquel, Nancy Qian, and Yang Yao. 2011. "Do Local Elections in Non-Democracies Increase Accountability? Evidence from Rural China." *National Bureau of Economic Research Working Paper Series.*

Maskin, Eric, Yingyi Qian, and Chenggang Xu. 2000. "Incentives, Information, and Organizational Form." *Review of Economic Studies* 67 (2): 359–378.

Matray, James I. 2012. "Irreconcilable Differences? Realism and Idealism in Cold War Korean-American Relations." *Journal of American-East Asian Relations* 19 (1): 1–26.

Maxfield, Sylvia, and Ben Ross Schneider. 1997. *Business and the State in Developing Countries*. New York, NY: Cornell University Press.

McMillan, John, John Whalley, and Lijing Zhu. 1989. "The Impact of China's Economic Reforms on Agricultural Productivity Growth." *Journal of Political Economy* 97 (4): 781–807.

Medeiros, Evan S. 2009. *China's International Behavior: Activism, Opportunism, and Diversification*. Santa Monica, CA: Rand Corporation.

Miller, Alice L. 2018. "The 19th Central Committee Politburo." *China Leadership Monitor* (January 23). https://www.hoover.org/research/19th-central-committee-politburo.

Minami, Ryoshin. 1986. *The Economic Development of Japan: A Qantitative Study*. New York, NY: St. Martin's Press.

Minns, John. 2001. "Of Miracles and Models: the Rise and Decline of the Developmental State in South Korea." *Third World Quarterly* 22 (6): 1025–1043.

Mo, Jongryn, and Barry R. Weingast. 2013. *Korean Political and Economic Development: Crisis, Security, and Institutional Rebalancing*. Cambridge, MA: Harvard University Asia Center.

Mochizuki, Mike M. 1983–1984. "Japan's Search for Strategy." *International Security* 8 (3): 152–179.

Moon, Chung-in, and In Taek Hyun. 1992. "Muddling through Security, Growth and Welfare: The Political Economy of Defense Spending in South Korea." In *Defense, Welfare and Growth*, edited by Steve Chan and Alex Mintz, 137–162. London, UK: Routledge.

Moon, Chung-in, and Sunghack Lim. 2001. "The Politics of Economic Rise and Decline in South Korea." In *Understanding Korean Politics: An Introduction*, edited by Soong Hoom Kil and Chung-in Moon, 201–230. Albany, NY: SUNY Press.

Moon, Chung-in, and Sunghack Lim. 2014. *Industry and Technology Policies in Korea*. OECD. doi:10.1787/9789264213227-en.

Moon, Myung-jae, and Patricia Ingraham. 1998. "Shaping Administrative Reform and Governance: An Examination of the Political Nexus Triads in Three Asian Countries." *Governance* 11 (1): 77–100.

Moon, Seungsook. 2010. "The Interplay between the State, the Market, and Culture in Shaping Civil Society: A Case Study of the People's Solidarity for Participatory Democracy in South Korea." *The Journal of Asian Studies* 69 (2): 479–505.

Morrison, Wayne M. 2018. *China-U.S. Trade Issues*. Washington DC: Congressional Research Service.

Nakamura, Akira, and Ronald J. Hrebenar. 2015. "The Liberal Democratic Party: The Persistent Ruling Party of Japan." In *Party Politics in Japan: Political Chaos and Stalemate in the Twenty-first Century*, edited by Ronald J. Hrebenar and Akira Nakamura, 118–147. New York, NY: Routledge.

Nakanishi, Hiroshi. 2015. "Reorienting Japan? Security Transformation under the Second Abe Cabinet." *Asian Perspective* 39 (3): 405–421.

Nathan, Andrew J., and Andrew Scobell. 2012 *China's Search for Security*. New York, NY: Columbia University Press.

Nathan, Andrew J., and Andrew Scobell. 2016. "Globalization as a Security Strategy: Power and Vulnerability in the "China Model." *Political Science Quarterly* 131 (2): 313–339.

Naughton, Barry. 2007. *The Chinese Economy: Transitions and Growth*. Cambridge, MA: MIT Press.

Noble, Gregory W. 2013. "Koizumi's Complementary Coalition for (Mostly) Neoliberal Reform in Japan." In *Syncretism: The Politics of Economic Restructuring and System Reform in Japan*, edited by Kenji E. Kushida, Kay Shimizu, and Jean C. Oi, 115–145. Stanford, CT: Walter H. Shorenstein Asia-Pacific Research Center.

Noesselt, Nele. 2014. "Microblogs and the Adaptation of the Chinese Party-State's Governance Strategy." *Governance* 27 (3): 449–468.

Nolan, Marcus. 2007. "From Industrial Policy to Innovation Policy: Japan's Pursuit of Competitive Advantage." *Asian Economic Policy Review* 2 (2): 251–268.

Nolan, Peter. 2014. "Globilization and Industrial Policy: The Case of China." *The World Economy* 37 (6): 747–764.

O'Brien, Kevin J., and Rongbin Han. 2009. "Path to Democracy? Assessing Village Elections in China." *Journal of Contemporary China* 18 (60): 359–378.

OECD. 2009. "OECD Rural Policy Reviews: China." Paris, France: OECD. doi:10.1787/9789264059573-en.

OECD. 2010. *OECD Economic Survey of China*. Paris, France: OECD.

OECD. 2017a. *A Decade of Social Protection Development in Selected Asian Countries*. Paris, France: OECD. doi:http://dx.doi.org/10.1787/9789264272262-en.

OECD. 2017b. *OECD Economic Surveys: China 2017*. Paris, France: OECD. doi:http://dx.doi.org/10.1787/eco_surveys-chn-2017-en.

OECD. 2018. *OECD Economic Surveys: Korea*. Paris, France: OECD.

Ogawa, Akihiro. 2014. "Civil Society: Past, Presdent, and Future." In *Critical Issues in Contemporary Japan*, edited by Jeff Kingston, 52–63. New York, NY: Routledge.

Oh, Jennifer S. 2012. "Strong State and Strong Civil Society in Contemporary South Korea: Challenges to Democratic Governance." *Asian Survey* 52 (3): 528–549.

Oi, Jean C. 1999. *Rural China Takes Off: Institutional Foundations of Economic Reform*. Berkely, CA: University of California Press.

Okuno-Fujiwara, Masahiro. 1991. "Industrial Policy in Japan: A Political Economy View." In *Trade with Japan: Has the Door Opened Wider?*, edited by Paul Krugman, 271–304. Chicago, IL: University of Chicago Press.

Olson, Mancur. 1971. *The Logic of Collective Action: Public Goods and the Theory of Groups*. Cambridge, MA: Harvard University Press.

Oros, Andrew. 2008. *Normalizing Japan: Politics, Identity, and the Evolution of Security Practice*. Stanford, CA: Stanford University Press.

Panda, Jagannath P. 2013. "Competing Realities in China-India Multilateral Discourse: Asia's Enduring Power Rivalry." *Journal of Contemporary China* 22 (82): 669–690.

Park, Chan Wook. 2002. "Elections in Democratizing Korea." In *How Asia Votes*, edited by John Fuh-sheng Hsieh and David Newman, 118–146. New York, NY: Seven Bridges Press.

Park, Chong-Min, and Doh Chull Shin. 2006. "Do Asian Values Deter Popular Support for Democracy in South Korea?" *Asian Survey* 46 (3): 341–361.

Park, Jae-Jeok. 2011. "A Comparative Case Study of the U.S.-Philippines Alliance in the 1990s and the U.S.-South Korea Alliance bettween 1998 and 2008: Alliance (Dis)Continuation." *Asian Survey* 51 (2): 268–289.

Pearson, Margaret M. 1997. *China's New Business Elite: The Political Consequences of Economic Reform*. Berkeley, CA: University of California Press.

Pekkanen, Robert. 2000. "Japan's New Politics: The Case of the NPO Law." *Journal of Japanese Studies* 26 (1): 111–148.

Pempel, T. J. 1982. *Policy and Politics in Japan: Creative Conservatism*. Philadelphia, PA: Temple University Press.

Pempel, T. J. 1998. *Regime Shift: Comparative Dynamics of the Japanese Political Economy*. Ithaca, NY: Cornell University Press.

Pempel, T. J. 2002. "Labor Exclusion and Privatised Welfare." In *Models of Capitalism*, edited by Evelyne Huber, 277–300. University Park, PA: Pennsylvania State University Press.

Pempel, T. J. 2017. "Japan in 2016: Smooth Sailing despite Occasional Crosswinds." *Asian Survey* 57 (1): 79–92.

Peng, Ito. 2003. "Pushing for Social Care Expansion: Demography, Gender and the New Politics of the Social Welfare State in Japan." *American Asian Review* 21 (2): 25–55.

Przeworski, Adam, and Fernando Limongi. 1993. "Political Regimes and Economic Growth." *Journal of Economic Perspectives* 7 (3): 51–69.

Pyle, Kenneth B. 1982. "The Future of Japanese Nationalism: An Essay in a Contemporary History." *Journal of Japanese Studies* 8 (2): 223–263.

Ramo, Joshua Cooper. 2004. *The Beijing Consensus*. London, UK: Foreign Policy Center.

Ramsayer, Mark, and Frances McCall Rosenbluth. 1993. *Japan's Political Marketplace*. Cambridge, MA: Harvard University Press.

Reed, Steven, and Michael F. Thies. 2000. *The Causes of Electoral Reform in Japan*. Oxford, UK: Oxford University Press.

Reilly, Benjamin. 2007. "Electoral Systems and Party Systems in East Asia." *Journal of East Asian Studies* 7 (2): 185–202.

Reimann, Kim. 2003. "Building Global Civil Society from the Outside In? Japanese International Development NGOs, the State, and International Norms." In *The State of Civil Society in Japan*, edited by Frank J. Schwartz and Susan J. Pharr, 298–315. Cambridge, MA: Cambridge University Press.

Rich, Timothy S. 2014. "Is Duverger's Law Working in South Korea? An Analysis of District-Level Elections 1988–2012." *Asian Journal of Political Science* 22 (2): 164–180.

Ringen Stein, Huck-ju Kwon, Ilcheong Yi, Taekyoon Kim, and Jooha Lee. 2011. *The Korean State and Social Policy: How South Korea Lifted Itself from Poverty and Dictatorship to Affluence and Democracy.* New York, NY: Oxford University Press.

Rodan, Garry. 1989. *The Political Economy of Singapore's Industrialization: National State and International Capital.* New York, NY: St. Martin's Press, 1989.

Rodrik, Dani. 2006. "Goodbye Washington Consensus, Hello Washington Confusion? A Review of the World Bank's Economic Growth in the 1990s: Learning from a Decade of Reform." *Journal of Economic Literature* 44 (4): 973–987.

Roehrig, Terence. 2017. "Stability or Instability? The US Response to North Korean Nuclear Weapons." In *North Korea and Nuclear Weapons: Entering the New Era of Deterrence*, edited by Sung Chull Kim and Michael D. Cohen, 129–155. Washington, DC: Georgetown University Press.

Roy, Denny. 2013. *Return of the Dragon: Rising China and Regional Security.* New York, NY: Columbia University Press.

Ru, Jiang, and Leonard Ortolano. 2008. "Corporatist Control of Environmental Non-governmental Organizations: A State Perspective." In *Embedded Environmentalism: Opportunities and Constraints of a Socialist Movement In China*, by Peter Ho and Richard Louis Edmonds, 44–68. New York, NY: Routledge.

Sachs, Jeffrey D., and Wing Thye Woo. 2000. "Understanding China's Economic Performance." *Journal of Policy Reform* 4 (1): 1–50.

Saich, Tony. 2000. "Negotiating the State: The Development of Social Organizations in China." *China Quarterly* 161: 124–141.

Salditt, Felix, Peter Whiteford, and Willem Adema. 2007. *Pension Reform in China: Progress and Prospects.* OECD Social, Employment and Migration Working Papers. Paris, France: OECD.

Salmenkari, Taru. 2013. "Theoretical Poverty in the Research on Chinese Civil Society." *Modern Asian Studies* 47 (2): 682–711.

Salmenkari, Taru. 2014. "Encounters between Chinese NGOs and the State: Distance, Roles and Voice." *Issues & Studies* 50 (2): 143–177.

Samuels, Richard J. 2004. *Politics, Security Policy, and Japan's Cabinet Legislation Bureau: Who Elected These Guys, Anyway?* Japan Policy Research Institute.

Samuels, Richard J. 2007. *Securing Japan: Tokyo's Grand Strategy and the Future of East Asia.* Ithaca, NY: Cornell University Press.

Satake, Tomohiko. 2016. "The New Guidelines for Japan-U.S. Defense Cooperation and an Expanding Japanese Security Role." *Asian Politics & Policy* 8 (1): 27–38.

Scalapino, Robert, and Junnosuke Masumi. 1962. *Parties and Politics in Contemporary Japan*. Berkeley, CA: University of California Press.

Schaede, Urike. 2001. *Cooperative Capitalism: Self-regulation, Trade Associations, and the Anti-Monopoly Law in Japan*. New York, NY: Oxford University Press.

Schaede, Ulrike. 2004. "What Happened to the Japanese Model?" *Review of International Economics* 12 (2): 277–294.

Schaede, Ulrike. 2008. *Choose and Focus—Japanese Business Strategies for the 21st Century*. Ithaca, NY: Cornell University Press.

Schultz, Theodore W. 1961. "Investment in Human Capital." *American Economic Review* 51 (1): 1–17.

Schulze, Kai. 2018. "Japan's New Assertiveness: Institutional Change and Japan's Securitization of China." *International Relations of the Asia-Pacific* 18 (2): 221–247.

Schurmann, Franz. 1968. *Ideology and Organization in Communist China*. Second edition. Berkeley, CA: University of California Press.

Schwartz, Frank. 1998. *Advice and Consent: The Politics of Consultation in Japan*. New York, NY: Cambridge University Press.

Scobell, Andrew, and Phillip C. Saunders. 2015. *PLA Influence on China's National Security Policymaking*. Stanford, CA: Stanford Unviersity Press.

Seers, Dudley. 1969. "The Meaning of Development." *International Development Review* 11 (4): 3–4.

Seith, M. J. 2011. *A History of Korea: From Antiquity to the Present*. Lanham, MD: Rowman & Littlefield.

Seo, Jungmin, and Sungmoon Kim. 2015. "Civil Society under Authoritarian Rule: Bansanghoe and Extraordinary Everyday-ness in Korean Neighborhoods." *Korea Journal* 55 (1): 59–85.

Shambaugh, David. 2008. *China's Communist Party: Atrophy and Adaptation*. Berkeley: University of California Press, CA.

Sheehan, Spencer. 2017. "China's Struggle with Demographic Change: Will China's Aging Population Bring Down the Economy?" *The Diplomat*. https://thediplomat.com/2017/06/chinas-struggle-with-demographic-change.

Shieh, Shawn. 2009. "Beyond Corporatism and Civil Society: Three Modes of State-NGO Interaction in China." In *State and Society Responses to Social Welfare Needs in China*, edited by Jonathan Schwartz and Shawn Shieh, 22–41. London UK: Routledge.

Shieh, Shawn, and Guosheng Deng. 2011. "An Emerging Civil Society: The Impact of the 2008 Sichuan Earthquake on Grass-roots Associations in China." *China Journal* 65: 181–194.

Shin, Doh Chull. 1999. *Mass Politics and Culture in Democratizing Korea*. Cambridge, UK: Cambridge University Press.

Shinoda, Tomohito. 2013. *Contemporary Japanese Politics: Institutional Changes and Power Shifts*. New York, NY: Columbia University Press.

Snyder, Scott A., and Leaf-Eric Easley. 2014. "South Korea's Foreign Relations and Security Policies." In *The Oxford Handbook of the Interantional Relations of Asia*, edited by Saadia Pekkanen, John Ravenhill, and Rosemary Foot, 446–461. Oxford, UK: Oxford University Press.

Sohn, Yul, and Won-Taek Kang. 2013. "South Korea in 2012: An Election Year under Rebalancing Challenges." *Asian Survey* 54 (1): 198–205.

Sonn, Hochul. 2003. "Regional Cleavage in Korean Politics and Elections." *Korea Journal* 43 (2): 32–54.

Steinberg, David I., ed. 2005. *Korean Attitudes toward the United States: Changing Dynamics*. New York, NY: M. E. Sharpe.

Steinberg, David I., and Myung Shin. 2006."Tensions in South Korean Political Parties in Transition: From Entourage to Ideology?" *Asian Survey* 46 (4): 517–537.

Struver, Georfe. 2017. "China's Partnership Diplomacy: International Alignment Based on Interests or Ideology." *The Chinese Journal of International Politics* 10 (1): 31–65.

Sugimoto, Yoshio. 1997. *An Introduction to Japanese Society*. Cambridge, UK: Cambridge University Press.

Sugita, Yoneyuki. 2016. "The Yoshida Doctrine as a Myth." *The Japanese Journal of American Studies* 27: 123–143.

Sun, Xin. 2014. "Autocrats' Dilemma: The Dual Impacts of Village Elections on Public Opinion in China." *The China Journal* 71: 109–131.

Sun, Ying. 2013. "Independent Candidates in Mainland China: Origin, Development, and Implications for China's Democratization." *Asian Survey* 53 (2): 245–268.

Sun, Ying. 2014. "Municipal People's Congress Elections in the PRC: A Process of Co-option." *Journal of Contemporary China* 23 (85): 183–195.

Sun, Yun. 2013. *Chinese National Security Decision-making: Process and Challenges*. Washington, DC: Brookings Institution.

Takao, Yasuo. 2007. *Reinventing Japan: From Merchant Nation to Civic Nation*. New York, NY: Palgrave Macmillan.

Takegawa, Shogo. 2009. "International Circumstances as Factors in Building a Welfare State: Welfare Regimes in Europe, Japan and Korea." *International Journal of Japanese Sociology* 18 (1): 79–96.

Teets, Jessica C. 2009. "Post-Earthquake Relief and Reconstruction Efforts: The Emergence of Civil Society in China?" *China Quarterly* 198: 330–347.

Tsujinaka, Yutaka. 2003. "From Developmentalism to Maturity: Japan's Civil Society Organizations in Comparative Perspective." In *The State of Civil Society in Japan*, edited by Frank J. Schwartz and Susan J. Pharr, 83–115. Cambridge, UK: Cambridge University Press.

van Wolferen, Karel. 1989. *The Enigma of Japanese Power: People and Politics in a Stateless Nation*. New York, NY: Alfred A. Knopf.

Vogel, Steven K. 2006. *Japan Remodeled: How Government and Industry Are Reforming Japanese Capitalism*. Ithaca, NY: Cornell University Press.

von Staden, Peter. 2012. "Fettered by the Past in the March Forward: Ideology as an Explanation for Today's Malaise in Japan." *Asia Pacific Business Review* 18 (2): 187–202.

Wade, Robert. 1990. *Governing the Market: Economic Theory and the Role of Government in East Asian Industrialization.* Princeton, NJ: Princeton University Press.

Wang, Dong. 2017. "Grand Strategy, Power Politics, and China's Policy toward the United States in the 1960s." *Diplomatic History* 41 (2): 265–287.

Wang, Fei-ling. 2005."Preservation, Prosperity and Power: What Motivates China's Foreign Policy?" *Journal of Contemporary China* 14 (45): 669–694.

Wang, Jisi. 2011. "China's Search for a Grand Strategy: A Rising Great Power Finds Its Way." *Foreign Affairs* 90 (2): 68–79.

Wang, Shaoguang. 2000. "The Social and Political Implications of China's WTO Membership." *Journal of Contemporary China* 9 (25): 373–405.

Wang, Zheng. 2015. "The Legacy of Historical Memory and China's Foreign Policy in the 2010s." In *Misunderstanding Asia: International Relations Theory and Asian Studies over Half a Century,* edited by G. Rozman, 227–239. New York, NY: Palgrave Macmillan.

Watanuki, Joji. 1967. "Patterns of Politics in Present-Day Japan." In *Party Systems and Voter Alignments: Cross-National Perspectives,* edited by Seymour M. Lipset and Stein Rokkan, 447–466. New York, NY: Free Press.

Weitz, Richard. 2012. "The Russian-China Axis." *World Affairs* 175 (4): 71–78.

Westphal, Larry E., Linsu Kim, and Carl J. Dahlman. 1984. *Reflections on Korea's Acquisition of Technological Capability.* Development Research Department Discussion Paper. Washington, DC: World Bank.

Wezeman, Siemon T. 2017. *China, Russia, and the Shifting Landscape of Arms Sales.* Stockholm International Peace Research Institute (July 5). https://www.sipri.org/commentary/topical-backgrounder/2017/china-russia-and-shifting-landscape-arms-sales.

Whang, In-Joung. 1987. "The Role of Government in Economic Development: The Korean Experience." *Asian Development Review* 5 (2): 70–88.

Wong, Edward. 2016. "China Approves Strict Control of Foreign NGOs." *New York Times.* http://www.nytimes.com/2016/04/29/world/asia/china-foreign-ngo-law.html?hp&action=click&pgtype=Homepage&clickSource=story-heading&module=first-column-region&region=top-news&WT.nav=top-news&_r=0.

Woodall, Brian. 2015. "Japanese Political Finance and Its Dark Side." In *Party Politics in Japan: Political Chaos and Stalemate in the Twenty-First Century,* edited by Ronald J. Hrebenar and Akira Nakamura, 56–79. New York, NY: Routledge.

World Bank. 1993. *The East Asian Miracle: Economic Growth and Public Policy.* New York, NY: Oxford University Press.

World Bank. 1997. *Sharing Rising Incomes: Disparities in China.* Washington, DC: World Bank.

World Bank. 2013. *China 2030: Building a Modern, Harmonious, and Creative Society.* Washington, DC: World Bank.

World Bank & Development Research Center of the State Council, PRC. 2013. *China 2030: Building a Modern, Harmonious, and Creative Society*. Washington DC: World Bank.

Wu, Fengshi, and Kin-man Chan. 2012. "Graduated Control and Beyond: The Evolving Government-NGO Relations." *China Perspectives* 3: 9–17.

Wu, Guoguang. 2011. "China in 2010: Dilemmas of "Scientific Development." *Asian Survey* 51 (1): 18–32.

Yan, Xuetong. 2014. "From Keeping a Low Profile to Striving for Achievement." *The Chinese Journal of International Politics* 7 (2): 153–184.

Yao, Yang. 2010. "The End of Beijing Consensus: Can China's Model of Authoritarian Growth Survive?" *Foreign Affairs* (February 2). https://www.foreignaffairs.com/articles/china/2010–02–02/end-beijing-consensus.

Yeo, Yukyung. 2009. "Remaking the Chinese State and the Nature of Economic Governance? The Early Appraisal of the 2008 'Super-Ministry' Reform." *Journal of Contemporary China* 18 (62): 729–743.

Yoon, Seoyeon. 2015. "South Korea's Wartime Operational Control Transfer Debate: From an Organizational Perspective." *Journal of International and Area Studies* 22 (2): 89–108.

Zhao, Ziyang. 2010. *Prisoner of the State: The Secret Journal of Zhao Ziyang*. New York, NY: Simon & Schuster.

Zheng, Yongnian. 2010. "Central-Local Relations: The Power to Dominate." In *China Today, China Tomorrow: Domestic Politics, Econommy, and Society*, edited by Joseph Fewsmith, 193–222. Lanham, MD: Rowman & Littlefield.

Zheng, Yongnian. 2012. "China in 2011: Anger, Political Consciousness, Anxiety, and Uncertainty." *Asian Survey* 52 (1): 28–41.

Index

42017057R00195